OUR COMMON FUTURE

Members of the Commission

Our Common Future

WORLD COMMISSION ON
ENVIRONMENT AND DEVELOPMENT

Oxford   New York

OXFORD UNIVERSITY PRESS

Oxford University Press, Walton Street, Oxford OX2 6DP

Oxford New York
Athens Auckland Bangkok Bombay
Calcutta Cape Town Dar es Salaam Delhi
Florence Hong Kong Istanbul Karachi
Kuala Lumpur Madras Madrid Melbourne
Mexico City Nairobi Paris Singapore
Taipei Tokyo Toronto

and associated companies in
Berlin Ibadan

Oxford is a trade mark of Oxford University Press

First published 1987

British Library Cataloguing in Publication Data
Data available

Library of Congress Cataloging in Publication Data
Our common future
"April 1987."
1. Economic development—Environmental aspects.
2. Man—Influence on nature. 3. Environmental policy.
4. Human ecology.   I. World Commission on Environment
and Development.
HD75.6.097   1987   363.7   87-7853
ISBN 0-19-282080-X (pbk.)

17 19 20 18

Printed in Great Britain by
Clays Ltd
Bungay, Suffolk

Contents

Throughout this report, edited quotes from some of the many people who spoke at
WCED Public Hearings appear, to illustrate the range of opinions the Commission
was exposed to during its three years of work. They do not necessarily reflect the views
of the Commission.

List of Tables

List of Boxes

Acronym List

ATS	Antarctic Treaty System
CCAMLR	Commission for the Conservation of Antarctic Marine Living Resources
CIDIE	Committee of International Development Institutions on the Environment
CMEA	Council for Mutual Economic Assistance
DIESA	United Nations Department for International Economic and Social Affairs
ECB	United Nations Environment Co-ordination Board
ECE	Economic Commission for Europe
EEC	European Economic Community
EEZ	Exclusive Economic Zone
ELC	Environment Liaison Centre
FAO	Food and Agriculture Organization of the United Nations
GATT	General Agreement on Tariffs and Trade
GDP	gross domestic product
GEMS	Global Environment Monitoring System
GESAMP	Group of Experts on Scientific Aspects of Marine Pollution
GNP	gross national product
IAEA	International Atomic Energy Agency
ICRP	International Commission on Radiological Protection
ICSU	International Council of Scientific Unions
IDA	International Development Association
IGBP	International Geosphere Biosphere Project (of ICSU)
IIED	International Institute for Environment and Development
ILO	International Labour Organization
IMF	International Monetary Fund
ITU	International Telecommunications Union
IUCN	International Union for the Conservation of Nature and Natural Resources
IWC	International Whaling Commission
MVA	manufacturing value added
NCS	National Conservation Strategy

NGO	non-governmental organizations
NICs	newly industrialized countries
NUSS	Nuclear Safety Standards
OECD	Organisation for Economic Co-operation and Development
ODA	official development assistance
PPP	Polluter Pays Principle
SCAR	Scientific Committee on Antarctic Research
TNCs	transnational corporations
UNCHS	United Nations Centre for Human Settlements (HABITAT)
UNCTAD	United Nations Conference on Trade and Development
UNEP	United Nations Environment Programme
UNESCO	United Nations Educational, Scientific, and Cultural Organization
UNIDO	United Nations Industrial Development Organization
WHO	World Health Organization
WMO	World Meteorological Organization
WRI	World Resources Institute
WWF	World Wildlife Fund

Note on Terminology

The grouping of countries in the presentation of data is indicated in the appropriate places. The terms 'industrial countries' and 'developed countries' generally encompass the UN categories of developed market economies and the socialist countries of Eastern Europe and the USSR. Unless otherwise indicated, the term 'developing country' refers to the UN grouping of developing-country market economies and the socialist countries of Asia. The term 'Third World', unless the context implies otherwise, generally refers to the developing-country market economies as defined by the UN.

Unless indicated otherwise, tons are metric (1,000 kilogrammes, or 2.204.6 pounds). Dollars are current U.S. dollars or U.S. dollars for the year specified.

CHAIRMAN'S FOREWORD

'A global agenda for change'—this was what the World Commission on Environment and Development was asked to formulate. It was an urgent call by the General Assembly of the United Nations:

- to propose long-term environmental strategies for achieving sustainable development by the year 2000 and beyond;
- to recommend ways concern for the environment may be translated into greater co-operation among developing countries and between countries at different stages of economic and social development and lead to the achievement of common and mutually supportive objectives that take account of the interrelationships between people, resources, environment, and development;
- to consider ways and means by which the international community can deal more effectively with environmental concerns; and
- to help define shared perceptions of long-term environmental issues and the appropriate efforts needed to deal successfully with the problems of protecting and enhancing the environment, a long-term agenda for action during the coming decades, and aspirational goals for the world community.

When I was called upon by the Secretary-General of the United Nations in December 1983 to establish and chair a special, independent commission to address this major challenge to the world community, I was acutely aware that this was no small task and obligation, and that my day-to-day responsibilities as Party leader made it seem plainly prohibitive. What the General Assembly asked for also seemed to be unrealistic and much too ambitious. At the same time, it was a clear demonstration of the widespread feeling of frustration and inadequacy in the international community about our own ability to address the vital global issues and deal effectively with them.

That fact is a compelling reality, and should not easily be dismissed. Since the answers to fundamental and serious concerns are not at hand, there is no alternative but to keep on trying to find them.

All this was on my mind when the Secretary-General presented me with an argument to which there was no convincing rebuttal: No other political leader had become Prime Minister with a background of several years of political struggle, nationally and internationally, as an environment minister. This gave some hope that the environment was not destined to remain a side issue in central, political decision making.

In the final analysis, I decided to accept the challenge. The challenge of facing the future, and of safeguarding the interests of coming generations. For it was abundantly clear: We needed a mandate for change.

*   *   *   *   *

We live in an era in the history of nations when there is greater need than ever for co-ordinated political action and responsibility. The United Nations and its Secretary-General are faced with an enormous task and burden. Responsibly meeting humanity's goals and aspirations will require the active support of us all.

My reflections and perspective were also based on other important parts of my own political experience: the preceding work of the Brandt Commission on North-South issues, and the Palme Commission on security and disarmament issues, on which I served.

I was being asked to help formulate a third and compelling call for political action: After Brandt's *Programme for Survival* and *Common Crisis*, and after Palme's *Common Security*, would come *Common Future*. This was my message when Vice Chairman Mansour Khalid and I started work on the ambitious task set us by the United Nations. This report, as presented to the UN General Assembly in 1987, is the result of that process.

*   *   *   *   *

Perhaps our most urgent task today is to persuade nations of the need to return to multilateralism. The challenge of reconstruction after the Second World War was the real motivating power behind the establishment of our post-war international economic system. The challenge of finding sustainable development paths ought to provide the impetus—indeed the imperative—for a renewed search for multilateral solutions and a restructured international economic system of co-operation. These challenges cut across the divides of national sovereignty, of limited strategies for economic gain, and of separated disciplines of science.

After a decade and a half of a standstill or even deterioration in global co-operation, I believe the time has come for higher expectations, for common goals pursued together, for an increased political will to address our common future.

There was a time of optimism and progress in the 1960s, when there was greater hope for a braver new world, and for progressive international ideas. Colonies blessed with natural resources were becoming nations. The ideals of co-operation and sharing seemed to be seriously pursued. Paradoxically, the 1970s slid slowly into moods of reaction and isolation while at the same time a series of UN conferences offered hope for greater co-operation on major issues. The 1972 UN Conference on the Human Environment brought the industrialized and developing nations together to delineate the 'rights' of the human family to a healthy and productive environment. A string of such meetings followed: on the rights of people to adequate food, to sound housing, to safe water, to access to means of choosing the size of their families.

The present decade has been marked by a retreat from social concerns. Scientists bring to our attention urgent but complex problems bearing on our very survival: a warming globe, threats to the Earth's ozone layer, deserts consuming agricultural land. We respond by demanding more details, and by assigning the problems to institutions ill equipped to cope with them. Environmental degradation, first seen as mainly a problem of the rich nations and a side effect of industrial wealth, has become a survival issue for developing nations. It is part of the downward spiral of linked ecological and economic decline in which many of the poorest nations are trapped. Despite official hope expressed on all sides, no trends identifiable today, no programmes or policies, offer any real hope of narrowing the growing gap between rich and poor nations. And as part of our 'development', we have amassed weapons arsenals capable of diverting the paths that evolution has followed for millions of years and of creating a planet our ancestors would not recognize.

When the terms of reference of our Commission were originally being discussed in 1982, there were those who wanted its considerations to be limited to 'environmental issues' only. This would have been a grave mistake. The environment does not exist as a sphere separate from human actions, ambitions, and needs, and attempts to defend it in isolation from human concerns have given the very word 'environment' a connotation of naivety in some political circles. The word 'development' has also been narrowed by some into a very limited focus, along the lines of 'what poor nations should do to become richer', and thus again is automatically dismissed by many in the international arena as being a concern of specialists, of those involved in questions of 'development assistance'.

But the 'environment' is where we all live; and 'development' is what we all do in attempting to improve our lot within that abode. The two are inseparable. Further, development issues must be seen as crucial by the political leaders who feel that their countries have reached a plateau towards which other nations must strive. Many of the development paths of the industrialized nations are clearly unsustainable. And the development decisions of these countries, because of their great economic and political power, will have a profound effect upon the ability of all peoples to sustain human progress for generations to come.

Many critical survival issues are related to uneven development, poverty, and population growth. They all place unprecedented pressures on the planet's lands, waters, forests, and other natural resources, not least in the developing countries. The downward spiral of poverty and environmental degradation is a waste of opportunities and of resources. In particular, it is a waste of human resources. These links between poverty, inequality, and environmental degradation formed a major theme in our analysis and recommendations. What is needed now is a new era of economic growth—growth that is forceful and at the same time socially and environmentally sustainable.

Due to the scope of our work, and to the need to have a wide perspective, I was very much aware of the need to put together a highly qualified and influential political and scientific team, to constitute a truly independent Commission. This was an essential part of a successful process. Together, we should span the globe, and pull together to formulate an interdisciplinary, integrated approach to global concerns and our common future. We needed broad participation and a clear majority of members from developing countries, to reflect world realities. We needed people with wide experience, and from all political fields, not only from environment or development as political disciplines, but from all areas of vital decision making that influence economic and social progress, nationally and internationally.

We therefore come from widely differing backgrounds: foreign ministers, finance and planning officials, policymakers in agriculture, science, and technology. Many of the Commissioners are cabinet ministers and senior economists in their own nations, concerned largely with the affairs of those countries. As Commissioners, however, we were acting not in our national roles but as individuals; and as we worked, nationalism and the artificial divides between 'industrialized' and 'developing', between East and West, receded. In their place emerged a common concern for the planet and the interlocked ecological and economic threats with which its people, institutions, and governments now grapple.

During the time we met as a Commission, tragedies such as the

African famines, the leak at the pesticides factory at Bhopal, India, and the nuclear disaster at Chernobyl, USSR appeared to justify the grave predictions about the human future that were becoming commonplace during the mid-1980s. But at public hearings we held on five continents, we also heard from the individual victims of more chronic, widespread disasters: the debt crisis, stagnating aid to and investment in developing countries, falling commodity prices and falling personal incomes. We became convinced that major changes were needed, both in attitudes and in the way our societies are organized.

The questions of population—of population pressure, of population and human rights—and the links between these related issues and poverty, environment, and development proved to be one of the more difficult concerns with which we had to struggle. The differences of perspective seemed at the outset to be unbridgeable, and they required a lot of thought and willingness to communicate across the divides of cultures, religions, and regions.

Another such concern was the whole area of international economic relations. In these and in a number of other important aspects of our analysis and recommendations, we were able to develop broad agreement.

The fact that we all became wiser, learnt to look across cultural and historical barriers, was essential. There were moments of deep concern and potential crisis, moments of gratitude and achievement, moments of success in building a common analysis and perspective. The result is clearly more global, more realistic, more forward-looking than any one of us alone could have created. We joined the Commission with different views and perspectives, different values and beliefs, and very different experiences and insights. After these three years of working together, travelling, listening, and discussing, we present a unanimous report.

I am deeply grateful to all the Commissioners for their dedication, their foresight and personal commitment to our common endeavour. It has been a truly wonderful team. The spirit of friendship and open communication, the meeting of minds and the process of learning and sharing, have provided an experience of optimism, something of great value to all of us, and, I believe, to the report and its message. We hope to share with others our learning process, and all that we have experienced together. It is something that many others will have to experience if global sustainable development is to be achieved.

The Commission has taken guidance from people in all walks of life. It is to these people—to all the peoples of the world—that the

Commission now addresses itself. In so doing we speak to people directly as well as to the institutions that they have established.

The Commission is addressing governments, directly and through their various agencies and ministries. The congregation of governments, gathered in the General Assembly of the United Nations, will be the main recipient of this report.

The Commission is also addressing private enterprise, from the one-person business to the great multinational company with a total economic turnover greater than that of many nations, and with possibilities for bringing about far-reaching changes and improvements.

But first and foremost our message is directed towards people, whose well-being is the ultimate goal of all environment and development policies. In particular, the Commission is addressing the young. The world's teachers will have a crucial role to play in bringing this report to them.

If we do not succeed in putting our message of urgency through to today's parents and decision makers, we risk undermining our children's fundamental right to a healthy, life-enhancing environment. Unless we are able to translate our words into a language that can reach the minds and hearts of people young and old, we shall not be able to undertake the extensive social changes needed to correct the course of development.

The Commission has completed its work. We call for a common endeavour and for new norms of behaviour at all levels and in the interests of all. The changes in attitudes, in social values, and in aspirations that the report urges will depend on vast campaigns of education, debate, and public participation.

To this end, we appeal to citizens' groups, to non-governmental organizations, to educational institutions, and to the scientific community. They have all played indispensable roles in the creation of public awareness and political change in the past. They will play a crucial part in putting the world onto sustainable development paths, in laying the groundwork for Our Common Future.

The process that produced this unanimous report proves that it is possible to join forces, to identify common goals, and to agree on common action. Each one of the Commissioners would have chosen different words if writing the report alone. Still, we managed to agree on the analysis, the broad remedies, and the recommendations for a sustainable course of development.

In the final analysis, this is what it amounts to: furthering the common understanding and common spirit of responsibility so clearly needed in a divided world.

*   *   *   *   *

Thousands of people all over the world have contributed to the work of the Commission, by intellectual means, by financial means, and by sharing their experiences with us through articulating their needs and demands. I am sincerely grateful to everyone who has made such contributions. Many of their names are found in Annexe 2 of the report. My particular gratitude goes to Vice Chairman Mansour Khalid, to all the other members of the Commission, and to Secretary General Jim MacNeill and his staff at our secretariat, who went above and beyond the call of duty to assist us. Their enthusiasm and dedication knew no limits. I want to thank the chairmen and members of the Intergovernmental Inter-sessional Preparatory Committee, who co-operated closely with the Commission and provided inspiration and support. I thank also the Executive Director of the United Nations Environment Programme, Dr. Mostafa Tolba, for his valuable, continuous support and interest.

Gro Harlem Brundtland
Oslo, 20 March 1987

FROM ONE EARTH TO ONE WORLD

An Overview by the World Commission on Environment and Development

In the middle of the 20th century, we saw our planet from space for the first time. Historians may eventually find that this vision had a greater impact on thought than did the Copernican revolution of the 16th century, which upset the human self-image by revealing that the Earth is not the centre of the universe. From space, we see a small and fragile ball dominated not by human activity and edifice but by a pattern of clouds, oceans, greenery, and soils. Humanity's inability to fit its doings into that pattern is changing planetary systems, fundamentally. Many such changes are accompanied by life-threatening hazards. This new reality, from which there is no escape, must be recognized—and managed.

Fortunately, this new reality coincides with more positive developments new to this century. We can move information and goods faster around the globe than ever before; we can produce more food and more goods with less investment of resources; our technology and science gives us at least the potential to look deeper into and better understand natural systems. From space, we can see and study the Earth as an organism whose health depends on the health of all its parts. We have the power to reconcile human affairs with natural laws and to thrive in the process. In this our cultural and spiritual heritages can reinforce our economic interests and survival imperatives.

This Commission believes that people can build a future that is more prosperous, more just, and more secure. Our report, *Our Common Future*, is not a prediction of ever increasing environmental decay, poverty, and hardship in an ever more polluted world among ever decreasing resources. We see instead the possibility for a new era of economic growth, one that must be based on policies that sustain and expand the environmental resource base. And we believe such growth to be absolutely essential to relieve the great poverty that is deepening in much of the developing world.

But the Commission's hope for the future is conditional on decisive political action now to begin managing environmental resources to ensure both sustainable human progress and human survival. We are not forecasting a future; we are serving a notice—an urgent notice based on the latest and best scientific evidence—that the time has come to take the decisions needed to secure the resources to sustain this and coming generations. We do not offer a detailed blueprint for action, but instead a pathway by which the peoples of the world may enlarge their spheres of co-operation.

I. THE GLOBAL CHALLENGE

Successes and Failures

Those looking for success and signs of hope can find many: Infant mortality is falling; human life expectancy is increasing; the proportion of the world's adults who can read and write is climbing; the proportion of children starting school is rising; and global food production increases faster than the population grows.

But the same processes that have produced these gains have given rise to trends that the planet and its people cannot long bear. These have traditionally been divided into failures of 'development' and failures in the management of our human environment. On the development side, in terms of absolute numbers there are more hungry people in the world than ever before, and their numbers are increasing. So are the numbers who cannot read or write, the numbers without safe water or safe and sound homes, and the numbers short of woodfuel with which to cook and warm themselves. The gap between rich and poor nations is widening—not shrinking—and there is little prospect, given present trends and institutional arrangements, that this process will be reversed.

There are also environmental trends that threaten to radically alter the planet, that threaten the lives of many species upon it, including the human species. Each year another 6 million hectares of productive dryland turns into worthless desert. Over three decades, this would amount to an area roughly as large as Saudi Arabia. More than 11 million hectares of forests are destroyed yearly, and this, over three decades, would equal an area about the size of India. Much of this forest is converted to low-grade farmland unable to support the farmers who settle it. In Europe, acid precipitation kills forests and lakes and damages the artistic and architectural heritage of nations; it may have acidified vast tracts of soil beyond reasonable hope of repair. The burning of fossil fuels puts into the atmosphere carbon dioxide, which is causing gradual global warming. This 'greenhouse effect' may by early next century have increased average global temperatures enough to shift agricultural production areas, raise sea

The World Commission on Environment and Development first met in October 1984, and published its report 900 days later, in April 1987. Over those few days:

- The drought-triggered, environment-development crisis in Africa peaked, putting 35 million people at risk, killing perhaps a million.
- A leak from a pesticides factory in Bhopal, India, killed more than 2,000 people and blinded and injured over 200,000 more.
- Liquid gas tanks exploded in Mexico City, killing 1,000 and leaving thousands more homeless.
- The Chernobyl nuclear reactor explosion sent nuclear fallout across Europe, increasing the risks of future human cancers.
- Agricultural chemicals, solvents, and mercury flowed into the Rhine River during a warehouse fire in Switzerland, killing millions of fish and threatening drinking water in the Federal Republic of Germany and the Netherlands.
- An estimated 60 million people died of diarrhoeal diseases related to unsafe drinking water and malnutrition; most of the victims were children.

levels to flood coastal cities, and disrupt national economies. Other industrial gases threaten to deplete the planet's protective ozone shield to such an extent that the number of human and animal cancers would rise sharply and the oceans' food chain would be disrupted. Industry and agriculture put toxic substances into the human food chain and into underground water tables beyond reach of cleansing.

There has been a growing realization in national governments and multilateral institutions that it is impossible to separate economic development issues from environment issues; many forms of development erode the environmental resources upon which they must be based, and environmental degradation can undermine economic development. Poverty is a major cause and effect of global environmental problems. It is therefore futile to attempt to deal with environmental problems without a broader perspective that encompasses the factors underlying world poverty and international inequality.

These concerns were behind the establishment in 1983 of the World Commission on Environment and Development by the UN General Assembly. The Commission is an independent body, linked to but outside the control of governments and the UN system. The Commission's mandate gave it three objectives: to re-examine the critical environment and development issues and to formulate realistic proposals for dealing with them; to propose new forms of international co-operation on these issues that will influence policies and events in the direction of needed changes; and to raise the levels of understanding and commitment to action of individuals, voluntary organizations, businesses, institutes, and governments.

Through our deliberations and the testimony of people at the public hearings we held on five continents, all the commissioners came to focus on one central theme: many present development trends leave increasing numbers of people poor and vulnerable, while at the same time degrading the environment. How can such development serve next century's world of twice as many people relying on the same environment? This realization broadened our view of development. We came to see it not in its restricted context of economic growth in developing countries. We came to see that a new development path was required, one that sustained human progress not just in a few places for a few years, but for the entire planet into the distant future. Thus 'sustainable development' becomes a goal not just for the 'developing' nations, but for industrial ones as well.

The Interlocking Crises

Until recently, the planet was a large world in which human activities and their effects were neatly compartmentalized within nations, within sectors (energy, agriculture, trade), and within broad areas of concern (environmental, economic, social). These compartments have begun to dissolve. This applies in particular to the various global 'crises' that have seized public concern, particularly over the past decade. These are not separate crises: an environmental crisis, a development crisis, an energy crisis. They are all one.

The planet is passing through a period of dramatic growth and fundamental change. Our human world of 5 billion must make room in a finite environment for another human world. The population could stabilize at between 8 billion and 14 billion sometime next century, according to UN projections. More than 90 per cent of the increase will occur in the poorest countries, and 90 per cent of that growth in already bursting cities.

Economic activity has multiplied to create a $13 trillion world economy, and this could grow five- or tenfold in the coming half-century. Industrial production has grown more than fiftyfold over the past century, four-fifths of this growth since 1950. Such figures reflect and presage profound impacts upon the biosphere, as the world invests in houses, transport, farms, and industries. Much of the economic growth pulls raw material from forests, soils, seas, and waterways.

A mainspring of economic growth is new technology, and while this technology offers the potential for slowing the dangerously rapid consumption of finite resources, it also entails high risks, including new forms of pollution and the introduction to the planet of new variations of life forms that could change evolutionary pathways. Meanwhile, the industries most heavily reliant on environmental resources and most heavily polluting are growing most rapidly in the developing world, where there is both more urgency for growth and less capacity to minimize damaging side effects.

These related changes have locked the global economy and global ecology together in new ways. We have in the past been concerned about the impacts of economic growth upon the environment. We are now forced to concern ourselves with the impacts of ecological stress—degradation of soils, water regimes, atmosphere, and forests— upon our economic prospects. We have in the more recent past been forced to face up to a sharp increase in economic interdependence among nations. We are now forced to accustom ourselves to an accelerating ecological interdependence among nations. Ecology and economy are becoming ever more interwoven—locally, regionally, nationally, and globally—into a seamless net of causes and effects.

Impoverishing the local resource base can impoverish wider areas: Deforestation by highland farmers causes flooding on lowland farms; factory pollution robs local fishermen of their catch. Such grim local cycles now operate nationally and regionally. Dryland degradation sends environmental refugees in their millions across national borders. Deforestation in Latin America and Asia is causing more floods, and more destructive floods, in downhill, downstream nations. Acid precipitation and nuclear fallout have spread across the borders of Europe. Similar phenomena are emerging on a global scale, such as global warming and loss of ozone. Internationally traded hazardous chemicals entering foods are themselves internationally traded. In the next century, the environmental pressure causing population movements may increase sharply, while barriers to that movement may be even firmer than they are now.

Over the past few decades, life-threatening environmental concerns have surfaced in the developing world. Countrysides are coming under pressure from increasing numbers of farmers and the landless. Cities are filling with people, cars, and factories. Yet at the same time these developing countries must operate in a world in which the resources gap between most developing and industrial nations is widening, in which the industrial world dominates in the rule-making of some key international bodies, and in which the industrial world has already used much of the planet's ecological capital. This inequality is the planet's main 'environmental' problem; it is also its main 'development' problem.

International economic relationships pose a particular problem for environmental management in many developing countries. Agriculture, forestry, energy production, and mining generate at least half the gross national product of many developing countries and account for even larger shares of livelihoods and employment. Exports of natural resources remain a large factor in their economies, especially for the least developed. Most of these countries face enormous economic pressures, both international and domestic, to overexploit their environmental resource base.

The recent crisis in Africa best and most tragically illustrates the ways in which economics and ecology can interact destructively and trip into disaster. Triggered by drought, its real causes lie deeper. They are to be found in part in national policies that gave too little attention, too late, to the needs of smallholder agriculture and to the threats posed by rapidly rising populations. Their roots extend also to a global economic system that takes more out of a poor continent than it puts in. Debts that they cannot pay force African nations relying on commodity sales to overuse their fragile soils, thus turning good land to desert. Trade barriers in the wealthy nations—and in many developing ones—make it hard for Africans to sell their goods for reasonable returns, putting yet more pressure on ecological systems. Aid from donor nations has not only been inadequate in scale, but too often has reflected the priorities of the nations giving the aid, rather than the needs of the recipients.   The production base of other developing world areas suffers similarly both from local failures and from the workings of international economic systems. As a consequence of the 'debt crisis' of Latin America, that region's natural resources are now being used not for development but to meet financial obligations to creditors abroad. This approach to the debt problem is short-sighted from several standpoints: economic, political, and environmental. It requires relatively poor countries simultaneously to accept growing poverty while exporting growing amounts of scarce resources.

A majority of developing countries now have lower per capita incomes than when the decade began. Rising poverty and unemployment have increased pressure on environmental resources as more people have been forced to rely more directly upon them. Many governments have cut back efforts to protect the environment and to bring ecological considerations into development planning.

The deepening and widening environmental crisis presents a threat

The Commission has sought ways in which global development can be put on a sustainable path into the 21st century. Some 5,000 days will elapse between the publication of our report and the first day of the 21st century. What environmental crises lie in store over those 5,000 days?

During the 1970s, twice as many people suffered each year from 'natural' disasters as during the 1960s. The disasters most directly associated with environment/development mismanagement—droughts and floods—affected the most people and increased most sharply in terms of numbers affected. Some 18.5 million people were affected by drought annually in the 1960s, 24.4 million in the 1970s. There were 5.2 million flood victims yearly in the 1960s, 15.4 million in the 1970s. Numbers of victims of cyclones and earthquakes also shot up as growing numbers of poor people built unsafe houses on dangerous ground.

The results are not in for the 1980s. But we have seen 35 million afflicted by drought in Africa alone and tens of millions affected by the better managed and thus less-publicized Indian drought. Floods have poured off the deforested Andes and Himalayas with increasing force. The 1980s seem destined to sweep this dire trend on into a crisis-filled 1990s.

---

to national security—and even survival—that may be greater than well-armed, ill-disposed neighbours and unfriendly alliances. Already in parts of Latin America, Asia, the Middle East, and Africa, environmental decline is becoming a source of political unrest and international tension. The recent destruction of much of Africa's dryland agricultural production was more severe than if an invading army had pursued a scorched-earth policy. Yet most of the affected governments still spend far more to protect their people from invading armies than from the invading desert.

Globally, military expenditures total about $1 trillion a year and continue to grow. In many countries, military spending consumes such a high proportion of gross national product that it itself does great damage to these societies' development efforts. Governments tend to base their approaches to 'security' on traditional definitions. This is most obvious in the attempts to achieve security through the development of potentially planet-destroying nuclear weapons systems. Studies suggest that the cold and dark nuclear winter following even a limited nuclear war could destroy plant and animal ecosystems and leave any human survivors occupying a devastated planet very different from the one they inherited.

The arms race—in all parts of the world—pre-empts resources that might be used more productively to diminish the security threats created by environmental conflict and the resentments that are fuelled by widespread poverty.

Many present efforts to guard and maintain human progress, to meet human needs, and to realize human ambitions are simply unsustainable—in both the rich and poor nations. They draw too heavily, too quickly, on already overdrawn environmental resource accounts to be affordable far into the future without bankrupting those accounts. They may show profits on the balance sheets of our generation, but our children will inherit the losses. We borrow environmental capital from future generations with no intention or prospect of repaying. They may damn us for our spendthrift ways, but they can never collect on our debt to them. We act as we do because we can get away with it: future generations do not vote; they have no political or financial power; they cannot challenge our decisions.

But the results of the present profligacy are rapidly closing the options for future generations. Most of today's decision makers will be dead before the planet feels the heavier effects of acid precipitation, global warming, ozone depletion, or widespread desertification and species loss. Most of the young voters of today will still be alive. In the Commission's hearings it was the young, those who have the most to lose, who were the harshest critics of the planet's present management.

Sustainable Development

Humanity has the ability to make development sustainable—to ensure that it meets the needs of the present without compromising the ability of future generations to meet their own needs. The concept of sustainable development does imply limits—not absolute limits but limitations imposed by the present state of technology and social organization on environmental resources and by the ability of the biosphere to absorb the effects of human activities. But technology and social organization can be both managed and improved to make way for a new era of economic growth. The Commission believes that widespread poverty is no longer inevitable. Poverty is not only an evil in itself, but sustainable development requires meeting the basic needs of all and extending to all the opportunity to fulfil their aspirations for a better life. A world in which poverty is endemic will always be prone to ecological and other catastrophes.

Meeting essential needs requires not only a new era of economic growth for nations in which the majority are poor, but an assurance that those poor get their fair share of the resources required to sustain that growth. Such equity would be aided by political systems that secure effective citizen participation in decision making and by greater democracy in international decision making.

Sustainable global development requires that those who are more affluent adopt life-styles within the planet's ecological means—in their use of energy, for example. Further, rapidly growing populations can increase the pressure on resources and slow any rise in living standards; thus sustainable development can only be pursued if population size and growth are in harmony with the changing productive potential of the ecosystem.

Yet in the end, sustainable development is not a fixed state of harmony, but rather a process of change in which the exploitation of resources, the direction of investments, the orientation of technological development, and institutional change are made consistent with future as well as present needs. We do not pretend that the process is easy or straightforward. Painful choices have to be made. Thus, in the final analysis, sustainable development must rest on political will.

The Institutional Gaps

The objective of sustainable development and the integrated nature of the global environment/development challenges pose problems for institutions, national and international, that were established on the basis of narrow preoccupations and compartmentalized concerns. Governments' general response to the speed and scale of global changes has been a reluctance to recognize sufficiently the need to change themselves. The challenges are both interdependent and integrated, requiring comprehensive approaches and popular participation.

Yet most of the institutions facing those challenges tend to be independent, fragmented, working to relatively narrow mandates with closed decision processes. Those responsible for managing natural resources and protecting the environment are institutionally separated from those responsible for managing the economy. The real world of interlocked economic and ecological systems will not change; the policies and institutions concerned must.

There is a growing need for effective international co-operation to manage ecological and economic interdependence. Yet at the same time, confidence in international organizations is diminishing and support for them dwindling.

The other great institutional flaw in coping with environment/ development challenges is governments' failure to make the bodies whose policy actions degrade the environment responsible for ensuring that their policies prevent that degradation. Environmental concern arose from damage caused by the rapid economic growth following the Second World War. Governments, pressured by their citizens, saw a need to clean up the mess, and they established environmental ministries and agencies to do this. Many had great success—within the limits of their mandates—in improving air and water quality and enhancing other resources. But much of their work has of necessity been after-the-fact repair of damage: reforestation, reclaiming desert lands, rebuilding urban environments, restoring natural habitats, and rehabilitating wild lands.

The existence of such agencies gave many governments and their citizens the false impression that these bodies were by themselves able to protect and enhance the environmental resource base. Yet many industrialized and most developing countries carry huge economic burdens from inherited problems such as air and water pollution, depletion of ground-water, and the proliferation of toxic chemicals and hazardous wastes. These have been joined by more recent problems—erosion, desertification, acidification, new chemicals, and new forms of waste—that are directly related to agricultural, industrial, energy, forestry, and transportation policies and practices.

The mandates of the central economic and sectoral ministries are also often too narrow, too concerned with quantities of production or growth. The mandates of ministries of industry include production targets, while the accompanying pollution is left to ministries of environment. Electricity boards produce power, while the acid pollution they also produce is left to other bodies to clean up. The present challenge is to give the central economic and sectoral ministries the responsibility for the quality of those parts of the human environment affected by their decisions, and to give the environmental agencies more power to cope with the effects of unsustainable development.

The same need for change holds for international agencies concerned with development lending, trade regulation, agricultural development, and so on. These have been slow to take the environmental effects of their work into account, although some are trying to do so.

The ability to anticipate and prevent environmental damage requires that the ecological dimensions of policy be considered at the same time as the economic, trade, energy, agricultural, and other dimensions. They should be considered on the same agendas and in the same national and international institutions.

This reorientation is one of the chief institutional challenges of the 1990s and beyond. Meeting it will require major institutional development and reform. Many countries that are too poor or small or that have limited managerial capacity will find it difficult to do this unaided. They will need financial and technical assistance and training. But the changes required involve all countries, large and small, rich and poor.

II. THE POLICY DIRECTIONS

The Commission has focused its attention in the areas of population, food security, the loss of species and genetic resources, energy, industry, and human settlements—realizing that all of these are connected and cannot be treated in isolation one from another. This section contains only a few of the Commission's many recommendations.

Population and Human Resources

In many parts of the world, the population is growing at rates that cannot be sustained by available environmental resources, at rates that are outstripping any reasonable expectations of improvements in housing, health care, food security, or energy supplies.

The issue is not just numbers of people, but how those numbers relate to available resources. Thus the 'population problem' must be dealt with in part by efforts to eliminate mass poverty, in order to assure more equitable access to resources, and by education to improve human potential to manage those resources.

Urgent steps are needed to limit extreme rates of population growth. Choices made now will influence the level at which the population stabilizes next century within a range of 6 billion people. But this is not just a demographic issue; providing people with facilities and education that allow them to choose the size of their families is a way of assuring—especially for women—the basic human right of self-determination.

Governments that need to do so should develop long-term, multifaceted population policies and a campaign to pursue broad demographic goals: to strengthen social, cultural, and economic motivations for family planning, and to provide to all who want them the education, contraceptives, and services required.

Human resource development is a crucial requirement not only to build up technical knowledge and capabilities, but also to create new values to help individuals and nations cope with rapidly changing social, environmental, and development realities. Knowledge shared globally would assure greater mutual understanding and create greater willingness to share global resources equitably.

Tribal and indigenous peoples will need special attention as the forces of economic development disrupt their traditional life-styles— life-styles that can offer modern societies many lessons in the management of resources in complex forest, mountain, and dryland ecosystems. Some are threatened with virtual extinction by insensitive development over which they have no control. Their traditional rights should be recognized and they should be given a decisive voice in formulating policies about resource development in their areas. (See Chapter 4 for a wider discussion of these issues and recommendations.)

Food Security: Sustaining the Potential

Growth in world cereal production has steadily outstripped world population growth. Yet each year there are more people in the world who do not get enough food. Global agriculture has the potential to grow enough food for all, but food is often not available where it is needed.

Production in industrialized countries has usually been highly subsidized and protected from international competition. These subsidies have encouraged the overuse of soil and chemicals, the pollution of both water resources and foods with these chemicals, and the degradation of the countryside. Much of this effort has produced surpluses and their associated financial burdens. And some of this surplus has been sent at concessional rates to the developing world, where it has undermined the farming policies of recipient nations. There is, however, growing awareness in some countries of the environmental and economic consequences of such paths, and the emphasis of agricultural policies is to encourage conservation.

Many developing countries, on the other hand, have suffered the opposite problem: farmers are not sufficiently supported. In some, improved technology allied to price incentives and government services has produced a major breakthrough in food production. But elsewhere, the food-growing small farmers have been neglected. Coping with often inadequate technology and few economic incentives, many are pushed onto marginal land: too dry, too steep, lacking in nutrients. Forests are cleared and productive drylands rendered barren.

Most developing nations need more effective incentive systems to encourage production, especially of food crops. In short, the 'terms of trade' need to be turned in favour of the small farmer. Most industrialized nations, on the other hand, must alter present systems in order to cut surpluses, to reduce unfair competition with nations that may have real comparative advantages, and to promote eco-logically sound farming practices.

Food security requires attention to questions of distribution, since hunger often arises from lack of purchasing power rather than lack of available food. It can be furthered by land reforms, and by policies to protect vulnerable subsistence farmers, pastoralists, and the landless—groups who by the year 2000 will include 220 million households. Their greater prosperity will depend on integrated rural development that increases work opportunities both inside and outside agriculture. (See Chapter 5 for a wider discussion of these issues and recommendations.)

Species and Ecosystems: Resources for Development

The planet's species are under stress. There is a growing scientific consensus that species are disappearing at rates never before witnessed on the planet, although there is also controversy over those rates and the risks they entail. Yet there is still time to halt this process.

The diversity of species is necessary for the normal functioning of ecosystems and the biosphere as a whole. The genetic material in wild species contributes billions of dollars yearly to the world economy in the form of improved crop species, new drugs and medicines, and raw materials for industry. But utility aside, there are also moral, ethical, cultural, aesthetic, and purely scientific reasons for conserving wild beings.

A first priority is to establish the problem of disappearing species and threatened ecosystems on political agendas as a major economic and resource issue.

Governments can stem the destruction of tropical forests and other reservoirs of biological diversity while developing them economically. Reforming forest revenue systems and concession terms could raise billions of dollars of additional revenues, promote more efficient, long-term forest resource use, and curtail deforestation.

The network of protected areas that the world will need in the future must include much larger areas brought under some degree of protection. Therefore, the cost of conservation will rise—directly and in terms of opportunities for development foregone. But over the long term the opportunities for development will be enhanced. International development agencies should therefore give com-prehensive and systematic attention to the problems and opportunities of species conservation.

Governments should investigate the prospect of agreeing to a

'Species Convention', similar in spirit and scope to other international conventions reflecting principles of 'universal resources'. They should also consider international financial arrangements to support the implementation of such a convention. (See Chapter 6 for a wider discussion of these issues and recommendations.)

Energy: Choices for Environment and Development

A safe and sustainable energy pathway is crucial to sustainable development; we have not yet found it. Rates of increase in energy use have been declining. However, the industrialization, agricultural development, and rapidly growing populations of developing nations will need much more energy. Today, the average person in an industrial market economy uses more than 80 times as much energy as someone in sub-Saharan Africa. Thus any realistic global energy scenario must provide for substantially increased primary energy use by developing countries.

To bring developing countries' energy use up to industrialized country levels by the year 2025 would require increasing present global energy use by a factor of five. The planetary ecosystem could not stand this, especially if the increases were based on non-renewable fossil fuels. Threats of global warming and acidification of the environment most probably rule out even a doubling of energy use based on present mixes of primary sources.

Any new era of economic growth must therefore be less energy-intensive than growth in the past. Energy efficiency policies must be the cutting edge of national energy strategies for sustainable development, and there is much scope for improvement in this direction. Modern appliances can be redesigned to deliver the same amounts of energy-services with only two-thirds or even one-half of the primary energy inputs needed to run traditional equipment. And energy efficiency solutions are often cost-effective.

After almost four decades of immense technological effort, nuclear energy has become widely used. During this period, however, the nature of its costs, risks, and benefits have become more evident and the subject of sharp controversy. Different countries world-wide take up different positions on the use of nuclear energy. The discussion in the Commission also reflected these different views and positions. Yet all agreed that the generation of nuclear power is only justifiable if there are solid solutions to the unsolved problems to which it gives rise. The highest priority should be accorded to research and development on environmentally sound and ecologically viable alternatives, as well as on means of increasing the safety of nuclear energy.

Energy efficiency can only buy time for the world to develop 'low-energy paths' based on renewable sources, which should form the foundation of the global energy structure during the 21st century. Most of these sources are currently problematic, but given innovative development, they could supply the same amount of primary energy the planet now consumes. However, achieving these use levels will require a programme of coordinated research, development, and demonstration projects commanding funding necessary to ensure the rapid development of renewable energy. Developing countries will require assistance to change their energy use patterns in this direction.

Millions of people in the developing world are short of fuelwood, the main domestic energy of half of humanity, and their numbers are growing. The wood-poor nations must organize their agricultural sectors to produce large amounts of wood and other plant fuels.

The substantial changes required in the present global energy mix will not be achieved by market pressures alone, given the dominant role of governments as producers of energy and their importance as consumers. If the recent momentum behind annual gains in energy efficiency is to be maintained and extended, governments need to make it an explicit goal of their policies for energy pricing to consumers. Prices needed to encourage the adoption of energy-saving measures may be achieved through several means. Although the Commission expresses no preference, 'conservation pricing' requires that governments take a long-term view in weighing the costs and benefits of the various measures. Given the importance of oil prices on international energy policy, new mechanisms for encouraging dialogue between consumers and producers should be explored.

A safe, environmentally sound, and economically viable energy pathway that will sustain human progress into the distant future is clearly imperative. It is also possible. But it will require new dimensions of political will and institutional co-operation to achieve it. (See Chapter 7 for a wider discussion of these issues and recommendations.)

Industry: Producing More with Less

The world manufactures seven times more goods today than it did as recently as 1950. Given population growth rates, a five- to tenfold increase in manufacturing output will be needed just to raise developing-world consumption of manufactured goods to industrialized world levels by the time population growth rates level off next century.

Experience in the industrialized nations has proved that anti-pollution technology has been cost-effective in terms of health, property, and environmental damage avoided, and that it has made many industries more profitable by making them more resource-efficient. While economic growth has continued, the consumption of raw materials has held steady or even declined, and new technologies offer further efficiencies.

Nations have to bear the costs of any inappropriate industrialization, and many developing countries are realizing that they have neither the resources nor—given rapid technological change—the time to damage their environments now and clean up later. But they also need assistance and information from industrialized nations to make the best use of technology. Transnational corporations have a special responsibility to smooth the path of industrialization in the nations in which they operate.

Emerging technologies offer the promise of higher productivity, increased efficiency, and decreased pollution, but many bring risks of new toxic chemicals and wastes and of major accidents of a type and scale beyond present coping mechanisms. There is an urgent need for tighter controls over the export of hazardous industrial and agricultural chemicals. Present controls over the dumping of hazardous wastes should be tightened.

Many essential human needs can be met only through goods and services provided by industry, and the shift to sustainable development must be powered by a continuing flow of wealth from industry. (See Chapter 8 for a wider discussion of these issues and recommendations.)

The Urban Challenge

By the turn of the century, almost half of humanity will live in urban centres; the world of the 21st century will be a largely urban world. Over only 65 years, the developing world's urban population has increased tenfold, from around 100 million in 1920 to 1 billion today. In 1940, one person in 100 lived in a city of 1 million or more inhabitants; by 1980, one in 10 lived in such a city. Between 1985 and the year 2000, Third World cities could grow by another three-quarters of a billion people. This suggests that the developing world must, over the next few years, increase by 65 per cent its capacity to produce and manage its urban infrastructure, services, and shelter merely to maintain today's often extremely inadequate conditions.

Few city governments in the developing world have the power, resources, and trained personnel to provide their rapidly growing populations with the land, services, and facilities needed for an adequate human life: clean water, sanitation, schools, and transport. The result is mushrooming illegal settlements with primitive facilities, increased overcrowding, and rampant disease linked to an unhealthy environment. Many cities in industrial countries also face problems— deteriorating infrastructure, environmental degradation, inner-city decay, and neighbourhood collapse. But with the means and resources to tackle this decline, the issue for most industrial countries is ultimately one of political and social choice. Developing countries are not in the same situation. They have a major urban crisis on their hands.

Governments will need to develop explicit settlements strategies to guide the process of urbanization, taking the pressure off the largest urban centres and building up smaller towns and cities, more closely integrating them with their rural hinterlands. This will mean examining and changing other policies—taxation, food pricing, transportation, health, industrialization—that work against the goals of settlements strategies.

Good city management requires decentralization—of funds, political power, and personnel—to local authorities, which are best placed to appreciate and manage local needs. But the sustainable development of cities will depend on closer work with the majorities of urban poor who are the true city builders, tapping the skills, energies, and resources of neighbourhood groups and those in the 'informal sector'. Much can be achieved by 'site and service' schemes that provide households with basic services and help them to get on with building sounder houses around these. (See Chapter 9 for a wider discussion of these issues and recommendations.)

III. INTERNATIONAL CO-OPERATION AND INSTITUTIONAL REFORM

The Role of the International Economy

Two conditions must be satisfied before international economic exchanges can become beneficial for all involved. The sustainability of ecosystems on which the global economy depends must be guaranteed. And the economic partners must be satisfied that the basis of exchange is equitable. For many developing countries, neither condition is met.

Growth in many developing countries is being stifled by depressed commodity prices, protectionism, intolerable debt burdens, and declining flows of development finance. If living standards are to grow so as to alleviate poverty, these trends must be reversed.

A particular responsibility falls to the World Bank and the International Development Association as the main conduit for multilateral finance to developing countries. In the context of consistently increased financial flows, the World Bank can support environmentally sound projects and policies. In financing structural adjustment, the International Monetary Fund should support wider and longer term development objectives than at present: growth, social goals, and environmental impacts.

The present level of debt service of many countries, especially in Africa and Latin America, is not consistent with sustainable development. Debtors are being required to use trade surpluses to service debts, and are drawing heavily on non-renewable resources to do so. Urgent action is necessary to alleviate debt burdens in ways that represent a fairer sharing between both debtors and lenders of the responsibilities and burdens.

Current arrangements for commodities could be significantly improved: More compensatory financing to offset economic shocks would encourage producers to take a long-term view, and not to overproduce commodities; and more assistance could be given from diversification programmes. Commodity-specific arrangements can build on the model of the International Tropical Timber Agreement, one of the few that specifically includes ecological concerns.

Multinational companies can play an important role in sustainable development, especially as developing countries come to rely more on foreign equity capital. But if these companies are to have a positive influence on development, the negotiating capacity of developing countries vis à vis transnationals must be strengthened so they can secure terms that respect their environmental concerns.

However, these specific measures must be located in a wider context of effective co-operation to produce an international economic system geared to growth and the elimination of world poverty. (See Chapter 3 for a more detailed discussion of issues and recommendations on the international economy.)

Managing the Commons

Traditional forms of national sovereignty raise particular problems in managing the 'global commons' and their shared ecosystems—the oceans, outer space, and Antarctica. Some progress has been made in all three areas; much remains to be done.

The UN Conference on the Law of the Sea was the most ambitious attempt ever to provide an internationally agreed regime for the management of the oceans. All nations should ratify the Law of the Sea

Treaty as soon as possible. Fisheries agreements should be strengthened to prevent current overexploitation, as should conventions to control and regulate the dumping of hazardous wastes at sea.

There are growing concerns about the management of orbital space, centring on using satellite technology for monitoring planetary systems, on making the most effective use of the limited capacities of geosynchronous orbit for communications satellites, and on limiting space debris. The orbiting and testing of weapons in space would greatly increase this debris. The international community should seek to design and implement a space regime to ensure that space remains a peaceful environment for the benefit of all.

Antarctica is managed under the 1959 Antarctic Treaty. However, many nations outside of that pact view the Treaty System as too limited, both in participation and in the scope of its conservation measures. The Commission's recommendations deal with the safeguarding of present achievements, the incorporation of any minerals development into a management regime, and various options for the future. (See Chapter 10 for more discussion on issues and recommendations on the management of the commons.)

Peace, Security, Development, and the Environment

Among the dangers facing the environment, the possibility of nuclear war is undoubtedly the gravest. Certain aspects of the issues of peace and security bear directly upon the concept of sustainable development. The whole notion of security as traditionally understood— in terms of political and military threats to national sovereignty— must be expanded to include the growing impacts of environmental stress—locally, nationally, regionally, and globally. There are no military solutions to 'environmental insecurity'.

Governments and international agencies should assess the cost-effectiveness, in terms of achieving security, of money spent on armaments compared with money spent on reducing poverty or restoring a ravaged environment.

But the greatest need is to achieve improved relations among those major powers capable of deploying weapons of mass destruction. This is needed to achieve agreement on tighter control over the proliferation and testing of various types of weapons of mass destruction—nuclear and non-nuclear—including those that have environmental implications. (See Chapter 11 for more discussion of issues and recommendations on the links between peace, security, development, and the environment.)

Institutional and Legal Change

The report that follows contains throughout (and especially in Chapter 12) many specific recommendations for institutional and legal change. These cannot be adequately summarized here. However, the Commission's main proposals are embodied in six priority areas.

Getting at the Sources

Governments must begin now to make the key national, economic, and sectoral agencies directly responsible and accountable for ensuring that their policies, programmes, and budgets support development that is economically and ecologically sustainable.

By the same token, the various regional organizations need to do more to integrate environment fully in their goals and activities. New regional arrangements will especially be needed among developing countries to deal with transboundary environmental issues.

All major international bodies and agencies should ensure that their programmes encourage and support sustainable development, and they should greatly improve their coordination and co-operation. The Secretary-General of the United Nations Organization should provide a high-level centre of leadership for the UN system to assess, advise, assist, and report on progress made towards this goal.

Dealing with the Effects

Governments should also reinforce the roles and capacities of environmental protection and resource management agencies. This is needed in many industrialized countries, but most urgently in developing countries, which will need assistance in strengthening their institutions. The UN Environment Programme (UNEP) should be strengthened as the principal source on environmental data, assessment, and reporting and as the principal advocate and agent for change and international co-operation on critical environment and natural resource protection issues.

Assessing Global Risks

The capacity to identify, assess, and report on risks of irreversible damage to natural systems and threats to the survival, security, and well-being of the world community must be rapidly reinforced and extended. Governments, individually and collectively, have the principal responsibility to do this. UNEP's Earthwatch programme should be the centre of leadership in the UN system on risk assessment.

However, given the politically sensitive nature of many of the most critical risks, there is also a need for an independent but complementary capacity to assess and report on critical global risks. A new international programme for co-operation among largely non-governmental organizations, scientific bodies, and industry groups should therefore be established for this purpose.

Making Informed Choices

Making the difficult choices involved in achieving sustainable development will depend on the widespread support and involvement of an informed public and of non-governmental organizations, the scientific community, and industry. Their rights, roles, and participation in development planning, decision making, and project implementation should be expanded.

Providing the Legal Means

National and international law is being rapidly outdistanced by the accelerating pace and expanding scale of impacts on the ecological basis of development. Governments now need to fill major gaps in existing national and international law related to the environment, to find ways to recognize and protect the rights of present and future generations to an environment adequate for their health and well-being, to prepare under UN auspices a universal Declaration on environmental protection and sustainable development and a subsequent Convention, and to strengthen procedures for avoiding or resolving disputes on environment and resource management issues.

Investing in Our Future

Over the past decade, the overall cost-effectiveness of investments in halting pollution has been demonstrated. The escalating economic and ecological damage costs of not investing in environmental protection and improvement have also been repeatedly demonstrated—often in grim tolls of flood and famine. But there are large financial implications: for renewable energy development, pollution control, and achieving less resource-intensive forms of agriculture.

Multilateral financial institutions have a crucial role to play. The World Bank is presently reorienting its programmes towards greater environmental concerns. This should be accompanied by a fundamental commitment to sustainable development by the Bank. It is also essential that the regional Development Banks and the International Monetary Fund incorporate similar objectives in their policies and programmes. A new priority and focus is also needed in bilateral aid agencies.

Given the limitations on increasing present flows of international aid, proposals for securing additional revenue from the use of international commons and natural resources should now be seriously considered by governments.

IV. A CALL FOR ACTION

Over the course of this century, the relationship between the human world and the planet that sustains it has undergone a profound change.

When the century began, neither human numbers nor technology had the power radically to alter planetary systems. As the century closes, not only do vastly increased human numbers and their activities have that power, but major, unintended changes are occurring in the atmosphere, in soils, in waters, among plants and animals, and in the relationships among all of these. The rate of change is outstripping the ability of scientific disciplines and our current capabilities to assess and advise. It is frustrating the attempts of political and economic institutions, which evolved in a different, more fragmented world, to adapt and cope. It deeply worries many people who are seeking ways to place those concerns on the political agendas.

The onus lies with no one group of nations. Developing countries face the obvious life-threatening challenges of desertification, deforestation, and pollution, and endure most of the poverty associated with environmental degradation. The entire human family of nations would suffer from the disappearance of rain forests in the tropics, the loss of plant and animal species, and changes in rainfall patterns. Industrial nations face the life-threatening challenges of toxic chemicals, toxic wastes, and acidification. All nations may suffer from the releases by industrialized countries of carbon dioxide and of gases that react with the ozone layer, and from any future war fought with the nuclear arsenals controlled by those nations. All nations will have a role to play in changing trends, and in righting an international economic system that increases rather than decreases inequality, that increases rather than decreases numbers of poor and hungry.

The next few decades are crucial. The time has come to break out of past patterns. Attempts to maintain social and ecological stability through old approaches to development and environmental protection will increase instability. Security must be sought through change. The Commission has noted a number of actions that must be taken to reduce risks to survival and to put future development on paths that are sustainable. Yet we are aware that such a reorientation on a continuing basis is simply beyond the reach of present decision-making structures and institutional arrangements, both national and international.

This Commission has been careful to base our recommendations on the realities of present institutions, on what can and must be accomplished today. But to keep options open for future generations, the present generation must begin now, and begin together.

To achieve the needed changes, we believe that an active follow-up of this report is imperative. It is with this in mind that we call for the UN General Assembly, upon due consideration, to transform this report into a UN Programme on Sustainable Development. Special follow-up conferences could be initiated at the regional level. Within an appropriate period after the presentation of this report to the General Assembly, an international conference could be convened to review progress made, and to promote follow-up arrangements that will be needed to set benchmarks and to maintain human progress.

First and foremost, this Commission has been concerned with people—of all countries and all walks of life. And it is to people that we address our report. The changes in human attitudes that we call for depend on a vast campaign of education, debate, and public participation. This campaign must start now if sustainable human progress is to be achieved.

The members of the World Commission on Environment and Development came from 21 very different nations. In our discussions, we disagreed often on details and priorities. But despite our widely differing backgrounds and varying national and international responsibilities, we were able to agree to the lines along which change must be drawn.

We are unanimous in our conviction that the security, well-being, and very survival of the planet depend on such changes, now.

Part I

COMMON CONCERNS

1

A THREATENED FUTURE

The Earth is one but the world is not. We all depend on one biosphere for sustaining our lives. Yet each community, each country, strives for survival and prosperity with little regard for its impact on others. Some consume the Earth's resources at a rate that would leave little for future generations. Others, many more in number, consume far too little and live with the prospect of hunger, squalor, disease, and early death.

Yet progress has been made. Throughout much of the world, children born today can expect to live longer and be better educated than their parents. In many parts, the new-born can also expect to attain a higher standard of living in a wider sense. Such progress provides hope as we contemplate the improvements still needed, and also as we face our failures to make this Earth a safer and sounder home for us and for those who are to come.

The failures that we need to correct arise both from poverty and from the short-sighted way in which we have often pursued prosperity. Many parts of the world are caught in a vicious downwards spiral: Poor people are forced to overuse environmental resources to survive from day to day, and their impoverishment of their environment further impoverishes them, making their survival ever more difficult and uncertain. The prosperity attained in some parts of the world is often precarious, as it has been secured through farming, forestry, and industrial practices that bring profit and progress only over the short term.

Societies have faced such pressures in the past and, as many desolate ruins remind us, sometimes succumbed to them. But generally these pressures were local. Today the scale of our interventions in nature is increasing and the physical effects of our decisions spill across national frontiers. The growth in economic interaction between nations amplifies the wider consequences of national decisions. Economics and ecology bind us in ever-tightening networks. Today, many regions face risks of irreversible damage to the human environment that threaten the basis for human progress.

These deepening interconnections are the central justification for establishment of this Commission. We travelled the world for nearly three years, listening. At special public hearings organized by the Commission, we heard from government leaders, scientists, and experts, from citizens' groups concerned about a wide range of environment and development issues, and from thousands of individuals—farmers, shanty-town residents, young people, industrialists, and indigenous and tribal peoples.

We found everywhere deep public concern for the environment, concern that has led not just to protests but often to changed behaviour. The challenge is to ensure that these new values are more adequately reflected in the principles and operations of political and economic structures.

We also found grounds for hope: that people can cooperate to build a future that is more prosperous, more just, and more secure; that a new era of economic growth can be attained, one based on policies that sustain and expand the Earth's resource base; and that the progress that some have known over the last century can be experienced by all in the years ahead. But for this to happen, we must understand better the symptoms of stress that confront us, we must identify the causes, and we must design new approaches to managing environmental resources and to sustaining human development.

I. SYMPTOMS AND CAUSES

Environmental stress has often been seen as the result of the growing demand on scarce resources and the pollution generated by the rising living standards of the relatively affluent. But poverty itself pollutes the environment, creating environmental stress in a different way. Those who are poor and hungry will often destroy their immediate environment in order to survive: They will cut down forests; their livestock will overgraze grasslands; they will overuse marginal land; and in growing numbers they will crowd into congested cities. The cumulative effect of these changes is so far-reaching as to make poverty itself a major global scourge.

On the other hand, where economic growth has led to improvements in living standards, it has sometimes been achieved in ways that are globally damaging in the longer term. Much of the improvement in the past has been based on the use of increasing amounts of raw materials, energy, chemicals, and synthetics and on the creation of pollution that is not adequately accounted for in figuring the costs of production processes. These trends have had unforeseen effects on the environment. Thus today's environmental challenges arise both from the lack of development and from the unintended consequences of some forms of economic growth.

Poverty

There are more hungry people in the world today than ever before in human history, and their numbers are growing. In 1980, there were 340 million people in 87 developing countries not getting enough calories to prevent stunted growth and serious health risks. This total was very slightly below the figure for 1970 in terms of share of the world population, but in terms of sheer numbers, it represented a 14 per cent increase. The World Bank predicts that these numbers are likely to go on growing.[1]

The number of people living in slums and shanty towns is rising, not falling. A growing number lack access to clean water and sanitation and hence are prey to the diseases that arise from this lack. There is some progress, impressive in places. But, on balance, poverty persists and its victims multiply.

The pressure of poverty has to be seen in a broader context. At the international level there are large differences in per capita income, which ranged in 1984 from $190 in low-income countries (other than China and India) to $11,430 in the industrial market economies. (See Table 1.1.)

Such inequalities represent great differences not merely in the quality of life today, but also in the capacity of societies to improve their quality of life in the future. Most of the world's poorest countries depend for increasing export earnings on tropical agricultural products that are vulnerable to fluctuating or declining terms of trade. Expansion can often only be achieved at the price of ecological stress. Yet diversification in ways that will alleviate both poverty and ecological stress is hampered by disadvantageous terms of technology transfer, by protectionism, and by declining financial flows to those countries that most need international finance.[2]

Within countries, poverty has been exacerbated by the unequal distribution of land and other assets. The rapid rise in population has compromised the ability to raise living standards. These factors, combined with growing demands for the commercial use of good land, often to grow crops for exports, have pushed many subsistence farmers onto poor land and robbed them of any hope of participating in their nations' economic lives. The same forces have meant that traditional shifting cultivators, who once cut forests, grew crops, and then gave the forest time to recover, now have neither land enough

TABLE 1.1

Population Size and Per Capita GNP by Groups of Countries

Country Group	Population (million)	Per Capita GNP (1984 dollars)	Average Annual Growth Rate of Per Capita GNP, 1965–84 (per cent)
Low-income Economies (excl. China, India)	611	190	0.9
China and India	1,778	290	3.3
Lower Middle-income Economies	691	740	3.0
Upper Middle-income Economies	497	1,950	3.3
High-income Oil Exporters	19	11,250	3.2
Industrial Market Economies	733	11,430	2.4

Source: Based on data in World Bank, *World Development Report 1986* (New York: Oxford University Press, 1986).

nor time to let forests re-establish. So forests are being destroyed, often only to create poor farmland that cannot support those who till it. Extending cultivation onto steep slopes is increasing soil erosion in many hilly sections of both developing and developed nations. In many river valleys, areas chronically liable to floods are now farmed.

These pressures are reflected in the rising incidence of disasters. During the 1970s, six times as many people died from 'natural disasters' each year as in the 1960s, and twice as many suffered from such disasters. Droughts and floods, disasters among whose causes are widespread deforestation and overcultivation, increased most in terms of numbers affected. There were 18.5 million people affected by droughts annually in the 1960s, but 24.4 million in the 1970s; 5.2 million people were victims of floods yearly in the 1960s, compared with 15.4 million in the 1970s.[3] The results are not in for the 1980s, but this disaster-prone decade seems to be carrying forward the trend, with droughts in Africa, India, and Latin America, and floods throughout Asia, parts of Africa, and the Andean region of Latin America.

Such disasters claim most of their victims among the impoverished in poor nations, where subsistence farmers must make their land more liable to droughts and floods by clearing marginal areas, and where the poor make themselves more vulnerable to all disasters by living on steep slopes and unprotected shores—the only lands left for their shanties. Lacking food and foreign exchange reserves, their economically vulnerable governments are ill equipped to cope with such catastrophes.

'I think this Commission should give attention on how to look into the question of more participation for those people who are the object of development. Their basic needs include the right to preserve their cultural identity, and their right not to be alienated from their own society, and their own community. So the point I want to make is that we cannot discuss environment or development without discussing political development. And you cannot eradicate poverty, at least not only by redistributing wealth or income, but there must be more redistribution of power.'

Aristides Katoppo
Publisher
WCED Public Hearing, Jakarta, 26 March 1985

The links between environmental stress and developmental disaster are most evident in sub-Saharan Africa. Per capita food production, declining since the 1960s, plummeted during the drought of the 1980s, and at the height of the food emergency some 35 million people were exposed to risk. Human overuse of land and prolonged drought threaten to turn the grasslands of Africa's Sahel region into desert.[4] No other region more tragically suffers the vicious cycle of poverty leading to environmental degradation, which leads in turn to even greater poverty.

Growth

In some parts of the world, particularly since the mid-1950s, growth and development have vastly improved living standards and the quality of life. Many of the products and technologies that have gone into this improvement are raw material- and energy-intensive and entail a substantial amount of pollution. The consequent impact on the environment is greater than ever before in human history.

Over the past century, the use of fossil fuels has grown nearly thirtyfold, and industrial production has increased more than fiftyfold. The bulk of this increase, about three-quarters in the case of fossil fuels and a little over four-fifths in the case of industrial production, has taken place *since* 1950. The annual increase in industrial production today is perhaps as large as the total production in Europe around the end of the 1930s.[5] Into every year we now squeeze the decades of industrial growth—and environmental disruption—that formed the basis of the pre-war European economy.

Environmental stresses also arise from more traditional forms of production. More land has been cleared for settled cultivation in the

'If people destroy vegetation in order to get land, food, fodder, fuel, or timber, the soil is no longer protected. Rain creates surface runoff, and the soil erodes. When the soil is gone, no water is retained and the land can no longer produce enough food, fodder, fuel, or timber, so people need to turn to new land and start the process all over again.

All major disaster problems in the Third World are essentially unsolved development problems. Disaster prevention is thus primarily an aspect of development, and this must be a development that takes place within the sustainable limits.'

Odd Grann
Secretary General, Norwegian Red Cross
WCED Public Hearing, Oslo, 24–25 June 1985

past 100 years than in all the previous centuries of human existence. Interventions in the water cycles have increased greatly. Massive dams, most of them built after 1950, impound a large proportion of the river flow. In Europe and Asia, water use has reached 10 per cent of the annual run-off, a figure that is expected to rise to 20–25 per cent by the end of the century.[6]

The impact of growth and rising income levels can be seen in the distribution of world consumption of a variety of resource-intensive products. The more affluent industrialized countries use most of the world's metals and fossil fuels. Even in the case of food products a sharp difference exists, particularly in the products that are more resource-intensive. (See Table 1.2.)

In recent years, industrial countries have been able to achieve economic growth using less energy and raw materials per unit of output. This, along with the efforts to reduce the emission of pollutants, will help to contain the pressure on the biosphere. But with the increase in population and the rise in incomes, per capita consumption of energy and materials will go up in the developing countries, as it has to if essential needs are to be met. Greater attention to resource efficiency can moderate the increase, but, on balance, environmental problems linked to resource use will intensify in global terms.

Survival

The scale and complexity of our requirements for natural resources have increased greatly with the rising levels of population and production. Nature is bountiful, but it is also fragile and finely balanced. There are thresholds that cannot be crossed without

TABLE 1.2

Distribution of World Consumption, Averages for 1980–82

Commodity	Units of Per Capita Consumption	Developed Countries (26 per cent of population)		Developing Countries (74 per cent of population)	
		Share in World Consumption (per cent)	Per Capita	Share in World Consumption (per cent)	Per Capita
Food:					
Calories	Kcal/day	34	3,395	66	2,389
Protein	gms/day	38	99	62	58
Fat	gms/day	53	127	47	40
Paper	kg/year	85	123	15	8
Steel	kg/year	79	455	21	43
Other Metals	kg/year	86	26	14	2
Commercial Energy	mtce/year	80	5.8	20	0.5

Source: WCED estimates based on country-level data from FAO, UN Statistical Office, UNCTAD, and American Metal Association.

endangering the basic integrity of the system. Today we are close to many of these thresholds; we must be ever mindful of the risk of endangering the survival of life on Earth. Moreover, the speed with which changes in resource use are taking place gives little time in which to anticipate and prevent unexpected effects.

The 'greenhouse effect', one such threat to life-support systems, springs directly from increased resource use. The burning of fossil fuels and the cutting and burning of forests release carbon dioxide (CO_2). The accumulation in the atmosphere of CO_2 and certain other gases traps solar radiation near the Earth's surface, causing global warming. This could cause sea level rises over the next 45 years large enough to inundate many low-lying coastal cities and river deltas. It could also drastically upset national and international agricultural production and trade systems.[7]

Another threat arises from the depletion of the atmospheric ozone layer by gases released during the production of foam and the use of refrigerants and aerosols. A substantial loss of such ozone could have catastrophic effects on human and livestock health and on some life forms at the base of the marine food chain. The 1986 discovery of a hole in the ozone layer above the Antarctic suggests the possibility of a more rapid depletion than previously suspected.[8]

*❛The remarkable achievements of the celebrated Industrial Revolution
are now beginning seriously to be questioned principally because the
environment was not considered at the time. It was felt that the sky was
so vast and clear nothing could ever change its colour, our rivers so big
and their water so plentiful that no amount of human activity could ever
change their quality, and there were trees and natural forests so plentiful
that we will never finish them. After all, they grow again.*

*Today we should know better. The alarming rate at which the Earth's
surface is being denuded of its natural vegetative cover seems to indicate
that the world may soon become devoid of trees through clearing for
human developments.❜*

Hon. Victoria Chitepo
Minister of Natural Resources and Tourism, Government of Zimbabwe
WCED Opening Ceremony, Harare, 18 Sept 1986

A variety of air pollutants are killing trees and lakes and damaging
buildings and cultural treasures, close to and sometimes thousands
of miles from points of emission. The acidification of the environment
threatens large areas of Europe and North America. Central Europe
is currently receiving more than one gramme of sulphur on every
square metre of ground each year.[9] The loss of forests could bring
in its wake disastrous erosion, siltation, floods, and local climatic
change. Air pollution damage is also becoming evident in some newly
industrialized countries.

In many cases the practices used at present to dispose of toxic wastes,
such as those from the chemical industries, involve unacceptable risks.
Radioactive wastes from the nuclear industry remain hazardous for
centuries. Many who bear these risks do not benefit in any way from
the activities that produce the wastes.

Desertification—the process whereby productive arid and semi-arid
land is rendered economically unproductive—and large-scale deforestation are other examples of major threats to the integrity of
regional ecosystems. Desertification involves complex interactions
between humans, land, and climate. The pressures of subsistence food
production, commercial crops, and meat production in arid and
semi-arid areas all contribute to this process.

Each year another 6 million hectares are degraded to desert-like
conditions.[10] Over three decades, this would amount to an area
roughly as large as Saudi Arabia. More than 11 million hectares of
tropical forests are destroyed per year and this, over 30 years, would
amount to an area about the size of India.[11] Apart from the direct
and often dramatic impacts within the immediate area, nearby regions

are affected by the spreading of sands or by changes in water regimes and increased risks of soil erosion and siltation.

The loss of forests and other wild lands extinguishes species of plants and animals and drastically reduces the genetic diversity of the world's ecosystems. This process robs present and future generations of genetic material with which to improve crop varieties, to make them less vulnerable to weather stress, pest attacks, and disease. The loss of species and subspecies, many as yet unstudied by science, deprives us of important potential sources of medicines and industrial chemicals. It removes forever creatures of beauty and parts of our cultural heritage; it diminishes the biosphere.

Many of the risks stemming from our productive activity and the technologies we use cross national boundaries; many are global. Though the activities that give rise to these dangers tend to be concentrated in a few countries, the risks are shared by all, rich and poor, those who benefit from them and those who do not. Most who share in the risks have little influence on the decision processes that regulate these activities.

Little time is available for corrective action. In some cases we may already be close to transgressing critical thresholds. While scientists continue to research and debate causes and effects, in many cases we already know enough to warrant action. This is true locally and regionally in the cases of such threats as desertification, deforestation, toxic wastes, and acidification; it is true globally for such threats as climate change, ozone depletion, and species loss. The risks increase faster than do our abilities to manage them.

Perhaps the greatest threat to the Earth's environment, to sustainable human progress, and indeed to survival is the possibility of nuclear war, increased daily by the continuing arms race and its spread to outer space. The search for a more viable future can only be meaningful in the context of a more vigorous effort to renounce and eliminate the development of means of annihilation.

The Economic Crisis

The environmental difficulties that confront us are not new, but only recently have we begun to understand their complexity. Previously our main concerns centred on the effects of development on the environment. Today, we need to be equally concerned about the ways in which environmental degradation can dampen or reverse economic development. In one area after another, environmental degradation is eroding the potential for development. This basic connection was brought into sharp focus by the environment and development crises of the 1980s.

TABLE 1.3

*Annual Rate of Increase of GDP in Developing Countries,
1976–85 (per cent)*

Indicator	1976–80	1981	1982	1983	1984	1985
Gross Domestic Product:						
All Developing Countries	4.9	1.3	0.2	0.8	2.1	2.5
Developing Countries Excluding Large Countries	4.5	1.0	−0.6	0.1	1.5	1.4
Per Capita GDP:						
All Developing Countries	2.4	−1.0	−2.1	−1.5	−0.2	−0.2
Developing Countries Excluding Large Countries	1.9	−1.5	−3.1	−2.4	−1.0	−1.1

Source: Department of International Economic and Social Affairs, *Doubling Development Finance: Meeting a Global Challenge, Views and Recommendations of the Committee on Development Planning* (New York: UN, 1986).

The slowdown in the momentum of economic expansion and the stagnation in world trade in the 1980s challenged all nations' abilities to react and adjust. Developing countries that rely on the export of primary products have been hit particularly hard by falling commodity prices. Between 1980 and 1984, developing countries lost about $55 billion in export earnings because of the fall in commodity prices, a blow felt most keenly in Latin America and Africa.[12]

As a consequence of this period of slow growth in the world economy—together with rising debt service obligations and a decline in the inflow of finance—many developing countries have faced severe economic crises. Over half of all developing countries actually experienced declining per capita gross domestic product (GDP) in the years 1982–85 and per capita GDP has fallen, for developing countries as a whole, by around 10 per cent in the 1980s. (See Table 1.3.)

The heaviest burden in international economic adjustment has been carried by the world's poorest people. The consequence has been a considerable increase in human distress and the overexploitation of land and natural resources to ensure survival in the short term.

Many international economic problems remain unresolved: Developing country indebtedness remains serious; commodity and energy markets are highly unstable; financial flows to developing countries are seriously deficient; protectionism and trade wars are a serious threat. Yet at a time when multilateral institutions, and rules, are more than ever necessary, they have been devalued. And the notion of an international responsibility for development has virtually disappeared. The trend is towards a decline in multilateralism and an assertion of national dominance.

II. NEW APPROACHES TO ENVIRONMENT AND DEVELOPMENT

Human progress has always depended on our technical ingenuity and a capacity for cooperative action. These qualities have often been used constructively to achieve development and environmental progress: in air and water pollution control, for example, and in increasing the efficiency of material and energy use. Many countries have increased food production and reduced population growth rates. Some technological advances, particularly in medicine, have been widely shared.

But this is not enough. Failures to manage the environment and to sustain development threaten to overwhelm all countries. Environment and development are not separate challenges; they are inexorably linked. Development cannot subsist upon a deteriorating environmental resource base; the environment cannot be protected when growth leaves out of account the costs of environmental destruction. These problems cannot be treated separately by fragmented institutions and policies. They are linked in a complex system of cause and effect.

First, environmental stresses are linked one to another. For example, deforestation, by increasing run-off, accelerates soil erosion and siltation of rivers and lakes. Air pollution and acidification play their part in killing forests and lakes. Such links mean that several different problems must be tackled simultaneously. And success in one area, such as forest protection, can improve chances of success in another area, such as soil conservation.

Second, environmental stresses and patterns of economic development are linked one to another. Thus agricultural policies may lie at the root of land, water, and forest degradation. Energy policies are associated with the global greenhouse effect, with acidification, and with deforestation for fuelwood in many developing nations. These stresses all threaten economic development. Thus economics and ecology must be completely integrated in decision-making and lawmaking processes not just to protect the environment, but also to protect and promote development. Economy is not just about the

How long can we go on and safely pretend that the environment is not the economy, is not health, is not the prerequisite to development, is not recreation? Is it realistic to see ourselves as managers of an entity out there called the environment, extraneous to us, an alternative to the economy, too expensive a value to protect in difficult economic times? When we organize ourselves starting from this premise, we do so with dangerous consequences to our economy, health, and industrial growth.

We are now just beginning to realize that we must find an alternative to our ingrained behaviour of burdening future generations resulting from our misplaced belief that there is a choice between economy and the environment. That choice, in the long term, turns out to be an illusion with awesome consequences for humanity.

Charles Caccia,
Member of Parliament, House of Commons
WCED Public Hearing, Ottawa, 26–27 May 1986

production of wealth, and ecology is not just about the protection of nature; they are both equally relevant for improving the lot of humankind.

Third, environmental and economic problems are linked to many social and political factors. For example, the rapid population growth that has so profound an impact on the environment and on development in many regions is driven partly by such factors as the status of women in society and other cultural values. Also, environmental stress and uneven development can increase social tensions. It could be argued that the distribution of power and influence within society lies at the heart of most environment and development challenges. Hence new approaches must involve programmes of social development, particularly to improve the position of women in society, to protect vulnerable groups, and to promote local participation in decision making.

Finally, the systemic features operate not merely within but also between nations. National boundaries have become so porous that traditional distinctions between matters of local, national, and international significance have become blurred. Ecosystems do not respect national boundaries. Water pollution moves through shared rivers, lakes, and seas. The atmosphere carries air pollution over vast distances. Major accidents—particularly those at nuclear reactors or at plants or warehouses containing toxic materials—can have widespread regional effects.

Many environment-economy links also operate globally. For instance, the highly subsidized, incentive-driven agriculture of in-

'To successfully advance in solving global problems, we need to develop new methods of thinking, to elaborate new moral and value criteria, and, no doubt, new patterns of behaviour.

Mankind is on the threshold of a new stage in its development. We should not only promote the expansion of its material, scientific, and technical basis, but, what is most important, the formation of new value and humanistic aspirations in human psychology, since wisdom and humaneness are the 'eternal truths' that make the basis of humanity. We need new social, moral, scientific, and ecological concepts, which should be determined by new conditions in the life of mankind today and in the future.'

I. T. Frolov
Editor-in-Chief, Communist Magazine
WCED Public Hearing, Moscow, 8 Dec 1986

dustrialized market economies generates surpluses that depress prices and erode the viability of the often neglected agriculture of developing countries. Soils and other environmental resources suffer in both systems. Each country may devise national agricultural policies to secure short-term economic and political gains, but no nation alone can devise policies to deal effectively with the financial, economic, and ecological costs of the agricultural and trade policies of other nations.

In the past, responsibility for environmental matters has been placed in environmental ministries and institutions that often have had little or no control over destruction caused by agricultural, industrial, urban development, forestry, and transportation policies and practices. Society has failed to give the responsibility for preventing environmental damage to the 'sectoral' ministries and agencies whose policies cause it. Thus our environmental management practices have focused largely upon after-the-fact repair of damage: reforestation, reclaiming desert lands, rebuilding urban environments, restoring natural habitats, and rehabilitating wild lands. The ability to anticipate and prevent environmental damage will require that the ecological dimensions of policy be considered at the same time as the economic, trade, energy, agricultural, and other dimensions.

In most countries, environmental policies are directed at the symptoms of harmful growth; these policies have brought progress and rewards and must be continued and strengthened. But that will not be enough. What is required is a new approach in which all nations aim at a type of development that integrates production with resource conservation and enhancement, and that links both to the

❛You talk very little about life, you talk too much about survival. It is very important to remember that when the possibilities for life are over, the possibilities for survival start. And there are peoples here in Brazil, especially in the Amazon region, who still live, and these peoples that still live don't want to reach down to the level of survival.❜

Speaker from the floor
WCED Public Hearing, Sao Paulo, 28–29 Oct 1985

provision for all of an adequate livelihood base and equitable access to resources.

The concept of sustainable development provides a framework for the integration of environment policies and development strategies—the term 'development' being used here in its broadest sense. The word is often taken to refer to the processes of economic and social change in the Third World. But the integration of environment and development is required in all countries, rich and poor. The pursuit of sustainable development requires changes in the domestic and international policies of every nation.

Sustainable development seeks to meet the needs and aspirations of the present without compromising the ability to meet those of the future. Far from requiring the cessation of economic growth, it recognizes that the problems of poverty and underdevelopment cannot be solved unless we have a new era of growth in which developing countries play a large role and reap large benefits.

Economic growth always brings risk of environmental damage, as it puts increased pressure on environmental resources. But policy makers guided by the concept of sustainable development will necessarily work to assure that growing economies remain firmly attached to their ecological roots and that these roots are protected and nurtured so that they may support growth over the long term. Environmental protection is thus inherent in the concept of sustainable development, as is a focus on the sources of environmental problems rather than the symptoms.

No single blueprint of sustainability will be found, as economic and social systems and ecological conditions differ widely among countries. Each nation will have to work out its own concrete policy implications. Yet irrespective of these differences, sustainable development should be seen as a global objective.

No country can develop in isolation from others. Hence the pursuit of sustainable development requires a new orientation in international relations. Long-term sustainable growth will require far-reaching changes to produce trade, capital, and technology flows that are more equitable and better synchronized to environmental imperatives.

The mechanics of increased international cooperation required to assure sustainable development will vary from sector to sector and in relation to particular institutions. But it is fundamental that the transition to sustainable development be managed jointly by all nations. The unity of human needs requires a functioning multilateral system that respects the democratic principle of consent and accepts that not only the Earth but also the world is one.

In the chapters that follow we examine these issues in greater detail and make a number of specific proposals for responding to the crises of a threatened future. Overall, our report carries a message of hope. But it is hope conditioned upon the establishment of a new era of international cooperation based on the premise that every human being—those here and those who are to come—has the right to life, and to a decent life. We confidently believe that the international community can rise, as it must, to the challenge of securing sustainable human progress.

Notes

1 World Bank, *Poverty and Hunger: Issues and Options for Food Security in Developing Countries* (Washington, DC: 1986).

2 Department of International Economic and Social Affairs, *Doubling Development Finance: Meeting a Global Challenge, Views and Recommendations of the Committee on Development Planning* (New York: UN, 1986).

3 G. Hagman et al., *Prevention Better Than Cure*, Report on Human and Environmental Disasters in the Third World (Stockholm: Swedish Red Cross, 1984).

4 UN, General Assembly, 'The Critical Economic Situation in Africa: Report of the Secretary General', A/S-13/z, New York, 20 May 1986.

5 Based on data from W. W. Rostow, *The World Economy: History and Prospect* (Austin: University of Texas Press, 1978); UN, *World Energy Supplies in Selected Years 1929-1950* (New York: 1952); UN, *Statistical Yearbook 1982* (New York: 1985); UNCTAD, *Handbook of International Trade and Development Statistics 1985 Supplement* (New York: 1985); W. S. and E. S. Woytinsky, *World Population and Production Trends and Outlook* (New York: Twentieth Century Fund, 1953).

6 USSR Committee for the International Hydrological Decade, *World Water Balance and Water Resources of the Earth* (Paris: UNESCO, 1978).

7 WMO, *A Report of the International Conference on the Assessment of Carbon Dioxide and Other Greenhouse Gases in Climate Variations and Associated Impacts*, Villach, Austria, 9–15 October 1985, WMO No.661 (Geneva: WMO/ICSU/UNEP, 1986).

8 National Science Foundation, 'Scientists Closer to Identifying Cause of Antarctic Ozone Layer Depletion', news release, Washington, DC, 20 October 1986.

9 J. Lehmhaus et al., 'Calculated and Observed Data for 1980 Compared at EMEP Measurement Stations', Norwegian Meteorological Institute, EMEP/MSC-W Report 1–86, 1986.

10 UNEP, 'General Assessment of Progress in the Implementation of the Plan of Action to Combat Desertification 1978–1984', Nairobi, 1984; WCED Advisory Panel on Food Security, Agriculture, Forestry and Environment, *Food Security* (London: Zed Books, 1987).

11 World Resources Institute/International Institute for Environment and Development, *World Resources 1986* (New York: Basic Books, 1986).

12 UNCTAD, *Trade and Development Report 1986* (New York: 1986).

2

TOWARDS SUSTAINABLE DEVELOPMENT

Sustainable development is development that meets the needs of the present without compromising the ability of future generations to meet their own needs. It contains within it two key concepts:

- the concept of 'needs', in particular the essential needs of the world's poor, to which overriding priority should be given; and
- the idea of limitations imposed by the state of technology and social organization on the environment's ability to meet present and future needs.

Thus the goals of economic and social development must be defined in terms of sustainability in all countries—developed or developing, market-oriented or centrally planned. Interpretations will vary, but must share certain general features and must flow from a consensus on the basic concept of sustainable development and on a broad strategic framework for achieving it.

Development involves a progressive transformation of economy and society. A development path that is sustainable in a physical sense could theoretically be pursued even in a rigid social and political setting. But physical sustainability cannot be secured unless development policies pay attention to such considerations as changes in access to resources and in the distribution of costs and benefits. Even the narrow notion of physical sustainability implies a concern for social equity between generations, a concern that must logically be extended to equity within each generation.

I. THE CONCEPT OF SUSTAINABLE DEVELOPMENT

The satisfaction of human needs and aspirations is the major objective of development. The essential needs of vast numbers of people in developing countries—for food, clothing, shelter, jobs—are not being met, and beyond their basic needs these people have legitimate aspirations for an improved quality of life. A world in which poverty and inequity are endemic will always be prone to ecological and other crises. Sustainable development requires meeting the basic needs of all and extending to all the opportunity to satisfy their aspirations for a better life.

Living standards that go beyond the basic minimum are sustainable only if consumption standards everywhere have regard for long-term sustainability. Yet many of us live beyond the world's ecological means, for instance in our patterns of energy use. Perceived needs are socially and culturally determined, and sustainable development requires the promotion of values that encourage consumption standards that are within the bounds of the ecological possible and to which all can reasonably aspire.

Meeting essential needs depends in part on achieving full growth potential, and sustainable development clearly requires economic growth in places where such needs are not being met. Elsewhere, it can be consistent with economic growth, provided the content of growth reflects the broad principles of sustainability and non-exploitation of others. But growth by itself is not enough. High levels of productive activity and widespread poverty can coexist, and can endanger the environment. Hence sustainable development requires that societies meet human needs both by increasing productive potential and by ensuring equitable opportunities for all.

An expansion in numbers can increase the pressure on resources and slow the rise in living standards in areas where deprivation is widespread. Though the issue is not merely one of population size but of the distribution of resources, sustainable development can only be pursued if demographic developments are in harmony with the changing productive potential of the ecosystem.

A society may in many ways compromise its ability to meet the essential needs of its people in the future—by overexploiting resources, for example. The direction of technological developments may solve some immediate problems but lead to even greater ones. Large sections of the population may be marginalized by ill-considered development.

Settled agriculture, the diversion of watercourses, the extraction of minerals, the emission of heat and noxious gases into the atmosphere, commercial forests, and genetic manipulation are all examples of human intervention in natural systems during the course of development. Until recently, such interventions were small in scale and their impact limited. Today's interventions are more drastic in scale and impact, and more threatening to life-support systems both locally and globally. This need not happen. At a minimum, sustainable

⁶A communications gap has kept environmental, population, and development assistance groups apart for too long, preventing us from being aware of our common interest and realizing our combined power. Fortunately, the gap is closing. We now know that what unites us is vastly more important than what divides us.

We recognize that poverty, environmental degradation and population growth are inextricably related and that none of these fundamental problems can be successfully addressed in isolation. We will succeed or fail together.

Arriving at a commonly accepted definition of 'sustainable development' remains a challenge for all the actors in the development process.⁹

'Making Common Cause'
U.S.-Based Development, Environment, Population NGOs
WCED Public Hearing, Ottawa, 26–27 May 1986

---

development must not endanger the natural systems that support life on Earth: the atmosphere, the waters, the soils, and the living beings.

Growth has no set limits in terms of population or resource use beyond which lies ecological disaster. Different limits hold for the use of energy, materials, water, and land. Many of these will manifest themselves in the form of rising costs and diminishing returns, rather than in the form of any sudden loss of a resource base. The accumulation of knowledge and the development of technology can enhance the carrying capacity of the resource base. But ultimate limits there are, and sustainability requires that long before these are reached, the world must ensure equitable access to the constrained resource and reorient technological efforts to relieve the pressure.

Economic growth and development obviously involve changes in the physical ecosystem. Every ecosystem everywhere cannot be preserved intact. A forest may be depleted in one part of a watershed and extended elsewhere, which is not a bad thing if the exploitation has been planned and the effects on soil erosion rates, water regimes, and genetic losses have been taken into account. In general, renewable resources like forests and fish stocks need not be depleted provided the rate of use is within the limits of regeneration and natural growth. But most renewable resources are part of a complex and interlinked ecosystem, and maximum sustainable yield must be defined after taking into account system-wide effects of exploitation.

As for non-renewable resources, like fossil fuels and minerals, their use reduces the stock available for future generations. But this does not mean that such resources should not be used. In general the rate of depletion should take into account the criticality of that resource, the availability of technologies for minimizing depletion, and the likelihood of substitutes being available. Thus land should not be degraded beyond reasonable recovery. With minerals and fossil fuels, the rate of depletion and the emphasis on recycling and economy of use should be calibrated to ensure that the resource does not run out before acceptable substitutes are available. Sustainable development requires that the rate of depletion of non-renewable resources should foreclose as few future options as possible.

Development tends to simplify ecosystems and to reduce their diversity of species. And species, once extinct, are not renewable. The loss of plant and animal species can greatly limit the options of future generations; so sustainable development requires the conservation of plant and animal species.

So-called free goods like air and water are also resources. The raw materials and energy of production processes are only partly converted to useful products. The rest comes out as wastes. Sustainable development requires that the adverse impacts on the quality of air, water, and other natural elements are minimized so as to sustain the ecosystem's overall integrity.

In essence, sustainable development is a process of change in which the exploitation of resources, the direction of investments, the orientation of technological development, and institutional change are all in harmony and enhance both current and future potential to meet human needs and aspirations.

II. EQUITY AND THE COMMON INTEREST

Sustainable development has been described here in general terms. How are individuals in the real world to be persuaded or made to act in the common interest? The answer lies partly in education, institutional development, and law enforcement. But many problems of resource depletion and environmental stress arise from disparities in economic and political power. An industry may get away with unacceptable levels of air and water pollution because the people who bear the brunt of it are poor and unable to complain effectively. A forest may be destroyed by excessive felling because the people living there have no alternatives or because timber contractors generally have more influence than forest dwellers.

Ecological interactions do not respect the boundaries of individual ownership and political jurisdiction. Thus:

- In a watershed, the ways in which a farmer up the slope uses land directly affect run-off on farms downstream.
- The irrigation practices, pesticides, and fertilizers used on one farm affect the productivity of neighbouring ones, especially among small farms.
- The efficiency of a factory boiler determines its rate of emission of soot and noxious chemicals and affects all who live and work around it.
- The hot water discharged by a thermal power plant into a river or a local sea affects the catch of all who fish locally.

Traditional social systems recognized some aspects of this interdependence and enforced community control over agricultural practices and traditional rights relating to water, forests, and land. This enforcement of the 'common interest' did not necessarily impede growth and expansion though it may have limited the acceptance and diffusion of technical innovations.

Local interdependence has, if anything, increased because of the technology used in modern agriculture and manufacturing. Yet with this surge of technical progress, the growing 'enclosure' of common lands, the erosion of common rights in forests and other resources, and the spread of commerce and production for the market, the responsibilities for decision making are being taken away from both groups and individuals. This shift is still under way in many developing countries.

It is not that there is one set of villains and another of victims. All would be better off if each person took into account the effect of his or her acts upon others. But each is unwilling to assume that others will behave in this socially desirable fashion, and hence all continue to pursue narrow self-interest. Communities or governments can compensate for this isolation through laws, education, taxes, subsidies, and other methods. Well-enforced laws and strict liability legislation can control harmful side effects. Most important, effective participation in decision-making processes by local communities can help them articulate and effectively enforce their common interest.

Interdependence is not simply a local phenomenon. Rapid growth in production has extended it to the international plane, with both physical and economic manifestations. There are growing global and regional pollution effects, such as in the more than 200 international river basins and the large number of shared seas.

The enforcement of common interest often suffers because areas of political jurisdictions and areas of impact do not coincide. Energy policies in one jurisdiction cause acid precipitation in another. The

'If the desert is growing, forest disappearing, malnutrition increasing, and people in urban areas living in very bad conditions, it is not because we are lacking resources but the kind of policy implemented by our rulers, by the elite group. Denying people rights and peoples' interests is pushing us to a situation where it is only the poverty that has a very prosperous future in Africa. And it is our hope that your Commission, the World Commission, will not overlook these problems of human rights in Africa and will put emphasis on it. Because it is only free people, people who have rights, who are mature and responsible citizens, who then participate in the development and in the protection of the environment.'

Speaker from the floor
WCED Public Hearing, Nairobi, 23 Sept 1986

fishing policies of one state affect the fish catch of another. No supranational authority exists to resolve such issues, and the common interest can only be articulated through international cooperation.

In the same way, the ability of a government to control its national economy is reduced by growing international economic interactions. For example, foreign trade in commodities makes issues of carrying capacities and resource scarcities an international concern. (See Chapter 3.) If economic power and the benefits of trade were more equally distributed, common interests would be generally recognized. But the gains from trade are unequally distributed, and patterns of trade in, say, sugar affect not merely a local sugar-producing sector, but the economies and ecologies of the many developing countries that depend heavily on this product.

The search for common interest would be less difficult if all development and environment problems had solutions that would leave everyone better off. This is seldom the case, and there are usually winners and losers. Many problems arise from inequalities in access to resources. An inequitable landownership structure can lead to overexploitation of resources in the smallest holdings, with harmful effects on both environment and development. Internationally, monopolistic control over resources can drive those who do not share in them to excessive exploitation of marginal resources. The differing capacities of exploiters to commandeer 'free' goods—locally, nationally, and internationally—is another manifestation of unequal access to resources. 'Losers' in environment/development conflicts include those who suffer more than their fair share of the health, property, and ecosystem damage costs of pollution.

As a system approaches ecological limits, inequalities sharpen. Thus when a watershed deteriorates, poor farmers suffer more because they cannot afford the same anti-erosion measures as richer farmers. When urban air quality deteriorates, the poor, in their more vulnerable areas, suffer more health damage than the rich, who usually live in more pristine neighbourhoods. When mineral resources become depleted, late-comers to the industrialization process lose the benefits of low-cost supplies. Globally, wealthier nations are better placed financially and technologically to cope with the effects of possible climatic change.

Hence, our inability to promote the common interest in sustainable development is often a product of the relative neglect of economic and social justice within and amongst nations.

III. STRATEGIC IMPERATIVES

The world must quickly design strategies that will allow nations to move from their present, often destructive, processes of growth and development onto sustainable development paths. This will require policy changes in all countries, with respect both to their own development and to their impacts on other nations' development possibilities. (This chapter concerns itself with national strategies. The required reorientation in international economic relations is dealt with in Chapter 3.)

Critical objectives for environment and development policies that follow from the concept of sustainable development include:

- reviving growth;
- changing the quality of growth;
- meeting essential needs for jobs, food, energy, water, and sanitation;
- ensuring a sustainable level of population;
- conserving and enhancing the resource base;
- reorienting technology and managing risk; and
- merging environment and economics in decision making.

Reviving Growth

As indicated earlier, development that is sustainable has to address the problem of the large number of people who live in absolute poverty—that is, who are unable to satisfy even the most basic of their needs. Poverty reduces people's capacity to use resources in a sustainable manner; it intensifies pressure on the environment. Most

---

Box 2-1. Growth, Redistribution, and Poverty

The poverty line is that level of income below which an individual or household cannot afford on a regular basis the necessities of life. The percentage of the population below that line will depend on per capita national income and the manner in which it is distributed. How quickly can a developing country expect to eliminate absolute poverty? The answer will vary from country to country, but much can be learned from a typical case.

Consider a nation in which half the population lives below the poverty line and where the distribution of household incomes is as follows: The top one-fifth of households have 50 per cent of total income, the next fifth have 20 per cent, the next fifth have 14 per cent, the next fifth have 9 per cent, and the bottom fifth have just 7 per cent. This is a fair representation of the situation in many low-income developing countries.

In this case, if the income distribution remains unchanged, per capita national income would have to double before the poverty ratio drops from 50 to 10 per cent. If income is redistributed in favour of the poor, this reduction can occur sooner. Consider the case in which 25 per cent of the incremental income of the richest one-fifth of the population is redistributed equally to the others.

---

such absolute poverty is in developing countries; in many, it has been aggravated by the economic stagnation of the 1980s. A necessary but not a sufficient condition for the elimination of absolute poverty is a relatively rapid rise in per capita incomes in the Third World. It is therefore essential that the stagnant or declining growth trends of this decade be reversed.

While attainable growth rates will vary, a certain minimum is needed to have any impact on absolute poverty. It seems unlikely that, taking developing countries as a whole, these objectives can be accomplished with per capita income growth of under 3 per cent. (See Box 2-1.) Given current population growth rates, this would require overall national income growth of around 5 per cent a year in the developing economies of Asia, 5.5 per cent in Latin America, and 6 per cent in Africa and West Asia.

Are these orders of magnitude attainable? The record in South and East Asia over the past quarter-century and especially over the last five years suggests that 5 per cent annual growth can be attained in most countries, including the two largest, India and China. In Latin America, average growth rates on the order of 5 per cent were achieved during the 1960s and 1970s, but fell well below that in the first half of this decade, mainly because of the debt crisis.[1] A revival of Latin American growth depends on the resolution of this crisis. In Africa, growth rates during the 1960s and 1970s were around 4–

The assumptions here about redistribution reflect three judgements. First, in most situations redistributive policies can only operate on increases in income. Second, in low-income developing countries the surplus that can be skimmed off for redistribution is available only from the wealthier groups. Third, redistributive policies cannot be so precisely targeted that they deliver benefits only to those who are below the poverty line, so some of the benefits will accrue to those who are just a little above it.

The number of years required to bring the poverty ratio down from 50 to 10 per cent ranges from:
- 18–24 years if per capita income grows at 3 per cent,
- 26–36 years if it grows at 2 per cent, and
- 51–70 years if it grows only at 1 per cent.

In each case, the shorter time is associated with the redistribution of 25 per cent of the incremental income of the richest fifth of the population and the longer period with no redistribution.

So with per capita national income growing only at 1 per cent a year, the time required to eliminate absolute poverty would stretch well into the next century. If, however, the aim is to ensure that the world is well on its way towards sustainable development by the beginning of the next century, it is necessary to aim at a minimum of 3 per cent per capita national income growth *and* to pursue vigorous redistributive policies.

4.5 per cent, which at current rates of population growth would mean per capita income growth of only a little over 1 per cent.[2] Moreover, during the 1980s, growth nearly halted and in two-thirds of the countries per capita income declined.[3] Attaining a minimum level of growth in Africa requires the correction of short-term imbalances, and also the removal of deep-rooted constraints on the growth process.

Growth must be revived in developing countries because that is where the links between economic growth, the alleviation of poverty, and environmental conditions operate most directly. Yet developing countries are part of an interdependent world economy; their prospects also depend on the levels and patterns of growth in industrialized nations. The medium-term prospects for industrial countries are for growth of 3–4 per cent, the minimum that international financial institutions consider necessary if these countries are going to play a part in expanding the world economy. Such growth rates could be environmentally sustainable if industrialized nations can continue the recent shifts in the content of their growth towards less material- and energy-intensive activities and the improvement of their efficiency in using materials and energy.

As industrialized nations use less materials and energy, however, they will provide smaller markets for commodities and minerals from the developing nations. Yet if developing nations focus their efforts upon eliminating poverty and satisfying essential human needs, then domestic demand will increase for both agricultural products and manufactured goods and some services. Hence the very logic of sustainable development implies an internal stimulus to Third World growth.

Nonetheless, in large numbers of developing countries markets are very small; and for all developing countries high export growth, especially of non-traditional items, will also be necessary to finance imports, demand for which will be generated by rapid development. Thus a reorientation of international economic relations will be necessary for sustainable development, as discussed in Chapter 3.

Changing the Quality of Growth

Sustainable development involves more than growth. It requires a change in the content of growth, to make it less material- and energy-intensive and more equitable in its impact. These changes are required in all countries as part of a package of measures to maintain the stock of ecological capital, to improve the distribution of income, and to reduce the degree of vulnerability to economic crises.

The process of economic development must be more soundly based upon the realities of the stock of capital that sustains it. This is rarely done in either developed or developing countries. For example, income from forestry operations is conventionally measured in terms of the value of timber and other products extracted, minus the costs of extraction. The costs of regenerating the forest are not taken into account, unless money is actually spent on such work. Thus figuring profits from logging rarely takes full account of the losses in future revenue incurred through degradation of the forest. Similar incomplete accounting occurs in the exploitation of other natural resources, especially in the case of resources that are not capitalized in enterprise or national accounts: air, water, and soil. In all countries, rich or poor, economic development must take full account in its measurements of growth of the improvement or deterioration in the stock of natural resources.

Income distribution is one aspect of the quality of growth, as described in the preceding section, and rapid growth combined with deteriorating income distribution may be worse than slower growth combined with redistribution in favour of the poor. For instance, in many developing countries the introduction of large-scale commercial agriculture may produce revenue rapidly, but may also dispossess a large number of small farmers and make income distribution more inequitable. In the long run, such a path may not be sustainable; it

‘People have acquired, often for the first time in history, both an idea of their relative poverty and a desire to emerge from it and improve the quality of their lives. As people advance materially, and eat and live better, what were once luxuries tend to be regarded as necessities. The net result is that the demand for food, raw materials, and power increases to an even greater degree than the population. As demand increases, a greater and greater strain is put on the finite area of the world's land to produce the products needed.’

Dr. I. P. Garbouchev
Bulgarian Academy of Sciences
WCED Public Hearing, Moscow, 11 Dec 1986

impoverishes many people and can increase pressures on the natural resource base through overcommercialized agriculture and through the marginalization of subsistence farmers. Relying more on small-holder cultivation may be slower at first, but more easily sustained over the long term.

Economic development is unsustainable if it increases vulnerability to crises. A drought may force farmers to slaughter animals needed for sustaining production in future years. A drop in prices may cause farmers or other producers to overexploit natural resources to maintain incomes. But vulnerability can be reduced by using technologies that lower production risks, by choosing institutional options that reduce market fluctuations, and by building up reserves, especially of food and foreign exchange. A development path that combines growth with reduced vulnerability is more sustainable than one that does not.

Yet it is not enough to broaden the range of economic variables taken into account. Sustainability requires views of human needs and well-being that incorporate such non-economic variables as education and health enjoyed for their own sake, clean air and water, and the protection of natural beauty. It must also work to remove disabilities from disadvantaged groups, many of whom live in ecologically vulnerable areas, such as many tribal groups in forests, desert nomads, groups in remote hill areas, and indigenous peoples of the Americas and Australasia.

Changing the quality of growth requires changing our approach to development efforts to take account of all of their effects. For instance, a hydropower project should not be seen merely as a way of producing more electricity; its effects upon the local environment and the livelihood of the local community must be included in any balance sheets. Thus the abandonment of a hydro project because it will disturb a rare ecological system could be a measure of progress, not a setback to development.[4] Nevertheless, in some cases, sustainability considerations will involve a rejection of activities that are financially attractive in the short run.

Economic and social development can and should be mutually reinforcing. Money spent on education and health can raise human productivity. Economic development can accelerate social development by providing opportunities for underprivileged groups or by spreading education more rapidly.

Meeting Essential Human Needs

The satisfaction of human needs and aspirations is so obviously an objective of productive activity that it may appear redundant to assert its central role in the concept of sustainable development. All too often poverty is such that people cannot satisfy their needs for survival and well-being even if goods and services are available. At the same time, the demands of those not in poverty may have major environmental consequences.

The principal development challenge is to meet the needs and aspirations of an expanding developing world population. The most basic of all needs is for a livelihood: that is, employment. Between 1985 and 2000 the labour force in developing countries will increase by nearly 900 million, and new livelihood opportunities will have to be generated for 60 million persons every year.[5] The pace and pattern of economic development have to generate sustainable work opportunities on this scale and at a level of productivity that would enable poor households to meet minimum consumption standards.

More food is required not merely to feed more people but to attack undernourishment. For the developing world to eat, person for person, as well as the industrial world by the year 2000, annual increases of 5.0 per cent in calories and 5.8 per cent in proteins are needed in Africa; of 3.4 and 4.0 per cent, respectively, in Latin America; and of 3.5 and 4.5 per cent in Asia.[6] Foodgrains and starchy roots are the primary sources of calories, while proteins are obtained primarily from products like milk, meat, fish, pulses, and oil-seeds.

Though the focus at present is necessarily on staple foods, the projections given above also highlight the need for a high rate of growth of protein availability. In Africa, the task is particularly challenging given the recent declining per capita food production and the current constraints on growth. In Asia and Latin America, the required growth rates in calorie and protein consumption seem to be

'In the developing world, mostly in the Third World, we realize that the main problem we have is that we do not have employment opportunities, and most of these people who are unemployed move from rural areas and they migrate into the cities and those who remain behind always indulge in processes—for example charcoal burning—and all this leads to deforestation. So maybe the environmental organizations should step in and look for ways to prevent this kind of destruction.'

Kennedy Njiro
Student, Kenya Polytechnic
WCED Public Hearing, Nairobi, 23 Sept 1986

more readily attainable. But increased food production should not be based on ecologically unsound production policies and compromise long-term prospects for food security.

Energy is another essential human need, one that cannot be universally met unless energy consumption patterns change. The most urgent problem is the requirements of poor Third World households, which depend mainly on fuelwood. By the turn of the century, 3 billion people may live in areas where wood is cut faster than it grows or where fuelwood is extremely scarce.[7] Corrective action would both reduce the drudgery of collecting wood over long distances and preserve the ecological base. The minimum requirements for cooking fuel in most developing countries appear to be on the order of 250 kilogrammes of coal equivalent per capita per year. This is a fraction of the household energy consumption in industrial countries.

The linked basic needs of housing, water supply, sanitation, and health care are also environmentally important. Deficiencies in these areas are often visible manifestations of environmental stress. In the Third World, the failure to meet these key needs is one of the major causes of many communicable diseases such as malaria, gastro-intestinal infestations, cholera, and typhoid. Population growth and the drift into cities threaten to make these problems worse. Planners must find ways of relying more on supporting community initiatives and self-help efforts and on effectively using low-cost technologies.

Ensuring a Sustainable Level of Population

The sustainability of development is intimately linked to the dynamics of population growth. The issue, however, is not simply one of global population size. A child born in a country where levels of material and energy use are high places a greater burden on the Earth's resources than a child born in a poorer country. A similar argument applies within countries. Nonetheless, sustainable development can be pursued more easily when population size is stabilized at a level consistent with the productive capacity of the ecosystem.

In industrial countries, the overall rate of population growth is under 1 per cent, and several countries have reached or are approaching zero population growth. The total population of the industrialized world could increase from its current 1.2 billion to about 1.4 billion in the year 2025.[8]

The greater part of global population increase will take place in developing countries, where the 1985 population of 3.7 billion may increase to 6.8 billion by 2025.[9] The Third World does not have the option of migration to 'new' lands, and the time available for adjustment is much less than industrial countries had. Hence the challenge now is to quickly lower population growth rates, especially in regions such as Africa, where these rates are increasing.

Birth rates declined in industrial countries largely because of economic and social development. Rising levels of income and urbanization and the changing role of women all played important roles. Similar processes are now at work in developing countries. These should be recognized and encouraged. Population policies should be integrated with other economic and social development programmes—female education, health care, and the expansion of the livelihood base of the poor. But time is short, and developing countries will also have to promote direct measures to reduce fertility, to avoid going radically beyond the productive potential to support their populations. In fact, increased access to family planning services is itself a form of social development that allows couples, and women in particular, the right to self-determination.

Population growth in developing countries will remain unevenly distributed between rural and urban areas. UN projections suggest that by the first decade of the next century, the absolute size of rural populations in most developing countries will start declining. Nearly 90 per cent of the increase in the developing world will take place in urban areas, the population of which is expected to rise from 1.15 billion in 1985 to 3.85 billion in 2025.[10] The increase will be particularly marked in Africa and, to a lesser extent, in Asia.

Developing-country cities are growing much faster than the capacity of authorities to cope. Shortages of housing, water, sanitation, and mass transit are widespread. A growing proportion of city-dwellers live in slums and shanty towns, many of them exposed to air and water pollution and to industrial and natural hazards. Further deterioration is likely, given that most urban growth will take place in the largest cities. Thus more manageable cities may be the principal gain from slower rates of population growth.

Urbanization is itself part of the development process. The challenge is to manage the process so as to avoid a severe deterioration in the quality of life. Thus the development of smaller urban centres needs to be encouraged to reduce pressures in large cities. Solving the impending urban crisis will require the promotion of self-help housing and urban services by and for the poor, and a more positive approach to the role of the informal sector, supported by sufficient funds for water supply, sanitation, and other services.

Conserving and Enhancing the Resource Base

If needs are to be met on a sustainable basis the Earth's natural resource base must be conserved and enhanced. Major changes in policies will be needed to cope with the industrial world's current high levels of consumption, the increases in consumption needed to meet minimum standards in developing countries, and expected population growth. However, the case for the conservation of nature should not rest only with development goals. It is part of our moral obligation to other living beings and future generations.

Pressure on resources increases when people lack alternatives. Development policies must widen people's options for earning a sustainable livelihood, particularly for resource-poor households and in areas under ecological stress. In a hilly area, for instance, economic self-interest and ecology can be combined by helping farmers shift from grain to tree crops by providing them with advice, equipment, and marketing assistance. Programmes to protect the incomes of farmers, fishermen, and foresters against short-term price declines may decrease their need to overexploit resources.

The conservation of agricultural resources is an urgent task because in many parts of the world cultivation has already been extended to marginal lands, and fishery and forestry resources have been overexploited. These resources must be conserved and enhanced to meet the needs of growing populations. Land use in agriculture and forestry should be based on a scientific assessment of land capacity, and the annual depletion of topsoil, fish stock, or forest resources must not exceed the rate of regeneration.

The pressures on agricultural land from crop and livestock production can be partly relieved by increasing productivity. But shortsighted, short-term improvements in productivity can create different forms of ecological stress, such as the loss of genetic diversity in

❝I work with rubber trees in the Amazon. I am here to speak about the tropical forest.

We live from this forest they want to destroy. And we want to take this opportunity of having so many people here gathered with the same objective in mind to defend our habitat, the conservation of forest, of tropical forest.

In my area, we have about 14–15 native products that we extract from the forest, besides all the other activities we have. So I think this must be preserved. Because it is not only with cattle, not only with pasture lands, and not only with highways that we will be able to develop the Amazon.

When they think of falling trees, they always think of building roads and the roads bring destruction under a mask called progress. Let us put this progress where the lands have already been deforested, where it is idle of labour and where we have to find people work, and where we have to make the city grow. But let us leave those who want to live in the forest, who want to keep it as it.

We have nothing written. I don't have anything that was created in somebody's office. There is no philosophy. It is just the real truth, because this is what our life is.❞

Jaime da Silva Araujo
National Council of Rubber Tappers
WCED Public Hearing, Sao Paulo, 28–29 Oct 1985

standing crops, salinization and alkalization of irrigated lands, nitrate pollution of ground-water, and pesticide residues in food. Ecologically more benign alternatives are available. Future increases in productivity, in both developed and developing countries, should be based on the better controlled application of water and agrochemicals, as well as on more extensive use of organic manures and non-chemical means of pest control. These alternatives can be promoted only by an agricultural policy based on ecological realities. (See Chapter 5.)

In the case of fisheries and tropical forestry, we rely largely on the exploitation of the naturally available stocks. The sustainable yield from these stocks may well fall short of demand. Hence it will be necessary to turn to methods that produce more fish, fuelwood, and forest products under controlled conditions. Substitutes for fuelwood can be promoted.

The ultimate limits to global development are perhaps determined by the availability of energy resources and by the biosphere's capacity to absorb the by-products of energy use.[11] These energy limits may be approached far sooner than the limits imposed by other material resources. First, there are the supply problems: the depletion of oil reserves, the high cost and environmental impact of coal mining, and the hazards of nuclear technology. Second, there are emission problems, most notably acid pollution and carbon dioxide build-up leading to global warming.

Some of these problems can be met by increased use of renewable energy sources. But the exploitation of renewable sources such as fuelwood and hydropower also entails ecological problems. Hence sustainability requires a clear focus on conserving and efficiently using energy.

Industrialized countries must recognize that their energy consumption is polluting the biosphere and eating into scarce fossil fuel supplies. Recent improvements in energy efficiency and a shift towards less energy-intensive sectors have helped limit consumption. But the process must be accelerated to reduce per capita consumption and encourage a shift to non-polluting sources and technologies. The simple duplication in the developing world of industrial countries' energy use patterns is neither feasible nor desirable. Changing these patterns for the better will call for new policies in urban development, industry location, housing design, transportation systems, and the choice of agricultural and industrial technologies.

Non-fuel mineral resources appear to pose fewer supply problems. Studies done before 1980 that assumed an exponentially growing demand did not envisage a problem until well into the next century.[12] Since then, world consumption of most metals has remained nearly constant, which suggests that the exhaustion of non-fuel minerals is even more distant. The history of technological developments also suggests that industry can adjust to scarcity through greater efficiency in use, recycling, and substitution. More immediate needs include modifying the pattern of world trade in minerals to allow exporters a higher share in the value added from mineral use, and improving the access of developing countries to mineral supplies, as their demands increase.

The prevention and reduction of air and water pollution will remain a critical task of resource conservation. Air and water quality come under pressure from such activities as fertilizer and pesticide use, urban sewage, fossil fuel burning, the use of certain chemicals, and various other industrial activities. Each of these is expected to increase the pollution load on the biosphere substantially, particularly in developing countries. Cleaning up after the event is an expensive solution. Hence all countries need to anticipate and prevent these pollution problems, by, for instance, enforcing emission standards that reflect likely long-term effects, promoting low-waste technologies, and anticipating the impact of new products, technologies, and wastes.

Reorienting Technology and Managing Risk

The fulfilment of all these tasks will require the reorientation of technology—the key link between humans and nature. First, the capacity for technological innovation needs to be greatly enhanced in developing countries so that they can respond more effectively to the challenges of sustainable development. Second, the orientation of technology development must be changed to pay greater attention to environmental factors.

The technologies of industrial countries are not always suited or easily adaptable to the socio-economic and environmental conditions of developing countries. To compound the problem, the bulk of world research and development addresses few of the pressing issues facing these countries, such as arid-land agriculture or the control of tropical diseases. Not enough is being done to adapt recent innovations in materials technology, energy conservation, information technology, and biotechnology to the needs of developing countries. These gaps must be covered by enhancing research, design, development, and extension capabilities in the Third World.

In all countries, the processes of generating alternative technologies, upgrading traditional ones, and selecting and adapting imported technologies should be informed by environmental resource concerns. Most technological research by commercial organizations is devoted to product and process innovations that have market value. Technologies are needed that produce 'social goods', such as improved air quality or increased product life, or that resolve problems normally outside the cost calculus of individual enterprises, such as the external costs of pollution or waste disposal.

The role of public policy is to ensure, through incentives and disincentives, that commercial organizations find it worthwhile to take fuller account of environmental factors in the technologies they develop. (See Chapter 8.) Publicly funded research institutions also need such direction, and the objectives of sustainable development and environmental protection must be built into the mandates of the institutions that work in environmentally sensitive areas.

The development of environmentally appropriate technologies is closely related to questions of risk management. Such systems as nuclear reactors, electric and other utility distribution networks, communication systems, and mass transportation are vulnerable if

Indigenous peoples are the base of what I guess could be called the environmental security system. We are the gate-keepers of success or failure to husband our resources. For many of us, however, the last few centuries have meant a major loss of control over our lands and waters. We are still the first to know about changes in the environment, but we are now the last to be asked or consulted.

We are the first to detect when the forests are being threatened, as they are under the slash and grab economics of this country. And we are the last to be asked about the future of our forests. We are the first to feel the pollution of our waters, as the Ojibway peoples of my own homelands in northern Ontario will attest. And, of course, we are the last to be consulted about how, when, and where developments should take place in order to assure continuing harmony for the seventh generation.

The most we have learned to expect is to be compensated, always too late and too little. We are seldom asked to help avoid the need for compensation by lending our expertise and our consent to development.

Louis Bruyere
President, Native Council of Canada
WCED Public Hearing, Ottawa, 26–27 May 1986

stressed beyond a certain point. The fact that they are connected through networks tends to make them immune to small disturbances but more vulnerable to unexpected disruptions that exceed a finite threshold. Applying sophisticated analyses of vulnerabilities and past failures to technology design, manufacturing standards, and contingency plans in operations can make the consequences of a failure or accident much less catastrophic.

The best vulnerability and risk analysis has not been applied consistently across technologies or systems. A major purpose of large system design should be to make the consequences of failure or sabotage less serious. There is thus a need for new techniques and technologies—as well as legal and institutional mechanisms—for safety design and control, accident prevention, contingency planning, damage mitigation, and provision of relief.

Environmental risks arising from technological and developmental decisions impinge on individuals and areas that have little or no influence on those decisions. Their interests must be taken into account. National and international institutional mechanisms are needed to assess potential impacts of new technologies before they are widely used, in order to ensure that their production, use,

'The issues that have been brought forward here, I think, are wide-ranging and maybe you know, maybe you don't know, the answers to all those issues. But at least by hearing all those questions, stories, all these expressions that have been put forward, at least you could have some idea.

You don't know the answers nor the solutions, but you could suggest the way to solve many problems and this is by suggesting either to governments, or the UN, or international agencies, to solve any problem the best way: that is to include those with direct interests in it. The beneficiaries, as well as the victims of any development issue should be included, should be heard.

I think that is the one thing maybe that all of us are hearing here, or expecting: that in every development planning or development issue as much as possible to listen and to include, to consult the people concerned. If that is taken care of, at least one step of the problem is resolved.'

Ismid Hadad
Chief Editor, Prisma
WCED Public Hearing, Jakarta, 26 March 1985

and disposal do not overstress environmental resources. Similar arrangements are required for major interventions in natural systems, such as river diversion or forest clearance. In addition, liability for damages from unintended consequences must be strengthened and enforced.

Merging Environment and Economics in Decision Making

The common theme throughout this strategy for sustainable development is the need to integrate economic and ecological considerations in decision making. They are, after all, integrated in the workings of the real world. This will require a change in attitudes and objectives and in institutional arrangements at every level.

Economic and ecological concerns are not necessarily in opposition. For example, policies that conserve the quality of agricultural land and protect forests improve the long-term prospects for agricultural development. An increase in the efficiency of energy and material use serves ecological purposes but can also reduce costs. But the compatibility of environmental and economic objectives is often lost in the pursuit of individual or group gains, with little regard for the impacts on others, with a blind faith in science's ability to find solutions, and in ignorance of the distant consequences of today's decisions. Institutional rigidities add to this myopia.

One important rigidity is the tendency to deal with one industry or sector in isolation, failing to recognize the importance of intersectoral linkages. Modern agriculture uses substantial amounts of commercially produced energy and large quantities of industrial products. At the same time, the more traditional connection—in which agriculture is a source of raw materials for industry—is being diluted by the widening use of synthetics. The energy-industry connection is also changing, with a strong tendency towards a decline in the energy intensity of industrial production in industrial countries. In the Third World, however, the gradual shift of the industrial base towards the basic material-producing sectors is leading to an increase in the energy intensity of industrial production.

These intersectoral connections create patterns of economic and ecological interdependence rarely reflected in the ways in which policy is made. Sectoral organizations tend to pursue sectoral objectives and to treat their impacts on other sectors as side effects, taken into account only if compelled to do so. Hence impacts on forests rarely worry those involved in guiding public policy or business activities in the fields of energy, industrial development, crop husbandry, or foreign trade. Many of the environment and development problems that confront us have their roots in this sectoral fragmentation of responsibility. Sustainable development requires that such fragmentation be overcome.

Sustainability requires the enforcement of wider responsibilities for the impacts of decisions. This requires changes in the legal and institutional frameworks that will enforce the common interest. Some necessary changes in the legal framework start from the proposition that an environment adequate for health and well-being is essential for all human beings—including future generations. Such a view places the right to use public and private resources in its proper social context and provides a goal for more specific measures.

The law alone cannot enforce the common interest. It principally needs community knowledge and support, which entails greater public participation in the decisions that affect the environment. This is best secured by decentralizing the management of resources upon which local communities depend, and giving these communities an effective say over the use of these resources. It will also require promoting citizens' initiatives, empowering people's organizations, and strengthening local democracy.[13]

Some large-scale projects, however, require participation on a different basis. Public inquiries and hearings on the development and environment impacts can help greatly in drawing attention to different

‘It has not been too difficult to push the environment lobby of the North and the development lobby of the South together. And there is now in fact a blurring of the distinction between the two, so they are coming to have a common consensus around the theme of sustainable development.

The building blocks are there. Environmental concern is common to both sides. Humanitarian concern is common to both sides. The difference lies in the methods of each and the degree to which each side tries to achieve its own economic interest through the development assistance process.

The time is right for bridging this gap for some very pragmatic political reasons. First of all, the people of the North do not want to see their taxes wasted. Secondly, they do not want to see growing poverty, and they obviously care for the environment, be it the environment of the North, where they live, or of the South. And the majority of people in the South do not want short-term overpass solutions.

In effect, there is a political community of interest, North and South, in the concept of sustainable development that you can build upon.’

Richard Sandbrook
International Institute for Environment and Development
WCED Public Hearing, Oslo, 24–25 June 1985

points of view. Free access to relevant information and the availability of alternative sources of technical expertise can provide an informed basis for public discussion. When the environmental impact of a proposed project is particularly high, public scrutiny of the case should be mandatory and, wherever feasible, the decision should be subject to prior public approval, perhaps by referendum.

Changes are also required in the attitudes and procedures of both public and private-sector enterprises. Moreover, environmental regulation must move beyond the usual menu of safety regulations, zoning laws, and pollution control enactments; environmental objectives must be built into taxation, prior approval procedures for investment and technology choice, foreign trade incentives, and all components of development policy.

The integration of economic and ecological factors into the law and into decision-making systems within countries has to be matched at the international level. The growth in fuel and material use dictates that direct physical linkages between ecosystems of different countries will increase. Economic interactions through trade, finance, investment, and travel will also grow and heighten economic and ecological interdependence. Hence in the future, even more so than now, sustainable development requires the unification of economics and ecology in international relations, as discussed in the next chapter.

IV. CONCLUSION

In its broadest sense, the strategy for sustainable development aims to promote harmony among human beings and between humanity and nature. In the specific context of the development and environment crises of the 1980s, which current national and international political and economic institutions have not and perhaps cannot overcome, the pursuit of sustainable development requires:

- a political system that secures effective citizen participation in decision making,
- an economic system that is able to generate surpluses and technical knowledge on a self-reliant and sustained basis,
- a social system that provides for solutions for the tensions arising from disharmonious development,
- a production system that respects the obligation to preserve the ecological base for development,
- a technological system that can search continuously for new solutions,
- an international system that fosters sustainable patterns of trade and finance, and
- an administrative system that is flexible and has the capacity for self-correction.

These requirements are more in the nature of goals that should underlie national and international action on development. What matters is the sincerity with which these goals are pursued and the effectiveness with which departures from them are corrected.

Notes

1 UNCTAD, *Handbook of International Trade and Development Statistics 1985 Supplement* (New York: 1985).

2 Ibid.

3 Department of International Economic and Social Affairs (DIESA), *Doubling Development Finance: Meeting a Global Challenge, Views and Recommendations of the Committee for Development Planning* (New York: UN, 1986).

4 One example of such a decision to forgo a developmental benefit in the interest of conservation is provided by the dropping of the Silent Valley Hydro project in India.

5 Based on data from World Bank, *World Development Report 1984* (New York: Oxford University Press, 1984).

6 Based on per capita consumption data from FAO, *Production Yearbook 1984* (Rome: 1985) and population projections from DIESA, *World Population Prospects Estimates and Projections as Assessed in 1984* (New York: UN, 1986).

7 FAO, *Fuelwood Supplies in the Developing Countries*, Forestry Paper No. 42 (Rome: 1983).

8 DIESA, *World Population Prospects*, op. cit.

9 Ibid.

10 Ibid.

11 W. Häfele and W. Sassin, 'Resources and Endowments, An Outline of Future Energy Systems', in P.W. Hemily and M.N. Ozdas (eds.), *Science and Future Choice* (Oxford: Clarendon Press, 1979).

12 See, for example, OECD, *Interfutures: Facing the Future* (Paris: 1979) and Council on Environmental Quality and US Department of State, *The Global 2000 Report to the President: Entering the Twenty-First Century, The Technical Report, Vol. Two* (Washington, DC: U. S. Government Printing Office, 1980).

13 See 'For Municipal Initiative and Citizen Power', in INDERENA, *La Campana Verde y los Concejos Verdes* (Bogota, Colombia: 1985).

3

THE ROLE OF
THE INTERNATIONAL ECONOMY

Through the ages, people have reached beyond their own borders to obtain essential, valued, or exotic materials. Today's surer communications and larger trade and capital movements have greatly enlarged this process, quickened its pace, and endowed it with far-reaching ecological implications. Thus the pursuit of sustainability requires major changes in international economic relations.

I. THE INTERNATIONAL ECONOMY, THE ENVIRONMENT, AND DEVELOPMENT

Two conditions must be satisfied before international economic exchanges can become beneficial for all involved. The sustainability of ecosystems on which the global economy depends must be guaranteed. And the economic partners must be satisfied that the basis of exchange is equitable; relationships that are unequal and based on dominance of one kind or another are not a sound and durable basis for interdependence. For many developing countries, neither condition is met.

Economic and ecological links between nations have grown rapidly. This widens the impact of the growing inequalities in the economic development and strength of nations. The asymmetry in international economic relations compounds the imbalance, as developing nations are generally influenced by—but unable to influence—international economic conditions.

International economic relationships pose a particular problem for poor countries trying to manage their environments, since the export of natural resources remains a large factor in their economies, especially those of the least developed nations. The instability and adverse price trends faced by most of these countries make it impossible for them to manage their natural resource bases for sustained production. The rising burden of debt servicing and the decline in new capital flows intensify those forces that lead to

---

Box 3-1.   Cotton Produced for Export in the Sahel

In 1983–84, as drought and hunger were taking hold in the Sahel region of Africa, five Sahelian nations—Burkina Faso, Chad, Mali, Niger, and Senegal—produced record amounts of cotton. They harvested 154 million tons of cotton fibre, up from 22.7 million tons in 1961–62. The Sahel as a whole set another record in 1984: It imported a record 1.77 million tons of cereals, up from 200,000 tons yearly in the early 1960s. Over the period that Sahelian cotton harvests were steadily rising, world cotton prices were steadily falling in real terms. These figures do not suggest that Sahelian nations should plough up all cotton to plant sorghum and millet. But the fact that farmers who can grow cotton cannot grow enough food to feed themselves suggests that cash crops are getting too much attention and food crops too little.

Source: J. Giri, 'Retrospective de l'Economie Sahelienne', Club du Sahel, Paris, 1984.

---

environmental deterioration and resource depletion occurring at the expense of long-term development.

The trade in tropical timber, for example, is one factor underlying tropical deforestation. Needs for foreign exchange encourage many developing countries to cut timber faster than forests can be regenerated. This overcutting not only depletes the resource that underpins the world timber trade, it causes the loss of forest-based livelihoods, increases soil erosion and downstream flooding, and accelerates the loss of species and genetic resources. International trade patterns can also encourage the unsustainable development policies and practices that have steadily degraded the croplands and rangelands in the drylands of Asia and Africa; an example of that is provided by the growth of cotton production for export in the Sahel region. (See Box 3-1.)

Growth in many developing countries also requires external capital inflows. Without reasonable flows, the prospect for any improvements in living standards is bleak. As a result, the poor will be forced to overuse the environment to ensure their own survival. Long-term development thus becomes much harder, and in some cases impossible. Yet trends in the movement of capital are worrying. Net resource flows to developing countries have fallen in real terms; in aggregate, there is now actually an outflow. (See Table 3.1.) The increase of international capital flows to developing countries expected over the rest of the 1980s is only half that thought necessary to restore growth to levels where a reduction in poverty can occur.[1]

A mere increase in flows of capital to developing countries will not necessarily contribute to development. Domestic efforts are of

TABLE 3.1

Net Transfer of Resources to Capital-Importing Developing Countries (billion dollars)

Capital Flow	1979	1980	1981	1982	1983	1984	1985
Net Transfer from Loans (all IDCs)*	30.7	30.6	27.7	0.8	−8.6	−22.0	−41.0
Net Transfer from all Resource Flows (all IDCs)†	41.4	39.3	41.5	10.4	−0.3	−12.5	−31.0
Net Transfer from all Resource Flows to Latin America	15.6	11.9	11.4	−16.7	−25.9	−23.2	−30.0

* Net transfers on loans are net capital flows minus net interest paid. All loans, official and private, short- and long-term, are included together with IMF credit.

† Total net resource flows relate to net loan transfers, grants, and net direct investment (less net direct investment income).

Source: UN, *World Economic Survey 1986* (New York: 1986).

paramount importance. More external funding is also required, but it must come in ways that are sensitive to the environmental impacts. The point is that the reduction of poverty itself is a precondition for environmentally sound development. And resource flows from rich to poor—flows improved both qualitatively and quantitatively—are a precondition for the eradication of poverty.

II. DECLINE IN THE 1980s

The pressures of poverty and rising populations make it enormously difficult for developing countries to pursue environmentally sound policies even in the best of circumstances. But when international economic conditions are bad, the problems can become unmanageable. During the 1980s, economic growth rates declined sharply or even turned negative in much of the Third World, particularly in Africa and Latin America. Over the five years from 1981 to 1985, population growth outstripped economic growth in most developing countries.[2]

Deteriorating terms of trade, rising debt-service obligations, stagnating flows of aid, and growing protectionism in the developed market economies caused severe external payment problems. The increased cost of foreign borrowing, at a time when exports were depressed, also helped to plunge many developing countries into debt crises. Austerity programmes laid down by the International Monetary Fund (IMF) as a prerequisite for extending credit to meet short-term balance-of-payments needs became particularly onerous after the debt crisis. Growth was cut back and many social objectives fell by the wayside, including those having to do with employment, health, education, environment, and human settlements.

This was a radical change from the 1960s and 1970s. Then it was rapid economic growth that was seen as an ecological threat. Now it is recession, austerity, and falling living standards. The decline of the 1980s has aggravated pressures on the environment in several ways:

- Austerity measures and general recessionary conditions have brought sharp declines in per capita incomes and increased unemployment. This forces more people back into subsistence agriculture, where they draw heavily on the natural resource base and thus degrade it.
- Austerity programmes inevitably include government cutbacks in both the staff and expenditure of fledgling, weak environmental agencies, undermining even the minimal efforts being made to bring ecological considerations into development planning.
- Conservation always takes a back seat in times of economic stress. As economic conditions have worsened in developing countries and debt pressures have mounted, planners have tended to ignore environmental planning and conservation in both industrial and rural development projects.

The critical situations in sub-Saharan Africa and the debt-strapped countries of Latin America demonstrate, in an extreme way, the damaging impacts that unreformed international economic arrangements are having on both development and the environment.

The African Continent

Africa on the whole has been caught up in a series of downward spirals:

- poverty and hunger leading to environmental degradation, deteriorating agriculture, and hence more poverty and hunger;
- falling savings and a neglect of new investment in the wake of growing poverty;
- high infant mortality, poverty, and lack of education;
- high population growth rates; and
- a flight from rural hunger to the cities, leading to explosive levels

'We know that the world lives through an international finance crisis, which increases the misery and the poverty in the Third World and we sacrifice even more our environment, though we know that this situation can be reversed, if we can use correctly new technology and knowledge. But for this we have to find a new ethic that will include the relationship between man and nature above all.'

Sergio Dialetachi
Speaker from the floor
WCED Public Hearing, Sao Paulo, 28–29 Oct 1985

of urban growth and squalor, compounding the problems of inadequate food supplies.

The situation is not everywhere so bleak. Some nations have coped well, and some far-reaching and courageous policy reforms begun in the last few years have started to bear fruit. Encouragement also comes from South Asia, where a comparable crisis 20 years ago has given way to an upward spiral of rising food production, diminishing (but still vast) poverty, slowing population growth, rising savings and investment, and greater attention to the long-term questions of environmental management and appropriate technology.

Among the many causes of the African crisis, the workings of the international economy stand out. Sub-Saharan Africa's economic well-being depends even more than low-income Asia's on developments in the world economy. Within the last decade, many sub-Saharan countries have been hit by adverse trends in commodity terms of trade and external shocks such as higher oil prices, fluctuating exchange rates, and higher interest rates. Over the last 10 years, the prices of major commodities such as copper, iron ore, sugar, ground-nuts, rubber, timber, and cotton have fallen significantly. In 1985, the terms of trade of sub-Saharan countries (except oil-exporting countries) were 10 per cent below 1970 levels. In countries eligible for funds from the International Development Association (IDA), the average fall was well over 20 per cent, with even greater drops in some, including Ethiopia, Liberia, Sierra Leone, Zaire, and Zambia.[3]

The problem has been compounded by growing difficulties in attracting development capital from the industrial world. At the same time, debt repayments and interest charges have risen. Debt service rose in sub-Saharan Africa as a whole from 15 per cent of export earnings in 1980 to 31 per cent in 1986.[4] This combination of events has led to a situation where net resource transfers to the area fell from an estimated $10 billion a year in 1982 to $1 billion in 1985.[5]

6*The seriousness of the African crisis cannot be overemphasized and in its entirety, it should really engage the whole world. The lives of 400 million people living in Africa today are imperilled. And many more people yet to be born will face a very bleak future unless effective solutions are found and found quickly.*

*It requires of course very little imagination to appreciate the fact that it is not only Africa that is in danger. In the long term the entire world economy could be threatened not only because of the indivisibility of human welfare but because of Africa's crucial position in the global economy as a source of a large number of vital raw materials.*9

Maxime Ferrari
Director, UNEP Regional Office for Africa
WCED Public Hearing, Harare, 18 Sept 1986

Thus nations have been able to import far less. In countries eligible for IDA loans, the import volume per person in 1984 was only 62 per cent of the volume in 1970.[6] Imports for agriculture—machinery, fertilizers, and pesticides—and of essential supplies to meet basic needs have all been cut. The combination of adverse international and internal factors cut per capita incomes by 16 per cent in sub-Saharan Africa between 1980 and 1985.[7]

The economic difficulties of sub-Saharan countries have had devastating social impacts. Declining per capita food production has contributed to growing undernourishment. The recent drought placed some 35 million lives at risk in 1984/85, and as the drought receded some 19 million people continued to suffer famine.[8] Malnutrition and hunger have weakened much of the population, reducing their productivity, and made more of them (especially children and the old) more susceptible to debilitating diseases and premature death. The crisis has reversed progress in supplying safe drinking water and sanitation.

It is now more widely recognized that it is necessary to deal with the long-term causes rather than the symptoms. The vast misery brought on by the drought in Africa is now generally acknowledged, and the world community has responded with a substantial emergency programme. But emergency food aid is only a short-term reaction, and, at best, a partial answer. The roots of the problem lie in national and international policies that have so far prevented African economies from realizing their full potential for economic expansion and thus for easing poverty and the environmental pressures that it generates.

The resolution lies in large part with African decision makers, but the international community also has a heavy responsibility to support Africa's adjustment efforts with adequate aid and trade arrangements and to see to it that more capital flows into poorer nations than out. These two complementary aspects of the resolution of the problems have been fully recognized by the African countries themselves[9] and generally acknowledged by the international community.[10] The World Bank estimates that even if external economic conditions are favourable over the next five years, and even if African governments implement key policy reforms, a substantial gap will still remain between the finance or debt relief available on current donor policies and the amounts needed to prevent a further deterioration in the living standards of low-income Africa.[11] And there is no money in this grim equation for restoring the damaged environment.

The international community must realize that Africa cannot pull itself out of the planet's most serious economic and ecological crisis without much more long-term assistance than is currently envisioned. In addition, greatly increased external financing for development must be accompanied by policy changes that recognize the need to avoid environmental degradation.

Latin American Debt

Debt is an acute problem for many countries of Africa. But, because of the magnitudes of debt involved, it has had its most visible impact in some middle-income countries—particularly in Latin America. The debt crisis remains a threat to international financial stability, but its main impact so far has been on the process of development, both in its economic and ecological aspects. Of the total world debt of around $950 billion in 1985, roughly 30 per cent was owed by four countries: Argentina, Brazil, Mexico, and Venezuela. Their debts constitute roughly two-thirds of the outstanding loans of banks to developing countries.[12]

In the 1970s, Latin America's economic growth was facilitated by external borrowing. Commercial banks were happy to lend to growing countries rich in natural resources. Then major changes in international conditions made the debt unsustainable. A global recession restricted export markets, and tight monetary policies forced up global interest rates to levels far exceeding any in living memory. Bankers, alarmed by deteriorating creditworthiness, stopped lending. A flight of indigenous capital from developing countries compounded the problem.

The ensuing crisis forced governments into austerity policies to cut

⁶*The impact of the present crisis on Latin America has been compared, in its depth and extension, with the Great Depression of 1929–32. The crisis has made it clear that, although the need to protect the environment against the traditional problems of deterioration and depletion continues to be a valid objective, policy-makers responsible for environmental management ought to avoid negative attitudes in the face of the need for economic reactivation and growth.*

*The expansion, conservation, maintenance, and protection of the environment can make an essential contribution to the improvement of the standard of living, to employment, and to productivity.*⁹

Osvaldo Sunkel
Coordinator, Joint ECLA/UNEP Development and Environment Unit
WCED Public Hearing, Sao Paulo, 28–29 Oct 1985

back imports. As a result, Latin American imports fell by 40 per cent in real terms over three years.[13] The consequent economic contraction reduced per capita gross domestic product by an average of 8 per cent in the eight main Latin American countries.[14] Much of the burden was carried by the poor, as real wages fell and unemployment rose. Growing poverty and deteriorating environmental conditions are clearly visible in every major Latin American country.

Further, the lack of new credit and the continuing burden of debt service forced these countries to service their debts by running trade surpluses. The net transfers from seven major Latin American countries to creditors rose to almost $39 billion in 1984, and in that year 35 per cent of export earnings went to pay interest on overseas debt.[15] This massive drain represents 5 to 6 per cent of the region's gross domestic product, around a third of the internal savings, and nearly 40 per cent of export earnings. It has been achieved by adjustment policies that impose severe and regressively skewed cuts in wages, social services, investment, consumption, and employment, both public and private, further aggravating social inequity and widespread poverty. Pressures on the environment and resources have increased sharply in the search for new and expanded exports and replacements for imports, together with the deterioration and overexploitation of the environment brought about by the swelling number of the urban and rural poor in desperate struggle for survival. A substantial part of Latin America's rapid growth in exports are raw materials, food, and resource-based manufactured goods.

So Latin American natural resources are being used not for development or to raise living standards, but to meet the financial requirements of industrialized country creditors. This approach to the debt problem raises questions of economic, political, and environmental sustainability. To require relatively poor countries to simultaneously curb their living standards, accept growing poverty, and export growing amounts of scarce resources to maintain external creditworthiness reflects priorities few democratically elected governments are likely to be able to tolerate for long. The present situation is not consistent with sustainable development. This conflict is aggravated by the economic policies of some major industrial countries, which have depressed and destabilized the international economy. In order to bring about socially and environmentally sustainable development it is indispensable, among other elements, for industrial countries to resume internationally expansionary policies of growth, trade, and investment. The Commission noted that, in these circumstances, some debtor countries have felt forced to suspend or limit the net outflow of funds.

Growing numbers of creditor banks and official agencies are realizing that many debtors simply will not be able to keep servicing their debts unless the burden is eased. Measures under discussion include additional new lending, forgiveness of part of the debt, longer-term rescheduling, and conversion to softer terms. But a necessary sense of urgency is lacking. Any such measures must incorporate the legitimate interests of creditors and debtors and represent a fairer sharing of the burden of resolving the debt crisis.

III. ENABLING SUSTAINABLE DEVELOPMENT

Developing countries have sought, for many years, fundamental changes in international economic arrangements so as to make them more equitable, particularly with regard to financial flows, trade, transnational investment, and technology transfer.[16] Their arguments must now be recast to reflect the ecological dimensions, frequently overlooked in the past.

In the short run, for most developing countries except the largest a new era of economic growth hinges on effective and co-ordinated economic management among major industrial countries—designed to facilitate expansion, to reduce real interest rates, and to halt the slide to protectionism. In the longer term, major changes are also required to make consumption and production patterns sustainable in a context of higher global growth.

International co-operation to achieve the former is embryonic, and to achieve the latter, negligible. In practice, and in the absence of

❝The universal importance of ecological problems can hardly be denied. Their successful solution will increasingly require coordinated activities not only within every country's economy but also within the scope of international co-operation. Ecological problems are unprecedented in the history of mankind.❞

Dr. Todor I. Bozhinov
Committee for Environment Protection, Bulgaria
WCED Public Hearing, Moscow, 8 Dec 1986

global management of the economy or the environment, attention must be focused on the improvement of policies in areas where the scope for co-operation is already defined: aid, trade, transnational corporations, and technology transfer.

Enhancing the Flow of Resources to Developing Countries

Two interrelated concerns lie at the heart of our recommendations on financial flows: one concerns the quantity, the other the 'quality' of resource flows to developing countries. The need for more resources cannot be evaded. The idea that developing countries would do better to live within their limited means is a cruel illusion. Global poverty cannot be reduced by the governments of poor countries acting alone. At the same time, more aid and other forms of finance, while necessary, are not sufficient. Projects and programmes must be designed for sustainable development.

Increasing the Flow of Finance

As regards the quantity of resources, the stringency of external finance has already contributed to an unacceptable decline in living standards in developing countries. The patterns and the needs of the heavily indebted countries that rely mainly on commercial finance have been described, along with those of low-income countries that depend on aid. But there are other poor countries that have made impressive progress in recent years but still face immense problems, not least in countering environmental degradation. Low-income Asia has a continuing need for large amounts of aid; in general, the main recipients in this region have a good record of aid management. Without such aid it will be much more difficult to sustain the growth that, together with poverty-focused programmes, could improve the lot of hundreds of millions of the 'absolute poor'.

To meet such needs requires that the main donors and lending institutions re-examine their policies. Official development assistance

*'The industrialized world's demands for raw materials, higher pro-
ductivity, and material goods have imposed serious environmental impacts and high economic costs not only in our own countries, but also
on the developing world. The existing international patterns of financial,
economic, trade, and investment policies further add to the problems.*

*We must all be willing to examine our relations in international trade,
investments, development assistance, industry, and agriculture in light
of the consequences these may have for underdevelopment and environmental destruction in the Third World. We must even be willing
to go further and implement the means necessary to alleviate these
symptoms.'*

Rakel Surlien
Former Minister of Environment, Government of Norway
WCED Opening Ceremony, Oslo, 24 June 1985

levels have stagnated in absolute terms, and most donor countries fall
well short of internationally agreed targets. Commercial lending and
lending by export credit agencies has fallen sharply. As part of a
concerted effort to reverse these trends it is vitally important for
development that there should be a substantial increase in resources
available to the World Bank and IDA. Increased commercial bank
lending is also necessary for major debtors.

Lending for Sustainable Development

In the past, development assistance has not always contributed to
sustainable development and in some cases detracted from it. Lending
for agriculture, forestry, fishing, and energy has usually been made
on narrow economic criteria that take little account of environmental
effects. For instance, development agencies have sometimes promoted
chemical-dependent agriculture, rather than sustainable, regenerative
agriculture. It is important therefore that there should be a qualitative
as well as a quantitive improvement.

A larger portion of total development assistance should go to
investments needed to enhance the environment and the productivity
of the resource sectors. Such efforts include reforestation and fuelwood
development, watershed protection, soil conservation, agroforestry,
rehabilitation of irrigation projects, small-scale agriculture, low-cost
sanitation measures, and the conversion of crops into fuel. Experience
has shown that the most effective efforts of this type are small projects
with maximum grass-roots participation. The programmes most
directly related to the objective of sustainable development may

therefore involve higher local costs, a higher ratio of recurrent to capital costs, and a greater use of local technology and expertise.

A shift towards projects of this kind would also require donors to re-examine the content of their aid programmes, particularly with regard to commodity assistance, which has sometimes served to reduce rather than enhance the possibilities for sustainable development. (See Chapter 5.)

The major priority is for sustainability considerations to be diffused throughout the work of international financial institutions. The roles of the World Bank and the IMF are particularly crucial because their lending conditions are being used as benchmarks for parallel lending by other institutions—commercial banks and export credit agencies. It is important in this context that sustainability considerations be taken into account by the Bank in the appraisal of structural adjustment lending and other policy-oriented lending directed to resource-based sectors—agriculture, fishing, forestry, and energy in particular—as well as specific projects.

A similar shift of emphasis is required in respect of adjustment programmes undertaken by developing countries. To date, 'adjustment'—particularly under IMF auspices—has led more often than not to cutbacks in living standards in the interest of financial stabilization. Implicit in many suggested plans for coping with the debt crisis is the growing recognition that future adjustment should be growth-oriented. Yet it also needs to be environmentally sensitive.

The IMF also has a mandate for structural adjustment lending, as in its new Structural Adjustment Facility. There has been a strongly expressed demand from developing-country borrowers for the Fund to take into account wider and longer-term development objectives than financial stabilization: growth, social goals, and environmental impacts.

Development agencies, and the World Bank in particular, should develop easily usable methodologies to augment their own appraisal techniques and to assist developing countries to improve their capacity for environmental assessment.

Linking Trade, Environment, and Development

The importance of foreign trade to national development has greatly increased for most countries in the post-war period. (See Table 3.2.) This is one measure of the extent to which trade has made nations, economically and ecologically, more interdependent. Patterns of world trade also have changed markedly. First, the value of trade in manufactured goods grew at a faster rate than that in primary

TABLE 3.2

The Growing Importance of Trade (exports as a percentage
of GDP or NMP)

Economic Group	1950	1982
Developed Market Economies	7.7	15.3
Developing Market Economies	15.5	23.8
Socialist Countries of Eastern Europe	3.4*	16.6*
Socialist Countries of Asia	2.9*	9.7*

* percentages to net material product (NMP).

Source: Based on UNCTAD, *Handbook of International Trade and Development Statistics, 1985 Supplement* (New York: UN, 1985).

products other than fuel, and a growing number of developing countries have emerged as major exporters of such goods. Manufactured goods now account for twice the value of developing countries' non-oil exports.[17] (See Chapter 8.) Second, the industrialized market economies have come to depend more on fuel imports from developing countries, which accounted for 43 per cent of consumption in 1980–81 compared with only 16 per cent in 1959–60 and even less in pre-war years.[18]

The dependence of the developed market economies on other mineral imports from the developing countries has also grown, and the share of these imports in consumption increased from 19 per cent in 1959–60 to 30 per cent in 1980–81.[19] Non-renewable resources like fuels and minerals, as well as manufactured goods, are now far more important than tropical products and other agricultural materials in the flow of primary products from developing to industrial countries. In fact, the flow of foodgrains is in the opposite direction.

The main link between trade and sustainable development is the use of non-renewable raw materials to earn foreign exchange. Developing countries face the dilemma of having to use commodities as exports, in order to break foreign exchange constraints on growth, while also having to minimize damage to the environmental resource base supporting this growth. There are other links between trade and sustainable development; if protectionism raises barriers against manufactured exports, for example, developing nations have less scope for diversifying away from traditional commodities. And unsustainable development may arise not only from overuse of certain commodities but from manufactured goods that are potentially polluting.

❛I think it is also of importance for the Commission to note the problem of negotiation of contracts on resource development. We have been trying for 10 years to include provisions on environment. We have been successful only to get from the investors a very broad description of what should be done in environmental protection. If you go into details you get problems with the lawyers and so on. That hampers then the investment.

For us, of course, it is a choice of whether to loosen the grip a little bit or if you maintain that, then of course, there will be no investment in the country. If an appeal could be made to the multinationals, mainly to understand that what has been done in timber should also be applied to other agreements like coffee, tin, and others, I think this would be a great help.❜

Speaker from the floor, government agency
WCED Public Hearing, Jakarta, 26 March 1985

International Commodity Trade

Although a growing number of developing countries have diversified into manufactured exports, primary commodities other than petroleum continue to account for more than one-third of the export earnings of the group as a whole. Dependence on such exports is particularly high in Latin America (52 per cent) and Africa (62 per cent).[20] The countries recognized as 'least developed' for the purposes of the UN Special Programme use primary commodities for 73 per cent of their export earnings.[21]

Non-oil commodity prices fell during the early 1980s, not only in real but also in nominal terms. By early 1985, the UN Conference on Trade and Development (UNCTAD) commodity price index was 30 per cent below the 1980 average.[22] This recent weakness of commodity prices may not be only a temporary phenomenon. Commodity prices have not yet recovered from the depth of the world recession despite increased economic growth in consuming countries. The reasons may be partly technological (an acceleration in raw material substitution); partly monetary, caused by the high cost of holding stocks of commodities; and partly due to increases in supplies by countries desperate to earn foreign exchange.

These countries are turning the terms of trade against themselves, earning less while exporting more. The promotion of increased volumes of commodity exports has led to cases of unsustainable overuse of the natural resource base. While individual cases may not exactly fit this generalization, it has been argued that such processes have been at work in ranching for beef, fishing in both coastal and deep sea waters, forestry, and the growing of some cash crops. Moreover, the prices of commodity exports do not fully reflect the environmental costs to the resource base. In a sense, then, poor developing countries are being caused to subsidize the wealthier importers of their products.

The experience of oil has of course been different from that of most other commodities. (See Chapter 7.) It does provide one example of producers combining to restrict output and raise prices in ways that greatly increased export earnings while conserving the resource base and promoting energy saving and substitution on a large scale. Recent events suggest that regulation of the market by producers is very difficult in the long term, whether or not it is desirable in the wider, global interest, and in any event the conditions have not existed for other commodity exporters to operate in a like manner. Any arrangement encompassing measures to enhance the export earnings of producers, as well as to ensure the resource basis, would require consumer as well as producer support.

In recent years, Third World commodity exporters have sought to earn more by doing the first-stage processing of raw materials themselves. This first stage often involves subsidized energy, other concessions, and substantial pollution costs. But these countries often find that they do not gain much from this capital- and energy-intensive first-stage processing, as the price spread shifts in favour of down-stream products, most of which continue to be manufactured mainly in industrial countries. Tariff escalation in the industrial market economies reinforces this tendency.

The main international response to commodity problems has been the development of international commodity agreements to stabilize and raise developing countries' earnings from these exports. But real progress has been very limited and in fact there have been reversals. Moreover, environmental resource considerations have not played any part in commodity agreements, with the notable exception of the International Tropical Timber Agreement.[23]

Commodity agreements have not been easy to negotiate, and regulation of commodity trade has been notoriously controversial and difficult. Current arrangements could be improved in two crucial respects:

- Larger sums for compensatory financing to even out economic shocks—as under the IMF's Compensatory Financing Facility—would encourage producers to take a long-term view, and not to overproduce commodities where production is close to the

---

Box 3-2.   Sugar and Sustainable Development

Thirty million poor people in the Third World depend on sugar-cane for their survival. Many developing countries have a genuine comparative advantage in production and could earn valuable foreign exchange by expanding output. Some small states—Fiji, Mauritius, and several Caribbean islands—depend for their economic survival on cane sugar exports.

Industrial countries have actively promoted, and protected, beet sugar production, which competes with cane and has had quite damaging effects on developing countries: High-cost, protected beet production encourages artificial sweeteners; quotas have kept out Third World imports (except for some guaranteed imports as under the European Economic Community's Sugar Protocol); and surpluses are dumped on world markets, depressing prices.

In the 1986 *World Development Report*, the World Bank estimated that industrial countries' sugar policies cost developing countries about $7.4 billion in lost revenues during 1983, reduced their real income by about $2.1 billion and increased price instability by about 25 per cent.

Over and above the increased developing-country poverty that results from these practices, the promotion of beet production in industrial countries has had adverse ecological side effects. Modern beet growing is highly capital-intensive, it depends heavily on chemical herbicides, and the crop has poorer regenerative properties than others. The same product could be grown in developing countries, as cane, more cheaply, using more labour and fewer chemical additives.

---

limits of environmental sustainability during periods of market glut.

- Where producers need to diversify from traditional, single-crop production patterns, more assistance could be given for diversification programmes. The second window of the Common Fund could be used for promoting resource regeneration and conservation.[24]

Individual governments can better use renewable resources such as forests and fisheries to ensure that exploitation rates stay within the limits of sustainable yields and that finances are available to regenerate resources and deal with all linked environmental effects. As for non-renewable resources like minerals, governments should ensure that:

- the leaseholder undertakes exploration aimed at adding to proven reserves at least the amount extracted;
- that the ratio of production to proven reserve remains below a pre-specified limit;
- that the funds generated by royalties are used in a way that

compensates for the declining income when the resource deposit is exhausted; and

- that the leaseholder is responsible for land restoration and other environmental control measures in the area affected by mining.

Relevant international organizations such as various UN agencies, the World Bank, and regional groups could develop further their work on model contracts and guidelines incorporating these principles.

Protectionism and International Trade

The increase in protectionism in industrial countries stifles export growth and prevents diversification from traditional exports. The success of some Far Eastern developing countries in increasing exports of labour-intensive manufactured goods shows the development potential of such trade. However, other countries—especially low-income Asian and Latin American nations—seeking to follow the same route have found themselves severely handicapped by growing trade barriers, particularly in textiles and clothing. If developing countries are to reconcile a need for rapid export growth with a need to conserve the resource base, it is imperative that they enjoy access to industrial country markets for non-traditional exports where they enjoy a comparative advantage. In many cases, the problems of protectionism relate to manufactured goods; but there are cases—sugar is a good example—where industrial countries employ agricultural trade restrictions in ways that are damaging ecologically as well as economically. (See Box 3-2.)

'Pollution-intensive' Goods

The processing of certain raw materials—pulp and paper, oil, and alumina, for example—can have substantial environmental side effects. Industrial countries have generally been more successful than developing ones in seeing to it that export product prices reflect the costs of environmental damage and of controlling that damage. Thus in the case of exports from industrial countries, these costs are paid by consumers in importing nations, including those in the Third World. But in the case of exports from developing countries, such costs continue to be borne entirely domestically, largely in the form of damage costs to human health, property, and ecosystems.

In 1980 the industries of developing countries exporting to Organisation for Economic Co-operation and Development (OECD) members would have incurred direct pollution control costs of $5.5 billion if they had been required to meet the environmental standards then prevailing in the United States, according to a study conducted for this Commission.[25] If the pollution control expenditures associated with the materials that went into the final product are also counted, the costs would have mounted to $14.2 billion. The evidence also suggests that OECD imports from developing countries involve products that entail higher average environmental and resource damage costs than do overall OECD imports.[26] These hypothetical pollution control costs probably understate the real costs of environmental and resource damage in the exporting countries. Furthermore, these costs relate only to environmental pollution and not to the economic damage costs associated with resource depletion.

The fact that these costs remain hidden means that developing countries are able to attract more investment to export manufactured goods than they would under a more rigorous system of global environmental control. Many Third World policymakers see this as beneficial in that it gives developing countries a comparative advantage in 'pollution-intensive' goods that should be exploited. They also see that passing along more of the real costs could reduce the competitive position of their country in some markets, and thus regard any pressure in this direction as a form of disguised protectionism from established producers. Yet it is in developing countries' own long-term interests that more of the environmental and resource costs associated with production be reflected in prices. Such changes must come from the developing countries themselves.

The Mandates of Multilateral Trade Forums

Although a number of UNCTAD research projects have considered the links between trade and environment, these issues have not been taken up systematically by intergovernmental organizations. The mandates of these organizations—principally the General Agreement on Tariffs and Trade (GATT) and UNCTAD—should include sustainable development. Their activities should reflect concern with the impacts of trading patterns on the environment and the need for more effective instruments to integrate environment and development concerns into international trading arrangements.

International organizations dealing with trade will find it easier to reorientate their activities if each nation designates a lead agency with a broad mandate to assess the effects of international trade on sustaining the environmental and resource base of economic growth. This agency could be responsible for raising sustainability issues in the work of UNCTAD, GATT, OECD, the Council for Mutual Economic Assistance, and other relevant organizations.

Box 3-3. The Role of Transnational Corporations

- In 1983 chemicals accounted for roughly one-fourth of the stock of foreign direct investment in manufacturing in developing countries by companies from four leading countries—Japan (23 per cent), the United States (23 per cent), the United Kingdom (27 per cent), and the Federal Republic of Germany (14 per cent).
- Agriculture, mining, and other extractive industries accounted for 38 per cent of the stock of US investment in developing countries in 1983, 29 per cent of the stock of Japanese investment in 1983, 21 per cent of the total FRG investment in 1981–83, and 9 per cent of the stock of UK investment in 1978.
- Eighty to ninety per cent of the trade in tea, coffee, cocoa, cotton, forest products, tobacco, jute, copper, iron ore, and bauxite is controlled in the case of each commodity by the three to six largest transnationals.

Source: UN Centre on Transnational Corporations, *Environmental Aspects of the Activities of Transnational Corporations: A Survey* (New York: UN, 1985).

Ensuring Responsibility in Transnational Investment

Overseas investment activity by companies in market economies has grown substantially over the past 40 years. (See Box 3-3.) Foreign affiliates now account for 40 per cent of sales, 33 per cent of net assets, and 56 per cent of net earnings for 380 of the largest industrial corporations in the market economies, according to data compiled by the UN Centre for Transnational Corporations.[27] A high proportion of transnational investment is within industrial market economies, another aspect of the growing integration of these economies.

Transnational corporations (TNCs) play an important role as owners, as partners in joint ventures, and as suppliers of technology in the mining and manufacturing sectors in many developing countries, especially in such environmentally sensitive areas as petroleum, chemicals, metals, paper, and automobiles. They also dominate world trade in many primary commodities.

In recent years, many developing countries have begun to take a more positive view of the role TNC investment can play in their development process. This has been somewhat influenced by these countries' needs for foreign exchange and their awareness of the role that foreign investment might play in providing it. Effective co-operation with TNCs is possible in creating equal conditions for all parties. This can be attained by a strict observance of the principle of sovereignty of the host country. For their part, many corporations have recognized the need to share managerial skills and technological know-how with host-country nationals and to pursue profit-seeking objectives within a framework of long-term sustainable development. But mutual suspicions still exist, usually because of an asymmetry in bargaining power between large corporations and small, poor, developing countries. Negotiations are often made one-sided by a developing country's lack of information, technical unpreparedness, and political and institutional weaknesses. Suspicions and disagreements remain, particularly concerning the introduction of new technologies, the development of natural resources, and the use of the environment. If multinationals are to play a larger role in development, these conflicts and suspicions must be reduced.

Strengthening the bargaining posture and response of developing countries vis à vis transnationals is therefore critical. Where nations lack indigenous capacity to deal with large TNCs, regional and other international institutions should assist. As indicated earlier, they could expand existing help in the form of model agreements with transnationals for different situations, such as lease agreements for the exploitation of a mineral resource. They could also field technical assistance and advisory teams when a country negotiates with a transnational.

Transnationals can have a substantial impact on the environment and resources of other countries and on the global commons. Both the home and host countries of TNCs share responsibilities and should work together to strengthen policies in this sphere. For example, information on policies and standards applied to and followed by corporations when investing in their own home country, especially concerning hazardous technologies, should be provided to host countries. Moreover, the policies of some industrialized countries that major investments are subject to prior environmental assessment should be considered for application to investments made elsewhere and should be broadened to include sustainability criteria. The information and recommendations thus arrived at should be shared with the host countries, which of course would retain the final responsibility.

Despite their importance, international measures regarding transnationals have been generally lacking and have proved extremely difficult to negotiate. The codes of conduct for transnational corporations formulated by the OECD and under discussion in the UN should deal explicitly with environmental matters and the objective of sustainable development. More detailed and specific instruments are needed for other problems. In particular, when introducing a new technology, plant, product, or process, or when setting up a joint venture in a developing country, the parties involved must also recognize and accept certain special responsibilities. (See Chapter 8.)

Broadening the Technological Base

The promotion of resource productivity is largely the work of domestic economic policy. But the international economy impinges on possibilities for productivity improvement in several ways, particularly in the transfer of technology from one country to another.

The Diffusion of Environmentally Sound Technologies

The promotion of sustainable development will require an organized effort to develop and diffuse new technologies, such as for agricultural production, renewable energy systems, and pollution control. Much of this effort will be based on the international exchange of technology: through trade in improved equipment, technology-transfer agreements, provision of experts, research collaboration, and so on. Hence the procedures and policies that influence these exchanges must stimulate innovation and ensure ready and widespread access to environmentally sound technologies.

The real challenge is to ensure that the new technologies reach all those who need them, overcoming such problems as the lack of information and in some cases an inability to pay for commercially developed technologies. The measures required at the national level to deal with these problems are discussed in Part II of this report. However, both these issues also arise in the international diffusion of technology.

Developing countries paid about $2 billion in 1980 by way of royalties and fees, mainly to industrial countries.[28] The gap in scientific and technological capabilities is particularly wide in areas of direct relevance to the objectives of sustainable development, including biotechnology and genetic engineering, new energy sources, new materials and substitutes, and low-waste and non-polluting technologies.

The principal policy issue as regards the impact of payments is the impact of patents and proprietary rights. In 1980, industrialized market economies accounted for 65 per cent of the world total of patents granted, and the socialist countries of Eastern Europe held 29 per cent.[29] Developing countries held only 6 per cent, and most of these had been granted to non-residents. Proprietary rights are a key element in the commercial development of technology. But their application in certain areas may hamper the diffusion of environmentally sound technologies and may increase inequities.

'Transfer of technology should be also looked upon as being a social process. Actually, ideally, it is the people themselves who have to make the selection, not us. So, to sum it up I think, talking about technology it is very important to, perhaps, understand that we are dealing here with a process of change. Technologies cannot be directly transferred except by relating this to a social process. So, actually technology is not an independent variable in this case, but it is very much dependant on social change.'

M. Nashihin Hasan
Speaker from the floor
WCED Public Hearing, Jakarta, 26 March 1985

In the past, publicly funded research provided new technology to small producers, particularly farmers, on a full or subsidized basis. The situation is not very different now, and in areas such as new seed varieties there is some reason to believe proprietary rights could act as a major barrier to developing countries' acquisition of new technologies. International co-operation is essential to maintain the flow of genetic material and to ensure an equitable sharing of gains.

Building Up Technological Capabilities in Developing Countries

At present, most of the global research and development effort is devoted to military purposes or the commercial objectives of large corporations. Little of this is of direct relevance to conditions in developing countries. In many areas the gap in technological capabilities is narrowing, but these efforts must be supported by international assistance, especially in such key areas as biotechnology. Unless action is taken to accumulate biological knowledge, valuable information as well as vital genetic variety will be lost forever, and developing countries will be at a permanent disadvantage in adapting the new biotechnologies to their own needs.

Developing countries therefore have to work, individually and together, to build up their technological capabilities. The creation and enhancement of the infrastructure for research and technology is a precondition for such co-operation. The countries concerned could share the burden by establishing co-operative research projects along the lines of the International Agricultural Research Centres.[30] Mission-oriented co-operative research ventures could be developed in areas such as dryland agriculture, tropical forestry, pollution control in small enterprises, and low-cost housing. Specific responsibilities would be assigned to institutions and corporations in the participating countries, and the agreement could provide for the equitable sharing and widespread diffusion of the technologies developed.

IV. A SUSTAINABLE WORLD ECONOMY

If large parts of the developing world are to avert economic, social, and environmental catastrophes, it is essential that global economic growth be revitalized. In practical terms, this means more rapid economic growth in both industrial and developing countries, freer market access for the products of developing countries, lower interest rates, greater technology transfer, and significantly larger capital flows, both concessional and commercial.

But many people fear that a more rapidly growing world economy will apply environmental pressures that are no more sustainable than the pressures presented by growing poverty. The increased demand for energy and other non-renewable raw materials could significantly raise the price of these items relative to other goods.

The Commission's overall assessment is that the international economy must speed up world growth while respecting the environmental constraints. Some favourable trends have been noted in the pattern of consumption and production in industrial countries, which collectively still consume most of the world's non-renewable resources.

Sustaining these trends will make it easier for developing countries to grow by diversifying their own economies. But for them to emerge from dependence a general acceleration of global economic growth is not enough. This would mean a mere perpetuation of existing economic patterns, though perhaps at a higher level of incomes. It must be ensured that the economies of developing countries grow fast enough to outpace their growing internal problems and fast enough for that first leap needed to acquire momentum. A continuation of economic growth and diversification, along with the development of technological and managerial skills, will help developing countries mitigate the strains on the rural environment, raise productivity and consumption standards, and allow nations to move beyond dependence on one or two primary products for their export earnings.

Future patterns of agricultural and forestry development, energy use, industrialization, and human settlements can be made far less material-intensive (see Chapters 5, 7, 8, and 9), and hence both more economically and environmentally efficient. Under these conditions, a new era of growth in the world economy can widen the options available to developing countries.

Reforms at an international level are now needed to deal simultaneously with economic and ecological aspects in ways that allow the world economy to stimulate the growth of developing countries while giving greater weight to environmental concerns. Such an agenda requires deep commitment by all countries to the satisfactory working of multilateral institutions, such as the multilateral development banks; to the making and observance of international rules in fields such as trade and investment; and to constructive dialogue on the many issues where national interests do not immediately coincide but where negotiation could help to reconcile them.

The Commission therefore regrets but cannot ignore the recent decline in multilateral co-operation in general and a negative attitude to dialogue on development in particular. At first sight, the introduction of an environmental dimension further complicates the search for such co-operation and dialogue. But it also injects an additional element of mutual self-interest, since a failure to address the interaction between resource depletion and rising poverty will accelerate global ecological deterioration.

New dimensions of multilateralism are essential to human progress. The Commission feels confident that the mutual interests involved in environment and development issues can help generate the needed momentum and can secure the necessary international economic changes that it will make possible.

Notes

1 Department of International Economic and Social Affairs (DIESA), *Doubling Development Finance: Meeting a Global Challenge, Views and Recommendations of the Committee on Development Planning* (New York: UN, 1986).

2 Ibid.

3 World Bank, *Financing Adjustment with Growth in Sub-Saharan Africa* (Washington, DC: 1986).

4 IMF, *World Economic Outlook*, October 1986.

5 UN, *World Economic Survey 1986* (New York: 1986).

6 World Bank, op. cit.

7 Ibid.

8 UN General Assembly, 'The Critical Economic Situation in Africa: Report of the Secretary General', A/S-13/z, New York, 20 May 1986.

9 Organization of African Unity Assembly of Heads of State of Government, *Africa's Priority Programme of Action 1986-1991* (Addis Ababa: 1985).

10 UN General Assembly, *United Nations Programme of Action for African Economic Recovery and Development* (New York: 1986).

11 World Bank, op. cit.

12 Bank for International Settlements, *International Banking and Financial Markets Developments* (Basel: 1986).

13 Inter-American Development Bank, *Economic and Social Progress in Latin America* (Washington, DC: 1986).

14 Unpublished data from UN Economic Commission on Latin America.

15 Ibid.

16 See, for example, UN General Assembly, 'Programme of Action on a New International Economic Order', Resolution 3202 (S-V1), 1 May 1974.

17 See GATT, *International Trade 1985-86* (Geneva: 1986).

18 UNCTAD, *Handbook of International Trade and Development Statistics 1977* and *1985 Supplements* (New York: UN, 1977 and 1985).

19 Ibid.

20 UNCTAD, *Statistical Pocketbook* (New York: UN, 1984).

21 Ibid.

22 UNCTAD, *Trade and Development Report* (New York: UN, 1986).

23 Alister MacIntyre, UNCTAD, statement at WCED Public Hearings, Oslo, 1985.

24 The Common Fund is an international arrangement for the stabilization of prices for a group of commodities of particular interest to developing countries. The Second Window of the fund is meant to provide resources for promotional and research measures.

25 I. Walter and J.H. Loudon, 'Environmental Costs and the Patterns of North-South Trade', prepared for WCED, 1986.

26 Ibid.

27 UN Centre on Transnational Corporations, *Transnational Corporations in World Development Third Survey* (New York: UN, 1983).

28 Ibid.

29 Commonwealth Working Group, *Technological Change* (London: Commonwealth Secretariat, 1985).

30 The reference is to the activities of the international institutes that work under the umbrella of the Consultative Group on International Agricultural Research of the World Bank.

Part II

COMMON CHALLENGES

4

POPULATION AND HUMAN RESOURCES

In 1985, some 80 million people were added to a world population of 4.8 billion. Each year the number of human beings increases, but the amount of natural resources with which to sustain this population, to improve the quality of human lives, and to eliminate mass poverty remains finite. On the other hand, expanding knowledge increases the productivity of resources.

Present rates of population growth cannot continue. They already compromise many governments' abilities to provide education, health care, and food security for people, much less their abilities to raise living standards. This gap between numbers and resources is all the more compelling because so much of the population growth is concentrated in low-income countries, ecologically disadvantaged regions, and poor households.

Yet the population issue is not solely about numbers. And poverty and resource degradation can exist on thinly populated lands, such as the drylands and the tropical forests. People are the ultimate resource. Improvements in education, health, and nutrition allow them to better use the resources they command, to stretch them further. In addition, threats to the sustainable use of resources come as much from inequalities in people's access to resources and from the ways in which they use them as from the sheer numbers of people. Thus concern over the 'population problem' also calls forth concern for human progress and human equality.

Nor are population growth rates the challenge solely of those nations with high rates of increase. An additional person in an industrial country consumes far more and places far greater pressure on natural resources than an additional person in the Third World. Consumption patterns and preferences are as important as numbers of consumers in the conservation of resources.

Thus many governments must work on several fronts—to limit population growth; to control the impact of such growth on resources and, with increasing knowledge, enlarge their range and improve their productivity; to realize human potential so that people can better husband and use resources; and to provide people with forms of social security other than large numbers of children. The means of accomplishing these goals will vary from country to country, but all should keep in mind that sustainable economic growth and equitable access to resources are two of the more certain routes towards lower fertility rates.

Giving people the means to choose the size of their families is not just a method of keeping population in balance with resources; it is a way of assuring—especially for women—the basic human right of self-determination. The extent to which facilities for exercising such choices are made available is itself a measure of a nation's development. In the same way, enhancing human potential not only promotes development but helps to ensure the right of all to a full and dignified life.

I. THE LINKS WITH ENVIRONMENT AND DEVELOPMENT

Population growth and development are linked in complex ways. Economic development generates resources that can be used to improve education and health. These improvements, along with associated social changes, reduce both fertility and mortality rates. On the other hand, high rates of population growth that eat into surpluses available for economic and social development can hinder improvements in education and health.

In the past, the intensification of agriculture and the production of higher yields helped nations cope with the increasing population pressures on available land. Migration and international trade in food and fuels eased the pressure on local resources. They permitted and helped sustain the high population densities of some industrialized countries.

The situation is different in most of the developing world. There, improvements in medicine and public health have led to a sharp drop in mortality rates and have accelerated population growth rates to unprecedented levels. But fertility rates remain high; much human potential remains unrealized, and economic development is stalled. Agricultural intensification can go some way towards restoring a balance between food production and population, but there are limits beyond which intensification cannot go. (See Box 4-1.)

The very possibility of development can be compromised by high population growth rates. Moreover, most developing countries do not have the resources to wait for a few generations before population stabilizes. The option of migration to new lands is virtually closed.

'Since 1970 it has been fashionable to draw a distinction between population and environment as two crisis areas, but often times we forget that population is in fact a very integral part of the environment and therefore when we are addressing ourselves to population we are looking at not only the physical, biological, and chemical environments, we are also looking at the socio-cultural or socio-economic environment in which these development programmes are being set. And population makes much more sense if you are talking of population within a context.'

Dr. J. O. Oucho
Population Studies and Research Institute
WCED Public Hearing, Nairobi, 23 Sept 1986

And low levels of economic and social development combined with changing trade-production relationships limit possibilities of using international trade to augment access to resources. Hence, in the absence of deliberate measures, the imbalance between population growth and resource development will worsen.

Population pressure is already forcing traditional farmers to work harder, often on shrinking farms on marginal land, just to maintain household income. In Africa and Asia, rural population nearly doubled between 1950 and 1985, with a corresponding decline in land availability.[1] Rapid population growth also creates urban economic and social problems that threaten to make cities wholly unmanageable. (See Chapter 9.)

Larger investments will be needed just to maintain the current inadequate levels of access to education, health care, and other services. In many cases, the resources required are just not available. Health, housing conditions, and the quality of education and public services all deteriorate; unemployment, urban drift, and social unrest increase.

Industrial countries seriously concerned with high population growth rates in other parts of the world have obligations beyond simply supplying aid packages of family planning hardware. Economic development, through its indirect impact on social and cultural factors, lowers fertility rates. International policies that interfere with economic development thus interfere with a developing nation's ability to manage its population growth. A concern for population growth must therefore be a part of a broader concern for a more rapid rate of economic and social development in the developing countries.

Box 4-1. The Food/Population Balance

The potential population-supporting capacity of land in developing countries has been assessed in a joint study by FAO and the International Institute for Applied Systems Analysis. Data on soil and land characteristics were combined with climatic data to calculate the potential yields of major crops, to select the optimum crops, and to derive the overall potential for calorie production. Three levels of crop production were calculated: the first at a low level of technology with no fertilizer or chemicals, traditional crop varieties, and no soil conservation; the second at an intermediate level, where the most productive crop mix is used on half the land along with fertilizers, improved varieties, and some soil conservation; and the third at a high level of technology with an ideal crop mix and technology on all lands. The population-supporting capacity was determined by dividing the total calorie production by a minimum per capita intake level. This figure was then compared with the medium-variant UN population projections.

The 117 developing countries covered in the study, taken together, can produce enough food to feed one-and-a-half times their projected population in the year 2000, even at a low level of technology. But the picture is less hopeful in the cases of individual countries. At the low level of technology, 64 countries (with a population of around 1.1 billion) lack the resources to feed themselves. With the most advanced agricultural methods, the number of countries where food production potential would fall short of requirements drops to 19, with a total population of 100

In the final analysis, and in both the developed and developing worlds, the population issue is about humans and not about numbers. It is misleading and an injustice to the human condition to see people merely as consumers. Their well-being and security—old age security, declining child mortality, health care, and so on—are the goal of development. Almost any activity that increases well-being and security lessens people's desires to have more children than they and national ecosystems can support.

II. THE POPULATION PERSPECTIVE

Growth in Numbers

Population growth accelerated in the middle of the 18th century with the advent of the Industrial Revolution and associated improvements in agriculture, not just in the regions that are more developed but elsewhere as well. The recent phase of acceleration started around 1950 with the sharp reduction in mortality rates in the developing countries.

million. Most are high-income West Asian countries and some small island states. Many of these countries have the capacity to earn enough foreign exchange to import their food requirements. In the others, the real issue is the modernization of agriculture on a sustainable basis.

Some researchers have assessed the 'theoretical' potential for global food production. One study assumes that the area under food production can be around 1.5 billion hectares (close to the current level) and that average yields could go up to 5 tons of grain equivalent per hectare (as against the present average of 2 tons of grain equivalent). Allowing for production from rangelands and marine sources, the total 'potential' is placed at 8 billion tons of grain equivalent.

How many people can this sustain? The present global average consumption of plant energy for food, seed, and animal feed amounts to about 6,000 calories daily, with a range among countries of 3,000–15,000 calories, depending on the level of meat consumption. On this basis, the potential production could sustain a little more than 11 billion people. But if the average consumption rises substantially—say, to 9,000 calories—the population carrying capacity of the Earth comes down to 7.5 billion. These figures could be substantially higher if the area under food production and the productivity of 3 billion hectares of permanent pastures can be increased on a sustainable basis. Nevertheless, the data do suggest that meeting the food needs of an ultimate world population of around 10 billion would require some changes in food habits, as well as greatly improving the efficiency of traditional agriculture.

Sources: B. Gilland, 'Considerations on World Population and Food Supply', *Population and Development Review*, Vol. 9, No. 2, pp. 203–11; G.M. Higgins et al., *Potential Population Supporting Capacities of Lands in the Developing World* (Rome: FAO, 1982); D.J. Mahar (ed.), *Rapid Population Growth and Human Carrying Capacity*, Staff Working Papers No. 690 (Washington, DC: World Bank, 1985).

Between 1950 and 1985, world population grew at an annual rate of 1.9 per cent, compared with 0.8 per cent in the half-century preceding 1950.[2] Population growth is now concentrated in the developing regions of Asia, Africa, and Latin America, which accounted for 85 per cent of the increase of global population since 1950. (See Table 4.1.)

The processes of population growth are changing in most developing countries as birth and death rates fall. In the early 1950s, practically all developing countries had birth rates over 40 and death rates over 20, the major exception being the low death rates in Latin America. (These rates refer to the annual number of births and deaths per 1,000 population.) Today the situation is quite different:

- Thirty-two per cent of the people in the Third World live in countries—such as China and the Republic of Korea—with birth rates below 25 and death rates below 10.

Table 4.1

World Population 1950–85: Key Facts

Size and Rates	1950	1960	1970	1980	1985
Total Population (billions):					
World	2.5	3.0	3.7	4.4	4.8
More developed regions	0.83	0.94	1.05	1.14	1.17
Less developed regions	1.68	2.07	2.65	3.31	3.66
Annual Growth* (per cent):					
World		1.8	2.0	1.9	1.7
More developed regions		1.3	1.0	0.8	0.6
Less developed regions		2.1	2.5	2.3	2.0
Urban Population (per cent):					
World	29	34	37	40	41
More developed regions	54	67	67	70	72
Less developed regions	17	22	25	29	31

* Data are for growth over previous decade or, for last column, over previous five years.

Source: Department of International Economic and Social Affairs, *World Population Prospects: Estimates and Projections as Assessed in 1984* (New York: UN, 1986).

- Forty-one per cent are in countries where birth rates have fallen, but not as much as death rates, and their populations are growing at around 2 per cent—doubling, in other words, every 34 years. Such countries include Brazil, India, Indonesia, and Mexico.
- The remaining 27 per cent live in countries, such as Algeria, Bangladesh, Iran, and Nigeria, where death rates have fallen slightly but birth rates remain high. Overall population growth is in the range of 2.5 to 3 per cent (doubling every 28 to 23 years), with even higher growth rates in some countries, such as Kenya.[3]

In the industrial world, fertility rates have declined and the population is not growing rapidly. In fact, it has stabilized in many countries. Still, the population in North America, Europe, the USSR, and Oceania is expected to increase by 230 million by the year 2025, which is as many people as live in the United States today.

The acceleration of population growth in the Third World and the decline in fertility levels in industrial countries are changing age distribution patterns radically. In developing countries, the young predominate. In 1980, 39 per cent of developing-country populations were younger than 15; the figure for industrialized countries was only 23 per cent.[4] Yet in these countries, the proportion of the elderly is

TABLE 4.2

Current and Projected Population Size and Growth Rates*

Region	Population (billion)			Annual Growth Rate (per cent)		
				1950 to 1985	1985 to 2000	2000 to 2025
	1985	2000	2025			
World	4.8	6.1	8.2	1.9	1.6	1.2
Africa	0.56	0.87	1.62	2.6	3.1	2.5
Latin America	0.41	0.55	0.78	2.6	2.0	1.4
Asia	2.82	3.55	4.54	2.1	1.6	1.0
North America	0.26	0.30	0.35	1.3	0.8	0.6
Europe	0.49	0.51	0.52	0.7	0.3	0.1
USSR	0.28	0.31	0.37	1.3	0.8	0.6
Oceania	0.02	0.03	0.04	1.9	1.4	0.9

* Medium-variant projections.

Source: Department of International Economic and Social Affairs, *World Population Prospects: Estimates and Projections as Assessed in 1984* (New York: UN, 1986).

growing. Those 65 or older accounted for 11 per cent of the population in 1980; in developing countries, they represented only 4 per cent.[5] Thus in the industrial world, relatively fewer people of working age will bear the burden of supporting relatively larger numbers of older people.

A changing age structure helps to set patterns of future population growth. The large number of young people in developing countries means large numbers of future parents, so that even if each person produces fewer children, the total number of births will continue to increase. Population growth can continue to grow for some decades after fertility rates decline to the 'replacement level' of slightly over two children on average per couple. Thus in many nations, high population growth rates over the next few generations are assured.

Population projections indicate an increase in global population from 4.8 billion in 1985 to 6.1 billion by 2000, and to 8.2 billion by 2025. (See Table 4.2.) More than 90 per cent of this increase is expected in developing regions. Large differences exist among countries in these areas, and the momentum of population growth is higher in Africa than in Latin America or Asia. In some developing countries, such as China, population growth rates are already well below 2 per cent and are expected to fall below 1 per cent by the beginning of the next century.[6]

Reflecting the 'momentum' of population growth, long-term UN projections show that at the global level:

- if replacement-level fertility is reached in 2010, global population will stabilize at 7.7 billion by 2060;
- if this rate is reached in 2035, population will stabilize at 10.2 billion by 2095;
- if, however, the rate is reached only in 2065, global population in 2100 would be 14.2 billion.[7]

These projections show that the world has real choices. Policies to bring down fertility rates could make a difference of billions to the global population next century. The greater part of the differences between the three variants is accounted for by South Asia, Africa, and Latin America. Hence much depends on the effectiveness of population policies in these regions.

Changes in Mobility

The number of people in Europe, Japan, North America, and the Soviet Union quintupled between 1750 and 1950, and these regions' share in world population increased sharply over this period.[8] By the latter part of the 19th century, there was growing concern about population pressures in Europe. Migration to North America, Australia, and New Zealand helped to some extent. At its peak between 1881 and 1910, permanent emigration absorbed nearly 20 per cent of the increase in population in Europe.[9]

Today, however, migration is not a major factor in determining population distribution among countries. Between 1970 and 1980 permanent emigration as a percentage of population increase fell to 4 per cent in Europe and was only 2.5 per cent in Latin America. The corresponding percentages in Asia and Africa were very much lower.[10] Thus the option of emigration to new lands has not been and will not be a significant element in relieving demographic pressures in developing countries. In effect, this reduces the time available to bring population into balance with resources.

Within countries, populations are more mobile. Improved communications have enabled large movements of people, sometimes as a natural response to the growth of economic opportunities in different places. Some governments have actively encouraged migration from densely to sparsely settled areas. A more recent phenomenon is the flight of 'ecological refugees' from areas of environmental degradation.

Much of the movement is from countryside to city. (See Chapter 9.) In 1985, some 40 per cent of the world's population lived in cities;

TABLE 4.3

Health Indicators

Region	Life Expectancy at Birth (years)		Infant Mortality Rates (deaths per 1,000 live births)	
	1950–55	1980–85	1960–65	1980–85
World	49.9	64.6	117	81
Africa	37.5	49.7	157	114
Asia	41.2	57.9	133	87
South America	52.3	64.0	101	64
North America	64.4	71.1	43	27
Europe	65.3	73.2	37	16
USSR	61.7	70.9	32	25
Oceania	61.0	67.6	55	39

Source: WCED, based on data in World Resources Institute/International Institute for Environment and Development, *World Resources 1986* (New York: Basic Books, 1986).

the magnitude of the urban drift can be seen in the fact that since 1950, the increase in urban population has been larger than the increase in rural population both in percentage and in absolute terms. This shift is most striking in developing countries, where the number of city-dwellers quadrupled during this period.[11]

Improved Health and Education

Improvements in the health and education of all, but especially of women and in conjunction with other social changes that raise the status of women, can have a profound effect in bringing down population growth rates. In an initial period, however, better health care means that more babies live to reproduce and that women reproduce over longer time spans.

The 'health status' of a society is a complex concept that cannot be measured easily. Two widely available indicators that reflect at least some aspects of a given society's health are life expectancy and infant mortality rates. (See Table 4.3.) These statistics suggest that health has improved virtually everywhere; and, at least with regard to these two indicators, the gap between industrial and developing regions has narrowed.

Many factors can increase life expectancy and reduce mortality rates; two are worth emphasizing. First, although generally speaking

TABLE 4.4

Male and Female Enrolment Ratios, by Region, 1960 and 1982

	Male		Female	
Region	1960	1982	1960	1982
World				
First Level	92.2	101.3	71.1	87.3
Second Level	31.3	53.3	23.1	42.5
Africa				
First Level	56.2	89.2	32.0	72.1
Second Level	7.3	29.6	2.9	19.5
Latin America and Caribbean				
First Level	75.0	106.2	71.2	103.3
Second Level	14.9	46.6	13.6	48.5
North America				
First Level	117.4	119.7	116.4	119.9
Second Level	69.4	85.4	71.4	86.6
Asia				
First Level	94.9	100.1	63.1	79.9
Second Level	29.3	49.3	16.6	32.9
Europe and USSR				
First Level	103.4	105.4	102.7	104.5
Second Level	46.5	76.2	44.6	81.3
Oceania				
First Level	102.2	102.9	100.7	98.9
Second Level	53.8	71.1	58.8	72.0

Note: The figures are percentages of appropriate age groups receiving a given level of education. As many older children are in primary school, percentages can be over 100.

Source: WCED, based on data in UNESCO, 'A Summary Statistical Review of Education in the World, 1960–1982', Paris, July 1984.

national wealth buys national health, some relatively poor nations and areas, such as China, Sri Lanka, and the Indian state of Kerala, have achieved remarkable success in lowering infant mortality and improving health through increases in education, especially of women; the establishment of primary health clinics; and other health care programmes.[12] Second, the principal reductions in mortality rates in the industrial world came about before the advent of modern drugs; they were due to improved nutrition, housing, and hygiene. The recent gains in developing countries have also been largely due to public health programmes, particularly for the control of communicable diseases.

Education is another key dimension of 'population quality'. The past few decades have seen a great expansion of educational facilities in virtually all countries. In terms of school enrolment, literacy rates, the growth in technical education, and the development of scientific skills, much progress has been achieved. (See Table 4.4.)

III. A POLICY FRAMEWORK

Excessive population growth diffuses the fruits of development over increasing numbers instead of improving living standards in many developing countries; a reduction of current growth rates is an imperative for sustainable development. The critical issues are the balance between population size and available resources and the rate of population growth in relation to the capacity of the economy to provide for the basic needs of the population, not just today but for generations. Such a long-term view is necessary because attitudes to fertility rarely change rapidly and because, even after fertility starts declining, past increases in population impart a momentum of growth as people reach child-bearing age. However a nation proceeds towards the goals of sustainable development and lower fertility levels, the two are intimately linked and mutually reinforcing.

Measures to influence population size cannot be effective in isolation from other environment/development issues. The number, density, movement, and growth rate of a population cannot be influenced in the short run if these efforts are being overwhelmed by adverse patterns of development in other areas. Population policies must have a broader focus than controlling numbers: Measures to improve the quality of human resources in terms of health, education, and social development are as important.

A first step may be for governments to abandon the false division between 'productive' or 'economic' expenditures and 'social' expenditures. Policymakers must realize that spending on population activities and on other efforts to raise human potential is crucial to a nation's economic and productive activities and to achieving sustainable human progress—the end for which a government exists.

Managing Population Growth

Progress in population policies is uneven. Some countries with serious population problems have comprehensive policies. Some go no further than the promotion of family planning. Some do not do even that.

A population policy should set out and pursue broad national demographic goals in relation to other socio-economic objectives. Social and cultural factors dominate all others in affecting fertility. The most important of these is the roles women play in the family, the economy, and the society at large. Fertility rates fall as women's employment opportunities outside the home and farm, their access to education, and their age at marriage all rise. Hence policies meant to lower fertility rates not only must include economic incentives and disincentives, but must aim to improve the position of women in society. Such policies should essentially promote women's rights.

Poverty breeds high rates of population growth: Families poor in income, employment, and social security need children first to work and later to sustain elderly parents. Measures to provide an adequate livelihood for poor households, to establish and enforce minimum-age child labour laws, and to provide publicly financed social security will all lower fertility rates. Improved public health and child nutrition programmes that bring down infant mortality rates—so parents do not need 'extra' children as insurance against child death—can also help to reduce fertility levels.

All these programmes are effective in bringing down birth rates only when their benefits are shared by the majority. Societies that attempt to spread the benefits of economic growth to a wider segment of the population may do better at lowering birth rates than societies with both faster and higher levels of economic growth but a less even sharing of the benefits of that growth.

Thus developing-country population strategies must deal not only with the population variable as such but also with the underlying social and economic conditions of underdevelopment. They must be multifaceted campaigns: to strengthen social, cultural, and economic motivations for couples to have small families and, through family planning programmes, to provide to all who want them the education, technological means, and services required to control family size.

Family planning services in many developing countries suffer by being isolated from other programmes that reduce fertility and even from those that increase motivation to use such services. They remain separate both in design and implementation from such fertility-related programmes as nutrition, public health, mother and child care, and preschool education that take place in the same area and that are often funded by the same agency.

Such services must therefore be integrated with other efforts to improve access to health care and education. The clinical support needed for most modern contraceptive methods makes family planning services heavily dependent on the health system. Some gov-

‘The environment is the business of everybody, development is the business of everybody, life and living is the business of everybody. I think the solution will be found in encouraging mass environmental literacy so that there can be democratic and literate decisions, because if decisions are taken by a few without the incorporation of the opinion of the masses, the NGOs especially included, the likelihood is that the situations will not succeed. They will be imposed from above, the people will not respond positively to them, and the project is lost before it is launched.’

Joseph Ouma
Dean of School of Environmental Studies, Moi University
WCED Public Hearing, Nairobi, 23 Sept 1986

ernments have successfully combined population programmes with health, education, and rural development projects, and implemented them as part of major socio-economic programmes in villages or regions. This integration increases motivation, improves access, and raises the effectiveness of investments in family planning.

Only about 1.5 per cent of official development aid now goes for population assistance.[13] Regrettably, some donor countries have cut back on their assistance for multilateral population programmes and so weakened them; this must be reversed.

Zimbabwe is one nation that has successfully integrated its family planning efforts not only with its rural health services but also with efforts to improve women's abilities to organize group activities and earn money through their own labour. The government's initial efforts were aimed less at limiting population growth than at assisting women to space births in the interests of mother and child health and at helping infertile women to bear children. But gradually families have begun to use the contraceptives made available for child spacing as a way to limit fertility. Zimbabwe now leads sub-Saharan Africa in the use of modern contraceptive methods.[14]

Managing Distribution and Mobility

Population distribution across a country's different regions is influenced by the geographical spread of economic activity and opportunity. Most countries are committed in theory to balancing regional development, but are rarely able to do this in practice. Governments able to spread employment opportunities throughout their nations and especially through their countrysides will thus limit the rapid and often uncontrolled growth of one or two cities. China's

'Demographic phenomena constitute the heart of the African Development problematique. They are the data that lead most analysts to project a continuing and deepening crisis in Africa. There is no doubt of the imperative and urgent need for a far-reaching population policy to be adopted and vigorously implemented by African governments.

One issue of relevance that requires further research is the use of the tax system as a means for controlling population growth and discouraging rural-urban migration.

To slow down population growth, should families without children be given a tax incentive or tax break? Should a tax penalty be imposed for each child after a fixed number of children, considering that the tax system has not solved the population migration problem?'

Adebayo Adedeji
Executive Director, Economic Commission for Africa
WCED Public Hearing, Harare, 18 Sept 1986

effort to support village-level industries in the countryside is perhaps the most ambitious of this sort of national programme.

Migration from countryside to city is not in itself a bad thing; it is part of the process of economic development and diversification. The issue is not so much the overall rural-urban shift but the distribution of urban growth between large metropolitan cities and smaller urban settlements. (See Chapter 9.)

A commitment to rural development implies more attention to realizing the development potential of all regions, particularly those that are ecologically disadvantaged. (See Chapter 5.) This would help reduce migration from these areas due to lack of opportunities. But governments should avoid going too far in the opposite direction, encouraging people to move into sparsely populated areas such as tropical moist forests, where the land may not be able to provide sustainable livelihoods.

From Liability to Asset

When a population exceeds the carrying capacity of the available resources, it can become a liability in efforts to improve people's welfare. But talking of population just as numbers glosses over an important point: People are also a creative resource, and this creativity is an asset societies must tap. To nurture and enhance that asset, people's physical well-being must be improved through better nutrition, health care, and so on. And education must be provided to help them become more capable and creative, skilful, productive, and better able to deal with day-to-day problems. All this has to be achieved through access to and participation in the processes of sustainable development.

Improving Health

Good health is the foundation of human welfare and productivity. Hence a broad-based health policy is essential for sustainable development. In the developing world, the critical problems of ill health are closely related to environmental conditions and development problems.

Malaria is the most important parasitic disease in the tropics, and its prevalence is closely related to wastewater disposal and drainage. Large dams and irrigation systems have led to sharp increases in the incidence of schistosomiasis (snail fever) in many areas. Inadequacies in water supply and sanitation are direct causes of other widespread and debilitating diseases such as diarrhoeas and various worm infestations.

Though much has been achieved in recent years, 1.7 billion people lack access to clean water, and 1.2 billion to adequate sanitation.[15] Many diseases can be controlled not just through therapeutic interventions but also through improvements in rural water supply, sanitation, and health education. In this sense, they really require a developmental solution. In the developing world, the number of water taps nearby is a better indication of the health of a community than is the number of hospital beds.

Other examples of links between development, environmental conditions, and health include air pollution and the respiratory illnesses it brings, the impact of housing conditions on the spread of tuberculosis, the effects of carcinogens and toxic substances, and the exposure to hazards in the workplace and elsewhere.

Many health problems arise from the nutritional deficiencies that occur in virtually all developing countries, but most acutely in low-income areas. Most malnutrition is related to a shortage of calories or protein or both, but some diets also lack specific elements and compounds, such as iron and iodine. Health will be greatly improved in low-income areas by policies that lead to the production of more of the cheap foods the poor traditionally eat—coarse grains and root crops.

These health, nutrition, environment, and development links imply that health policy cannot be conceived of purely in terms of curative or preventive medicine, or even in terms of greater attention to public health. Integrated approaches are needed that reflect key health objectives in areas such as food production; water supply and sanitation; industrial policy, particularly with regard to safety and pollution; and the planning of human settlements. Beyond this, it is necessary to identify vulnerable groups and their health risks and to ensure that the socio-economic factors that underlie these risks are taken into account in other areas of development policy.

Hence, the World Health Organization's 'Health for All' strategy should be broadened far beyond the provision of medical workers and clinics, to cover health-related interventions in all development activities.[16] Moreover, this broader approach must be reflected in institutional arrangements to co-ordinate all such activities effectively.

Within the narrower area of health care, providing primary health care facilities and making sure that everyone has the opportunity to use them are appropriate starting points. Maternal and child health care are also particularly important. The critical elements here are relatively inexpensive and can have a profound impact on health and well-being. An organized system of trained birth attendants, protection against tetanus and other childbirth infections, and supplemental feeding can dramatically reduce maternal mortality. Similarly, low-cost programmes to assure immunization, teach and supply oral dehydration therapy against diarrhoeas, and encourage breast-feeding (which in turn can reduce fertility) can increase child survival rates dramatically.

Health care must be supplemented by effective health education. Some parts of the Third World may soon face growing numbers of the illnesses associated with life-styles in industrial nations—cancer and heart disease especially. Few developing nations can afford the expensive treatment required for the latter diseases, and should begin efforts now to educate their citizens on the dangers of smoking and of high-fat diets.

A rapid spread of acquired immune deficiency syndrome (AIDS) in both developed and developing nations could drastically alter all countries' health priorities. AIDS is threatening to kill millions of people and disrupt the economies of many countries. Governments should overcome any lingering shyness and rapidly educate their people about this syndrome and about the ways in which it is spread. International co-operation on research and the handling of the disease is essential.

Another major health problem with international ramifications is the increase in drug addiction. It is a problem closely linked to organized crime in the production of drugs, in large-scale international traffic in these drugs, and in the networks for distribution. It distorts

We in Asia, I feel, want to have an equilibrium between the spiritual and material life. I noticed that you have tried to separate religion from the technological side of life. Is that not exactly the mistake in the West in developing technology, without ethics, without religion? If that is the case, and we have the chance to develop a new direction, should we not advise the group on technology to pursue a different kind of technology which has as its base not only the rationality, but also the spiritual aspect? Is this a dream or is this something we cannot avoid?

Speaker from the floor
WCED Public Hearing, Jakarta, 26 March 1985

the economy in many poor producing areas and destroys people the world over. International co-operation is essential in tackling this scourge. Some countries have to deploy considerable financial resources to halt the production and traffic in narcotics and to promote crop diversification and rehabilitation schemes in the producing areas, which are generally impoverished. To sustain their efforts, greater international assistance is essential

Most medical research focuses on pharmaceuticals, vaccines, and other technological interventions for disease management. Much of this research is directed at the diseases of industrialized countries, as their treatment accounts for a substantial part of the sales of pharmaceutical companies. More research is urgently needed on the environmentally related tropical diseases that are the major health problem in the Third World. This research should focus not merely on new medicines, but also on public health measures to control these diseases. Existing arrangements for international collaboration on tropical disease research should be greatly strengthened.

Broadening Education

Human resource development demands knowledge and skills to help people improve their economic performance. Sustainable development requires changes in values and attitudes towards environment and development—indeed, towards society and work at home, on farms, and in factories. The world's religions could help provide direction and motivation in forming new values that would stress individual and joint responsibility towards the environment and towards nurturing harmony between humanity and environment.

Education should also be geared towards making people more capable of dealing with problems of overcrowding and excessive population densities, and better able to improve what could be called

6 Education and communication are vitally important in order to impress each individual of his or her responsibility regarding the healthy future of the Earth. The best way for students to recognize that their action can make a difference is to have projects organized by the school or community on which the students can work. Once convinced that they can help, people tend to change both their attitude and their behaviour. New attitudes towards the environment will be reflected in decisions at home and in corporate boardrooms around the world.9

Vanessa Allison
Student, North Toronto Collegiate High School
WCED Public Hearing, Ottawa, 26-27 May 1986

'social carrying capacities'. This is essential to prevent ruptures in the social fabric, and schooling should enhance the levels of tolerance and empathy required for living in a crowded world. Improved health, lower fertility, and better nutrition will depend on greater literacy and social and civic responsibility. Education can induce all these, and can enhance a society's ability to overcome poverty, increase incomes, improve health and nutrition, and reduce family size.

The investment in education and the growth in school enrolment during the past few decades are signs of progress. Access to education is increasing and will continue to do so. Today almost all the world's boys are getting some form of primary education. In Asia and Africa, however, enrolment rates for girls are much lower than for boys at all levels. A large gap also exists between developed and developing countries in enrolment rates beyond primary schools, as Table 4.4 indicated.

UN projections of enrolment rates for the year 2000 suggest a continuation of these trends. Thus despite the growth in primary education, illiteracy will continue to rise in terms of sheer numbers; there will be more than 900 million people unable to read and write at the end of the century. By then, girls' enrolment rates are still expected to be below the current rates for boys in Asia. As for secondary education, developing countries are not expected to attain even the 1960 industrial country levels by the year 2000.[17]

Sustainable development requires that these trends be corrected. The main task of education policy must be to make literacy universal and to close the gaps between male and female enrolment rates. Realizing these goals would improve individual productivity and earnings, as well as personal attitudes to health, nutrition, and child-bearing. It can also instill a greater awareness of everyday environmental factors. Facilities for education beyond primary school must be expanded to improve skills necessary for pursuing sustainable development.

A major problem confronting many countries is the widespread unemployment and the unrest that it leads to. Education has often been unable to provide the skills needed for appropriate employment. This is evident in the large numbers of unemployed people who have been trained for white-collar employment in swelling urban populations. Education and training should also be directed towards the acquisition of practical and vocational skills, and particularly towards making people more self-reliant. All this should be supported by efforts to nurture the informal sector and the participation of community organizations.

Providing facilities is only the beginning. Education must be improved in quality and in relevance to local conditions. In many areas, it should be integrated with children's participation in farm work, a process requiring flexibility in the school system. It should impart knowledge relevant for the proper management of local resources. Rural schools must teach about local soils, water, and the conservation of both, about deforestation and how the community and the individual can reverse it. Teachers must be trained and the curriculum developed so that students learn about the agricultural balance sheet of an area.

Most people base their understanding of environmental processes and development on traditional beliefs or on information provided by a conventional education. Many thus remain ignorant about ways in which they could improve traditional production practices and better protect the natural resource base. Education should therefore provide comprehensive knowledge, encompassing and cutting across the social and natural sciences and the humanities, thus providing insights on the interaction between natural and human resources, between development and environment.

Environmental education should be included in and should run throughout the other disciplines of the formal education curriculum at all levels—to foster a sense of responsibility for the state of the environment and to teach students how to monitor, protect, and improve it. These objectives cannot be achieved without the involvement of students in the movement for a better environment, through such things as nature clubs and special interest groups. Adult education, on-the-job training, television, and other less formal methods must be used to reach out to as wide a group of individuals as possible, as environmental issues and knowledge systems now change radically in the space of a lifetime.

A critical point of intervention is during teacher training. The attitudes of teachers will be key in increasing understanding of the environment and its links with development. To enhance the awareness and capabilities of teachers in this area, multilateral and bilateral agencies must provide support for the relevant curriculum development in teacher training institutions, for the preparation of teaching aids, and for other similar activities. Global awareness could be fostered by encouraging contacts among teachers from different countries, for instance in specialized centres set up for this purpose.

Empowering Vulnerable Groups

The processes of development generally lead to the gradual integration of local communities into a larger social and economic framework. But some communities—so-called indigenous or tribal peoples—remain isolated because of such factors as physical barriers to communication or marked differences in social and cultural practices. Such groups are found in North America, in Australia, in the Amazon Basin, in Central America, in the forests and hills of Asia, in the deserts of North Africa, and elsewhere.

The isolation of many such people has meant the preservation of a traditional way of life in close harmony with the natural environment. Their very survival has depended on their ecological awareness and adaptation. But their isolation has also meant that few of them have shared in national economic and social development; this may be reflected in their poor health, nutrition, and education.

With the gradual advance of organized development into remote regions, these groups are becoming less isolated. Many live in areas rich in valuable natural resources that planners and 'developers' want to exploit, and this exploitation disrupts the local environment so as to endanger traditional ways of life. The legal and institutional changes that accompany organized development add to such pressures.

Growing interaction with the larger world is increasing the vulnerability of these groups, since they are often left out of the processes of economic development. Social discrimination, cultural barriers, and the exclusion of these people from national political processes makes these groups vulnerable and subject to exploitation. Many groups become dispossessed and marginalized, and their traditional practices disappear. They become the victims of what could be described as cultural extinction.

These communities are the repositories of vast accumulations of traditional knowledge and experience that links humanity with its ancient origins. Their disappearance is a loss for the larger society,

❝I am here as the son of a small nation, the Krenak Indian Nation. We live in the valley of the Rio Doce, which is the frontier of Espirito Santo with the State of Minas Gerais. We are a micro-country—a micro-nation.

When the government took our land in the valley of Rio Doce, they wanted to give us another place somewhere else. But the State, the government will never understand that we do not have another place to go.

The only possible place for the Krenak people to live and to re-establish our existence, to speak to our Gods, to speak to our nature, to weave our lives is where our God created us. It is useless for the government to put us in a very beautiful place, in a very good place with a lot of hunting and a lot of fish. The Krenak people, we continue dying and we die insisting that there is only one place for us to live.

My heart does not become happy to see humanity's incapacity. I have no pleasure at all to come here and make these statements. We can no longer see the planet that we live upon as if it were a chess-board where people just move things around. We cannot consider the planet as something isolated from the cosmic.

We are not idiots to believe that there is possibility of life for us outside of where the origin of our life is. Respect our place of living, do not degrade our living condition, respect this life. We have no arms to cause pressure, the only thing we have is the right to cry for our dignity and the need to live in our land.❞

Ailton Krenak
Co-ordinator of Indian Nations' Union
WCED Public Hearing, Sao Paulo, 28–29 Oct 1985

which could learn a great deal from their traditional skills in sustainably managing very complex ecological systems. It is a terrible irony that as formal development reaches more deeply into rain forests, deserts, and other isolated environments, it tends to destroy the only cultures that have proved able to thrive in these environments.

The starting point for a just and humane policy for such groups is the recognition and protection of their traditional rights to land and the other resources that sustain their way of life—rights they may define in terms that do not fit into standard legal systems. These groups' own institutions to regulate rights and obligations are crucial for maintaining the harmony with nature and the environmental awareness characteristic of the traditional way of life. Hence the recognition of traditional rights must go hand in hand with measures to protect the local institutions that enforce responsibility in resource use. And this recognition must also give local communities a decisive voice in the decisions about resource use in their area.

Protection of traditional rights should be accompanied by positive measures to enhance the well-being of the community in ways appropriate to the group's life-style. For example, earnings from traditional activities can be increased through the introduction of marketing arrangements that ensure a fair price for produce, but also through steps to conserve and enhance the resource base and increase resource productivity.

Those promoting policies that have an impact on the lives of an isolated, traditional people must tread a fine line between keeping them in artificial, perhaps unwanted isolation and wantonly destroying their life-styles. Hence broader measures of human resource development are essential. Health facilities must be provided to supplement and improve traditional practices; nutritional deficiencies have to be corrected, and educational institutions established. These steps should precede new projects that open up an area to economic development. Special efforts should also be made to ensure that the local community can derive the full benefit of such projects, particularly through jobs.

In terms of sheer numbers, these isolated, vulnerable groups are small. But their marginalization is a symptom of a style of development that tends to neglect both human and environmental considerations. Hence a more careful and sensitive consideration of their interests is a touchstone of a sustainable development policy.

Notes

1 Department of International Economic and Social Affairs (DIESA), *World Population Prospects: Estimates and Projections as Assessed in 1984* (New York: UN, 1986).

2 Ibid.

3 Based on data from UNCTAD, *Handbook of International Trade and Development Statistics 1985 Supplement* (New York: 1985).

4 World Bank, *World Development Report 1984* (New York: Oxford University Press, 1984).

5 Ibid.

6 DIESA, op. cit.

7 UN, *Population Bulletin of the United Nations, No. 14, 1982* (New York: 1983).

8 C. Clark, *Population Growth and Land Use* (New York: St. Martin's Press, 1957).

9 World Bank, op. cit.

10 Ibid.

11 DIESA, op. cit.

12 WHO, *Intersectoral Linkages and Health Development, Case Studies in India (Kerala State), Jamaica, Norway, Sri Lanka and Thailand* (Geneva: 1984).

13 World Bank, op. cit.

14 L. Timberlake, *Only One Earth: Living for the Future* (London: BBC/Earthscan, 1987).

15 UNEP, *The State of the Environment: Environment and Health* (Nairobi: 1986).

16 WHO, *Global Strategy for Health for All by the Year 2000* (Geneva: 1981).

17 UNESCO, *A Summary Statistical Review of Education in the World, 1960–82* (Paris: 1984).

5

FOOD SECURITY: SUSTAINING
THE POTENTIAL

The world produces more food per head of population today than ever before in human history. In 1985, it produced nearly 500 kilogrammes per head of cereals and root crops, the primary sources of food.[1] Yet amid this abundance, more than 730 million people did not eat enough to lead fully productive working lives.[2] There are places where too little is grown; there are places where large numbers cannot afford to buy food. And there are broad areas of the Earth, in both industrial and developing nations, where increases in food production are undermining the base for future production.

The agricultural resources and the technology needed to feed growing populations are available. Much has been achieved over the past few decades. Agriculture does not lack resources; it lacks policies to ensure that the food is produced where it is needed and in a manner that sustains the livelihoods of the rural poor. We can meet this challenge by building on our achievements and devising new strategies for sustaining food and livelihood security.

I. ACHIEVEMENTS

Between 1950 and 1985, cereal production outstripped population growth, increasing from around 700 million tons to over 1,800 million tons, an annual growth rate of around 2.7 per cent.[3] This increase helped to meet escalating demands for cereals caused by population growth and rising incomes in developing countries and by growing needs for animal feed in developed countries. Yet regional differences in performance have been large. (See Table 5.1.)

As production has increased sharply in some regions and demand in others, the pattern of world trade in foods, especially cereals, has changed radically. North America exported barely 5 million tons of foodgrains yearly before the Second World War; it exported nearly 120 million tons during the 1980s. Europe's grain deficit is very much lower now, and the bulk of North American exports are to the USSR,

TABLE 5.1

Two Decades of Agricultural Development

Region	Per Capita Food Production (1961–64=100)		Per Capita Gross Cropped Area (hectares)		Per Hectare Fertilizer use (kilogrammes)	
	1961–64	1981–84	1964	1984	1964	1984
World	100	112	0.44	0.31	29.3	85.3
North America	100	121	1.05	0.90	47.3	93.2
Western Europe	100	131	0.31	0.25	124.4	224.3
Eastern Europe and USSR	100	128	0.84	0.71	30.4	122.1
Africa	100	88	0.74	0.35	1.8	9.7
Near East*	100	107	0.53	0.35	6.9	53.6
Far East†	100	116	0.30	0.20	6.4	45.8
Latin America	100	108	0.49	0.45	11.6	32.4
CPEs of Asia‡	100	135	0.17	0.10	15.8	170.3

* An FAO grouping that includes West Asia plus Egypt, Libya, and Sudan.
† An FAO grouping that covers South and South-East Asia excluding the centrally planned economies of Asia.
‡ An FAO grouping of centrally planned economies of Asia that covers China, Kampuchea, North Korea, Mongolia and Vietnam.

Source: Based on FAO data.

Asia, and Africa. Three countries—China, Japan, and the USSR—took half the world exports in the early 1980s; much of the rest went to relatively wealthy developing countries, such as Middle Eastern oil exporters. Several poor agricultural countries, especially in sub-Saharan Africa, have become net importers of foodgrains. Still, although one-fourth of sub-Saharan Africa's population relied on imported grains in 1984, that region's imports have accounted for less than 10 per cent of world grain trade thus far in the 1980s.[4]

Other foods besides grains are changing the patterns of world food demand and production. Demand for milk and meat is growing as incomes rise in societies that prefer animal protein, and much agricultural development in the industrialized nations has been devoted to meeting these demands. In Europe, meat production more than tripled between 1950 and 1984, and milk production nearly doubled.[5] Meat production for exports increased sharply, particularly in the rangelands of Latin America and Africa. World meat exports have risen from around 2 million tons in 1950–52 to over 11 million tons in 1984.[6]

To produce this milk and meat required in 1984 about 1.4 billion cattle and buffaloes, 1.6 billion sheep and goats, 800 million pigs, and a great deal of poultry—all of which weigh more than the people on the planet.[7] Most of these animals graze or browse or are fed local plants collected for them. However, rising demands for livestock feedgrains led to sharp increases in the production of cereals such as corn, which accounted for nearly two-thirds of the total increase in grain production in North America and Europe between 1950 and 1985.

This unprecedented growth in food production has been achieved partly by an extension of the production base: larger cropped areas, more livestock, more fishing vessels, and so on. But most of it is due to a phenomenal rise in productivity. Population increases have meant a decline in the area of cropped land in most of the world in per capita terms. And as the availability of arable land has declined, planners and farmers have focused on increasing productivity. In the past 35 years this has been achieved by:

- using new seed varieties designed to maximize yields, facilitate multiple cropping, and resist disease;
- applying more chemical fertilizers, the consumption of which rose more than ninefold[8] ;
- using more pesticides and similar chemicals, the use of which increased thirty-two-fold[9] ; and
- increasing irrigated area, which more than doubled.[10]

Global statistics mask substantial regional differences. (See Box 5-1.) The impacts of new technology have been uneven, and in some respects the agricultural technology gap has widened. For instance, average African foodgrain productivity declined in relation to European productivity from roughly one-half to about one-fifth over the past 35 years. Even in Asia, where new technology has spread rapidly, productivity in relation to European levels dropped.[11] Similar 'technology gaps' have emerged between regions within countries.

The past few decades have seen the emergence of three broad types of food production systems. 'Industrial agriculture', capital- and input-intensive and usually large-scale, is dominant in North America, Western and Eastern Europe, Australia and New Zealand, and in some small areas in developing countries. 'Green Revolution agriculture' is found in uniform, resource-rich, often flat and irrigated areas in the agricultural heartlands of some developing countries. It is more widespread in Asia but is also found in parts of Latin America and North Africa. Though initially the new technologies may have favoured large farmers, they are today accessible to a growing number of small producers. 'Resource-poor agriculture' relies on uncertain

Box 5-1. Regional Perspective on Agricultural Development

Africa
- a drop in per capita food output of about 1 per cent a year since the beginning of the 1970s
- a focus on cash crops and a growing dependence on imported food, fostered by pricing policies and foreign exchange compulsions
- major gaps in infrastructure for research, extension, input supply, and marketing
- degradation of the agricultural resource base due to desertification, droughts, and other processes
- large untapped potential of arable land, irrigation, and fertilizer use

West Asia and North Africa
- improvements in productivity due to better irrigation, the cultivation of high-yielding varieties, and higher fertilizer use
- limited arable land and considerable amounts of desert, making food self-sufficiency a challenge
- a need for controlled irrigation to cope with dry conditions

South and East Asia
- increased production and productivity, with some countries registering grain surpluses
- rapid growth in fertilizer use in some countries and extensive development of irrigation
- government commitments to be self-reliant in food, leading to national research centres, development of high-yielding seeds, and the fostering of location-specific technologies
- little unused land, and extensive, unabated deforestation
- growing numbers of rural landless

Latin America
- declining food imports since 1980, as food production kept pace with population growth over the last decade
- government support in the form of research centres to develop high-yielding seeds and other technologies
- inequitable distribution of land
- deforestation and degradation of the agricultural resource base, fueled partly by foreign trade and debt crisis
- a huge land resource and high productivity potential, though most of the potentially arable land is in the remote, lightly populated Amazon Basin, where perhaps only 20 per cent of the land is suitable for sustainable agriculture

North America and Western Europe

- North America the world's leading source of surplus foodgrain, though the rate of increase in output per hectare and in total productivity slowed in the 1970s
- subsidies for production that are ecologically and economically expensive
- depressing effect of surpluses on world markets and consequent impact on developing countries
- a resource base increasingly degraded through erosion, acidification, and water contamination
- in North America, some scope for future agricultural expansion in frontier areas that can be intensively farmed only at high cost

Eastern Europe and the Soviet Union

- food deficits met through imports, with the Soviet Union being the world's largest grain importer
- increased government investment in agriculture accompanied by eased farm distribution and organization to meet desires for food self-reliance, leading to production increases in meat and root crops
- pressures on agricultural resources through soil erosion, acidification, salinization, alkalization, and water contamination

---

rain rather than irrigation and is usually found in developing regions difficult to farm—drylands, highlands, and forests—with fragile soils. This includes most of sub-Saharan Africa and the remoter areas of Asia and Latin America. Here, per capita production has been declining and hunger is a critical problem. But today, all three systems of food production display signs of crises that endanger their growth.

II. SIGNS OF CRISIS

Agricultural policies in practically all countries have focused on output growth. Despite this, it has proved far more difficult to raise world agricultural output by a consistent 3 per cent a year in the mid-1980s than it was in the mid-1950s. Moreover, production records have been offset by the appearance of linked economic and ecological crises: Industrialized countries are finding it increasingly difficult to manage their surplus food production, the livelihood base of millions of poor producers in developing countries is deteriorating, and the resource base for agriculture is under pressure virtually everywhere.

Impact of Subsidies

The food surpluses in North America and Europe result mainly from subsidies and other incentives that stimulate production even in the absence of demand. Direct or indirect subsidies, which now cover virtually the entire food cycle, have become extremely expensive. In the United States, the cost of farm support has grown from $2.7 billion in 1980 to $25.8 billion in 1986. In the EEC, such costs have risen from $6.2 billion in 1976 to $21.5 billion in 1986.[12]

It has become politically more attractive, and usually cheaper, to export surpluses—often as food aid—rather than to store them. These heavily subsidized surpluses depress the international market prices of commodities such as sugar and have created severe problems for several developing countries whose economies are based on agriculture. Non-emergency food aid and low-priced imports also keep down prices received by Third World farmers and reduce the incentive to improve domestic food production.

The environmental consequences of a heavily subsidized production system are becoming evident within industrialized nations[13]:

- lower productivity as soil quality declines due to intensive soil cultivation and overuse of chemical fertilizers and pesticides[14] ;
- the destruction of the countryside, through clearing of hedgerows, park belts, and other protective cover and the levelling, occupation, and cultivation of marginal land and watershed protection areas; and
- nitrate pollution of ground-water aquifers due to the often subsidized overuse of nitrate fertilizers.

The financial, economic, and environmental effects of the current incentive systems are beginning to be questioned by many governments and groups, including farm organizations. A particular area of concern is the impact of these policies on developing countries. They depress international prices of products, such as rice and sugar, that are important exports for many developing countries and so reduce exchange earnings of developing countries. They increase the instability of world prices. And they discourage the processing of agricultural commodities in the producing countries.[15]

It is in the interests of all, including the farmers, that the policies be changed. Indeed, in recent years some conservation-oriented changes have taken place and some subsidy systems have increasingly stressed the need to retire land from production. The financial and economic burden of subsidies must be reduced. The harm that these policies do to the agriculture of developing countries by disrupting world markets must be eliminated.

Neglect of the Small Producer

The new technology behind increases in agricultural productivity

❛I think that at a forum like this there always tends to be someone standing up and saying you forgot my issue. I think my issue, as an NGO, is rather important; it is the issue of women. And I am sure that most of the people here have a serious sensitivity to women's role vis-à-vis the environment.

Especially in Africa, I think it has been clearly stated over and again that women are responsible for between 60 to 90 per cent of the food production, processing, and marketing. No one can really address the food crisis in Africa or many of the other crises that seem to exist here without addressing the question of women, and really seeing that women are participants in decision-making processes at the very basic all the way through up to the highest level.❜

Mrs. King
The Greenbelt Movement
WCED Public Hearing, Nairobi, 23 Sept 1986

requires scientific and technological skills, a system for technology extension and other services for farmers, and commercial orientation in farm management. In many parts of Asia, in particular, small farmers have shown a remarkable capacity to use new technology once they are given incentives and adequate financial and infrastructural support. Small cash-crop farmers in Africa have demonstrated the potential of the smallholder on that continent, and in the last few years successes have been recorded in food crops also. But ecologically disadvantaged areas and land-poor rural masses have not benefited from advances in technology and will not until governments are willing and able to redistribute land and resources, and give them the necessary support and incentives.

Agricultural support systems seldom take into account the special circumstances of subsistence farmers and herders. Subsistence farmers cannot afford the high cash outlay of modern inputs. Many are shifting cultivators who do not have a clear title to the land they use. They may plant a variety of crops on one plot to meet their own needs, and are thus unable to use methods developed for large stands of a single crop.

Many herders are nomadic and difficult to reach with education, advice, and equipment. They, like subsistence farmers, depend on certain traditional rights, which are threatened by commercial developments. They herd traditional breeds, which are hardy but rarely highly productive.

Women farmers, though they play a critical role in food production, are often ignored by programmes meant to improve production. In

Latin America, the Caribbean, and Asia they form a large agricultural labour force, while most of sub-Saharan Africa's food is grown by women. Yet almost all agricultural programmes tend to neglect the special needs of women farmers.

Degradation of the Resource Base

Short-sighted policies are leading to degradation of the agricultural resource base on almost every continent: soil erosion in North America; soil acidification in Europe; deforestation and desertification in Asia, Africa, and Latin America; and waste and pollution of water almost everywhere. Within 40–70 years, global warming may cause the flooding of important coastal production areas. Some of these effects arise from trends in energy use and industrial production. Some arise from the pressure of population on limited resources. But agricultural policies emphasizing increased production at the expense of environmental considerations have also contributed greatly to this deterioration.

Loss of Soil Resources

Increases in cropped areas in recent decades have often extended cultivation onto marginal lands prone to erosion. By the late 1970s, soil erosion exceeded soil formation on about a third of US cropland, much of it in the midwestern agricultural heartland.[16] In Canada, soil degradation has been costing farmers $1 billion a year.[17] In the USSR, the extension of cultivation to the so-called Virgin Lands was a major plank of agricultural policy, but now it is believed that much of this land is marginal.[18] In India, soil erosion affects 25–30 per cent of the total land under cultivation.[19] Without conservation measures, the total area of rainfed cropland in developing countries in Asia, Africa, and Latin America will shrink by 544 million hectares over the long term because of soil erosion and degradation, according to a Food and Agriculture Organization (FAO) study.[20]

Erosion makes soil less able to retain water, depletes it of nutrients, and reduces the depth available for the roots to take hold. Land productivity declines. Eroded topsoil is carried to rivers, lakes, and reservoirs; silts up ports and waterways; reduces reservoir storage capacity; and increases the incidence and severity of floods.

Poorly designed and implemented irrigation systems have caused waterlogging, salinization, and alkalization of soils. FAO and the UN Educational, Scientific, and Cultural Organization estimate that as much as half the world's irrigation schemes suffer in some degree from these problems.[21] These estimates indicate that some 10 million hectares of irrigated land are being abandoned each year.

Soil degradation erodes the overall resource base for agriculture. The loss of croplands encourages farmers to overuse the remaining land and to move into forests and onto rangelands. Sustainable agriculture cannot be based on methods that mine and deplete the soil.

Impact of Chemicals

Chemical fertilizers and pesticides have played a large role in production increases since the Second World War, but clear warnings have been raised against over-reliance on them. The run-off of nitrogen and phosphates from excess use of fertilizers damages water resources, and such damage is spreading.

Using chemicals to control insects, pests, weeds, and fungi enhances productivity, but overuse threatens the health of humans and the lives of other species. Continuing, long-term exposure to pesticide and chemical residues in food, water, and even in the air is hazardous, particularly to children. A 1983 study estimated that approximately 10,000 people died each year in developing countries from pesticide poisoning and about 400,000 suffered acutely.[22] The effects are not limited to the area where pesticides are used but travel through the food chain.

Commercial fisheries have been depleted, bird species endangered, and insects that prey on pests wiped out. The number of pesticide-resistant insect pest species worldwide has increased and many resist even the newest chemicals. The variety and severity of pest infestations multiply, threatening the productivity of agriculture in the areas concerned.

The use of agricultural chemicals is not in itself harmful. In fact, the level of use is still quite low in many regions. In these areas, response rates are high and the environmental consequences of residues are not yet a problem. Hence these regions would benefit by using more agrochemicals. However, the growth in the use of chemicals tends to be concentrated precisely where they may be doing more overall harm than good.

Pressure on Forests

Forests are crucial for maintaining and improving the productivity of agricultural land. Yet agricultural expansion, a growing world timber trade, and woodfuel demand have destroyed much forest cover. Although this destruction has occurred worldwide, today the greatest challenge is in developing countries, particularly in tropical forests. (See Chapter 6.)

'Small farmers are held responsible for environmental destruction as if they had a choice of resources to depend on for their livelihood, when they really don't. In the context of basic survival, today's needs tend to overshadow consideration for the environmental future. It is poverty that is responsible for the destruction of natural resources, not the poor.'

Geoffrey Bruce
Canadian International Development Agency
WCED Public Hearing, Ottawa, 26–27 May 1986

Growing populations and the decreasing availability of arable land lead poor farmers in these countries to seek new land in forests to grow more food. Some government policies encourage the conversion of forests to pastures and others encourage large resettlement schemes in forests. There is nothing inherently wrong with clearing forests for farming, provided that the land is the best there is for new farming, can support the numbers encouraged to settle upon it, and is not already serving a more useful function, such as watershed protection. But often forests are cleared without forethought or planning.

Deforestation most severely disrupts mountainous areas and upland watersheds and the ecosystems that depend on them. The uplands influence precipitation, and the state of their soil and vegetation systems influence how this precipitation is released into the streams and rivers and onto the croplands of the plains below. The growing numbers and growing severity of both floods and droughts in many parts of the world have been linked to the deforestation of upland watersheds.[23]

Advancing Deserts

Some 29 per cent of the earth's land area suffers slight, moderate, or severe desertification; an additional 6 per cent is classified as extremely severely desertified.[24] In 1984, the world's drylands supported some 850 million people, of whom 230 million were on lands affected by severe desertification.[25]

The process of desertification affects almost every region of the globe, but it is most destructive in the drylands of South America, Asia, and Africa; for these three areas combined, 18.5 per cent (870 million hectares) of productive lands are severely desertified. Of the drylands in developing countries, Africa's Sudano-Sahelian zones and, to a lesser extent, some countries south of this zone suffer the most. In their arid and semi-arid lands are to be found 80 per cent of the moderately affected and 85 per cent of the severely affected people.[26]

Land permanently degraded to desert-like conditions continues to grow at an annual rate of 6 million hectares.[27] Each year, 21 million additional hectares provide no economic return because of the spread of desertification.[28] These trends are expected to continue despite some local improvements. Desertification is caused by a complex mix of climatic and human effects. The human effects, over which we have more control, include the rapid growth of both human and animal populations, detrimental land use practices (especially deforestation), adverse terms of trade, and civil strife. The cultivation of cash crops on unsuitable rangelands has forced herders and their cattle onto marginal lands. The unfavourable international terms of trade for primary products and the policies of aid donors have reinforced pressures to encourage increasing cash-crop production at any cost.

A Plan of Action conceived by the UN Environment Programme and drawn up at the 1977 UN Conference on Desertification has led to some slight, mainly local gains.[29] Progress on the plan has been hampered by lack of financial support from the international community, by inadequacies of the regional organizations established to respond to the regional nature of the problem, and by the lack of involvement of grass-roots communities.

III. THE CHALLENGE

Food demand will increase as populations increase and their consumption patterns change. In the remaining years of this century, about 1.3 billion people will be added to the human family (see Chapter 4); rising incomes, however, may account for 30 to 40 per cent of the increased demand for food in developing countries and about 10 per cent in industrial nations.[30] Thus over the next few decades, the global food system must be managed to increase food production by 3 to 4 per cent yearly.

Global food security depends not only on raising global production, but on reducing distortions in the structure of the world food market and on shifting the focus of food production to food-deficit countries, regions, and households. Many of the countries not growing enough food to feed themselves possess the largest remaining reservoirs of untapped agricultural resources. Latin America and sub-Saharan Africa have much unused land, although its quality and quantity vary greatly from nation to nation and much of it is ecologically vulnerable.[31] The Soviet Union and parts of North America have

'There are many contradictions in agricultural development. The blind imitation of models developed under different circumstances will have to give way to the realities and conditions existing in Africa. Large areas of virgin land have been opened up for export crops whose prices keep declining. This is not in the interest of developing countries.

There are so many problems to be overcome that we forget that every problem is an opportunity to do something positive. This is an opportunity for us to think of conservation and environment in a broad educational context. In doing so, we will be able to capture the next generation and demonstrate the wonder and the benefits of the world around them.'

Adolfo Mascarenhas
IUCN Harare Office
WCED Public Hearing, Harare, 18 Sept 1986

significant amounts of frontier land suitable for agriculture; only Asia and Europe are truly land-starved.

Global food security also depends on ensuring that all people, even the poorest of the poor, can get food. While on the world scale this challenge requires a reappraisal of global food distribution, the task weighs more immediately and heavily on national governments. Inequitable distribution of production assets, unemployment, and underemployment are at the heart of the problem of hunger in many countries.

Rapid, sound agricultural development will mean not only more food but more opportunities for people to earn money to purchase food. Thus when countries with untapped agricultural resources provide food by importing more, they are effectively importing unemployment. By the same token, countries that are subsidizing food exports are increasing unemployment in food-importing countries. This marginalizes people, and marginalized people are forced to destroy the resource base to survive. Shifting production to food-deficit countries and to the resource-poor farmers within those countries is a way of securing sustainable livelihoods.

Conserving the agricultural resource base and livelihood security of the poor can be mutually supportive in three ways. First, secure resources and adequate livelihoods lead to good husbandry and sustainable management. Second, they ease rural-to-urban migration, stimulate agricultural production from resources that otherwise would be underused, and reduce the need for food to be produced elsewhere. Third, by combating poverty, they help to slow population growth.

Shifting the focus of production to food-deficit countries will also reduce pressures on agricultural resources in the industrialized market economies, enabling them to move towards more sustainable agricultural practices. Incentive structures can be changed so that instead of encouraging overproduction, they encourage farm practices that improve soil and water quality. Government budgets will be relieved of the burdens of storing and exporting surplus products.

This shift in agricultural production will be sustainable only if the resource base is secure. As indicated, this is far from the case today. Thus to achieve global food security, the resource base for food production must be sustained, enhanced, and, where it has been diminished or destroyed, restored.

IV. STRATEGIES FOR SUSTAINABLE FOOD SECURITY

Food security requires more than good conservation programmes, which can be—and usually are—overridden and undermined by inappropriate agricultural, economic, and trade policies. Nor is it just a matter of adding an environmental component to programmes. Food strategies must take into account all the policies that bear upon the threefold challenge of shifting production to where it is most needed, of securing the livelihoods of the rural poor, and of conserving resources.

Government Intervention

Government intervention in agriculture is the rule in both industrial and developing countries, and it is here to stay. Public investment in agricultural research and extension services, assisted farm credit and marketing services, and a range of other support systems have all played parts in the successes of the last half-century. In fact, the real problem in many developing countries is the weakness of these systems.

Intervention has taken other forms as well. Many governments regulate virtually the entire food cycle—inputs and outputs, domestic sales, exports, public procurement, storage and distribution, price controls and subsidies—as well as imposing various land use regulations: acreage, crop variety, and so on.

In general, patterns of government intervention suffer three basic defects. First, the criteria that underlie the planning of these interventions lack an ecological orientation and are often dominated by short-term considerations. These criteria should discourage environmentally unsound farm practices and encourage farmers to maintain and improve their soils, forests, and waters.

The second defect is that agricultural policy tends to operate within a national framework with uniform prices and subsidies, standardized criteria for the provision of support services, indiscriminate financing of infrastructure investments, and so forth. Policies that vary from region to region are needed to reflect different regional needs, encouraging farmers to adopt practices that are ecologically sustainable in their own areas.

The importance of regional policy differentiation can be easily illustrated:

- Hill areas may require incentive prices for fruits and subsidized supplies of foodgrains to induce farmers to shift towards horticulture, which may be ecologically more sustainable.
- In areas prone to wind and water erosion, public intervention through subsidies and other measures should encourage farmers to conserve soil and water.
- Farmers on land over recharge areas for underground aquifers subject to nitrate pollution might be given incentives to maintain soil fertility and increase productivity by means other than nitrate fertilizers.

The third defect in government intervention lies in incentive structures. In industrialized countries, overprotection of farmers and overproduction represent the accumulated result of tax reliefs, direct subsidies, and price controls. Such policies are now studded with contradictions that encourage the degradation of the agricultural resource base and, in the long run, do more harm than good to the agricultural industry. Some governments now recognize this and are making efforts to change the focus of the subsidies from production growth to conservation.

On the other hand, in most developing countries the incentive structure is weak. Market interventions are often ineffective for lack of an organizational structure for procurement and distribution. Farmers are exposed to a high degree of uncertainty, and price support systems have often favoured the urban dweller or are limited to a few commercial crops, leading to distortions of cropping patterns that add to destructive pressures on the resource base. In some cases, price controls reduce the incentive to produce. What is required, in many cases, is nothing less than a radical attempt to turn the 'terms of trade' in favour of farmers through pricing policy and government expenditure reallocation.

⁶*The problem in agriculture is not faceless. I as a farmer am a potential victim of the system that we now operate under. Why are approximately a quarter of Canadian farmers facing the immediate prospects of farm bankruptcy? It is directly related to the general concept of a cheap food policy that has constituted a cornerstone of federal agricultural policy since the beginning of settlement.*

*We regard the current cheap food policy as a form of economic violence that is contributing towards soil exploitation and the growing impersonal relationship between farmers and the soil for economic survival. It is a policy of industrialization that can lead only towards disaster economically—for us as farmers, and environmentally for us all as Canadians and as world citizens.*⁹

Wayne Easter
President, National Farmers' Union
WCED Public Hearing, Ottawa, 26–27 May 1986

Strengthening food security from a global point of view requires reducing incentives that force overproduction and non-competitive production in the developed market economies and enhancing those that encourage food production in developing countries. At the same time, these incentive structures must be redesigned to promote farming practices that conserve and enhance the agricultural resource base.

A Global Perspective

Trade in agricultural products tripled between 1950 and 1970; it has doubled since then. Yet, when it comes to farming, countries are at their most conservative, continuing to think mainly in local or national terms and concerned, above all, to protect their own farmers at the expense of competitors.

Shifting food production towards food-deficit countries will require a major shift in trading patterns. Countries must recognize that all parties lose through protectionist barriers, which reduce trade in food products in which some nations may have genuine advantage. They must begin by redesigning their trade, tax, and incentive systems using criteria that include ecological and economic sustainability and international comparative advantage.

The incentive-driven surpluses in developed market economies increase pressures to export these surpluses at subsidized prices or as non-emergency food aid. Donor and receiving countries should be responsible for the impacts of aid and use it for long-term objectives. It can be beneficially used in projects to restore degraded lands, build up rural infrastructure, and raise the nutrition level of vulnerable groups.

The Resource Base

Agricultural production can only be sustained on a long-term basis if the land, water, and forests on which it is based are not degraded. As suggested, a reorientation of public intervention will provide a framework for this. But more specific policies that protect the resource base are needed to maintain and even enhance agricultural productivity and the livelihoods of all rural dwellers.

Land Use

The initial task in enhancing the resource base will be to delineate broad land categories:

- enhancement areas, which are capable of sustaining intensive cropping and higher population and consumption levels;
- prevention areas, which by common consent should not be developed for intensive agriculture or, where developed, should be converted to other uses; and
- restoration areas, where land stripped of vegetative cover has either totally lost its productivity or had it drastically reduced.

Identifying land according to 'best use' criteria requires information that is not always available. Most industrial nations possess inventories and descriptions of their lands, forests, and waters that are detailed enough to provide a basis for delineating land categories. Few developing countries have such inventories, but they can and should develop them quickly using satellite monitoring and other rapidly changing techniques.[32]

Selection of land for each category could be made the responsibility of a board or commission representing the interests involved, especially the poor and more marginalized segments of the population. The process must be public in character, with publicly agreed criteria that combine the best use approach with the level of development required to sustain livelihood. Classifying land according to best use will determine variations in infrastructure provision, support services, promotional measures, regulatory restrictions, fiscal subsidies, and other incentives and disincentives.

Lands identified as prevention areas should be denied supports and subsidies that would encourage their development for intensive agriculture. But such areas might well support certain ecologically and economically sustainable uses such as grazing, fuelwood plantations, fruit farming, and forestry. Those redesigning support systems and incentives should focus on a broader range of crops, including those that enhance grazing, soil and water conservation, and so on.

In vast areas today natural factors and land use practices have reduced productivity to a point too low to sustain even subsistence farming. Treatment of these areas must vary from site to site. Governments should give priority to establishing a national policy and multidisciplinary programmes and to creating or strengthening institutions to restore such areas. Where these already exist, they should be better coordinated and designed. The UN Plan of Action to Combat Desertification, which is already in place, requires more support, particularly financial.

Restoration may require limits on human activities so as to permit the regeneration of vegetation. This can be difficult where there are large herds of animals or large numbers of people, for the agreement and participation of the local people are of the highest importance. The state, with the co-operation of those living locally, could protect these areas by declaring them national reserves. Where these areas are privately held, the state might wish either to purchase the land from the owners or to provide incentives for its restoration.

Water Management

Improvements in water management are essential to raise agricultural productivity and to reduce land degradation and water pollution. Critical issues concern the design of irrigation projects and the efficiency of water use.

Where water is scarce, an irrigation project should maximize productivity per unit of water; where water is plentiful, it must maximize productivity per unit of land. But local conditions will dictate how much water can be used without damaging the soil. Salinization, alkalization, and waterlogging can be avoided by a more careful approach to drainage, maintenance, cropping patterns, the regulation of water quantities, and more rational water charges. Many of these objectives will be easier to realize in small-scale irrigation projects. But whether small or large, the projects must be designed with the abilities and aims of the participating farmers in mind, and then involve them in the management.

In some areas excessive use of ground-water is rapidly lowering the water table—usually a case where private benefits are being realized at society's expense. Where ground-water use exceeds the recharge capacity of local aquifers, regulatory or fiscal controls become essential. The combined use of ground and surface water can improve the timing of water availability and stretch limited supplies.

Intensive agriculture may quickly exhaust the soil cover, causing its degradation, unless some special soil protection measures aimed at constant restoration and expanded reproduction of fertility are taken. The task of agriculture is thus not confined to obtaining the biological product but extends to constant maintenance and augmentation of soil fertility. Otherwise we will very quickly consume what by right belongs to our children, grandchildren, and great-grandchildren, to say nothing of more distant descendants. It is this misgiving—that our generation lives to a certain extent at the expense of the coming generations, thoughtlessly drawing on the basic reserves of soil fertility accumulated in the millennia of the biospheric development, instead of living off the current annual increment—that causes the increasing concern of scientists dealing with the state of the planetary soil cover.

B. G. Rozanov
Moscow State University
WCED Public Hearing, Moscow, 11 Dec 1986

Alternatives to Chemicals

Many countries can and should increase yields by greater use of chemical fertilizers and pesticides, particularly in the developing world. But countries can also improve yields by helping farmers to use organic nutrients more efficiently. Hence governments must encourage the use of more organic plant nutrients to complement chemicals. Pest control must also be based increasingly on the use of natural methods. (See Box 5-2.) These strategies require changes in public policies, which now encourage the increased use of chemical pesticides and fertilizers. The legislative, policy, and research capacity for advancing non-chemical and less-chemical strategies must be established and sustained.

Chemical fertilizers and pesticides are heavily subsidized in many countries. These subsidies promote chemical use precisely in the more commercially oriented agricultural areas where their environmental damage may already outweigh any increases in productivity they bring. Hence different regions will require different policies to regulate and promote chemical use.

Legislative and institutional frameworks for controlling agrochemicals must be greatly strengthened everywhere. Industrialized countries must tighten controls on pesticide exports. (See Chapter 8.) Developing countries must possess the basic legislative and

---

Box 5-2.   Natural Systems of Nutrient Supply and Pest Control

- Crop residues and farmyard manure are potential sources of soil nutrients.
- Organic wastes reduce run-off, increase the take-up of other nutrients, and improve soil's water-holding and erosion-resistance capacity.
- Using farmyard manure, especially in conjunction with intercropping and crop rotation, can greatly lower production costs.
- Overall systems efficiency is enhanced if manure or vegetable biomass is anaerobically digested in biogas plants, yielding energy for cooking and to run pumps, motors, or electric generators.
- Natural systems of biological nitrogen fixation through the use of certain annual plants, trees, and micro-organisms have a high potential.
- Integrated pest management (IPM) reduces the need for agrochemicals, improves a country's balance of payments, releases foreign exchange for other development projects, and creates jobs where they are most needed.
- IPM requires detailed information about pests and their natural enemies, seed varieties tailored to resist pests, integrated cropping patterns, and farmers who support the approach and are willing to modify farm practices to adopt it.

---

institutional instruments to manage the use of agricultural chemicals within their countries. And they will need technical and financial assistance to do so.

Forestry and Agriculture

Undisturbed forests protect watersheds, reduce erosion, offer habitats for wild species, and play key roles in climatic systems. They are also an economic resource providing timber, fuelwood, and other products. The crucial task is to balance the need to exploit forests against the need to preserve them.

Sound forest policies can be based only on an analysis of the capacity of the forests and the land under them to perform various functions. Such an analysis might lead to some forests being cleared for intensive cultivation, others for livestock; some forestland might be managed for increased timber production or agroforestry use and some left intact for watershed protection, recreation, or species conservation. The extension of agriculture into forest areas must be based on scientific classification of land capacities.

Programmes to preserve forest resources must start with the local people who are both victims and agents of destruction, and who will bear the burden of any new management scheme.[33] They should be at the centre of integrated forest management, which is the basis of sustainable agriculture.

Such an approach would entail changes in the way governments set development priorities, as well as the evolution of greater responsibility to local governments and communities. Contracts covering forest use will have to be negotiated, or renegotiated, to ensure sustainability of forest exploitation and overall environmental and ecosystem conservation. Prices for forest products need to reflect the true resource value of the goods.

Portions of forests may be designated as prevention areas. These are predominantly national parks, which could be set aside from agricultural exploitation to conserve soil, water, and wildlife. They may also include marginal lands whose exploitation accelerates land degradation through erosion or desertification. In this connection, the reforestation of degraded forest areas is of utmost importance. Conservation areas or national parks can also conserve genetic resources in their natural habitats. (See Chapter 6.)

Forestry can also be extended into agriculture. Farmers can use agroforestry systems to produce food and fuel. In such systems, one or more tree crop is combined with one or more food crop or animal farming on the same land, though sometimes at different times. Well-chosen crops reinforce each other and yield more food and fuel than when grown separately. The technology is particularly suitable for small farmers and for poor-quality lands. Agroforestry has been practised by traditional farmers everywhere. The challenge today is to revive the old methods, improve them, adapt them to the new conditions, and develop new ones.[34]

International forestry research organizations should work in various tropical countries in various ecosystems along the lines now followed by the Consultative Group on International Agricultural Research. There is considerable scope for institution building and additional research on forestry's role in agricultural production, for example by developing models that better predict the effects on water and soil loss of removing specific portions of forest cover.

Aquaculture

Fisheries and aquaculture are critical to food security in that they provide both protein and employment. The greater part of world fish supply comes from marine fisheries, which yielded 76.8 million tons in 1983. Landings have increased by 1 million tons per year over the past few years; by the end of the century, a catch of around 100 million tons should be possible.[35] This is well short of the projected demand. There are indications that much of the naturally available freshwater fish stocks are fully exploited or damaged by pollution. Aquaculture, or 'fish-farming', which differs from conventional fishing in that fish are deliberately reared in controlled water bodies, can help meet future needs. Yields from aquaculture have doubled during the last decade and now represent about 10 per cent of world production of fishery products.[36] A five- to tenfold increase is projected by the year 2000, given the necessary scientific, financial, and organizational support.[37] Aquaculture can be undertaken in paddy fields, abandoned mining excavations, small ponds, and many other areas with some water, as well as on various commercial scales: individual, family, co-operative, or corporate. The expansion of aquaculture should be given high priority in developing and developed countries.

Productivity and Yields

The conservation and enhancement of agriculture's resource base will increase production and productivity. But specific measures are required to make inputs more effective. This is best done by strengthening the technological and human resource base for agriculture in developing countries.

The Technological Base

Blends of traditional and modern technologies offer possibilities for improving nutrition and increasing rural employment on a sustainable basis. Biotechnology, including tissue culture techniques, technologies for preparing value-added products from biomass, micro-electronics, computer sciences, satellite imagery, and communication technology are all aspects of frontier technologies that can improve agricultural productivity and resource management.[38]

Providing sustainable livelihoods for resource-poor farmers presents a special challenge for agricultural research. The major advances in agricultural technology in recent decades are better suited to stable, uniform, resource-rich conditions with good soils and ample water supplies. New technologies are most urgently needed in sub-Saharan Africa and the remoter areas of Asia and Latin America, which typically have unreliable rainfall, uneven topography, and poorer soils, and hence are unsuited to Green Revolution technologies.

To serve agriculture in these areas, research has to be less centralized and more sensitive to farmers' conditions and priorities. Scientists will need to start talking to poor farmers and basing research priorities on growers' priorities. Researchers must learn from and develop the

Thus at the root of this environmental problem is a land problem that has to be solved if any serious ecological policy is to be taken—and reorientation of the agricultural policy has to be undertaken. I believe that any conservationist policy has to be followed by a coherent agricultural policy that will meet the need not only of preservation as such but also meet the needs of the Brazilian population.

Julio M.G. Gaiger
President, National Indian Support Association
WCED Public Hearing, Sao Paulo, 28–29 Oct 1985

innovations of farmers and not just the reverse. More adaptive research should be done right on the farm, using research stations for referral and with farmers eventually evaluating the results.

Commercial enterprises can help develop and diffuse technology, but public institutions must provide the essential framework for agricultural research and extension. Few academic and research institutions in developing regions are adequately funded. The problem is most acute in the low-income countries, where expenditure on agricultural research and extension amounts to 0.9 per cent of total agricultural income, as against 1.5 per cent in the middle-income countries.[39] Research and extension efforts must be greatly expanded, especially in areas where climate, soils, and terrain pose special problems.

These areas particularly will need new seed varieties, but so will much developing-country agriculture. At present, 55 per cent of the world's scientifically stored plant genetic resources is controlled by institutions in industrial countries, 31 per cent by institutions in developing countries, and 14 per cent by International Agricultural Research Centres.[40] Much of this genetic material originated in developing countries. These gene banks must increase their inventories of material, improve their storage techniques, and ensure that the resources are readily accessible to research centres in developing countries.

Private companies increasingly seek proprietary rights to improved seed varieties, often without recognizing the rights of the countries from which the plant matter was obtained. This could discourage countries rich in genetic resources from making these internationally available and thus reduce the options for seed development in all countries. The genetic research capabilities of developing countries are so limited that agriculture there could become excessively dependent on private gene banks and seed companies elsewhere. Thus international co-operation and a clear understanding on the sharing of gains are vital in critical areas of agricultural technology, such as the development of new seed varieties.

Human Resources

The technological transformation of traditional agriculture will be difficult without a matching effort to develop human resources. (See Chapter 4.) This means educational reforms to produce researchers more attuned to the needs of rural peoples and agriculture. Illiteracy is still widespread among the rural poor. But efforts to promote literacy should focus attention on functional literacy covering the efficient use of land, water, and forests.

Despite women's critical role in agriculture, their access to education and their representation in research, extension, and other support services is woefully inadequate. Women should be given the same educational opportunities as men. There should be more female extension workers, and women should participate in field visits. Women should be given more power to take decisions regarding agricultural and forestry programmes.

Productivity of Inputs

In traditional agriculture, local organic material provided farmers with sources of energy, nutrients, and ways of controlling pests. Today, these needs are increasingly met by electricity, petroleum products, chemical fertilizers, and pesticides. The cost of these inputs forms a growing proportion of agricultural costs, and wasteful use does economic and ecological harm.

One of the most important energy-related needs is mechanical power for irrigation. The efficiency of pumps could be greatly improved by providing appropriate incentives for equipment producers and farmers, and through effective extension work. Energy for irrigation pumps can also be provided by wind generators or by conventional internal combustion engines running on biogas produced from local biomass wastes. Solar dryers and solar coolers can save agricultural products. These non-conventional sources should be promoted, particularly in areas poor in energy resources.

Nutrients are lost when fertilizers are improperly applied. Often they leach away with the flow of water in a field and degrade local water supplies. Similar problems of waste and destructive side effects occur in the use of pesticides. Hence extension systems and chemical manufacturers will need to give priority to programmes to promote careful and economical use of these expensive, toxic materials.

Equity

The challenge of sustainable agriculture is to raise not just average productivity and incomes, but also the productivity and incomes of those poor in resources. And food security is not just a question of raising food production, but of ensuring that the rural and urban poor do not go hungry during the short term or midst a local food scarcity. All this requires the systematic promotion of equity in food production and distribution.

Land Reforms

In many countries where land is very unequally distributed land reform is a basic requirement. Without it, institutional and policy changes meant to protect the resource base can actually promote inequalities by shutting the poor off from resources and by favouring those with large farms, who are better able to obtain the limited credit and services available. By leaving hundreds of millions without options, such changes can have the opposite of their intended effect, ensuring the continued violation of ecological imperatives.

Given institutional and ecological variations, a universal approach to land reform is impossible. Each country should work out its own programme of land reform to assist the land-poor and to provide a base for co-ordinated resource conservation. The redistribution of land is particularly important where large estates and vast numbers of the land-poor coexist. Crucial components include the reform of tenancy arrangements, security of tenure, and the clear recording of land rights. In agrarian reforms the productivity of the land and, in forest areas, the protection of forests should be a major concern.

In areas where holdings are fragmented into many non-contiguous plots, land consolidation can ease the implementation of resource conservation measures. Promoting co-operative efforts by small farmers—in pest control or water management, for instance—would also help conserve resources.

In many countries women do not have direct land rights; titles go to men only. In the interests of food security, land reforms should recognize women's role in growing food. Women, especially those heading households, should be given direct land rights.

Subsistence Farmers and Pastoralists

Subsistence farmers, pastoralists, and nomads threaten the environmental resource base when processes beyond their control squeeze their numbers onto land or into areas that cannot support them.

❝As agriculture production is being developed, a rising number of farmers have been able to purchase tractors. But they find that, after using them for a year, it becomes much more expensive than they expected because they have to spend a tremendous amount of money on expensive spare parts. Perhaps we might recommend that Indonesia establish a factory that makes these spare parts, before they continue encouraging introduction of tractors in agriculture.

For this reason, a number of loans that the government has been providing for farmers to modernize their agricultural techniques, particularly buying tractors, have not been paid back. If the tractors were still running, they could probably pay back their loans. In fact, now these tractors are becoming a problem themselves, because they sit around getting rusty, and thus turning into pollution.❞

Andi Mappasala
Chairman, Yayasan Tellung Poccoe
WCED Public Hearing, Jakarta, 26 March 1985

The traditional rights of subsistence farmers, particularly shifting cultivators, pastoralists, and nomads, must therefore be protected from encroachments. Land tenure rights and communal rights in particular must be respected. When their traditional practices threaten the resource base, their rights may have to be curtailed, but only when alternatives have been provided. Most of these groups will need to be helped to diversify their livelihoods by entering the market economy through employment programmes and some cash-crop production.

Research should give early attention to the varied requirements of the mixed farming typical in subsistence agriculture. Extension and input supply systems must become more mobile to reach shifting cultivators and nomads and priority given to public investment to improve their cropland, grazing areas, and water sources.

Integrated Rural Development

Rural populations will continue to increase in many countries. With existing patterns of land distribution, the number of smallholders and landless households will increase by about 50 million, to nearly 220 million, by the year 2000.[41] Together, these groups represent three-quarters of the agricultural households in developing countries.[42] Without adequate livelihood opportunities, these resource-poor households will remain poor and be forced to overuse the resource base to survive.

Considerable effort has gone into creating strategies of integrated rural development, and the requirements and pitfalls are well known. Experience has shown that land reform is necessary but alone is not enough without support through the distribution of inputs and rural services. Smallholders, including—indeed especially—women, must be given preference when allocating scarce resources, staff, and credit. Small farmers must also be more involved in formulating agricultural policies.

Integrated rural development also requires resources to absorb the large increases in rural working populations expected in most developing countries through non-agricultural work opportunities, which should be promoted in rural areas. Successful agricultural development and the growth in incomes should open up opportunities in service activities and small-scale manufacturing if supported by public policy.

Food Availability Fluctuations

Environmental degradation can make food shortages more frequent and more severe. Hence sustainable agricultural development will reduce the season-to-season variability in food supplies. But such systems cannot eliminate it. There will be weather-induced fluctuations, and the growing dependence on only a few crop varieties over large areas may amplify the effects of weather and pest damage. Often it is the poorest households and the ecologically disadvantaged regions that suffer most from these shortages.

Food stocks are crucial in dealing with shortages. At present, the world stock of cereals is on the order of 20 per cent of annual consumption: The developing world controls about one-third of the stock and the industrial world, two-thirds. More than half the developing-country stock is in two countries—China and India. Stock levels in most of the others provide only for immediate operational requirements; there is little by way of a reserve.[43]

The food stocks of industrialized countries are essentially surpluses, and provide a basis for emergency assistance, which must be maintained. But emergency food aid is a precarious basis for food security; developing countries should build up national stocks in surplus years to provide reserves as well as encouraging development of food security at the household level. To do this, they will need an effective system of public support for measures facilitating the purchase, transportation, and distribution of food. The provision of strategically located storage facilities is critical both to reduce post-harvest losses and to provide a base for quick interventions in emergencies.

During most food shortages, poor households not only cannot produce food but also lose their usual sources of income and cannot buy the food that is available. Hence food security also requires that machinery is available promptly to put purchasing power in the hands of disaster-struck households, through emergency public works programme, and through measures to protect small farmers from crop failures.

V. FOOD FOR THE FUTURE

The challenge of increasing food production to keep pace with demand, while retaining the essential ecological integrity of production systems, is colossal both in its magnitude and complexity. But we have the knowledge we need to conserve our land and water resources. New technologies provide opportunities for increasing productivity while reducing pressures on resources. A new generation of farmers combine experience with education. With these resources at our command, we can meet the needs of the human family. Standing in the way is the narrow focus of agricultural planning and policies.

The application of the concept of sustainable development to the effort to ensure food security requires systematic attention to the renewal of natural resources. It requires a holistic approach focused on ecosystems at national, regional, and global levels, with co-ordinated land use and careful planning of water usage and forest exploitation. The goal of ecological security should be embedded firmly in the mandates of FAO, other UN organizations that deal with agriculture, and all other appropriate international agencies. It will also require an enhancement and reorientation of international assistance. (See Chapter 3.)

The agricultural systems that have been built up over the past few decades have contributed greatly to the alleviation of hunger and the raising of living standards. They have served their purposes up to a point. But they were built for the purposes of a smaller, more fragmented world. New realities reveal their inherent contradictions. These realities require agricultural systems that focus as much attention on people as they do on technology, as much on resources as on production, as much on the long term as on the short term. Only such systems can meet the challenge of the future.

Notes

The Commission accepts full responsibility for this chapter, but wishes to acknowledge that it draws on the report of its Advisory Panel on Food Security. (See Annexe 2 for a list of members.)

1 Based on data from FAO, *Production Yearbook 1985* (Rome: 1986).

2 Based on World Bank estimates for 1980, according to which 340 million people in developing countries (excluding China) did not have enough income to attain a minimum calorie standard that would prevent serious health risks and stunted growth in children, and 730 million were below a higher standard that would allow an active working life. See World Bank, *Poverty and Hunger Issues and Options for Food Security in Developing Countries* (Washington, DC: 1986).

3 FAO, *Yearbook of Food and Agriculture Statistics, 1951* (Rome: 1952); FAO, *Production Yearbook 1985*, op. cit.

4 FAO, *Yearbook of Food and Agricultural Statistics Trade Volume Part 2 1951* and *Trade Yearbook 1982* and *1984* (Rome: 1952, 1983, and 1985).

5 FAO, *Trade Yearbook 1968* and *Commodities Review and Outlook 1984–85* (Rome: 1969 and 1986).

6 FAO, *Yearbook of Food and Agricultural Statistics Trade Volume, Part 2 1954* (Rome: 1955); FAO, *Commodities Review*, op. cit.

7 FAO, *Production Yearbook 1984* (Rome: 1985).

8 L.R. Brown, 'Sustaining World Agriculture,' in L. R. Brown et al., *State of the World 1987* (London: W. W. Norton, 1987).

9 A. Gear (ed.), *The Organic Food Guide* (Essex: 1983).

10 USSR Committee for the International Hydrological Decade, *World Water Balance and Water Resources of the Earth* (Paris: UNESCO, 1978).

11 FAO, *Yearbook of Food and Agricultural Statistics 1951* and *Production Yearbook 1984*, op. cit.

12 'Dairy, Prairie', *The Economist*, 15 November 1986.

13 WCED Advisory Panel on Food Security, Agriculture, Forestry and Environment, *Food Security* (London: Zed Books, 1987).

14 The term pesticides is used in a generic sense in this report and covers insecticides, herbicides, fungicides, and similar agricultural inputs.

15 World Bank, *World Development Report 1986* (New York: Oxford University Press, 1986).

16 Brown, op. cit.

17 Standing Committee on Agriculture, Fisheries and Forestry, *Soil at Risk: Canada's Eroding Future*, A Report on Soil Conservation to the Senate of Canada (Ottawa: 1984).

18 Brown, op. cit.

19 Centre for Science and Environment, *The State of India's Environment 1984–85* (New Delhi: 1985).

20 FAO, *Land, Food and People* (Rome: 1984).

21 I. Szabolcs, 'Agrarian Change', prepared for WCED, 1985.

22 Gear, op. cit.

23 J. Bandyopadhyay, 'Rehabilitation of Upland Watersheds', prepared for WCED, 1985.

24 UNEP, 'General Assessment of Progress in the Implementation of the Plan of

Action to Combat Desertification 1978-1984', Nairobi, 1984; WCED Advisory Panel, op. cit.

25 UNEP, op. cit.

26 Ibid.

27 Ibid.

28 Ibid.

29 Ibid.

30 FAO, *Agriculture Towards 2000* (Rome: 1981).

31 FAO, *Potential Population Supporting Capacities of Lands in the Developing World* (Rome: 1982).

32 The land capability classification developed by the US Bureau of Land Management is an example of how the problem could be approached. A broader type of classification is implicit in FAO, *Potential Population Supporting Capacities*.

33 INDERENA, *Caguan-Caqueta Report* (Bogota, Colombia: 1985).

34 The agroforestry programmes implemented in India are examples of such an approach. They have been adopted enthusiastically by many farmers.

35 FAO, *World Food Report* (Rome: 1985); WCED Advisory Panel, op. cit.

36 WCED Advisory Panel, op. cit.

37 Ibid.

38 Ibid.

39 FAO, *World Food Report*, op. cit.

40 Data from Dag Hammarskjold Foundation, Sweden, in Centre for Science and Environment, op. cit.

41 FAO estimates quoted in WCED Advisory Panel, op. cit.

42 Ibid.

43 FAO, *Food Outlook* (Rome: 1986).

6

SPECIES AND ECOSYSTEMS: RESOURCES FOR DEVELOPMENT

Conservation of living natural resources—plants, animals, and micro-organisms, and the non-living elements of the environment on which they depend—is crucial for development. Today, the conservation of wild living resources is on the agenda of governments; nearly 4 per cent of the Earth's land area is managed explicitly to conserve species and ecosystems, and all but a small handful of countries have national parks. The challenge facing nations today is no longer deciding whether conservation is a good idea, but rather how it can be implemented in the national interest and within the means available in each country.

I. THE PROBLEM: CHARACTER AND EXTENT

Species and their genetic materials promise to play an expanding role in development, and a powerful economic rationale is emerging to bolster the ethical, aesthetic, and scientific cases for preserving them. The genetic variability and germplasm material of species make contributions to agriculture, medicine, and industry worth many billions of dollars per year.

Yet scientists have intensively investigated only one in every 100 of Earth's plant species, and a far smaller proportion of animal species. If nations can ensure the survival of species, the world can look forward to new and improved foods, new drugs and medicines, and new raw materials for industry. This—the scope for species to make a fast-growing contribution to human welfare in myriad forms—is a major justification for expanded efforts to safeguard Earth's millions of species.

Equally important are the vital life processes carried out by nature, including stabilization of climate, protection of watersheds and soil, preservation of nurseries and breeding grounds, and so on. Conserving these processes cannot be divorced from conserving the individual species within natural ecosystems. Managing species and ecosystems together is clearly the most rational way to approach the problem. Numerous examples of workable solutions to local problems are available.[1]

Species and natural ecosystems make many important contributions to human welfare. Yet these very important resources are seldom being used in ways that will be able to meet the growing pressures of future high demands for both goods and services that depend upon these natural resources.

There is a growing scientific consensus that species are disappearing at rates never before witnessed on the planet. But there is also controversy over those rates and the risks they entail. The world is losing precisely those species about which it knows nothing or little; they are being lost in the remotest habitats. The growing scientific concern is relatively new and the data base to support it fragile. But it firms yearly with each new field report and satellite study.

Many ecosystems that are rich biologically and promising in material benefits are severely threatened. Vast stocks of biological diversity are in danger of disappearing just as science is learning how to exploit genetic variability through the advances of genetic engineering. Numerous studies document this crisis with examples from tropical forests, temperate forests, mangrove forests, coral reefs, savannas, grasslands, and arid zones.[2] Although most of these studies are generalized in their documentation and few offer lists of individual species at risk or recently extinct, some present species-by-species details. (See Box 6-1.)

Habitat alteration and species extinction are not the only threat. The planet is also being impoverished by the loss of races and varieties within species. The variety of genetic riches inherent in one single species can be seen in the variability manifested in the many races of dogs, or the many specialized types of maize developed by breeders.[3]

Many species are losing whole populations at a rate that quickly reduces their genetic variability and thus their ability to adapt to climatic change and other forms of environmental adversity. For example, the remaining gene pools of major crop plants such as maize and rice amount to only a fraction of the genetic diversity they harboured only a few decades ago, even though the species themselves are anything but threatened. Thus there can be an important difference between loss of species and loss of gene reservoirs.

Some genetic variability inevitably will be lost, but all species should be safeguarded to the extent that it is technically, economically, and politically feasible. The genetic landscape is constantly changing through evolutionary processes, and there is more variability than

Box 6-1. Some Examples of Species Extinction

- In Madagascar, until about mid-century, there were 12,000 plant species and probably around 190,000 animal species, with at least 60 per cent of them endemic to the island's eastern strip of forest (that is, found nowhere else on Earth). At least 93 per cent of the original primary forest has been eliminated. Using these figures, scientists estimate that at least half the original species have already disappeared, or are on the point of doing so.
- Lake Malawi in Central Africa holds over 500 cichlid fish species, 99 per cent of them endemic. The lake is only one-eighth the size of North America's Great Lakes, which feature just 173 species, fewer than 10 per cent of which are endemic. Yet Lake Malawi is threatened through pollution from industrial installations and the proposed introduction of alien species.
- Western Ecuador is reputed to have once contained between 8,000 and 10,000 plant species, some 40 and 60 per cent of them endemic. Given that there are between 10 and 30 animal species for every one plant species in similar areas, western Ecuador must have contained about 200,000 species. Since 1960, almost all the forests of western Ecuador have been destroyed to make way for banana plantations, oil wells, and human settlements. The number of species thus eliminated is difficult to judge, but the total could well number 50,000 or more— all in just 25 years.
- The Pantanal area of Brazil contains 110,000 square kilometres of wetlands, probably the most extensive and richest in the world. They support the largest and most diversified populations of waterfowl in South America. The area has been classified by UNESCO as 'of international importance'. Yet it suffers increasingly from agricultural expansion, dam construction, and other forms of disruptive development.

Sources: W. Rauh, 'Problems of Biological Conservation in Madagascar', in D. Bramwell (ed.), *Plants and Islands* (London: Academic Press, 1979); D.C.N. Barel et al., 'Destruction of Fisheries in Africa's Lakes', *Nature*, Vol. 315, pp.19–20, 1985; A.H. Gentry, 'Patterns of Neotropical Plant Species Diversity', *Evolutionary Biology*, Vol. 15, pp. 1–84, 1982; D.A. Scott and M. Carbonell, 'A Directory of Neotropical Wetlands', IUCN, Gland, Switzerland, 1985.

can be expected to be protected by explicit government programmes. So in terms of genetic conservation, governments must be selective, and ask which gene reservoirs most merit a public involvement in protective measures. However, as a more general proposition, governments should enact national laws and public policies that encourage individual, community, or corporate responsibility for the protection of gene reservoirs.

But before science can focus on new ways to conserve species, policymakers and the general public for whom policy is made must

Our Atlantic forest, this mass of tropical forest that is a narrow stretch from the North to the South, has been reduced drastically.

The forest is characterized by a large number of endemic species, that is species that only exist in this area, and only exist in Brazil. And consequently, it is up to us, Brazilians, to shoulder the responsibility of keeping these species in existence.

Ibsen de Gusmao Camara
President, Brazilian Foundation for Preservation of Nature
WCED Public Hearing, Sao Paulo, 28–29 Oct 1985

grasp the size and the urgency of the threat. Species that are important to human welfare are not just wild plants that are relatives of agricultural crops, or animals that are harvested. Species such as earthworms, bees, and termites may be far more important in terms of the role they play in a healthy and productive ecosystem. It would be grim irony indeed if just as new genetic engineering techniques begin to let us peer into life's diversity and use genes more effectively to better the human condition, we looked and found this treasure sadly depleted.

II. EXTINCTION PATTERNS AND TRENDS

Extinction has been a fact of life since life first emerged. The present few million species are the modern-day survivors of the estimated half-billion species that have ever existed. Almost all past extinctions have occurred by natural processes, but today human activities are overwhelmingly the main cause of extinctions.

The average duration of a species is some 5 million years. The best current estimates are that on average 900,000 species have become extinct every 1 million years during the last 200 million years, so the average 'background rate' of extinction has been very roughly one in every one and one-ninth years.[4] The present human-caused rate is hundreds of times higher, and could easily be thousands of times higher.[5] We do not know. We have no accurate figures on the current rates of extinctions, as most of the species vanishing are those least documented, such as insects in tropical forests.

Although tropical moist forests are by far the richest biological units in terms of genetic diversity and by far the most threatened through human activities, other major ecological zones are also under pressure. Arid and semi-arid lands harbour only a very small number of species compared with tropical forests. But because of the adaptations of these species to harsh living conditions, they feature many potentially valuable biochemicals, such as the liquid wax of the jojoba shrub and the natural rubber of the guayule bush. Many of these are threatened by, among other things, the expansion of livestock herding.

Coral reefs, with an estimated half-million species in their 400,000 square kilometres, are being depleted at rates that may leave little but degraded remnants by early next century. This would be a great loss, in that coral-reef organisms, by virtue of the 'biological warfare' they engage in to ensure living space in crowded habitats, have generated an unusual number and variety of toxins valuable in modern medicine.[6]

Tropical moist forests cover only 6 per cent of the Earth's land surface but contain at least half the Earth's species (which totals 5 million at a minimum, but could be as many as 30 million). They may contain 90 per cent or even more of all species. The mature tropical forests that still exist cover only 900 million hectares, out of the 1.5–1.6 billion hectares that once stood. Between 7.6 million and 10 million hectares are eliminated outright each year, and at least a further 10 million hectares are grossly disrupted annually.[7] But these figures come from surveys of the late 1970s, and since then deforestation rates have probably accelerated.

By the end of the century, or shortly thereafter, there could be little virgin tropical moist forest left outside of the Zaire Basin and the western half of Brazilian Amazonia, plus some areas such as the Guyana tract of forest in northern South America and parts of the island of New Guinea. The forests in these zones are unlikely to survive beyond a few further decades, as world demand for their produce continues to expand and as the number of forestland farmers increases.

If deforestation were to continue in Amazonia at present rates until the year 2000, but then halted completely (which is unlikely), about 15 per cent of plant species would be lost. Were Amazonia's forest cover to be ultimately reduced to those areas now established as parks and reserves, 66 per cent of plant species would eventually disappear, together with almost 69 per cent of bird species and similar proportions of all other major categories of species. Almost 20 per cent of the Earth's species are found in Latin American forests outside of Amazonia; another 20 per cent are found in forests of Asia and Africa outside the Zaire Basin.[8] All these forests are threatened, and if they were to disappear, the species loss could amount to hundreds of thousands.

❛Twenty years ago, as we decided to intensify our forest exploitation, we just thought the resource is available, and we just took it. At the time, we also thought the intensive selecting out of the trees being cut wouldn't destroy forest regeneration. Because not all of the trees were being cut. But we forgot that we don't know yet about how the tropical forest should be rehabilitated.

An indigenous species such as meranti, I don't know the name in English, meranti, rami, is our high-valued wood, a timber that cannot make a shadow in its particular period of growth. And it cannot survive without that shadow. And we still didn't think about it, we just accepted the technology from the West that we have to cut, to exploit our forest.❜

Emmy H. Dharsono
NGO Network for Forest Conservation
WCED Public Hearing, Jakarta, 26 March 1985

Unless appropriate management measures are taken over the longer term, at least one-quarter, possibly one-third, and conceivably a still larger share of species existing today could be lost. Many experts suggest that at least 20 per cent of tropical forests should be protected, but to date well under 5 per cent has been afforded protection of any sort—and many of the tropical forest parks exist only on paper.

Even the most effectively managed parks and protected areas are unlikely to provide a sufficient answer. In Amazonia, if as much as half the forest were to be safeguarded in some way or another but the other half were to be eliminated or severely disrupted, there might well not be enough moisture in the Amazonian ecosystem to keep the remaining forest moist.[9] It could steadily dry up until it became more like an open woodland—with the loss of most of the species adapted to tropical moist forest conditions.

More widespread climatic changes are likely to emerge within the foreseeable future as the accumulation of 'greenhouse gases' in the atmosphere leads to global warming early in the next century. (See Chapter 7.) Such a change will produce considerable stress for all ecosystems, making it particularly important that natural diversity be maintained as a means of adaptation.

III. SOME CAUSES OF EXTINCTION

The tropics, which host the greatest number and diversity of species, also host most developing nations, where population growth is fastest and poverty is most widespread. If farmers in these countries are forced to continue with extensive agriculture, which is inherently unstable and leads to constant movement, then farming will tend to spread throughout remaining wildlife environments. But if they are helped and encouraged to practise more intensive agriculture, they could make productive use of relatively limited areas, with less impact on wildlands.

They will need help: training, marketing support, and fertilizers, pesticides, and tools they can afford. This will require the full support of governments, including ensuring that conservation policies are designed with the benefit of agriculture foremost in mind. It may be expedient to stress the value to farmers rather than to wildlife of this programme, but in fact the destinies of the two are intertwined. Species conservation is tied to development, and the problems of both are more political than technical.

Population growth is a major threat to conservation efforts in many developing nations. Kenya has allocated 6 per cent of its territory as parks and reserves in order to protect its wildlife and to earn foreign exchange through tourism. But Kenya's present population of 20 million people is already pressing so hard on parks that protected land is steadily being lost to invading farmers. And the country's population is projected to grow fourfold in the next 40 years.[10]

Similar population pressures threaten parks in Ethiopia, Uganda, Zimbabwe, and other countries in which a growing but impoverished peasantry is forced to depend on a dwindling natural resource base. The prospects are bleak for parks that do not make important and recognizable contributions to national development objectives.

Brazil, Colombia, Cote d'Ivoire, Indonesia, Kenya, Madagascar, Peru, the Philippines, Thailand, and other nations with an unusual abundance of species already suffer a massive flow of farmers from traditional homelands into virgin territories. These areas often include tropical forests, perceived by the migrants encouraged to farm there as 'free' lands available for unimpeded settlement. The people who are already living on such lands at low population densities and with only traditional rights to the land are often swept aside in the rush to develop lands that might better be left in extensively used forest.

Many tropical countries with large forest resources have provoked wasteful 'timber booms' by assigning harvesting rights to concessionaires for royalty, rent, and tax payments that are only a small fraction of the net commercial value of the timber harvest. They have compounded the damage caused by these incentives by offering only short-term leases, requiring concessionaires to begin harvesting at

'All of us in Africa are slowly waking up to the fact the African crisis is essentially an environmental problem that has precipitated such adverse symptoms as drought, famine, desertification, overpopulation, environmental refugees, political instability, widespread poverty, etc.

We are awaking to the fact that if Africa is dying it is because her environment has been plundered, overexploited, and neglected.

Many of us in Africa are also waking up to the realization that no good Samaritans will cross the seas to come to save the African environment. Only we Africans can and should be sufficiently sensitive to the well-being of our environment.'

Mrs. Rahab W. Mwatha
The Greenbelt Movement
WCED Public Hearing, Nairobi, 23 Sept 1986

once, and adopting royalty systems that induce loggers to harvest only the best trees while doing enormous damage to the remainder. In response, logging entrepreneurs in several countries have leased virtually the entire productive forest area within a few years and have overexploited the resource with little concern for future productivity (while unwittingly opening it for clearing by slash-and-burn cultivators).[11]

In Central and South America, many governments have encouraged the large-scale conversion of tropical forests to livestock ranches. Many of these ranches have proved ecologically and economically unsound, as the underlying soils are soon depleted of nutrients; weed species replace planted grasses, and pasture productivity declines abruptly. Yet tens of millions of hectares of tropical forest have been lost to such ranches, largely because governments have underwritten the conversions with large land grants, tax credits and tax holidays, subsidized loans, and other inducements.[12]

The promotion of tropical timber imports into certain industrial countries through low tariffs and favourable trade incentives, combined with weak domestic forest policies in tropical countries and with high costs and disincentives to harvesting in industrial countries, also drives deforestation. Some industrial countries typically import unprocessed logs either duty-free or at minimal tariff rates. This encourages developed country industries to use logs from tropical forests rather than their own, a pattern that is reinforced by domestic restrictions on the amounts that can be cut in domestic forests.

IV. ECONOMIC VALUES AT STAKE

Species conservation is not only justified in economic terms. Aesthetic, ethical, cultural, and scientific considerations provide ample grounds for conservation. But for those who demand an accounting, the economic values inherent in the genetic materials of species are alone enough to justify species preservation.

Today, industrialized nations record far greater financial benefits from wild species than do developing countries, though unrecorded benefits to people living in the tropical countryside can be considerable. But the industrial countries have the scientific and industrial capacity to convert the wild material for industrial and medical use. And they also trade a higher proportion of their agricultural produce than do developing nations. Northern crop breeders are increasingly dependent on genetic materials from wild relatives of maize and wheat, two crops that play leading roles in the international grain trade. The US Department of Agriculture estimates that contributions from plant genetic material lead to increases in productivity that average around 1 per cent annually, with a farm-gate value of well over $1 billion (1980 dollars).[13]

The US maize crop suffered a severe setback in 1970, when a leaf fungus blighted croplands, causing losses to farmers worth more than $2 billion. Then fungus-resistant genetic material was found in genetic stocks that had originated in Mexico.[14] More recently, a primitive species of maize was discovered in a montane forest of south-central Mexico.[15] This wild plant is the most primitive known relative of modern maize and was surviving in only three tiny patches covering a mere four hectares in an area threatened with destruction by farmers and loggers. The wild species is a perennial; all other forms of maize are annuals. Its cross-breeding with commercial varieties of maize opens up the prospect that farmers could be spared the annual expense of ploughing and sowing, since the plant would grow again yearly of its own accord. The genetic benefits of this wild plant, discovered when not more than a few thousand last stalks remained, could total several thousand million dollars a year.[16]

Wild species likewise contribute to medicine. Half of all prescriptions dispensed have their origins in wild organisms.[17] The commercial value of these medicines and drugs in the United States now amounts to some $14 billion a year.[18] World-wide, and including non-prescription materials plus pharmaceuticals, the estimated commercial value exceeds $40 billion a year.[19]

Industry also benefits from wildlife.[20] Wildlife-derived materials contribute gums, oils, resins, dyes, tannins, vegetable fats and waxes, insecticides, and many other compounds. Many wild plants bear oil-rich seeds that can help in the manufacture of fibres, detergents, starch, and general edibles. For instance, the *Fevillea* genus of rain-forest vines in western Amazonia bear seeds with such a high oil content that a hectare of such vines in an original forest could produce more oil than a hectare of commercial oil palm plantation.[21]

A few plant species contain hydrocarbons rather than carbo-hydrates.[22] Certain of these plants can flourish in areas that have been rendered useless through such activities as strip-mining. Hence land that has been degraded by extraction of hydrocarbons such as coal could be rehabilitated by growing hydrocarbons on the surface. Moreover, unlike an oil well, a 'petroleum plantation' need never run dry.

The emerging field of genetic engineering, by which science devises new variations of life forms, does not render wild genes useless. In fact, this new science must be based on existing genetic material and makes such material even more valuable and useful. Extinction, according to Professor Tom Eisner of Cornell University, 'no longer means the simple loss of one volume from the library of nature. It means the loss of a loose-leaf book whose individual pages, were the species to survive, would remain available in perpetuity for selective transfer and improvement of other species.'[23] And Professor Winston Brill of the University of Wisconsin has noted: 'We are entering an age in which genetic wealth, especially in tropical areas such as rain forests, until now a relatively inaccessible trust fund, is becoming a currency with high immediate value.'[24]

Genetic engineering may mean that agriculture's Green Revolution will be superseded by a 'Gene Revolution'. This technology raises hopes of eventually harvesting crops from deserts, from seawater, and from other environments that did not previously support farming. Medical researchers foresee their own Gene Revolution bringing more innovative advances during the last two decades of this century than occurred during the previous 200 years.

Many of the nations with the least capacity for managing living resources are those richest in species; the tropics, which contain at least two-thirds of all species and a still greater proportion of threatened species, roughly coincide with the area generally referred to as the Third World. Many developing nations recognize the need to safeguard threatened species but lack the scientific skills, institutional capacities, and funds necessary for conservation. In-dustrial nations seeking to reap some of the economic benefits of genetic resources should support the efforts of Third World nations to conserve species; they should also seek ways to help tropical nations—and particularly the rural people most directly involved with these species—realize some of the economic benefits of these resources.

V. A NEW APPROACH: ANTICIPATE AND PREVENT

The historical approach of establishing national parks that are somehow isolated from the greater society has been overtaken by a new approach to conservation of species and ecosystems that can be characterized as 'anticipate and prevent.' This involves adding a new dimension to the now-traditional and yet viable and necessary step of protected areas. Development patterns must be altered to make them more compatible with the preservation of the extremely valuable biological diversity of the planet. Altering economic and land use patterns seems to be the best long-term approach to ensuring the survival of wild species and their ecosystems.

This more strategic approach deals with the problems of species depletion at their sources in development policies, anticipates the obvious results of the more destructive policies, and prevents damage now. A useful tool in promoting this approach is the preparation of National Conservation Strategies (NCS), which bring the processes of conservation and development together. Preparing an NCS involves government agencies, non-governmental organizations, private interests, and the community at large in analysis of natural resource issues and assessment of priority actions. In this way, it is hoped that sectoral interests will better perceive their interrelationships with other sectors and new potentials for conservation and development will be revealed.

The link between conservation and development and the need to attack the problem at the source can be seen clearly in the case of tropical forests. Sometimes it is government policy, not economic necessity, that drives the overexploitation and destruction of these resources. The direct economic and fiscal costs of this over-exploitation—in addition to those of species extinction—are huge. The result has been wasteful exploitation of the tropical forests, the sacrifice of most of their timber and non-timber values, enormous losses of potential revenue to the government, and the destruction of rich biological resources.

Third World governments can stem the destruction of tropical forests and other reservoirs of biological diversity while achieving

‘It will not be possible to restore the population of ‘oomurasaki’—our purple emperor butterfly—to the previous level. The forest for oomurasaki requires weeding, planting of trees, and care and maintenance. The forest will be handed down to the succeeding generations. Isn't it wonderful to think that you are linked to the succeeding generations by handing down the forest where many oomurasaki fly and people enjoy themselves.

It would be nice if we could develop into the hearts of the children the love and affection for nature. We hope to make the forest we are making our gift to the children who will live in the 21st century.’

Mika Sakakibara
Student, Tokyo University of Agriculture and Technology
WCED Public Hearing, Tokyo, 27 Feb 1987

economic goals. They can conserve valuable species and habitat while reducing their economic and fiscal burdens. Reforming forest revenue systems and concession terms could raise billions of dollars of additional revenues, promote more efficient, long-term forest resource use, and curtail deforestation. Governments could save themselves enormous expense and revenue loss, promote more sustainable land uses, and slow down the destruction of tropical forests by eliminating incentives for livestock ranching.

The link between conservation and development also requires some changes in trade patterns. This has been recognized in the establishment in 1986 of the International Tropical Timber Organization, based in Yokohama, Japan, which seeks to rationalize trade flows. It has been set up to implement the first commodity agreement that incorporates a specific conservation component.

Numerous other opportunities can be found to encourage both species conservation and economic productivity. Many governments maintain unrealistically low taxes on rural land, while allowing settlers to establish title to 'virgin' land by converting it to farmland. Thus wealthy landowners can keep huge, underused estates at little or no cost, while land-hungry peasants are encouraged to clear forests to establish marginal holdings. Reforms of tax and tenure systems could increase productivity on existing holdings and reduce the pressures to expand cultivation into forests and upland watersheds.

Well-designed ecosystem conservation contributes to the predominant goals of sustainable development in a number of ways. Safeguards for critical tracts of wildlands can serve also to safeguard agricultural land, for example. This is particularly true for upland forests of the tropics, which protect valley fields from floods and erosion, and waterways and irrigation systems from siltation.

A case in point is the Dumoga-Bone Reserve in Indonesia's northern Sulawesi, covering some 3,000 square kilometres of upland forest. It protects large populations of most of Sulawesi's endemic mammals, and many of the island's 80 endemic bird species. It also protects the Dumoga Valley Irrigation Scheme, funded by a World Bank loan, set up in the flatlands below to achieve a tripling of rice production on more then 13,000 hectares of prime agricultural land.[25] Similar examples include the Canaima National Park in Venezuela, which protects domestic and industrial water supplies for a major hydropower facility that, in turn, provides electricity to the nation's key industrial centre and its capital city.

One conclusion from this connection is that governments could think of 'parks for development', insofar as parks serve the dual purpose of protection for species habitats and development processes at the same time. National efforts to anticipate and prevent the adverse consequences of development policies in any of these areas would surely yield much more for species conservation than all the measures of the past 10 years in support of park building, ranger patrols, anti-poaching units, and the other conventional forms of wildlife preservation. The 3rd World Congress on National Parks, held in Bali, Indonesia, in October 1982, brought this message from protected area managers to the policymakers of the world, demonstrating the many contributions that protected areas managed in the modern way are making to sustaining human society.

VI. INTERNATIONAL ACTION FOR NATIONAL SPECIES

Species and their genetic resources—whatever their origins—plainly supply benefits to all human beings. Wild genetic resources from Mexico and Central America serve the needs of maize growers and consumers globally. The principal cocoa-growing nations are in West Africa, while the genetic resources on which modern cocoa plantations depend for their continued productivity are found in the forests of western Amazonia.

Coffee growers and drinkers depend for the health of the crop on constant supplies of new genetic material from coffee's wild relatives, principally located in Ethiopia. Brazil, which supplies wild rubber germplasm to Southeast Asia's rubber plantation, itself depends on germplasm supplies from diverse parts of the world to sustain its sugar-cane, soybean, and other leading crops. Without access to foreign sources of fresh germplasm year by year, the nations of Europe and North America would quickly find their agricultural output declining.

The Earth's endowment of species and natural ecosystems will soon be seen as assets to be conserved and managed for the benefit of all humanity. This will necessarily add the challenge of species conservation to the international political agenda.

At the heart of the issue lies the fact that there is often a conflict between the short-term economic interest of the individual nations and the long-term interest of sustainable development and potential economic gains of the world community at large. A major thrust in actions to conserve genetic diversity must therefore be directed at making it more economically attractive both in the short term and in the longer perspective to protect wild species and their ecosystems. Developing countries must be ensured an equitable share of the economic profit from the use of genes for commercial purposes.

Some Current Initiatives

A number of international measures are already being tried. But they are limited in scope, only partially successful, and reactive in nature. The UN Educational, Scientific, and Cultural Organization (UNESCO) operates a clearing-house for information on natural areas and genetic resources. Its World Heritage Fund supports the management of a handful of exceptional ecosystems around the world, but all these activities receive small budgets. UNESCO has sought to establish a global system of Biosphere Reserves representing the Earth's 200 'biotic provinces' and harbouring sample communities of species. But only one-third of the needed reserves have been established, even though instituting and operating the rest would cost only about $150 million a year.[26]

UN agencies such as the Food and Agriculture Organization (FAO) and the UN Environment Programme (UNEP) run programmes concerned with threatened species, genetic resources, and outstanding ecosystems. But their combined activities are tiny in the face of the large needs. Among national agencies, the US Agency for International Development leads the field in recognizing the value of species conservation. Legislation passed by the US Congress in 1986 will make available $2.5 million a year for this purpose.[27] Again, this should be considered an important gesture compared with what has been done to date by bilateral agencies, but trifling compared with the needs and opportunities.

‘As deforestation progresses, it reduces the quality of life of millions of people in developing countries; their survival is threatened by the loss of the vegetation upon which they depend for their sources of household energy and many other goods. If tropical forests continue to be cleared at the current rate, at least 556 million acres (225 million hectares) will be cleared by the year 2000; if destruction of the tropical rain forests continues unabated, an estimated 10 to 20 per cent of the Earth's plant and animal life will be gone by the year 2000.

Reversing deforestation depends on political leadership and appropriate policy changes by developing-country governments to support community-level initiatives. The key ingredient is active participation by the millions of small farmers and landless people who daily use forests and trees to meet their needs.’

J. Gustave Speth
President, World Resources Institute
WCED Public Hearing, Sao Paulo, 28–29 Oct 1985

The International Union for the Conservation of Nature and Natural Resources (IUCN), working in close collaboration with UNEP, the World Wildlife Fund, the World Bank, and various international technical assistance agencies, has established a 'Conservation Monitoring Centre', to provide data on species and ecosystems for any part of the world quickly and easily. This service, which is available to all, can help ensure that development projects are designed with full information available about the species and ecosystems that might be affected. Technical assistance is also available for nations, sectors, and organizations interested in establishing local data bases for their own applications.

Species problems tend to be perceived largely in scientific and conservationist terms rather than as a leading economic and resource concern. Thus the issue lacks political clout. One important initiative that attempts to put conservation more squarely on the agenda of international development concerns has been the Tropical Forestry Action Plan. This collaborative effort coordinated by FAO involves the World Bank, IUCN, the World Resources Institute, and the UN Development Programme, along with numerous other collaborating institutions. The broad-based effort proposes the formulation of national forestry reviews, national forestry plans, identification of new projects, enhanced co-operation between development aid agencies at work in the forestry sector, and increased flows of technical and financial resources into forestry and related fields such as smallholder agriculture.

Establishing norms and procedures with respect to resource issues is at least as important as increased funding. Precedents for such norms include the Convention on Wetlands of International Importance, the proposed Convention on Conservation of Islands for Science (both of which safeguard prime habitats and their species), and the Convention on International Trade in Endangered Species. These three precedents all help, although the first two are essentially reactive attempts to devise 'species refuges'.

Setting Priorities

A first priority is to establish the problem of disappearing species and threatened ecosystems on political agendas as a major resource issue. The World Charter for Nature, adopted by the UN in October 1982, was an important step towards this objective.

Governments should investigate the prospect of agreeing to a 'Species Convention', similar in spirit and scope to the Law of the Sea Treaty and other international conventions reflecting principles of 'universal resources'. A Species Convention, such as a draft prepared by IUCN, should articulate the concept of species and genetic variability as a common heritage.

Collective responsibility for the common heritage would not mean collective international rights to particular resources within nations. This approach need not interfere with concepts of national sovereignty. But it would mean that individual nations would no longer be left to rely on their own isolated efforts to protect species within their borders.

Such a Convention would need to be supported by a financial arrangement that would have the active backing of the community of nations. Any such arrangement, and there are several possibilities, must not only seek to ensure the conservation of genetic resources for all people, but assure that the nations that possess many of these resources obtain an equitable share of the benefits and earnings derived from their development. This would greatly encourage the conservation of species. One such arrangement might be a Trust Fund to which all nations could contribute, with those benefiting most from the use of these resources contributing an appropriate share. Governments of tropical forest nations could receive payments to support the conservation of given areas of forest, with such payments rising or falling depending on the degree to which the forests are maintained and protected.[28]

The sums required for effective conservation are large. Traditional-type conservation needs in tropical forests alone require outlays of $170 million a year for at least five years.[29] However, the network of protected areas that the world will need by the year 2050 must include much larger areas brought under some degree of protection and a sophisticated degree of flexibility in management techniques.[30]

More funds will also be required for conservation activities outside protected areas: wildlife management, ecodevelopment areas, education campaigns, and so on. Other approaches of a less expensive sort include the conservation of wild gene reservoirs of special significance through 'genetic conservation areas' in countries well endowed with biological wealth. Much of this work can be carried out by citizens' groups and other non-governmental means.

International development agencies—the World Bank and other major lending banks, UN agencies, and bilateral agencies—should give comprehensive and systematic attention to the problems and opportunities of species conservation. Although the international trade in wildlife and wildlife products is considerable, to date the economic values inherent in genetic variability and ecological processes have been generally disregarded. Possible measures include environmental impact analyses of development projects with particular attention to species' habitats and life-support systems, identification of crucial localities featuring exceptional concentrations of species with exceptional levels of endemism that face exceptional degrees of threat, and special opportunities for linking species conservation with development aid.

VII. SCOPE FOR NATIONAL ACTION

As indicated earlier, governments need to follow a new approach in this field—one of anticipating the impact of their policies in numerous sectors and acting to prevent undesirable consequences. They should review programmes in areas such as agriculture, forestry, and settlements that serve to degrade and destroy species' habitats. Governments should determine how many more protected areas are needed, especially in the spirit of how such areas can contribute to national development objectives, and make further provision for protection of gene reservoirs (for instance, primitive cultivated varieties) that may not normally be preserved through conventional protected areas.

In addition, governments need to reinforce and expand existing strategies. Urgent needs include better wildlife and protected-area management, more protected areas of a non-conventional type (such as the ecological stations that are proving reasonably successful in Brazil), more game cropping and ranching projects (such as the crocodile schemes in India, Papua New Guinea, Thailand, and

'The world is unfortunately not what we would like it to be. The problems are many and great. Actually, they can only be solved with cooperation and quick-wittedness.

I represent an organization called 'Nature and Youth'. I know that I have full support among our members when I say that we are worried about the future if drastic changes do not take place, concerning the world's way of treating our essential condition, nature.

We who work with youth, and are youth ourselves in Norway today, know very well how the destroying of nature leads to an apathetic fear among youth concerning their future and how it will turn out.

It is of great importance that common people get the chance to take part in deciding how nature should be treated.'

Frederic Hauge
Nature and Youth
WCED Public Hearing, Oslo, 24–25 June 1985

Zimbabwe), more promotion of wildlife-based tourism, and stronger anti-poaching measures (even though relatively few species are threatened by poaching, compared with the vast numbers threatened by habitat loss). National Conservation Strategies, such as those already prepared in over 25 countries, can be important tools for coordinating conservation and development programmes.

Other measures governments could take to confront the crisis of disappearing species, recognizing that it constitutes a major resource and development challenge, include consideration of species conservation needs and opportunities in land use planning and the explicit incorporation of their genetic resource stocks into national accounting systems. This could entail establishing a natural-resource accounting system that directs particular attention to species as high-value yet little-appreciated resources. Finally, they should support and expand programmes of public education to ensure that the species question receives the attention it deserves throughout the entire population.

Every nation has only limited resources at its disposal for dealing with conservation priorities. The dilemma is how to use these resources most effectively. Cooperation with neighbouring nations sharing species and ecosystems can help streamline programmes as well as share expenses for regional initiatives. Explicit efforts to save particular species will be possible for only relatively few of the more spectacular or important ones. Agonizing as it will be to make such choices, planners need to make conservation strategies as systematically selective as possible. No one cares for the prospect of consigning threatened species to oblivion. But insofar as choices are already being made, unwittingly, they should be made with selective discretion that takes into account the impact of the extinction of a species upon the biosphere or on the integrity of a given ecosystem. But even though public effort may be concentrated on a few species, all species are important and deserve some degree of attention; this might take the form of tax credits to farmers willing to maintain primitive cultivars, an end to incentives to clear virgin forest, the promotion of research attention from local universities, and the preparation of basic inventories of native flora and fauna by national institutions.

VIII. THE NEED FOR ACTION

There are numerous signs that the loss of species and their ecosystems is being taken seriously as a phenomenon that carries practical implications for people all around the world, now and for generations to come.

The recent rise in public concern can be seen in such developments as the growth in Kenya's Wildlife Clubs, now numbering more than 1,500 school clubs with around 100,000 members.[31] A parallel development in conservation education has occurred in Zambia. In Indonesia, some 400 conservation groups have joined together under the banner of the Indonesian Environmental Forum and exert strong political influence.[32] In the United States, membership of the Audubon Society reached 385,000 in 1985.[33] In the Soviet Union, nature clubs have over 35 million members.[34] All of these indicate that the public puts a value on nature that is beyond the normal economic imperatives.

In response to this popular concern, governments have been moving to help species threatened within their borders, primarily through the establishment of additional protected areas. Today, the worldwide network of protected areas totals more than 4 million square kilometres, roughly equivalent to the size of most of the countries of Western Europe combined, or twice the size of Indonesia. In terms of continental coverage, protected areas in Europe (outside the USSR) amounted by 1985 to 3.9 per cent of territory; in the USSR, to 2.5 per cent; in North America, to 8.1 per cent; in South America, to 6.1 per cent; in Africa, to 6.5 per cent; and in Asia (outside the USSR) and Australia, to 4.3 per cent each.[35]

Since 1970, the networks have expanded in extent by more than 80 per cent, around two-thirds of which are in the Third World. But a great deal more remains to be done; a consensus of professional opinion suggests that the total expanse of protected areas needs to be at least tripled if it is to constitute a representative sample of Earth's ecosystems.[36]

There is still time to save species and their ecosystems. It is an indispensable prerequisite for sustainable development. Our failure to do so will not be forgiven by future generations.

Notes

1 J. McNeely and K. Miller (eds.), *National Parks Conservation and Development: The Role of Protected Areas in Sustaining Society*, Proceedings of the World Congress on National Parks (Washington, DC: Smithsonian Institution Press, 1984).

2 W.B. Banage, 'Policies for the Maintenance of Biological Diversity', prepared for WCED, 1986; P.R. Ehrlich and A.H. Ehrlich, *Extinction* (New York: Random House, 1981); D. Western (ed.), *Conservation 2100*, Proceedings of Wildlife Conservation International and New York Zoological Society Conference, 21-24 October 1986 (New York: Zoological Society, in press); N. Myers, 'Tropical Deforestation and Species Extinctions, The Latest News', *Futures*, October 1985; R. Lewin, 'A Mass Extinction Without Asteroids', *Science*, 3 October 1986; P.H. Raven, 'Statement from Meeting of IUCN/WWF Plant Advisory Group', Las Palmas, Canary Islands, 24-25 November 1985; M.E. Soule (ed.), *Conservation Biology: Science of Scarcity and Diversity* (Sunderland, Mass.: Sinauer Associates, 1986); E.O. Wilson (ed.), *Biodiversity*, Proceedings of National Forum held by National Academy of Sciences and Smithsonian Institution, 21-24 September 1986 (Washington, DC: National Academy Press, in press).

3 O.H. Frankel and M.E. Soule, *Conservation and Evolution* (Cambridge: Cambridge University Press, 1981); C.M. Schonewald-Cox et al. (eds.), *Genetics and Conservation* (Menlo Park, Calif.: Benjamin/Cummings Publishing Company Inc., 1983).

4 D.D. Raup, 'Biological Extinction in Earth History', *Science*, 28 March 1986.

5 Wilson, op. cit.; Ehrlich and Ehrlich, op. cit.; Myers, 'The Latest News', op. cit.; Soule, op. cit.

6 G.D. Ruggieri and N.D. Rosenberg, *The Healing Sea* (New York: Dodd Mead and Co., 1978).

7 FAO/UNEP, *Tropical Forest Resources*, Forestry Paper No. 30 (Rome: 1982); J.M. Melillo et al., 'A Comparison of Recent Estimates of Disturbance in Tropical Forests', *Environmental Conservation*, Spring 1985; N. Myers, *The Primary Source* (New York: W.W. Norton, 1984); Myers 'The Latest News', op. cit.; J. Molofsky et al., 'A Comparison of Tropical Forest Surveys', Carbon Dioxide Program, US Department of Energy, Washington DC, 1986.

8 D. Simberloff, 'Are We On the Verge of a Mass Extinction in Tropical Rain Forests?' in D.K. Elliott (ed.), *Dynamics of Extinction* (Chicester, UK: John Wiley & Sons, 1986); Raven, op. cit.

9 E. Salati and P.B. Vose, 'Amazon Basin: A System in Equilibrium', *Science*, 13 July 1984.

10 Department of International Economic and Social Affairs, *World Population Prospects: Estimates and Projections as Assessed in 1984* (New York: UN, 1986).

11 R. Repetto, 'Creating Incentives for Sustainable Forestry Development', World Resources Institute, Washington, DC, August 1985.

12 Ibid.

13 Agricultural Research Service, *Introduction, Classification, Maintenance, Evaluation and Documentation of Plant Germplasm* (Washington, DC: US Department of Agriculture, 1985).

14 L.A. Tatum, 'The Southern Corn Leaf Blight Epidemic', *Science*, Vol. 171, pp. 1113-16, 1971.

15 H.H. Iltis et al., 'Zea diploperennis (Gramineae), a New Teosinte from Mexico', *Science*, 12 January 1979.

16 A.C. Fisher, 'Economic Analysis and the Extinction of Species', Department of Energy and Resources, University of California, Berkeley, 1982.

17 N.R. Farnsworth and D.D. Soejarto, 'Potential Consequence of Plant Extinction in the United States on the Current and Future Availability of Prescription Drugs', *Economic Botany*, Vol. 39, pp. 231-40, 1985.

18 N. Myers, *A Wealth of Wild Species* (Boulder, Colo.: Westview Press, 1983).

19 Ibid.

20 M.L. Oldfield, 'The Value of Conserving Genetic Resources', National Park Service, US Department of the Interior, Washington, DC, 1984; L.H. Princen, 'New Crop Development for Industrial Oils', *Journal of the American Oil Chemists' Society*, Vol. 56, pp. 845-48, 1979.

21 A.H. Gentry and R. Wettach, 'Fevillea—A New Oilseed from Amazonian Peru', *Economic Botany*, Vol. 40, pp. 177-85, 1986.

22 M. Calvin, 'Hydrocarbons from Plants: Analytical Methods and Observations', *Naturwissenschaften*, Vol. 67, pp. 525-33, 1980; C.W. Hinman et al., 'Five Potential New Crops for Arid Lands', *Environmental Conservation*, Winter 1985.

23 T. Eisner, 'Chemicals, Genes, and the Loss of Species', *Nature Conservancy News*, Vol. 33, No. 6, pp. 23-24, 1983.

24 W.J. Brill, 'Nitrogen Fixation: Basic to Applied', *American Scientist*, Vol. 67, pp. 458-65, 1979.

25 McNeely and Miller, op. cit.

26 UNESCO, *International Coordinating Council of Man and the Biosphere*, MAB Report Series No.58 (Paris: 1985).

27 Letter to N. Myers, Consultant in Environment and Development, from Senator W. Roth (R-Del.), US Congress, Washington, DC.

28 R.A. Sedjo, Testimony before the Subcommittee on Human Rights and International Organizations, Foreign Affairs Committee, US House of Representatives, 12 September 1984.

29 International Task Force, *Tropical Forests: A Call for Action* (Washington, DC: World Resources Institute, 1985).

30 R.L. Peters and J.D.S. Darling, 'The Greenhouse Effect of Nature Reserves', *Bioscience*, Vol. 35, pp. 707-17, 1984.

31 'Kenya's Wildlife Clubs' (Brochure), Ed Wilson, WWF Regional Office for East and Central Africa, personal communication, 3 February 1987.

32 Centre for Environmental Studies, *Environmental NGO's in Developing Countries* (Copenhagen: 1985).

33 Membership figure from *Audubon* circulation in *Ulrich's Periodicals* (New York: R.W. Bowker, 1985).

34 Prof. Yazan, IUCN Vice-President and Regional Counsellor, *IUCN Bulletin*, Vol. 17, Nos. 7-9.

35 *List of National Parks and Equivalent Reserves* (IUCN: 1985).

36 McNeely and Miller, op. cit.

7

ENERGY: CHOICES FOR ENVIRONMENT AND DEVELOPMENT

Energy is necessary for daily survival. Future development crucially depends on its long-term availability in increasing quantities from sources that are dependable, safe, and environmentally sound. At present, no single source or mix of sources is at hand to meet this future need.

Concern about a dependable future for energy is only natural since energy provides 'essential services' for human life—heat for warmth, cooking, and manufacturing, or power for transport and mechanical work. At present, the energy to provide these services comes from fuels—oil, gas, coal, nuclear, wood, and other primary sources (solar, wind, or water power)—that are all useless until they are converted into the energy-services needed, by machines or other kinds of end-use equipment, such as stoves, turbines, or motors. In many countries world-wide, a lot of primary energy is wasted because of the inefficient design or running of the equipment used to convert it into the services required, though there is an encouraging growth in awareness of energy conservation and efficiency.

Today's primary sources of energy are mainly non-renewable: natural gas, oil, coal, peat, and conventional nuclear power. There are also renewable sources, including wood, plants, dung, falling water, geothermal sources, and solar, tidal, wind, and wave energy, as well as human and animal muscle-power. Nuclear reactors that produce their own fuel ('breeders') and eventually fusion reactors are also in this category. In theory, all the various energy sources can contribute to the future energy mix worldwide. But each has its own economic, health, and environmental costs, benefits, and risks—factors that interact strongly with other governmental and global priorities. Choices must be made, but in the certain knowledge that choosing an energy strategy inevitably means choosing an environmental strategy.

Patterns and changes of energy use today are already dictating patterns well into the next century. We approach this question from

Box 7-1. Energy Units

A variety of units are used to measure energy production and use in physical terms. This chapter uses the kilowatt (kW); the Gigawatt (GW), which is equal to 1 million kW; and the Terawatt (TW), which is equal to 1 billion kilowatts. One kilowatt—a thousand watts of energy—if emitted continuously for a year is 1kW year. Consuming 1 kW year/year is equivalent to the energy liberated by burning 1,050 kilogrammes—approximately 1 ton—of coal annually. Thus a TW year is equal to approximately 1 billion tons of coal. Throughout the chapter, TW years/year is written as TW.

the standpoint of sustainability. The key elements of sustainability that have to be reconciled are:

- sufficient growth of energy supplies to meet human needs (which means accommodating a minimum of 3 per cent per capita income growth in developing countries);
- energy efficiency and conservation measures, such that waste of primary resources is minimized;
- public health, recognizing the problems of risks to safety inherent in energy sources; and
- protection of the biosphere and prevention of more localized forms of pollution.

The period ahead must be regarded as transitional from an era in which energy has been used in an unsustainable manner. A generally acceptable pathway to a safe and sustainable energy future has not yet been found. We do not believe that these dilemmas have yet been addressed by the international community with a sufficient sense of urgency and in a global perspective.

I. ENERGY, ECONOMY, AND ENVIRONMENT

The growth of energy demand in response to industrialization, urbanization, and societal affluence has led to an extremely uneven global distribution of primary energy consumption.[1] The consumption of energy per person in industrial market economies, for example, is more than 80 times greater than in sub-Saharan Africa. (See Table 7.1.) And about a quarter of the world's population consumes three-quarters of the world's primary energy.

In 1980, global energy consumption stood at around 10TW.[2] (See Box 7-1.) If per capita use remained at the same levels as today, by 2025 a global population of 8.2 billion[3] would need about 14TW (over 4TW in developing and over 9TW in industrial countries)—an

TABLE 7.1

Global Primary Energy Consumption Per Capita, 1984

World Bank GNP Economy Category	GNP Per Capita (1984 dollars)	Energy Consumption (kW per capita*)	Mid–1984 Population (million)	Total Consumption (TW)
Low Income	260	0.41	2,390	0.99
Sub-Saharan Africa	210	0.08	258	0.02
Middle Income	1,250	1.07	1,188	1.27
Lower-middle	740	0.57	691	0.39
Upper-middle	1,950	1.76	497	0.87
Sub-Saharan Africa	680	0.25	148	0.04
High-Income Oil Exporters	11,250	5.17	19	0.10
Industrial Market Economies	11,430	7.01	733	5.14
East European Non-Market Economies	—	6.27	389	2.44
World	—	2.11†	4,718	9.94

* kW per capita is kW years/year per capita.

† Population-weighted average energy consumption (kW/capita) for first three main categories is 0.654 and for industrial market and East European categories is 6.76.

Source: Based on World Bank, *World Development Report 1986* (New York: Oxford University Press, 1986).

increase of 40 per cent over 1980. But if energy consumption per head became uniform world-wide at current industrial country levels, by 2025 that same global population would require about 55TW.

Neither the 'low' nor the 'high' figure is likely to prove realistic, but they give a rough idea of the range within which energy futures could move, at least hypothetically. Many other scenarios can be generated in-between, some of which assume an improved energy base for the developing world. For instance, if the average energy consumption in the low- and middle-income economies trebled and doubled, respectively, and if consumption in the high-income oil-exporting and industrial market and non-market countries remained the same as today, then the two groups would be consuming about the same amounts of energy. The low- and middle-income categories would need 10.5TW and the three 'high' categories would use 9.3TW—totalling 20TW globally, assuming that primary energy is used at the same levels of efficiency as today.

Box 7-2. Two Indicative Energy Scenarios

Case A-High Scenario

By the year 2030, a 35TW future would involve producing 1.6 times as much oil, 3.4 times as much natural gas, and nearly 5 times as much coal as in 1980. This increase in fossil fuel use implies bringing the equivalent of a new Alaska pipeline into production every one to two years. Nuclear capacity would have to be increased 30 times over 1980 levels— equivalent to installing a new nuclear power station generating 1 gigawatt of electricity every two to four days. This 35TW scenario is still well below the 55TW future that assumes today's levels of energy consumption per capita in industrial countries are achieved in all countries.

Case B-Low Scenario

Taking the 11.2TW scenario as a highly optimistic example of a strong conservation strategy, 2020 energy demand in developing and industrial countries is quoted as 7.3TW and 3.9TW respectively, as compared with 3.3TW and 7.0TW in 1980. This would mean a saving of 3.1TW in industrial countries by 2020 and an additional requirement of 4.0TW in developing countries. Even if developing countries were able to acquire the liberated primary resource, they would still be left with a shortfall of 0.9TW in primary supply. Such a deficit is likely to be much greater (possibly two to three times), given the extreme level of efficiency required for this scenario, which is unlikely to be realized by most governments. In 1980, the following breakdown of primary supply was quoted: oil, 4.2TW; coal, 2.4; gas, 1.7; renewables, 1.7; and nuclear, 0.2. The question is—where will the shortfall in primary energy supply come from? This rough calculation serves to illustrate that the postulated average growth of around 30 per cent per capita in primary consumption in developing countries will still require considerable amounts of primary supply even under extremely efficient energy usage regimes.

Sources: The 35TW scenario was originated in Energy Systems Group of the International Institute for Applied Systems Analysis, *Energy in a Finite World: A Global Systems Analysis* (Cambridge, Mass.: Ballinger, 1981); all other calculations are from J. Goldemberg et al., 'An End-Use Oriented Global Energy Strategy', *Annual Review of Energy, Vol. 10*, 1985.

How practical are any of these scenarios? Energy analysts have conducted many studies of global energy futures to the years 2020 and 2030.[4] Such studies do not provide forecasts of future energy needs, but they explore how various technical, economic, and environmental factors may interact with supply and demand. Two of these are reviewed in Box 7-2, though a much wider range of scenarios—from 5TW up to 63TW—are available.

In general, the lower scenarios (14.4TW by 2030,[5] 11.2TW by 2020,[6] and 5.2 by 2030[7]) require an energy efficiency revolution. The higher scenarios (18.8TW by 2025,[8] 24.7TW by 2020,[9] and 35.2 by 2030[10]) aggravate the environmental pollution problems that we have experienced since the Second World War.

The economic implications of a high energy future are disturbing. A recent World Bank Study indicates that for the period 1980-95, a 4.1 per cent annual growth in energy consumption, approximately comparable to Case A in Box 7-2, would require an average annual investment of some $130 billion (in 1982 dollars) in developing countries alone. This would involve doubling the share of energy investment in terms of aggregate gross domestic product.[11] About half of this would have to come from foreign exchange and the rest from internal spending on energy in developing countries.

The environmental risks and uncertainties of a high energy future are also disturbing and give rise to several reservations. Four stand out:

- the serious probability of climate change generated by the 'greenhouse effect' of gases emitted to the atmosphere, the most important of which is carbon dioxide (CO_2) produced from the combustion of fossil fuels[12];
- urban-industrial air pollution caused by atmospheric pollutants from the combustion of fossil fuels[13];
- acidification of the environment from the same causes[14] ; and
- the risks of nuclear reactor accidents, the problems of waste disposal and dismantling of reactors after their service life is over, and the dangers of proliferation associated with the use of nuclear energy.

Along with these, a major problem arises from the growing scarcity of fuelwood in developing countries. If trends continue, by the year 2000 around 2.4 billion people may be living in areas where wood is extremely scarce.[15]

These reservations apply at even lower levels of energy use. A study that proposed energy consumption at only half the levels of Case A (Box 7-2) drew special attention to the risks of global warming from CO_2.[16] The study indicated that a realistic fuel mix—a virtual quadrupling of coal and a doubling of gas use, along with 1.4 times as much oil—could cause significant global warming by the 2020s. No technology currently exists to remove CO_2 emissions from fossil fuel combustion. The high coal use would also increase emissions of oxides of sulphur and nitrogen, much of which turns to acids in the atmosphere. Technologies to remove these latter emissions are now required in some countries in all new and even some old facilities, but they can increase investment costs by 15-25 per cent.[17] If countries

'Energy is, put most simply, the fundamental unit of the physical world. As such, we cannot conceive of development without changes in the extent or the nature of energy flows. And because it is so fundamental, every one of those changes of flows has environmental implications. The implications of this are profound. It means that there is no such thing as a simple energy choice. They are all complex. And they all involve trade-offs. However, some of the choices and some of the trade-offs appear to be unequivocally better than others, in the sense that they offer more development and less environmental damage.'

David Brooks
Friends of the Earth
WCED Public Hearing, Ottawa, 26-27 May 1986

are not prepared to incur these expenses, this path becomes even more infeasible, a limitation that applies much more to the higher energy futures that rely to a greater extent on fossil fuels. A near doubling of global primary energy consumption will be difficult without encountering severe economic, social, and environmental constraints.

This raises the desirability of a lower energy future, where gross domestic product (GDP) growth is not constrained but where investment effort is switched away from building more primary supply sources and put into the development and supply of highly efficient fuel-saving end-use equipment. In this way, the energy-services needed by society could be supplied at much reduced levels of primary energy production. Case B in Box 7-2 allows for a 50 per cent fall in per capita primary energy consumption in industrial countries and a 30 per cent increase in developing countries.[18] By using the most energy-efficient technologies and processes now available in all sectors of the economy, annual global per capita GDP growth rates of around 3 per cent can be achieved. This growth is at least as great as that regarded in this report as a minimum for reasonable development. But this path would require huge structural changes to allow market penetration of efficient technologies, and it seems unlikely to be fully realizable by most governments during the next 40 years.

The crucial point about these lower, energy-efficient futures is not whether they are perfectly realizable in their proposed time frames. Fundamental political and institutional shifts are required to re-structure investment potential in order to move along these lower, more energy-efficient paths.

The Commission believes that there is no other realistic option open to the world for the 21st century. The ideas behind these lower scenarios are not fanciful. Energy efficiency has already shown cost-effective results. In many industrial countries, the primary energy required to produce a unit of GDP has fallen by as much as a quarter or even a third over the last 13 years, much of it from implementing energy efficiency measures.[19] Properly managed, efficiency measures could allow industrial nations to stabilize their primary energy consumption by the turn of the century. They would also enable developing countries to achieve higher levels of growth with much reduced levels of investment, foreign debt, and environmental damage. But by the early decades of the 21st century they will not alleviate the ultimate need for substantial new energy supplies globally.

II. FOSSIL FUELS: THE CONTINUING DILEMMA

Many forecasts of recoverable oil reserves and resources suggest that oil production will level off by the early decades of the next century and then gradually fall during a period of reduced supplies and higher prices. Gas supplies should last over 200 years and coal about 3,000 years at present rates of use. These estimates persuade many analysts that the world should immediately embark on a vigorous oil conservation policy.

In terms of pollution risks, gas is by far the cleanest fuel, with oil next and coal a poor third. But they all pose three interrelated atmospheric pollution problems: global warming,[20] urban industrial air pollution,[21] and acidification of the environment.[22] Some of the wealthier industrial countries may possess the economic capacity to cope with such threats. Most developing countries do not.

These problems are becoming more widespread particularly in tropical and subtropical regions, but their economic, social, and political repercussions are as yet not fully appreciated by society. With the exception of CO_2, air pollutants can be removed from fossil fuel combustion processes at costs usually below the costs of damage caused by pollution.[23] However, the risks of global warming make heavy future reliance upon fossil fuels problematic.

Managing Climatic Change

The burning of fossil fuels and, to a lesser extent, the loss of vegetative cover, particularly forests, through urban-industrial growth increase the accumulation of CO_2 in the atmosphere. The pre-industrial

'It is difficult to imagine an issue with more global impacts on human societies and the natural environment than the greenhouse effect. The signal is unclear but we may already be witnessing examples, if not actual greenhouse effects, in Africa.

The ultimate potential impacts of a greenhouse warming could be catastrophic. It is our considered judgement that it is already very late to start the process of policy consideration. The process of heightening public awareness, of building support for national policies, and finally for developing multilateral efforts to slow the rate of emissions growth will take time to implement.

The greenhouse issue is an opportunity as well as a challenge; not surprisingly, it provides another important reason to implement sustainable development strategies.'

Irving Mintzer
World Resources Institute
WCED Public Hearing, Oslo, 24–25 June 1985

concentration was about 280 parts of carbon dioxide per million parts of air by volume. This concentration reached 340 in 1980 and is expected to double to 560 between the middle and the end of the next century.[24] Other gases also play an important role in this 'greenhouse effect', whereby solar radiation is trapped near the ground, warming the globe and changing the climate.

After reviewing the latest evidence on the greenhouse effect in October 1985 at a meeting in Villach, Austria, organized by the World Meteorological Organization (WMO), the UN Environment Programme (UNEP), and the International Council of Scientific Unions (ICSU), scientists from 29 industrialized and developing countries concluded that climate change must be considered a 'plausible and serious probability'. They further concluded that: 'Many important economic and social decisions are being made today on . . . major water resource management activities such as irrigation and hydropower; drought relief; agricultural land use; structural designs and coastal engineering projects; and energy planning—all based on the assumption that past climatic data, without modification, are a reliable guide to the future. This is no longer a good assumption'.[25]

They estimated that if present trends continue, the combined concentration of CO_2 and other greenhouse gases in the atmosphere would be equivalent to a doubling of CO_2 from pre-industrial levels, possibly as early as the 2030s, and could lead to a rise in global mean temperatures 'greater than any in man's history'.[26] Current modelling studies and 'experiments' show a rise in globally averaged surface temperatures, for an effective CO_2 doubling, of somewhere between 1.5° C and 4.5° C, with the warming becoming more pronounced at higher latitudes during winter than at the equator.

An important concern is that a global temperature rise of 1.5-4.5° C, with perhaps a two to three times greater warming at the poles, would lead to a sea level rise of 25-140 centimetres.[27] A rise in the upper part of this range would inundate low-lying coastal cities and agricultural areas, and many countries could expect their economic, social, and political structures to be severely disrupted. It would also slow the 'atmospheric heat-engine', which is driven by the differences between equatorial and polar temperatures, thus influencing rainfall regimes.[28] Experts believe that crop and forest boundaries will move to higher latitudes; the effects of warmer oceans on marine ecosystems or fisheries and food chains are also virtually unknown.

There is no way to prove that any of this will happen until it actually occurs. The key question is: How much certainty should governments require before agreeing to take action? If they wait until significant climate change is demonstrated, it may be too late for any countermeasures to be effective against the inertia by then stored in this massive global system. The very long time lags involved in negotiating international agreement on complex issues involving all nations have led some experts to conclude that it is already late.[29] Given the complexities and uncertainties surrounding the issue, it is urgent that the process start now. A four-track strategy is needed, combining:

- improved monitoring and assessment of the evolving phenomena;
- increased research to improve knowledge about the origins, mechanisms, and effects of the phenomena;
- the development of internationally agreed policies for the reduction of the causative gases; and
- adoption of strategies needed to minimize damage and cope with the climate changes and rising sea level.

No nation has either the political mandate or the economic power to combat climatic change alone. However, the Villach statement recommended such a four-track strategy for climate change, to be promoted by governments and the scientific community through WMO, UNEP, and ICSU—backed by a global convention if necessary.[30]

While these strategies are being developed, more immediate policy measures can and should be adopted. The most urgent are those required to increase and extend the recent steady gains in energy efficiency and to shift the energy mix more towards renewables. Carbon dioxide output globally could be significantly reduced by energy efficiency measures without any reduction of the tempo of GDP growth.[31] These measures would also serve to abate other emissions and thus reduce acidification and urban-industrial air pollution. Gaseous fuels produce less carbon dioxide per unit of energy output than oil or coal and should be promoted, especially for cooking and other domestic uses.

Gases other than carbon dioxide are thought to be responsible for about one-third of present global warming, and it is estimated that they will cause about half the problem around 2030.[32] Some of these, notably chlorofluorocarbons used as aerosols, refrigeration chemicals, and in the manufacture of plastics, may be more easily controlled than CO_2. These, although not strictly energy-related, will have a decisive influence on policies for managing carbon dioxide emissions.

Apart from their climatic effect, chlorofluorocarbons are responsible to a large extent for damage to the Earth's stratospheric ozone.[33] The chemical industry should make every effort to find replacements, and governments should require the use of such replacements when found (as some nations have outlawed the use of these chemicals as aerosols). Governments should ratify the existing ozone convention and develop protocols for the limitation of chlorofluorocarbon emissions, and systematically monitor and report implementation.

A lot of policy development work is needed. This should proceed hand in hand with accelerated research to reduce remaining scientific uncertainties. Nations urgently need to formulate and agree upon management policies for all environmentally reactive chemicals released into the atmosphere by human activities, particularly those that can influence the radiation balance on earth. Governments should initiate discussions leading to a convention on this matter.

If a convention on chemical containment policies cannot be implemented rapidly, governments should develop contingency strategies and plans for adaptation to climatic change. In either case, WMO, UNEP, ICSU, the World Health Organization, and other relevant international and national bodies should be encouraged to coordinate and accelerate their programmes to develop a carefully integrated strategy of research, monitoring, and assessment of the likely impacts on climate, health, and environment of all environmentally reactive chemicals released into the atmosphere in significant quantities.

Reducing Urban-Industrial Air Pollution

The past three decades of generally rapid growth worldwide have seen dramatic increases in fuel consumption for heating and cooling, automobile transport, industrial activities, and electricity generation. Concern over the effects of increasing air pollution in the late 1960s resulted in the development of curative measures, including air-quality criteria, standards, and add-on control technologies that can remove pollutants cost-effectively. All these greatly reduced emissions of some of the principal pollutants and cleaned air over many cities. Despite this, air pollution has today reached serious levels in the cities of several industrial and newly industrialized countries as well as in those of most developing countries, which in some cases are by now the world's most polluted urban areas.

The fossil fuel emissions of principal concern in terms of urban pollution, whether from stationary or mobile sources, include sulphur dioxide, nitrogen oxides, carbon monoxide, various volatile organic compounds, fly ash, and other suspended particles. They can injure human health and the environment, bringing increased respiratory complaints, some potentially fatal. But these pollutants can be contained so as to protect human health and the environment and all governments should take steps to achieve acceptable levels of air quality.

Governments can establish and monitor air quality goals and objectives, allowable atmospheric loadings, and related emission criteria or standards, as some successfully do already. Regional organizations can support this effort. Multilateral and bilateral development assistance agencies and development banks should encourage governments to require that the most energy-efficient technology be used when industries and energy utilities plan to build new or extend existing facilities.

Damage from the Long-Range Transport of Air Pollution

Measures taken by many industrialized countries in the 1970s to control urban and industrial air pollution (high chimney stacks, for example) greatly improved the quality of the air in the cities concerned. However, it quite unintentionally sent increasing amounts of pollution across national boundaries in Europe and North America, contributing to the acidification of distant environments and creating new pollution problems. This was manifest in growing damage to lakes, soils, and communities of plants and animals.[34] Failure to control automobile pollution in some regions has seriously contributed to the problem.

'*A forest is an ecosystem that exists under certain environmental conditions, and if you change the conditions, the system is going to change. It is a very difficult task for ecologists to foresee what changes are going to be because the systems are so enormously complex.*

The direct causes behind an individual tree dying can be far removed from the primary pressure that brought the whole system into equilibrium. One time it might be ozone, another time it may be SO_2, a third time it may be aluminium poisoning.

I can express myself by an analogy: If there is famine, there are relatively few people who die directly from starvation; they die from dysentery or various infectious diseases. And in such a situation, it is not of very much help to send medicine instead of food. That means that in this situation, it is necessary to address the primary pressures against the ecosystem.'

Alf Johnels
Swedish Museum of Natural History
WCED Public Hearing, Oslo, 24–25 June 1985

Thus atmospheric pollution, once perceived only as a local urban-industrial problem involving people's health, is now also seen as a much more complex issue encompassing buildings, ecosystems, and maybe even public health over vast regions. During transport in the atmosphere, emissions of sulphur and nitrogen oxides and volatile hydrocarbons are transformed into sulphuric and nitric acids, ammonium salts, and ozone. They fall to the ground, sometimes many hundreds or thousands of kilometres from their origins, as dry particles or in rain, snow, frost, fog, and dew. Few studies of their socio-economic costs are available, but these demonstrate that they are quite large and suggest that they are growing rapidly.[35] They damage vegetation, contribute to land and water pollution, and corrode buildings, metallic structures and vehicles, causing billions of dollars in damage annually.

Damage first became evident in Scandinavia in the 1960s. Several thousand lakes in Europe, particularly in southern Scandinavia[36], and several hundreds in North America[37] have registered a steady increase in acidity levels to the point where their natural fish populations have declined or died out. The same acids enter the soil and groundwater, increasing corrosion of drinking water piping in Scandinavia.[38]

The circumstantial evidence indicating the need for action on the sources of acid precipitation is mounting with a speed that gives scientists and governments little time to assess it scientifically. Some of the greatest observed damage has been reported in Central Europe, which is currently receiving more than one gramme of sulphur on every square metre of ground each year, at least five times greater than natural background.[39] There was little evidence of tree damage in Europe in 1970. In 1982, the Federal Republic of Germany reported visible leaf damage in its forest plot samples nationwide, amounting in 1983 to 34 per cent, and rising in 1985 to 50 per cent.[40] Sweden reported light to moderate damage in 30 per cent of its forests, and various reports from other countries in Eastern and Western Europe are extremely disquieting. So far an estimated 14 per cent of all European forestland is affected.[41]

The evidence is not all in, but many reports show soils in parts of Europe becoming acid throughout the tree-rooting layers,[42] particularly nutrient-poor soils such as those of Southern Sweden.[43] The precise damage mechanisms are not known, but all theories include an air pollution component. Root damage[44] and leaf damage appear to interact, affecting the ability of the trees both to take up water from the soil and to retain it in the foliage, so that they become particularly vulnerable to dry spells and other stresses. Europe may be experiencing an immense change to irreversible acidification, the remedial costs of which could be beyond economic reach.[45] (See Box 7-3.) Although there are many options for reducing sulphur, nitrogen, and hydrocarbon emissions, no single pollutant control strategy is likely to be effective in dealing with forest decline. It will require a total integrated mix of strategies and technologies to improve air quality, tailored for each region.

Evidence of local air pollution and acidification in Japan and also in the newly industrialized countries of Asia, Africa, and Latin America is beginning to emerge. China and the Republic of Korea seem particularly vulnerable, as do Brazil, Colombia, Ecuador, and Venezuela. So little is known about the likely environmental loading of sulphur and nitrogen in these regions and about the acid-neutralizing capacity of tropical lakes and forest soils that a comprehensive programme of investigation should be formulated without delay.[46]

Where actual or potential threats from acidification exist, governments should map sensitive areas, assess forest damage annually and soil impoverishment every five years according to regionally agreed protocols, and publish the findings. They should support transboundary monitoring of pollution being carried out by agencies in their region and, where there is no such agency, create one or give the job to any suitable regional body. Governments in many regions could gain significantly from early agreement to prevent trans-

Box 7-3. The Damage and Control Costs of Air Pollution

- It is very difficult to quantify damage control costs, not least because cost figures are highly dependent on the control strategy assumed. However, in the eastern United States, it has been estimated that halving the remaining sulphur dioxide emissions from existing sources would cost $5 billion a year, increasing present electricity rates by 2–3 per cent. If nitrogen oxides are figured in, the additional costs might be as high as $6 billion a year. Materials corrosion damage alone is estimated to cost $7 billion annually in 17 states in the eastern United States.

- Estimates of the annual costs of securing a 55 to 65 per cent reduction in the remaining sulphur emissions in the countries of the European Economic Community between 1980 and 2000 range from $4.6 billion to $6.7 billion (1982 dollars) per year. Controls on stationary boilers to reduce nitrogen levels by only 10 per cent annually by the year 2000 range between $100,000 and $400,000 (1982 dollars). These figures translate into a one-time increase of about 6 per cent in the price of electrical power to the consumer. Studies place damage costs due to material and fish losses alone at $3 billion a year, while damage to crops, forests, and health are estimated to exceed $10 billion per year. Technologies for drastically reducing oxides of nitrogen and hydrocarbons from automobile exhaust gases are readily available and routinely used in North America and Japan, but not in Europe.

- Japanese laboratory studies indicate that air pollution and acid rain can reduce some wheat and rice crop production, perhaps by as much as 30 per cent.

Sources: US Congress, Office of Technology Assessment, *Acid Rain and Transported Air Pollutants: Implications for Public Policy* (Washington, DC: US Government Printing Office, 1985); US Environmental Protection Agency, *Acid Deposition Assessment* (Washington, DC: 1985); I.M. Torrens, 'Acid Rain and Air Pollution: A Problem of Industrialization', prepared for WCED, 1985; P. Mandelbaum, *Acid Rain - Economic Assessment* (New York: Plenum Press, 1985); M. Hashimoto, 'National Air Quality Management Policy of Japan', prepared for WCED, 1985; OECD, *The State of the Environment* (Paris: 1985).

boundary air pollution and the enormous damage to their economic base now being experienced in Europe and North America. Even though the exact causes of the damage are hard to prove, reduction strategies are certainly within reach and economic. They could be viewed as a cheap insurance policy compared with the vast amount of potential damage these strategies avoid.

III. NUCLEAR ENERGY: UNSOLVED PROBLEMS

The Peaceful Atom

In the years following the Second World War, the nuclear knowledge that under military control had led to the production of atomic weapons was redeployed for peaceful 'energy' purposes by civilian technologists. Several benefits were obvious at the time.

It was also realized that no energy source would ever be risk-free. There was the danger of nuclear war, the spread of atomic weapons, and nuclear terrorism. But intensive international co-operation and a number of negotiated agreements suggested that these dangers could be avoided. For instance, the Nonproliferation Treaty (NPT), drafted in its final form in 1969, included a promise by signatory governments possessing nuclear weapons and expertise to pursue and undertake nuclear disarmament and also to assist the non-nuclear signatories in developing nuclear power, but strictly for peaceful purposes only. Other problems, such as radiation risks, reactor safety, and nuclear waste disposal were all acknowledged as very important but, with the right amount of effort, containable.

And now, after almost four decades of immense technological effort to support nuclear development, nuclear energy has become widely used. Some 30 governments produce from nuclear generators a total of about 15 per cent of all the electricity used globally. Yet it has not met earlier expectations that it would be the key to ensuring an unlimited supply of low-cost energy. However, during this period of practical experience with building and running nuclear reactors, the nature of the costs, risks, and benefits have become much more evident and, as such, the subject of sharp controversy.

The Growing Understanding of Nuclear Issues

The potential for the spread of nuclear weapons is one of the most serious threats to world peace. It is in the interest of all nations to prevent proliferation of nuclear weapons. All nations therefore should contribute to the development of a viable non-proliferation regime. The nuclear-weapon states must deliver on their promise to reduce the number and ultimately eliminate nuclear weapons in their arsenals and the role those weapons play in their strategies. And the non-nuclear-weapon states must co-operate in providing credible assurances that they are not moving towards a nuclear weapon capability.

Most schemes for non-proliferation mandate an institutional separation between military and civilian uses of nuclear energy. But for countries with full access to the complete nuclear fuel cycle, no technical separation really exists. Not all states operate the necessary clear-cut administrative separation of civilian and military access. Co-operation is needed also among suppliers and buyers of civilian nuclear facilities and materials and the International Atomic Energy

Agency (IAEA), in order to provide credible safeguards against the diversion of civilian reactor programmes to military purposes, especially in countries that do not open all their nuclear programmes to IAEA inspection. Thus, there still remains a danger of the proliferation of nuclear weapons.

Costs

The costs of construction and the relative economics of electricity generating stations—whether powered by nuclear energy, coal, oil, or gas—are conditioned by the following factors throughout the service-life of a plant:

- the cost of borrowing money to finance plant construction;
- the impact of inflation;
- the duration of the period of planning, licensing, and construction;
- the cost of fuel and maintenance;
- the costs of protective measures to ensure safe operation; and
- waste-disposal costs (land, air, and water pollution containment) and the costs of dismantling at the end of service-life.

All these factors vary widely depending on differing institutional, legal, and financial arrangements in different countries. Cost generalizations and comparisons are therefore unhelpful or misleading. However, costs associated with several of these factors have increased more rapidly for nuclear stations during the last 5-10 years, so that the earlier clear cost advantage of nuclear over the service-life of the plant has been reduced or lost altogether.[47] Nations should therefore look very closely at cost comparisons to obtain the best value when choosing an energy path.

Health and Environment Risks

Very strict codes of safety practice are implemented in nuclear plants so that under officially approved operating conditions the danger from radiation to reactor personnel and especially to the general public is negligible. However, an accident occurring in a reactor may in certain very rare cases be serious enough to cause an external release of radioactive substances. Depending upon the level of exposure, people are under a certain level of risk of becoming ill from various forms of cancer or from alteration of genetic material, which may result in hereditary defects.

Since 1928, the International Commission on Radiological Protection (ICRP) has issued recommendations on radiation dosage levels above which exposure is unacceptable. These have been

'The health risks for the development of peaceful uses of nuclear technology, including nuclear electricity, are very small when compared with the benefits from the use of nuclear radiation for medical diagnosis treatment.

The safe application of nuclear radiation technology promises many benefits in environmental clean-up and in increasing world food supplies by eliminating spoilage.

With a recent and very notable exception, the international co-operation that has marked the development of nuclear power technology provides an excellent model by which to address common environmental and ethical problems posed by the development of other technologies.'

Ian Wilson
Vice-President, Canadian Nuclear Association
WCED Public Hearing, Ottawa, 26–27 May 1986

developed for occupationally exposed workers and for the general public. The 'Nuclear Safety Standards' (NUSS) codes of IAEA were developed in 1975 to reduce safety differences among member states. Neither system is in any way binding on governments. If an accident occurs, individual governments have the responsibility of deciding at what level of radioactive contamination pasture land, drinking water, milk, meat, eggs, vegetables, and fish are to be banned for consumption by livestock or humans.

Different countries—even different local government authorities within a country—have different criteria. Some have none at all, ICRP and NUSS notwithstanding. States with more rigorous standards may destroy large amounts of food or may ban food imports from a neighbour state with more permissive criteria. This causes great hardship to farmers who may not receive any compensation for their losses. It may also cause trade problems and political tension between states. Both of these difficulties occurred following the Chernobyl disaster, when the need to develop at least regionally conformable contamination criteria and compensation arrangements was overwhelmingly demonstrated.

Nuclear Accident Risks

Nuclear safety returned to the newspaper headlines following the Three Mile Island (Harrisburg, United States) and the Chernobyl (USSR) accidents. Probabilistic estimates of the risks of component failure leading to a radioactive release in Western-style light-water reactors were made in 1975 by the US Nuclear Regulatory Commission.[48] The most serious category of release through containment failure was placed at around 1 in 1,000,000 years of reactor operation. Post-accident analysis of both Harrisburg and Chernobyl—a completely different type of reactor—have shown that in both cases, human operator error was the main cause. They occurred after about 2,000 and 4,000 reactor-years respectively.[49] The frequencies of such occurrences are well nigh impossible to estimate probabilistically. However, available analyses indicate that although the risk of a radioactive release accident is small, it is by no means negligible for reactor operations at the present time.

The regional health and environment effects of an accident are largely predictable from radioactive fall-out studies following early atomic weapons testing in the atmosphere and have been confirmed in practice following the Chernobyl accident. What could not be confidently predicted before Chernobyl were the local effects of such an accident. A much clearer picture is now emerging as a result of the experiences there when a reactor exploded, following a series of infringements of the official safety regulations, on 26 April 1986, causing the worst reactor accident ever experienced. As a result, the whole district had to be managed on something like a 'war footing' and efforts resembling a large military operation were needed to contain the damage.

Radioactive Waste Disposal

Civil nuclear energy programmes world-wide have already generated many thousands of tons of spent fuel and high-level waste. Many governments have embarked on large-scale programmes to develop ways of isolating these from the biosphere for the many hundreds of thousands of years that they will remain hazardously radioactive.

But the problem of nuclear waste disposal remains unsolved. Nuclear waste technology has reached an advanced level of sophistication.[50] This technology has not however been fully tested or utilized and problems remain about disposal. There is particular concern about future recourse to ocean dumping and the disposal of contaminated waste in the territories of small or poor states that lack the capacity to impose strict safeguards. There should be a clear presumption that all countries that generate nuclear waste dispose of it within their own territories or under strictly monitored agreements between states.

The Current International Situation

During the last 25 years, a growing awareness of the difficulties outlined above has resulted in a wide range of reactions from technical experts, the public, and governments. Many experts still feel that so much can be learned from the problems experienced up to now. They argue that if the public climate allows them to solve the nuclear waste disposal and decommissioning issues and the cost of borrowing money remains reasonably below its 1980–82 peak, in the absence of viable new supply alternatives there is no reason why nuclear energy should not emerge as a strong runner in the 1990s. At the other extreme, many experts take the view that there are so many unsolved problems and too many risks for society to continue with a nuclear future. Public reactions also vary. Some countries have exhibited little public reaction; in others there appears to be a high level of anxiety that expresses itself in anti-nuclear results in public opinion polls or large anti-nuclear campaigns.

And so, whilst some states still remain nuclear-free, today nuclear reactors supply about 15 per cent of all the electricity generated. Total electricity production world-wide is in turn equivalent to around 15 per cent of global primary energy supply. Roughly one-quarter of all countries world-wide have reactors. In 1986, there were 366 working and a further 140 planned,[51] with 10 governments possessing about 90 per cent of all installed capacity (more than 5 GW (e)). Of these, there are 8 with a total capacity of more than 9 GW (e),[52] which provided the following percentages of electric power in 1985: France, 65; Sweden, 42; Federal Republic of Germany, 31; Japan, 23; United Kingdom, 19; United States, 16; Canada, 13; and USSR, 10. According to IAEA, in 1985 there were 55 research reactors world-wide, 33 of them in developing countries.[53]

Nevertheless, there is little doubt that the difficulties referred to above have in one way or another contributed to a scaling back of future nuclear plans—in some countries, to a de facto nuclear pause. In Western Europe and North America, which today have almost 75 per cent of current world capacity, nuclear provides about one-third of the energy that was forecast for it 10 years ago. Apart from France, Japan, the USSR, and several other East European countries that have decided to continue with their nuclear programmes, ordering, construction, and licensing prospects for new reactors in many other countries look poor. In fact, between 1972 and 1986, earlier global projections of estimated capacity for the year 2000 have been revised downwards by a factor of nearly seven. Despite this, the growth of nuclear at around 15 per cent a year over the last 20 years is still impressive.[54]

Following Chernobyl, there were significant changes in the nuclear

'Today the assessment of practical consequences can be based on practical experience. The consequences of Chernobyl has made Soviet specialists once again pose a question: Is not the development of nuclear energy on an industrial scale premature? Will it not be fatal to our civilization, to the ecosystem of our planet? On our planet so rich in all sorts of energy sources, this question can be discussed quite calmly. We have a real choice in this, both on a state and a governmental level, and also on the level of individuals and professionals.

We must put all our efforts to improve the technology itself, to develop and elaborate strict standards and norms of quality, of safety of a technology. We must work for the creation of antiaccident centres and centres devoting themselves to compensating for the losses to the environment. The upgrading of the industrial level of safety and the solution of the problem of the relations between man and machine would be a lot more natural thing to do than concentrating the efforts on only one element of the energy structure in the world. This would benefit the whole of humanity.'

V. A. Legasov
Member, Academy of Sciences of the USSR
WCED Public Hearing, Moscow, 8 Dec 1986

stance of certain governments. Several—notably China, the Federal Republic of Germany, France, Japan, Poland, United Kingdom, United States, and the USSR—have maintained or reaffirmed their pro-nuclear policy. Others with a 'no nuclear' or a 'phase-out' policy (Australia, Austria, Denmark, Luxembourg, New Zealand, Norway, Sweden—and Ireland with an unofficial anti-nuclear position) have been joined by Greece and the Philippines. Meanwhile, Finland, Italy, the Netherlands, Switzerland, and Yugoslavia are re-investigating nuclear safety and/or the anti-nuclear arguments, or have introduced legislation tying any further growth of nuclear energy and export/import of nuclear reactor technology to a satisfactory solution of the problem of disposal of radioactive wastes. Several countries have been concerned enough to conduct referendums to test public opinion regarding nuclear power.

Conclusions and Recommendations

These national reactions indicate that as they continue to review and update all the available evidence, governments tend to take up three possible positions:

- remain non-nuclear and develop other sources of energy;

- regard their present nuclear power capacity as necessary during a finite period of transition to safer alternative energy sources; or
- adopt and develop nuclear energy with the conviction that the associated problems and risks can and must be solved with a level of safety that is both nationally and internationally acceptable.

The discussion in the Commission also reflected these tendencies, views, and positions.

But whichever policy is adopted, it is important that the vigorous promotion of energy-efficient practices in all energy sectors and large-scale programmes of research, development, and demonstration for the safe and environmentally benign use of all promising energy sources, especially renewables, be given the highest priority.

Because of potential transboundary effects, it is essential that governments co-operate to develop internationally agreed codes of practice covering technical, economic, social (including health and environment aspects), and political components of nuclear energy. In particular, international agreement must be reached on the following specific items:

- full governmental ratification of the conventions on 'Early Notification of a Nuclear Accident' (including the development of an appropriate surveillance and monitoring system) and on 'Assistance in the Case of a Nuclear Accident or Radiological Emergency' as recently developed by IAEA;
- emergency response training—for accident containment and for decontamination and long-term clean-up of affected sites, personnel, and ecosystems;
- the transboundary movement of all radioactive materials, including fuels, spent fuels, and other wastes by land, sea, or air;
- a code of practice on liability and compensation;
- standards for operator training and international licensing;
- codes of practice for reactor operation, including minimum safety standards;
- the reporting of routine and accidental discharges from nuclear installations;
- effective, internationally harmonized minimum radiological protection standards;
- agreed site selection criteria as well as consultation and notification prior to the siting of all major civil nuclear-related installations;
- standards for waste repositories;

- standards for the decontamination and dismantling of time-expired nuclear reactors; and
- problems posed by the development of nuclear-powered shipping.

For many reasons, especially including the failure of the nuclear-weapons states to agree on disarmament, the Nonproliferation Treaty has not proved to be a sufficient instrument to prevent the proliferation of nuclear weapons, which still remains a serious danger to world peace. We therefore recommend in the strongest terms the construction of an effective international regime covering all dimensions of the problem. Both nuclear-weapons states and non-nuclear-weapons states should undertake to accept safeguards in accordance with the statutes of IAEA.

Additionally, an international regulatory function is required, including inspection of reactors internationally. This should be quite separate from the role of IAEA in promoting nuclear energy.

The generation of nuclear power is only justifiable if there are solid solutions to the presently unsolved problems to which it gives rise. The highest priority must be accorded to research and development on environmentally sound and economically viable alternatives, as well as on means of increasing the safety of nuclear energy.

IV. WOOD FUELS: THE VANISHING RESOURCE

Seventy per cent of the people in developing countries use wood and, depending on availability, burn anywhere between an absolute minimum of about 350 kilogrammes to 2,900 kilogrammes of dry wood annually, with the average being around 700 kilogrammes per person.[55] Rural woodfuel supplies appear to be steadily collapsing in many developing countries, especially in sub-Saharan Africa.[56] At the same time, the rapid growth of agriculture, the pace of migration to cities, and the growing numbers of people entering the money economy are placing unprecedented pressures on the biomass base[57] and increasing the demand for commercial fuels: from wood and charcoal to kerosene, liquid propane, gas, and electricity. To cope with this, many developing-country governments have no option but to immediately organize their agriculture to produce large quantities of wood and other plant fuels.

Wood is being collected faster than it can regrow in many developing countries that still rely predominantly on biomass—wood, charcoal, dung, and crop residues—for cooking, for heating their dwellings, and even for lighting. Food and Agriculture Organization estimates suggest that in 1980, around 1.3 billion people lived in wood-deficit areas.[58] If this population-driven overharvesting continues at present rates, by the year 2000 some 2.4 billion people may be living in areas where wood is 'acutely scarce or has to be obtained elsewhere'. These figures reveal great human hardship. Precise data on supplies are unavailable because much of the wood is not commercially traded but collected by the users, principally women and children. But there is no doubt that millions are hard put to find substitute fuels, and their numbers are growing.

The fuelwood crisis and deforestation—although related—are not the same problems. Wood fuels destined for urban and industrial consumers do tend to come from forests. But only a small proportion of that used by the rural poor comes from forests. Even in these cases, villagers rarely chop down trees; most collect dead branches or cut them from trees.[59]

When fuelwood is in short supply, people normally economize; when it is no longer available, rural people are forced to burn such fuels as cow dung, crop stems and husks, and weeds. Often this does no harm, since waste products such as cotton stalks are used. But the burning of dung and certain crop residues may in some cases rob the soil of needed nutrients. Eventually extreme fuel shortages can reduce the number of cooked meals and shorten the cooking time, which increases malnourishment.

Many urban people rely on wood, and most of this is purchased. Recently, as the price of wood fuels has been rising, poor families have been obliged to spend increasing proportions of their income on wood. In Addis Ababa and Maputo, families may spend a third to half of their incomes this way.[60] Much work has been done over the past 10 years to develop fuel-efficient stoves, and some of these new models use 30–50 per cent less fuel. These, as well as aluminium cooking pots and pressure cookers that also use much less fuel, should be made more widely available in urban areas.

Charcoal is a more convenient, cleaner fuel than wood, and its smoke causes less eye irritation and respiratory trouble than wood smoke.[61] But the usual methods for making it waste tremendous quantities of wood. Deforestation rates around cities could be greatly reduced if more efficient charcoal-making techniques, such as brick or metal kilns, were introduced.

Commercial forestry operations are rarely effective in providing fuelwood in rural areas, but they help to meet urban and industrial needs. Commercial farm forestry, or, on a larger scale, dedicated

> *Fuelwood and charcoal are, and will remain, the major sources of energy for the great majority of rural people in developing countries. The removal of trees in both semiarid and humid land in African countries is a result to a large extent of increasing energy needs from an increasing population, both rural and urban. The most visible results are desertification, soil erosion, and general environmental degradation.*
>
> *The reasons behind these disappointments are many, but a central cause is undoubtedly a singular focus on trees as the object of attention, rather than people. Forestry must enlarge its horizons: beyond trees—to the people who must exploit them.*

Rutger Engelhard
Beijer Institute's Centre for Energy and Development in Africa
WCED Public Hearing, Nairobi, 23 Sept 1986

energy plantations, can be viable enterprises. Green belts round large urban areas can also provide wood fuels for the urban consumers, and such an urban green zone brings other environmental amenities. Some iron and steel industries in developing countries are based on charcoal produced from wood in such dedicated energy plantations. Unfortunately, most still draw their wood supplies from native forests, without reforestation. Often, especially in the initial stages, fiscal and tax incentives are necessary to get planting projects going. Later these can be tied to success rates for tree growth, and can eventually be phased out. In urban areas, there are also good prospects for increasing the supplies of alternative energy sources, such as electricity, liquid propane gas, kerosene, and coal.

These strategies, however, will not be able to help most rural people, particularly the poor, who collect their wood. For them wood is a 'free good' until the last available tree is cut down. Rural areas require totally different strategies. Given the basic need for domestic fuel, and the few substitutes available, it seems that the only way out of this problem in the short and medium term is to treat fuelwood like food and grow it as a subsistence crop. This is best done through employing various agroforestry techniques, some of which have, in fact, been used for generations. (See Chapter 5.)

But in most rural areas, simply growing more trees does not necessarily solve the problem. In some districts where there are many trees, fuelwood is not available to those who need it. The trees may be owned by only a few people. Or tradition may dictate that women play no role in the cash economy and cannot buy or sell wood.[62] The communities concerned will have to work out local solutions to these problems. But such local issues mean that governments and aid and development organizations that want to help the fuelwood situation in developing countries will have to work harder to understand the role fuelwood plays in rural areas, and the social relations governing its production and use.

V. RENEWABLE ENERGY: THE UNTAPPED POTENTIAL

Renewable energy sources could in theory provide 10–13TW annually—equal to current global energy consumption.[63] Today they provide about 2TW annually, about 21 per cent of the energy consumed worldwide, of which 15 per cent is biomass and 6 per cent hydropower. However, most of the biomass is in the form of fuelwood and agricultural and animal wastes. As noted above, fuelwood can no longer be thought of as a 'renewable' resource in many areas, because consumption rates have overtaken sustainable yields.

Although worldwide reliance on all these sources has been growing by more than 10 per cent a year since the late 1970s, it will be some time before they make up a substantial portion of the world's energy budget. Renewable energy systems are still in a relatively primitive stage of development. But they offer the world potentially huge primary energy sources, sustainable in perpetuity and available in one form or another to every nation on Earth. But it will require a substantial and sustained commitment to further research and development if their potential is to be realized.

Wood as a renewable energy source is usually thought of as naturally occurring trees and shrubs harvested for local domestic use. Wood, however, is becoming an important feedstock, specially grown for advanced energy conversion processes in developing as well as industrial countries—for the production of process heat, electricity, and potentially for other fuels, such as combustible gases and liquids.

Hydropower, second to wood among the renewables, has been expanding at nearly 4 per cent annually. Although hundreds of thousands of megawatts of hydropower have been harnessed throughout the world, the remaining potential is huge.[64] In neighbouring developing countries, interstate co-operation in hydropower development could revolutionize supply potential, especially in Africa.

Solar energy use is small globally, but it is beginning to assume an important place in the energy consumption patterns of some countries. Solar water and household heating is widespread in many parts of Australia, Greece, and the Middle East. A number of East European and developing countries have active solar energy programmes, and the United States and Japan support solar sales of several hundred million dollars a year. With constantly improving solar thermal and solar electric technologies, it is likely that their contribution will increase substantially. The cost of photovoltaic equipment has fallen from around $500-600 per peak watt to $5 and is approaching the $1-2 level where it can compete with conventional electricity production.[65] But even at $5 per peak watt, it still provides electricity to remote places more cheaply than building power lines.

Wind power has been used for centuries—mainly for pumping water. Recently its use has been growing rapidly in regions such as California and Scandinavia. In these cases the wind turbines are used to generate electricity for the local electricity grid. The costs of wind-generated electricity, which benefited initially from substantial tax incentives, have fallen dramatically in California in the last five years and may possibly be competitive with other power generated there within a decade.[66] Many countries have successful but small wind programmes, but the untapped potential is still high.

The fuel alcohol programme in Brazil produced about 10 billion litres of ethanol from sugar-cane in 1984 and replaced about 60 per cent of the gasoline that would have been required.[67] The cost has been estimated at $50-60 per barrel of gasoline replaced. When subsidies are removed, and a true exchange rate is used, this is competitive at 1981 oil prices. With present lower oil prices, the programme has become uneconomical. But it saves the nation hard currency, and it provides the additional benefits of rural development, employment generation, increased self-reliance, and reduced vulnerability to crises in the world oil markets.

The use of geothermal energy, from natural underground heat sources, has been increasing at more than 15 per cent per year in both industrial and developing countries. The experience gained during the past decades could provide the basis for a major expansion of geothermal capacity.[68] By contrast, technologies for low-grade heat via heat pumps or from solar ponds and ocean thermal gradients are promising but still mostly at the research and development stage.

These energy sources are not without their health and environment risks. Although they range from rather trivial to very serious problems, public reactions to them are not necessarily in proportion to the damage sustained. For instance, some of the commonest difficulties with solar energy are, somewhat surprisingly, the injuries from roof falls during solar thermal maintenance and the nuisance of sun-glare off their glass surfaces. Or a modern wind turbine can be a significant

‘*In the choice of resources to be utilized we should not stare at renewable resources of energy blindly, we should not blow it out of proportion, we should not promote it for the sake of the environment per se. Instead we should develop and utilize all resources available, renewable sources of energy included, as a long-term endeavour requiring a continuous and sustained effort that will not be subject to short-term economic fluctuations, in order that we, in Indonesia, will achieve a successful and orderly transition to a more diversified and balanced structure of energy supply and environmentally sound energy supply system, which is the ultimate goal of our policy.*’

Speaker from the floor
WCED Public Hearing, Jakarta, 26 March 1985

noise nuisance to people living nearby. Yet, these apparently small problems often arouse very strong public reactions.

But these are still minor issues compared with the ecosystem destruction at hydropower sites or the uprooting of homesteads in the areas to be flooded, as well as the health risks from toxic gases generated by rotting submerged vegetation and soils, or from waterborne diseases such as schistosomiasis (snail fever). Hydrodams also act as an important barrier to fish migration and frequently to the movement of land animals. Perhaps the worst problem they pose is the danger of catastrophic rupture of the dam-wall and the sweeping away or flooding of human settlements downstream—about once a year somewhere in the world. This risk is small but not insignificant.

One of the most widespread chronic problems is the eye and lung irritation caused by woodsmoke in developing countries. When agricultural wastes are burned, pesticide residues inhaled from the dusts or smoke of the crop material can be a health problem. Modern biofuel liquids have their own special hazards. Apart from competing with food crops for good agricultural land, their production generates large quantities of organic waste effluent, which if not used as a fertilizer can cause serious water pollution. Such fuels, particularly methanol, may produce irritant or toxic combustion products. All these and many other problems, both large and small, will increase as renewable energy systems are developed.

Most renewable energy systems operate best at small to medium scales, ideally suited for rural and suburban applications. They are also generally labour-intensive, which should be an added benefit where there is surplus labour. They are less susceptible than fossil fuels to wild price fluctuations and foreign exchange costs. Most countries have some renewable resources, and their use can help nations move towards self-reliance.

The need for a steady transition to a broader and more sustainable mix of energy sources is beginning to become accepted. Renewable energy sources could contribute substantially to this, particularly with new and improved technologies, but their development will depend in the short run on the reduction or removal of certain economic and institutional constraints to their use. These are formidable in many countries. The high level of hidden subsidies for conventional fuels built into the legislative and energy programmes of most countries distorts choices against renewables in research and development, depletion allowances, tax write-offs, and direct support of consumer prices. Countries should undertake a full examination of all subsidies and other forms of support to various sources of energy and remove those that are not clearly justified.

Although the situation is changing rapidly in some jurisdictions, electrical utilities in most have a supply monopoly on generation that allows them to arrange pricing policies that discriminate against other, usually small, suppliers.[69] In some countries a relaxation of this control, requiring utilities to accept power generated by industry, small systems, and individuals, has created opportunities for the development of renewables. Beyond that, requiring utilities to adopt an end-use approach in planning, financing, developing, and marketing energy can open the door to a wide range of energy-saving measures as well as renewables.

Renewable energy sources require a much higher priority in national energy programmes. Research, development, and demonstration projects should command funding necessary to ensure their rapid development and demonstration. With a potential of 10TW or so, even if 3–4TW were realized, it would make a crucial difference to future primary supply, especially in developing countries, where the background conditions exist for the success of renewables. The technological challenges of renewables are minor compared with the challenge of creating the social and institutional frameworks that will ease these sources into energy supply systems.

The Commission believes that every effort should be made to develop the potential for renewable energy, which should form the foundation of the global energy structure during the 21st century. A much more concerted effort must be mounted if this potential is to be realized. But a major programme of renewable energy development will involve large costs and high risks, particularly massive-scale solar and biomass industries. Developing countries lack the resources to finance all but a small fraction of this cost although they will be important users and possibly even exporters. Large-scale financial and technical assistance will therefore be required.

VI. ENERGY EFFICIENCY: MAINTAINING THE MOMENTUM

Given the above analysis, the Commission believes that energy efficiency should be the cutting edge of national energy policies for sustainable development. Impressive gains in energy efficiency have been made since the first oil price shock in the 1970s. During the past 13 years, many industrial countries saw the energy content of growth fall significantly as a result of increases in energy efficiency averaging 1.7 per cent annually between 1973 and 1983.[70] And this energy efficiency solution costs less, by savings made on the extra primary supplies required to run traditional equipment.

The cost-effectiveness of 'efficiency' as the most environmentally benign 'source' of energy is well established. The energy consumption per unit of output from the most efficient processes and technologies is one-third to less than one-half that of typically available equipment.[71]

This is true of appliances for cooking, lighting and refrigeration, and space cooling and heating—needs that are growing rapidly in most countries and putting severe pressures on the available supply systems. It is also true of agricultural cultivation and irrigation systems, of the automobile, and of many industrial processes and equipment.

Given the large disproportion in per capita energy consumption between developed and developing countries in general, it is clear that the scope and need for energy saving is potentially much higher in industrial than in developing countries. Nonetheless, energy efficiency is important everywhere. The cement factory, automobile, or irrigation pump in a poor country is fundamentally no different from its equivalent in the rich world. In both, there is roughly the same scope for reducing the energy consumption or peak power demand of these devices without loss of output or welfare. But poor countries will gain much more from such reductions.

The woman who cooks in an earthen pot over an open fire uses perhaps eight times more energy than an affluent neighbour with a gas stove and aluminium pans. The poor who light their homes with a wick dipped in a jar of kerosene get one-fiftieth of the illumination of a 100-watt electric bulb, but use just as much energy. These examples illustrate the tragic paradox of poverty. For the poor, the

‚We must change our attitude towards consumption goods in developed countries and we must create technological advances that will allow us to carry on economic development using less energy. We must ask ourselves can we solve the problems of underdevelopment without using or increasing the tremendous amount of energy used by these countries.

The idea that developing countries use very little energy is an incorrect idea. We find that the poorest countries of all have a different problem; their problem is inefficient use of energy. Medium countries such as Brazil use more efficient and modern sources of fuel. The great hope for these countries is that the future will be built not based on technologies of the past, but using advanced technology. This will allow them to leap forward in relation to countries that are already developed.‚

Jose Goldemberg
President, Companhia Energetica de Sao Paulo
WCED Public Hearing, Brasilia, 30 Oct 1985

shortage of money is a greater limitation than the shortage of energy. They are forced to use 'free' fuels and inefficient equipment because they do not have the cash or savings to purchase energy-efficient fuels and end-use devices. Consequently, collectively they pay much more for a unit of delivered energy-services.

In most cases, investments in improved end-use technologies save money over time through lowered energy-supply needs. The costs of improving the end-use equipment is frequently much less than the cost of building more primary supply capacity. In Brazil, for example, it has been shown that for a discounted, total investment of $4 billion in more efficient end-use technologies (such as more efficient refrigerators, street-lighting, or motors) it would be feasible to defer construction of 21 gigawatts of new electrical supply capacity, corresponding to a discounted capital savings for new supplies of $19 billion in the period 1986 to 2000.[72]

There are many examples of successful energy efficiency programmes in industrial countries. The many methods used successfully to increase awareness include information campaigns in the media, technical press, and schools; demonstrations of successful practices and technologies; free energy audits; energy 'labelling' of appliances; and training in energy-saving techniques. These should be quickly and widely extended. Industrialized countries account for such a large proportion of global energy consumption that even small gains in efficiency can have a substantial impact on conserving reserves and reducing the pollution load on the biosphere. It is particularly important that consumers, especially large commercial and industrial agencies, obtain professional audits of their energy use. This kind of energy 'book-keeping' will readily identify those places in their consumption patterns where significant savings can be made.

Energy pricing policies play a critical role in stimulating efficiency. At present, they sometimes include subsidies and seldom reflect the real costs of producing or importing the energy, particularly when exchange rates are undervalued. Very rarely do they reflect the external damage costs to health, property, and the environment. Countries should evaluate all hidden and overt subsidies to see how far real energy costs can be passed on to the consumer. The true economic pricing of energy—with safeguards for the very poor— needs to be extended in all countries. Large numbers of countries both industrial and developing are already adopting such policies.

Developing countries face particular constraints in saving energy. Foreign exchange difficulties can make it hard to purchase efficient but costly energy conversion and end-use devices. Energy can often be saved cost-effectively by fine-tuning already functioning systems.[73] But governments and aid agencies may find it less attractive to fund such measures than to invest in new, large-scale energy supply hardware that is perceived as a more tangible symbol of progress.

The manufacture, import, or sale of equipment conforming to mandatory minimal energy consumption or efficiency standards is one of the most powerful and effective tools in promoting energy efficiency and producing predictable savings. International co-operation may be required when such equipment is traded from nation to nation. Countries and appropriate regional organizations should introduce and extend increasingly strict efficiency standards for equipment and mandatory labelling of appliances.

Many energy efficiency measures cost nothing to implement. But where investments are needed, they are frequently a barrier to poor households and small-scale consumers, even when pay-back times are short. In these latter cases, special small loan or hire-purchase arrangements are helpful. Where investment costs are not insurmountable, there are many possible mechanisms for reducing or spreading the initial investment, such as loans with favourable repayment periods and 'invisible' measures such as loans repaid by topping up the new, reduced energy bills to the pre-conservation levels.

Transport has a particularly important place in national energy and development planning. It is a major consumer of oil, accounting for 50–60 per cent of total petroleum use in most developing countries.[74] It is often a major source of local air pollution and regional acidification of the environment in industrial and developing countries. Vehicle markets will grow much more rapidly in developing countries, adding greatly to urban air pollution, which in many cities already exceeds international norms. Unless strong action is taken, air pollution could become a major factor limiting industrial development in many Third World cities.

In the absence of higher fuel prices, mandatory standards providing for a steady increase in fuel economy may be necessary. Either way, the potential for substantial future gains in fuel economy is enormous. If momentum can be maintained, the current average fuel consumption of approximately 10 litres per 100 kilometres in the fleet of vehicles in use in industrial countries could be cut in half by the turn of the century.[75]

A key issue is how developing countries can rapidly improve the fuel economy of their vehicles when these are, on average, used for twice as long those as in industrial countries, cutting rates of renewal and improvement in half. Licensing and import agreements should be reviewed to ensure access to the best available fuel-efficient designs and production processes. Another important fuel-saving strategy especially in the growing cities of developing countries is the organizing of carefully planned public transport systems.

Industry accounts for 40-60 per cent of all energy consumed in industrial countries and 10-40 per cent in developing countries. (See Chapter 8.) There has been significant improvement in the energy efficiency of production equipment, processes, and products. In developing countries, energy savings of as much as 20-30 per cent could be achieved by such skilful management of industrial development.

Agriculture world-wide is only a modest energy consumer, accounting for about 3.5 per cent of commercial energy use in the industrial countries and 4.5 per cent in developing countries as a whole.[76] A strategy to double food production in the Third World through increases in fertilizers, irrigation, and mechanization would add 140 million tons of oil equivalent to their agricultural energy use. This is only some 5 per cent of present world energy consumption and almost certainly a small part of the energy that could be saved in other sectors in the developing world through appropriate efficiency measures.[77]

Buildings offer enormous scope for energy savings, and perhaps the most widely understood ways of increasing energy efficiency are in the home and workplace. Buildings in the tropics are now commonly designed to avoid as much direct solar heating as possible by having very narrow east- and west-facing walls, but with long sides facing north and south and protected from the overhead sun by recessed windows or wide sills.

An important method of heating buildings is by hot water produced during electricity production and piped around whole districts, providing both heat and hot water. This extremely efficient use of fossil fuels demands a co-ordination of energy supply with local physical planning, which few countries are institutionally equipped to handle.[78] Where it has been successful, there has usually been local authority involvement in or control of regional energy-services boards, such as in Scandinavia and the USSR. Given the development of these or similar institutional arrangements, the cogeneration of heat and electricity could revolutionize the energy efficiency of buildings world-wide.

VII. ENERGY CONSERVATION MEASURES

There is general agreement that the efficiency gains achieved by some industrialized countries over the past 13 years were driven largely by higher energy prices, triggered by higher oil prices. Prior to the recent fall in oil prices, energy efficiency was growing at a rate of 2.0 per cent annually in some countries, having increased gradually year by year.[79]

It is doubtful whether such steady improvements can be maintained and extended if energy prices are held below the level needed to encourage the design and adoption of more energy-efficient homes, industrial processes, and transportation vehicles. The level required will vary greatly within and between countries, depending on a wide range of factors. But whatever it is, it should be maintained. In volatile energy markets, the question is how.

Nations intervene in the 'market price' of energy in a variety of ways. Domestic taxes (or subsidies) on electrical power rates, oil, gas, and other fuels are most common. They vary greatly between and even within countries where different states, provinces, and sometimes even municipalities have the right to add their own tax. Although taxes on energy have seldom been levied to encourage the design and adoption of efficiency measures, they can have that result if they cause energy prices to rise beyond a certain level—a level that varies greatly among jurisdictions.

Some nations also maintain higher-than-market prices on energy through duties on imported electricity, fuel, and fuel products. Others have negotiated bilateral pricing arrangements with oil and gas producers in which they stabilize prices for a period of time.

In most countries, the price of oil eventually determines the price of alternative fuels. Extreme fluctuations in oil prices, such as the world has experienced recently, endanger programmes to encourage conservation. Many positive energy developments world-wide that made sense with oil above $25 per barrel are harder to justify at lower prices. Investments in renewables, energy-efficient industrial processes, transport vehicles, and energy-services may be reduced. Most are needed to ease the transition to a safer and more sustainable energy future beyond this century. This goal requires a long, uninterrupted effort to succeed.

Given the importance of oil prices on international energy policy, the Commission recommends that new mechanisms for encouraging dialogue between consumers and producers be explored.

If the recent momentum behind annual gains in energy efficiency is to be maintained and extended, governments need to make it an explicit goal of their policies for energy pricing to consumers. Prices needed to encourage the adoption of energy-saving measures may be achieved by any of the above means or by other means. Although the Commission expresses no preference, 'conservation pricing' requires that governments take a long-term view in weighing the costs and benefits of the various measures. They need to operate over extended periods, dampening wild fluctuations in the price of primary energy, which can impair progress towards energy conservation.

VIII. CONCLUSION

It is clear that a low energy path is the best way towards a sustainable future. But given efficient and productive uses of primary energy, this need not mean a shortage of essential energy-services. Within the next 50 years, nations have the opportunity to produce the same levels of energy-services with as little as half the primary supply currently consumed. This requires profound structural changes in socio-economic and institutional arrangements and is an important challenge to global society.

More importantly, it will buy the time needed to mount major programmes on sustainable forms of renewable energy, and so begin the transition to a safer, more sustainable energy era. The development of renewable sources will depend in part on a rational approach to energy pricing to secure a stable matrix for such progress. Both the routine practice of efficient energy use and the development of renewables will help take pressure off traditional fuels, which are most needed to enable developing countries to realize their growth potential world-wide.

Energy is not so much a single product as a mix of products and services, a mix upon which the welfare of individuals, the sustainable development of nations, and the life-supporting capabilities of the global ecosystem depend. In the past, this mix has been allowed to flow together haphazardly, the proportions dictated by short-term pressures on and short-term goals of governments, institutions, and companies. Energy is too important for its development to continue in such a random manner. A safe, environmentally sound, and economically viable energy pathway that will sustain human progress into the distant future is clearly imperative. It is also possible. But it will require new dimensions of political will and institutional co-operation to achieve it.

Notes

The Commission accepts full responsibility for this chapter, but wishes to acknowledge that it draws on the report of its Advisory Panel on Energy. (See Annexe 2 for a list of members.)

1 World Bank, *World Development Report 1986* (New York: Oxford University Press, 1986).

2 British Petroleum Company, *BP Statistical Review of World Energy* (London: 1986).

3 Medium variant in Department of International Economic and Social Affairs, *World Population Prospects as Assessed in 1980*, Population Studies No.78 (Annex), and *Long Range Population Projections of the World and Major Regions 2025-2150, Five Variants as Assessed in 1980* (New York: UN, 1981).

4 For a useful comparison of various scenarios, see J. Goldemberg et al., 'An End-Use Oriented Global Energy Strategy', *Annual Review of Energy*, Vol. 10, 1985; and W. Keepin et al., 'Emissions of CO_2 into the Atmosphere', in B. Bolin et al. (eds.), *The Greenhouse Effect Climate Change and Ecosystems* (Chichester, UK: John Wiley & Sons, 1986).

5 U. Colombo and O. Bernadini, 'A Low Energy Growth Scenario and the Perspectives for Western Europe', Report for the Commission of the European Communities Panel on Low Energy Growth, 1979.

6 Goldemberg et al., 'Global Energy Strategy', op. cit.

7 A.B. Lovins et al., 'Energy Strategy for Low Climatic Risk', Report for the German Federal Environment Agency, 1981.

8 J.A. Edmonds et al., 'An Analysis of Possible Future Atmospheric Retention of Fossil Fuel CO_2', Report for US Department of Energy, DOE/OR/21400-1, Washington, DC, 1984.

9 J-R Frisch (ed.), *Energy 2000-2020: World Prospects and Regional Stresses*, World Energy Conference (London: Graham and Trotman, 1983).

10 Energy Systems Group of the International Institute for Applied Systems Analysis, *Energy in a Finite World—A Global Systems Analysis* (Cambridge, Mass.: Ballinger, 1981).

11 World Bank, *The Energy Transition in Developing Countries* (Washington, DC: 1983).

12 World Meteorological Organisation, *A Report of the International Conference on*

the *Assessment of the Role of Carbon Dioxide and of Other Greenhouse Gases in Climate Variations and Associated Impacts*, Villach, Austria, 9–15 October 1985, WMO No.661 (Geneva: WMO/ICSU/UNEP, 1986).

13 B.N. Lohani, 'Evaluation of Air Pollution Control Programmes and Strategies in Seven Asian Capital Cities', prepared for WCED, 1985; H. Weidner, 'Air Pollution Control Strategies and Policies in the Federal Republic of Germany', prepared for WCED, 1985; M. Hashimoto, 'National Air Quality Management Policy of Japan', prepared for WCED, 1985; CETESB, 'Air Pollution Control Programme and Strategies in Brazil—Sao Paulo and Cubatao Areas 1985', prepared for WCED, 1985.

14 National Research Council, *Acid Deposition: Long Term Trends* (Washington, DC: National Academy Press, 1985); L.P. Muniz and H. Leiverstad, 'Acidification Effects on Freshwater Fish', in D. Drablos and A. Tollan (eds.), *Ecological Impact of Acid Precipitation* (Oslo: SNSF, 1980); L. Hallbcken and C.O. Tamm, 'Changes in Soil Acidity from 1927 to 1982-4 in a Forest Area of South West Sweden', *Scandinavian Journal of Forest Research*, No. 1, pp. 219–32, 1986.

15 FAO, *Fuelwood Supplies in the Developing Countries*, Forestry Paper No.42 (Rome: 1983); Z. Mikdashi, 'Towards a New Petroleum Order', *Natural Resources Forum*, October 1986.

16 Edmonds et al., op. cit.

17 I.M. Torrens, 'Acid Rain and Air Pollution, A Problem of Industrialization', prepared for WCED, 1985.

18 Goldemberg et al., 'Global Energy Strategy', op. cit.

19 British Petroleum Company, op. cit.

20 WMO, *Report of International Conference*, op. cit.; I. Mintzer, 'Societal Responses to Global Warming', submitted to WCED Public Hearings, Oslo, 1985; F. K. Hare, 'The Relevance of Climate', submitted to WCED Public Hearings, Ottawa, 1986.

21 Lohani, op. cit.; Weidner, op. cit.; Hashimoto, op. cit.; CETESB, op. cit.

22 Torrens, op. cit.; F. Lixun and D. Zhao, 'Acid Rain in China', prepared for WCED, 1985; H. Rodhe, 'Acidification in Tropical Countries', prepared for WCED, 1985; G. T. Goodman, 'Acidification of the Environment, A Policy Ideas Paper', prepared for WCED, 1986.

23 Torrens, op. cit.

24 Bolin et al., op. cit.

25 WMO, *Report of International Conference*, op. cit.

26 Ibid.

27 Ibid.

28 Goldemberg et al., 'Global Energy Strategy', op. cit.

29 Mintzer, op. cit.

30 WMO, *Report of International Conference*, op. cit.

31 D.J. Rose et al., *Global Energy Futures and CO_2-Induced Climate Change*, MITEL Report 83-015 (Cambridge, Mass.: Massachusetts Institute of Technology, 1983); A.M. Perry et al., 'Energy Supply and Demand Implication of CO_2', *Energy*, Vol. 7, pp. 991–1004, 1982.

32 Bolin et al., op. cit.

33 G. Brasseur, 'The Endangered Ozone Layer: New Theories on Ozone Depletion', *Environment*, Vol. 29, No. 1, 1987.

34 National Research Council, op. cit.; Muniz and Leiverstad, op. cit.

35 OECD, *The State of the Environment* (Paris: 1985).

36 Muniz and Leiverstad, op. cit.

37 National Research Council, op. cit.

38 National Swedish Environmental Protection Board, *Air Pollution and Acidification* (Solna, Sweden: 1986).

39 J. Lehmhaus et al., 'Calculated and Observed Data for 1980 Compared at EMEP Measurement Stations', Norwegian Meteorological Institute, EMEP/MSC-W Report 1-86, 1986; C.B. Epstein and M. Oppenheimer, 'Empirical Relation Between Sulphur Dioxide Emissions and Acid Deposition Derived from Monthly Data', *Nature*, No. 323, pp. 245-47, 1985.

40 'Neuartige Waldschaden in der Bundersrepublik Deutschland', Das Bundesministerium fur Ernhrung, Landwirtschaft und Forsten, 1983; 'Waldschaden Sernebungen', Das Bundesministerium fur Ernhrung, Landwirtschaft und Forsten, 1985; S. Nilsson, 'Activities of Teams of Specialists: Implications of Air Pollution Damage to Forests for Roundwood Supply and Forest Products Markets: Study on Extent of Damage', TIM/R 124 Add.1 (Restricted), 1986.

41 S. Postel, 'Stabilizing Chemical Cycles' (after *Allgemeine Forst Zeitschrift*, Nos. 46 (1985) and 41 (1986)), in L.R. Brown et al., *State of the World 1987* (London: W.W. Norton, 1987).

42 T. Paces, 'Weathering Rates of Eneiss and Depletion of Exchangeable Cations in Soils Under Environmental Acidification', *Journal Ecological Society*, No. 143, pp. 673-77, 1986; T. Paces, 'Sources of Acidification in Central Europe Estimated from Elemental Budgets in Small Basins', *Nature*, No. 315, pp. 31-36, 1985.

43 Hallbäcken and Tamm, op. cit.

44 G. Tyler et al., 'Metaller i Skogsmark—Deposition och omsättning', SNV PM 1692, Solna, Sweden, 1983.

45 'Neuartige Waldschäden', 1983, op. cit; Paces, 'Weathering Rates', op. cit.

46 Rodhe, op. cit.

47 R. Eden et al., *Energy Economics* (New York: Cambridge University Press, 1981); Nuclear Energy Agency, *Projected Costs of Generating Electricity from Nuclear and Coal-Fired Power Stations for Commissioning in 1995* (Paris: OECD, 1986).

48 Nuclear Regulatory Commission, *Physical Processes in Reactor Meltdown Accidents, Appendix VIII to Reactor Safety Study* (WASH-1400) (Washington, DC: US Government Printing Office, 1975).

49 S. Islam and K. Lindgren, 'How many reactor accidents will there be?' *Nature*, No. 322, pp. 691-92, 1986; A.W.F. Edwards, 'How many reactor accidents?' *Nature*, No. 324, pp. 417-18, 1986.

50 F.L. Parker et al., *The Disposal of High Level Radioactive Waste - 1984, Vols. 1 & 2* (Stockholm: The Beijer Institute, 1984); F.L. Parker and R.E. Kasperson, *International Radwaste Policies* (Stockholm: The Beijer Institute, in press).

51 International Atomic Energy Agency, *Nuclear Power: Status and Trends, 1986 Edition* (Vienna: 1986).

52 'World List of Nuclear Power Plants', *Nuclear News*, August 1986.

53 *IAEA Bulletin*, Summer 1986.

54 C. Flavin, 'Reassessing Nuclear Power', in Brown et al., op. cit.; British Petroleum Company, op. cit.

55 G. Foley, 'Wood Fuel and Conventional Fuel Demands in the Developing World', *Ambio*, Vol. 14, No. 5, 1985.

56 FAO, *Fuelwood Supplies*, op. cit.; FAO/UNEP, *Tropical Forest Resources*, Forestry Paper No. 30 (Rome: 1982).

57 The Beijer Institute, *Energy, Environment and Development in Africa, Vols. 1-10* (Uppsala, Sweden: Scandinavian Institute of African Studies, 1984-87); 'Energy Needs in Developing Countries', *Ambio*, Vol. 14, 1985; E.N. Chidumayo, 'Fuelwood and Social Forestry', prepared for WCED, 1985; G.T. Goodman, 'Forest-Energy in Developing Countries: Problems and Challenges', International Union of Forest Research Organizations, *Proceedings*, Ljubljana, Yugoslavia, 1986.

58 FAO, *Fuelwood Supplies*, op. cit.

59 Beijer Institute, op. cit.; J. Bandyopadhyay, 'Rehabilitation of Upland Watersheds', prepared for WCED, 1986.

60 Beijer Institute, op. cit.

61 R. Overend, 'Bioenergy Conversion Process: A Brief State of the Art and Discussion of Environmental Implications', International Union of Forestry Research Organization, *Proceedings*, Ljubljana, Yugoslavia, 1986.

62 W. Fernandes and S. Kulkarni (eds.), *Towards a New Forest Policy: People's Rights and Environmental Needs* (New Delhi, India: Indian Social Institute, 1983); P.N. Bradley et al., 'Development Research and Energy Planning in Kenya', *Ambio*, Vol. 14, No. 4, 1985; R. Hosier, 'Household Energy Consumption in Rural Kenya', *Ambio*, Vol. 14, No. 4, 1985; R. Engelhard et al., 'The Paradox of Abundant On-Farm Woody Biomass, Yet Critical Fuelwood Shortage: A Case Study of Kakamega District (Kenya)', International Union of Forest Research Organization, *Proceedings*, Ljubljana, Yugoslavia, 1986.

63 D. Deudney and C. Flavin, *Renewable Energy: The Power to Choose* (London: W.W. Norton, 1983).

64 World Resources Institute/International Institute for Environment and Development, *World Resources 1987* (New York: Basic Books, in press).

65 Ibid.

66 Ibid.

67 Goldemberg et al., 'Global Energy Strategy', op. cit.; J. Goldemberg et al., 'Ethanol Fuel: A Use of Biomass Energy in Brazil, *Ambio*, Vol. 14, pp. 293-98, 1985; J. Goldemberg et al., 'Basic Needs and Much More, With One Kilowatt Per Capita', *Ambio*, Vol. 14, pp. 190-201, 1985.

68 WRI/IIED, op. cit.

69 N.J.D. Lucas, 'The Influence of Existing Institutions on the European Transition from Oil', *The European*, pp. 173-89, 1981.

70 OECD, op. cit.

71 E. Hirst et al., 'Recent Changes in US Energy Consumption, What Happened and Why?' in D.J. Rose (ed.), *Learning About Energy* (New York: Plenum Press, 1986).

72 H.S. Geller, 'The Potential for Electricity Conservation in Brazil', Companhia Energetica de Sao Paulo, Sao Paulo, Brazil, 1985.

73 World Bank, *Energy Transition in Developing Countries*, op. cit.

74 G. Leach et al., *Energy and Growth: A Comparison of Thirteen Industrialized and Developing Countries* (London: Butterworth, 1986).

75 MIT International Automobile Program, *The Future of the Automobile* (London: George Allen & Unwin, 1984).

76 FAO, *Agriculture Towards 2000* (Rome: 1981).

77 Ibid.

78 Lucas, op. cit.

79 OECD, op. cit.

8

INDUSTRY:
PRODUCING MORE WITH LESS

Industry is central to the economies of modern societies and an indispensable motor of growth. It is essential to developing countries, to widen their development base and meet growing needs. And though industrialized countries are said to be moving into a post-industrial, information-based era, this shift must be powered by a continuing flow of wealth from industry.[1]

Many essential human needs can be met only through goods and services provided by industry. The production of food requires increasing amounts of agrochemicals and machinery. Beyond this, the products of industry form the material basis of contemporary standards of living. Thus all nations require and rightly aspire to efficient industrial bases to meet changing needs.

Industry extracts materials from the natural resource base and inserts both products and pollution into the human environment. It has the power to enhance or degrade the environment; it invariably does both. (See Chapter 2 for a discussion of the concept of sustainable development within the context of industry and resource use.)

I. INDUSTRIAL GROWTH AND ITS IMPACT

As recently as 1950, the world manufactured only one-seventh of the goods it does today, and produced only one-third of the minerals. Industrial production grew most rapidly between 1950 and 1973, with a 7 per cent annual growth in manufacturing and a 5 per cent growth in mining. Since then growth rates have slowed, to about 3 per cent yearly between 1973 and 1985 in manufacturing and virtually zero growth in mining.[2]

That earlier, rapid growth in production was reflected in the rising importance of manufacturing in the economies of virtually all countries. By 1982, the relative share of value added to gross domestic product (GDP) by manufacturing (the 'manufacturing value added', or MVA) ranged from 19 per cent in developing countries as a whole

TABLE 8.1

Share of Manufacturing Value Added in GDP, by Economic Grouping and Income Group (per cent)

Group of Countries	1960	1970	1980	1982
Developing Countries	14.2	16.6	19.0	19.0
Low income	11.2	13.8	15.0	15.0
Lower-middle income	11.0	13.5	16.4	16.6
Intermediate income	10.6	14.4	17.1	17.6
Upper-middle income	19.4	21.6	24.1	23.3
High income	17.2	16.2	17.2	17.9
Developed Market Economies	25.6	28.3	27.9	27.1
Centrally Planned Economies*	32.0	42.4	50.5	50.8

* Figures refer to the share of manufacturing value added (estimated) in new material product. Data are at constant (1975) prices.

Source: UNIDO, *World Industry: A Statistical Review 1985* (Vienna: 1986).

to 27 per cent in industrialized market economies and 51 per cent of net material product in centrally planned economies. (See Table 8.1.) If the extractive industries are taken into account, the share is even higher.

The Changing Structure of World Industry

In recent years, the trend of the 1950s and 1960s has been reversed: Manufacturing has declined in importance relative to other sectors of the economy. In many countries, this decline has been in progress since 1973. It is most noticeable in the case of industrial market economies, but the share of MVA in gross domestic product has also declined in nearly half the 95 developing countries surveyed by the UN Industrial Development Organization (UNIDO).[3] This may reflect the growing interaction between industry and all fields of science and technology and the increasing integration of industry and services, as well as industry's ability to produce more with less.

The relative importance of industry as an employer has been declining for some time in developed countries. But the shift in jobs towards the service sector has accelerated sharply over the past 15 years with the increasing adoption of new processes and technologies. Economists continue to argue over whether the advent of an information-based economy will further depress employment in industry or will expand job opportunities overall.[4]

Most developing countries started at independence with virtually no modern industry. Then during the 1960s and 1970s their industrial production, employment, and trade consistently grew faster than these sectors in developed market economies. By 1984, developing countries accounted for 11.6 per cent of world MVA (still well short of the 'Lima target' of 25 per cent adopted by UNIDO in 1975). The centrally planned economies of Eastern Europe had raised their share of world MVA from 15.2 per cent in 1963 to 24.9 per cent in 1984.[5]

The international trade in manufactured goods, which has consistently grown faster than has world manufacturing output, is one of the factors underlying the changing geography of industrialization. Many developing nations, particularly newly industrialized countries (NICs), have shared in this growth and made spectacular progress in industrialization. Taking the Third World as a whole, exports of manufactured goods have grown steadily relative to primary exports, rising from 13.3 per cent of their total non-oil exports in 1960 to 54.7 per cent in 1982. (See Table 8.2.)

In general, developing-country industrial production is diversifying and moving into more capital-intensive areas such as metal products, chemicals, machinery, and equipment. And heavy industries, traditionally the most polluting, have been growing in relation to light industries. At the same time, the share of industries involved in food products, and to a lesser extent in textiles and clothing, has fallen significantly.

Environmental Decline and Response

Industry and its products have an impact on the natural resource base of civilization through the entire cycle of raw materials exploration and extraction, transformation into products, energy consumption, waste generation, and the use and disposal of products by consumers. These impacts may be positive, enhancing the quality of a resource or extending its uses. Or they may be negative, as a result of process and product pollution and of depletion or degradation of resources.

The negative environmental impacts of industrial activity were initially perceived as localized problems of air, water, and land pollution. Industrial expansion following the Second World War took place without much awareness of the environment and brought with it a rapid rise in pollution, symbolized by the Los Angeles smog; the proclaimed 'death' of Lake Erie; the progressive pollution of major rivers like the Meuse, Elbe, and Rhine; and chemical poisoning by mercury in Minamata. These problems have also been found in many parts of the Third World as industrial growth, urbanization, and the use of automobiles spread.[6]

TABLE 8.2

Composition of the Merchandise Trade of Developing Countries

Item	Exports				Imports			
	1960	1970	1980	1982	1960	1970	1980	1982
	(billions of dollars)							
Primary Commodities	25	45	452	369	11	17	166	166
Non-oil	17	27	107	93	8	12	79	73
Petroleum	8	18	345	277	3	5	87	92
Manufactured Goods	3	9	101	112	17	39	288	296
Total	27	55	553	481	28	56	454	462
Total non-oil	20	36	208	204	25	51	367	370
	(per cent)							
Primary Commodities Including Oil	90.4	82.6	81.8	76.8	38.8	30.1	36.6	35.9
Non-oil	62.3	49.2	19.4	19.2	28.4	21.7	17.5	15.9
Petroleum	28.1	33.4	62.4	57.5	10.4	8.4	19.1	20.0
Manufactured Goods	9.6	17.4	18.1	23.2	61.2	69.9	63.4	64.1
	Share in Non-oil Exports				Share in Non-oil Imports			
Primary Commodities (Non-oil)	86.7	73.9	51.6	45.3	32.7	23.7	21.6	19.8
Manufactured Goods	13.3	26.1	48.4	54.7	68.3	76.3	78.4	80.2

Source: UNIDO, *Industry in a Changing World* (New York: 1983). For 1982, WCED estimates based on UN, *1983 International Trade Statistics Yearbook, Vol. 1* (New York: 1985).

Public concern grew rapidly and forced a broad debate on environment conservation and economic growth. The possibility that the process of industrial growth would run into material resource constraints became an important theme in this debate. Although non-renewable resources are by definition exhaustible, recent assessments suggest that few minerals are likely to run out in the near future.

By the late 1960s, growing awareness and public concern led to

'I am one of the patients of air pollution. When Japanese economy grew very rapidly, my asthma deteriorated. I am 39 years old. I was hospitalized when I was 18 until I was 23 because of my severe asthma. I had no joy of life, no joie de vivre in those five years. I got a job and went to work but I cannot work as long a time as ordinary people. For the last 10 years I can hardly work. And when the law was enacted, the law concerning the abatement of pollution, it has given me compensation. That is my only income, from the compensation that this law provides. And if I should suffer another disease on top of asthma, I really don't know what to do.'

Yoshi Suzuki
Association of Patients of Pollution and Their Families
WCED Public Hearing, Tokyo, 27 Feb 1987

action by governments and industry in both industrial and some developing countries. Environmental protection and resource conservation policies and programmes were established, along with agencies to administer them. Initially policies focused on regulatory measures aimed at reducing emissions. Later a range of economic instruments were considered—taxation, pollution charges, and subsidies for pollution control equipment—but only a few countries introduced them. Expenditures rose, gradually at first, reaching 1.0 per cent and as high as 2.0 per cent of gross national product in some industrial countries by the late 1970s.

Industry also responded to these problems by developing new technologies and industrial processes designed to reduce pollution and other adverse environmental impacts. Expenditures on pollution control measures rose rapidly in some highly polluting industries; and corporations began to set up their own environmental policy and control units. Guidelines and codes of conduct were published covering safety of products and plant operations, trade practices, technology transfer, and international co-operation.[7] National and international industry associations have also developed guidelines and voluntary codes of practice.[8]

The results were mixed, but during the decade a number of industrial countries experienced a significant improvement in environmental quality. There was a considerable roll back in air pollution in many cities and water pollution in many lakes and rivers. Certain chemicals were controlled.

But these achievements were limited to some industrial countries. Taking the world as a whole, fertilizer run-off and sewage discharges into rivers, lakes, and coastal waters have increased, with resulting impacts on fishing, drinking-water supply, navigation, and scenic beauty. The water quality of most major rivers has not markedly improved over the years. It is, in fact, worsening in many of them, as it is in many smaller rivers. Industrialized countries still suffer from 'traditional' forms of air and land pollution. Levels of sulphur and nitrogen oxides, suspended particulates, and hydrocarbons remain high and in some cases have increased. Air pollution in parts of many Third World cities has risen to levels worse than anything witnessed in the industrial countries during the 1960s.[9]

It is becoming increasingly clear that the sources and causes of pollution are far more diffuse, complex, and interrelated—and the effects of pollution more widespread, cumulative, and chronic—than hitherto believed. Pollution problems that were once local are now regional or even global in scale. Contamination of soils, ground-water, and people by agrochemicals is widening and chemical pollution has spread to every corner of the planet. The incidence of major accidents involving toxic chemicals has grown. Discoveries of hazardous waste disposal sites—at Love Canal in the United States, for example, and at Lekkerkek in the Netherlands, Vac in Hungary, and Georgswerder in the Federal Republic of Germany—have drawn attention to another serious problem.

In the light of this and the growth trends projected through the next century, it is evident that measures to reduce, control, and prevent industrial pollution will need to be greatly strengthened. If they are not, pollution damage to human health could become intolerable in certain cities and threats to property and ecosystems will continue to grow. Fortunately, the past two decades of environmental action have provided governments and industry with the policy experience and the technological means to achieve more sustainable patterns of industrial development.

At the beginning of the 1970s, both governments and industry were deeply worried about the costs of proposed environmental measures. Some felt that they would depress investment, growth, jobs, competitiveness, and trade, while driving up inflation. Such fears proved misplaced. A 1984 survey by the Organisation for Economic Co-operation and Development (OECD) of assessments undertaken in a number of industrial countries concluded that expenditures on environmental measures over the past two decades had a positive short-term effect on growth and employment as the increased demand they generated raised the output of economies operating at less than full capacity. The benefits, including health, property, and ecosystem

It is absolutely clear now that the present scale and rate of development of the productive forces require a different approach to the questions connected with environmental protection and rational utilization of natural resources. This is a task of immense economic and social significance. For actually it is a question of people's health and a caring approach to the national wealth of each country. Moreover, it is also a question of the future. And on the solution depends the conditions in which the coming generations will live.

A. P. Semyonov
Central Council of Trade Unions
WCED Public Hearing, Moscow, 8 Dec 1986

damages avoided, have been significant. More important, these benefits have generally exceeded costs.[10]

Costs and benefits have naturally varied among industries. One method of estimating the cost of pollution abatement in industry compares expenditures on new plants and equipment that have pollution control facilities to hypothetical expenditures on new plants without such features. Studies using this comparison in the United States found that pollution abatement expenditures for new plant and equipment for all manufacturing industries in that country in 1984 amounted to $4.53 billion, or 3.3 per cent of total new expenditures. The chemical industry spent $580 million (3.8 per cent) on such equipment.[11] Similar studies in the Japanese steel industry found that new investment in pollution control equipment reached as high as 21.3 per cent of total investment in 1976 and even today remains around 5 per cent.[12]

Firms involved in food processing, iron and steel, non-ferrous metals, automobiles, pulp and paper, chemicals, and electric power generation—all major polluters—have borne a high proportion of the total pollution control investment by industry. Such costs provided a strong incentive for many of these industries to develop a broad range of new processes and cleaner and more efficient products and technologies. In fact, some firms that a decade ago established teams to research and develop innovative technologies to meet new environmental standards are today among the most competitive in their fields, nationally and internationally.

Waste recycling and reuse have become accepted practices in many industrial sectors. In some industrialized countries technologies to scrub sulphur and nitrogen compounds from smokestack gases made remarkable advances in a relatively short time. New combustion techniques simultaneously raise combustion efficiency and reduce pollutant emissions.[13] Innovative products and process technologies are also currently under development that promise energy- and resource-efficient modes of production, reducing pollution and minimizing risks of health hazards and accidents.

Pollution control has become a thriving branch of industry in its own right in several industrialized countries. High-pollution industries such as iron and steel, other metals, chemicals, and energy production have often led in expanding into the fields of pollution control equipment, detoxification and waste disposal technology, measurement instruments, and monitoring systems. Not only have these industries become more efficient and competitive, but many have also found new opportunities for investment, sales, and exports. Looking to the future, a growing market for pollution control systems, equipment, and services is expected in practically all industrialized countries, including NICs.

II. SUSTAINABLE INDUSTRIAL DEVELOPMENT IN A GLOBAL CONTEXT

If industrial development is to be sustainable over the long term, it will have to change radically in terms of the quality of that development, particularly in industrialized countries. But this is not to suggest that industrialization has reached a quantitative limit, particularly in developing countries. Even today, according to UNIDO, world industrial output would have to be increased by a factor of 2.6 if consumption of manufactured goods in developing countries were to be raised to current industrial country levels.[14] Given expected population growth, a five- to tenfold increase in world industrial output can be anticipated by the time world population stabilizes sometime in the next century. Such growth has serious implications for the future of the world's ecosystems and its natural resource base.

In general, industries and industrial operations should be encouraged that are more efficient in terms of resource use, that generate less pollution and waste, that are based on the use of renewable rather than non-renewable resources, and that minimize irreversible adverse impacts on human health and the environment.

Industrialization in the Third World

Growing populations and high proportions of young people in the Third World are leading to large increases in the labour force.

Agriculture cannot absorb them. Industry must provide these expanding societies not only with employment but with products and services. They will experience massive increases in the production of basic consumer goods and a concomitant build-up of industrial infrastructure—iron and steel, paper, chemicals, building materials, and transportation. All this implies considerable increases in energy and raw material use, industrial hazards and wastes, accidents, and resource depletion.

The problems and prospects for industrial development vary among the countries of the Third World, which differ greatly in size and resources. There are some large countries with abundant natural resources and a substantial domestic market that provide a base for wide-ranging industrial development. Smaller, resource-rich countries are trying to build up an export-oriented processing industry. Several developing countries have based much of their industrial development on export industries in garments, consumer electronics, and light engineering. In many countries, however, industrial development is restricted to a few consumer-goods industries that cater to relatively small domestic markets.

The developing countries' share in world production of iron and steel rose from 3.6 per cent in 1955 to 17.3 per cent in 1984, when four countries—Brazil, China, India, and the Republic of Korea—produced more than 10 million tons of steel each, as much as in many medium-sized industrialized countries.[15] At the same time that this industry is contracting in many developed countries, it is expected to expand by 38 million tons between 1982 and 1990 in the developing world. Latin America is projected to account for 41 per cent of this rise, Southeast Asia for 36 per cent, the Middle East for 20 per cent, and Africa for 1.3 per cent.[16]

Many developing countries still depend heavily on their exports of minerals and other commodities, mostly in unprocessed or only intermediately processed forms. In the case of several major minerals such as aluminium and nickel, a few transnational corporations control the whole industry, from mining through final processing.[17] Some countries have been moderately successful in increasing the share of refined products in their exports. Yet most of these 'manufactured' goods are processed further in the industrial country that imports them. Thus in 1980, only 39 per cent of all Third World exports of manufactured goods were ready for final use, while 43 per cent of its total exports were unprocessed.[18] This ratio should improve as developing nations move into the further stages of processing. These improvements should be speeded up.

'Our ecological movement is not against industry, but we must think of the social function of industries and that pollution and progress are not the same thing. Pollution is not the synonym of progress and therefore time has come for new development concepts to come up. Pollution should not be a synonym of progress because we know that pollution is controlled and when you do not control pollution you are transferring this pollution to the community of the whole.'

Fabio Feldman
Lawyer for Victims of Cubatao
WCED Public Hearing, Sao Paulo, 28–29 Oct 1985

The expected growth in basic industries foreshadows rapid increases in pollution and resource degradation unless developing countries take great care to control pollution and waste, to increase recycling and reuse, and to minimize hazardous wastes. These countries do not have the resources to industrialize now and repair the damage later; nor will they have the time, given the rapid pace of technological progress. They can profit from the improvements in resource and environmental management being achieved in industrialized countries, and so avoid the need for expensive clean-ups. Such technologies can also help them reduce ultimate costs and stretch scarce resources. And they can learn from the mistakes of developed countries.

Economies of scale are no longer always the primary consideration. New technologies in communications, information, and process control allow the establishment of small-scale, decentralized, widely dispersed industries, thus reducing levels of pollution and other impacts on the local environment. There may, however, be trade-offs to be made: Small-scale raw material processing, for example, is often labour-intensive and widely dispersed but intensive in the use of energy. Such dispersed industries could relieve big cities of some of their population and pollution pressures. They could provide non-farming jobs in the countryside, produce consumer goods that cater to local markets, and help spread environmentally sound technologies.

Use of Energy and Raw Materials

Industrial growth is widely seen as inevitably accompanied by corresponding increases in energy and raw material consumption. In the past two decades, however, this pattern appears to have fundamentally changed. As growth has continued in the developed market economies, the demand for many basic materials, including energy and water, has levelled off; in some cases, it has actually declined in absolute terms.

Energy consumption per unit of GDP in OECD countries has been dropping at a rate of 1–3 per cent every year since the late 1960s. Between 1973 and 1983, these nations improved energy efficiency by 1.7 per cent annually.[19] Industrial water consumption per unit of production has also declined. Older pulp and paper mills typically used about 180 cubic metres of water per ton of pulp; those built during the 1970s, however, used only 70. With advanced techniques that keep water circulating within a closed system, and with proper staff training, use rates could be lowered to 20–30 cubic metres per ton of pulp.[20]

An integrated steel mill uses about 80–200 tons of water for every ton of crude steel. However, since only about 3 tons of water per ton of crude steel are lost, mostly by evaporation, recycling can greatly reduce consumption.[21] Closed water circulation systems are not unique to the steel industry or to developed market economies. Between 1975 and 1980, the chemical industry's output in the USSR increased by 76 per cent, but the total consumption of fresh water remained at the 1975 level.[22] And between 1981 and 1986, Soviet industrial output increased by 25 per cent but industrial water consumption remained constant.[23]

Declines in consumption of other raw materials began much earlier. In fact, the amount of raw materials needed for a given unit of economic output has been dropping over this entire century, except in wartime, for practically all non-agricultural commodities.[24] A recent study of consumption trends of seven basic materials in the United States bears this out,[25] as do studies in Japan. Japan used only 60 per cent as much raw materials for every unit of industrial production in 1984 as it used in 1973.[26] These efficiency trends do not result from a decline in manufacturing in favour of service industries, for over these periods the output of the manufacturing sector continued to grow. The productivity and efficiency of resource use are constantly improving, and industrial production is steadily switching away from heavily material-intensive products and processes.

The two oil price hikes of the 1970s shocked many countries into saving money by promoting conservation measures, switching to other fuels, and raising overall energy efficiency. These events demonstrated the importance of energy pricing policies that take into account their current stock, depletion rates, availability of substitutes, and any unavoidable environmental damage associated with their extraction or processing. (See Chapter 7.) They also indicated the potential of similar pricing policies for other raw materials.

Some have referred to these processes as the increasing 'dematerialization' of society and the world economy. Yet even the most industrially advanced economies still depend on a continued supply of basic manufactured goods. Whether made domestically or imported, their production will continue to require large amounts of raw materials and energy, even if developing countries progress rapidly in the adoption of resource-efficient technologies. To sustain production momentum on a global level, therefore, policies that inject resource efficiency considerations into economic, trade, and other related policy domains are urgently needed, particularly in industrial countries, along with strict observance of environmental norms, regulations, and standards.

Promises and Risks of New Technologies

Technology will continue to change the social, cultural, and economic fabric of nations and the world community. With careful management, new and emerging technologies offer enormous opportunities for raising productivity and living standards, for improving health, and for conserving the natural resource base. Many will also bring new hazards, requiring an improved capacity for risk assessment and risk management. (See Chapter 12.)

Information technology based chiefly on advances in microelectronics and computer science is of particular importance. Coupled with rapidly advancing means of communication, it can help improve the productivity, energy and resource efficiency, and organizational structure of industry.

New materials such as fine ceramics, rare metals and metal alloys, high-performance plastics, and new composites allow more flexible approaches to production. They also contribute to energy and resource conservation, as in general they require less energy to manufacture and, being lighter, contain less matter than conventional materials.

Biotechnology will have major implications for the environment. The products of genetic engineering could dramatically improve human and animal health. Researchers are finding new drugs, new therapies, and new ways of controlling disease vectors. Energy derived from plants could increasingly substitute for non-renewable fossil fuels. New high-yield crop varieties and those resistant to unfavourable weather conditions and pests could revolutionize agriculture. Integrated pest management will become more common.

‛I think there must be a persistent push, a persistent effort towards establishing some kind of international code for areas of technologies having high environmental risks. At the moment not many in Indonesia would be considered as very knowledgeable industries. We need also this kind of thing in order to guarantee some kind of minimum safety for countries like ours to develop within the context of international economic relations.’

Speaker from the floor
WCED Public Hearing, Jakarta, 26 March 1985

Biotechnology could also yield cleaner and more efficient alternatives to many wasteful processes and polluting products. New techniques to treat solid and liquid wastes could help solve the pressing problem of hazardous waste disposal.[27]

Advances in space technology, now the almost exclusive domain of industrial countries, also hold promise for the Third World, even for agriculture-based economies. Weather forecasting services provided through a satellite and communications network can help farmers in deciding when to plant, water, fertilize, and harvest crops. Remote sensing and satellite imagery could facilitate optimal use of the Earth's resources, permitting the monitoring and assessment of long-term trends in climatic change, marine pollution, soil erosion rates, and plant cover. (See Chapter 10.)

These new technologies and the Green Revolution blur the traditional distinctions between agriculture, industry, and services. And they make it possible for developments in one sector to more radically affect those in another. Agriculture has become virtually an 'industry' in developed countries. Agriculture-related services—especially for regional weather forecasting, storage, and transport—are becoming ever more important. New techniques of tissue culture and genetic engineering could soon generate plant strains able to fix nitrogen from the air, a development that would drastically affect the fertilizer industry, but that would also reduce the threat of pollution by agrochemicals.

The chemical and energy industries are moving increasingly into the seeds business, providing new seeds that meet specific local conditions and requirements—but that may also need specific fertilizers and pesticides. Here research and development, production, and marketing need to be carefully guided so as not to make the world even more dependent on a few crop varieties—or on the products of a few large transnationals.

Yet new technologies are not all intrinsically benign, nor will they have only positive impacts on the environment. The large-scale production and widespread use of new materials, for example, may create hitherto unknown health hazards (such as the use of gallium arsenate in the microchip industry.)[28] Riskier research might be carried out and products manufactured where safeguards are weak or where people are unaware of the dangers. The need for caution in introducing a new technology is reinforced by the experience of the Green Revolution, which, despite formidable achievements, raises concerns over dependence on relatively few crop strains and large doses of agrochemicals. New life forms produced by genetic engineering should be carefully tested and assessed for their potential impact on health and on the maintenance of genetic diversity and ecological balance before they are introduced to the market, and thus to the environment.[29]

III. STRATEGIES FOR SUSTAINABLE INDUSTRIAL DEVELOPMENT

Resource and environmental considerations must be integrated into the industrial planning and decision-making processes of government and industry. This will allow a steady reduction in the energy and resource content of future growth by increasing the efficiency of resource use, reducing waste, and encouraging resource recovery and recycling.

Establish Environmental Goals, Regulations, Incentives, and Standards

In dealing with industrial pollution and resource degradation, it is essential that industry, government, and the public have clear benchmarks. Where the workforce and financial resources permit, national governments should establish clear environmental goals and enforce environmental laws, regulations, incentives, and standards on industrial enterprises. In formulating such policies, they should give priority to public health problems associated with industrial pollution and hazardous wastes. And they must improve their environmental statistics and data base relating to industrial activities.

The regulations and standards should govern such matters as air and water pollution, waste management, occupational health and safety of workers, energy and resource efficiency of products or processes, and the manufacture, marketing, use, transport, and disposal of toxic substances. This should normally be done at the national level, with local governments being empowered to exceed, but not to lower, national norms. In preparing environmental regulations, it is important that flexible systems are adopted without specifying a particular process or technology and recognizing that governments differ greatly in their capacity to formulate legal standards and enforce them.

Regulations to control the impacts of industrial activity across national boundaries and on the international commons are also needed. Existing or future international conventions dealing with transfrontier pollution or management of shared natural resources should enshrine certain key principles:

- the responsibility of every state not to harm the health and environment of other nations,
- liability and compensation for any damage caused by transfrontier pollution, and
- equal right of access to remedial measures by all parties concerned.

Make More Effective Use of Economic Instruments

Pollution is a form of waste, and a symptom of inefficiency in industrial production. When industries recognize pollution as a cost, they are sometimes motivated to make investments in improved products and processes to increase efficiency and hence to reduce the pollution and waste they generate, particularly when there are economic incentives to do so. It largely depends on whether such investments will increase their economic performance.

But there are limits to what society can expect industry operating in competition with other industries to do voluntarily. Regulations imposing uniform performance standards are essential to ensure that industry makes the investments necessary to reduce pollution and waste and to enable them to compete on an equal footing.

Air and water have traditionally been regarded as 'free goods', but the enormous costs to society of past and present pollution show that they are not free. The environmental costs of economic activity are not encountered until the assimilative capacity of the environment has been exceeded. Beyond that point, they cannot be avoided. They will be paid. The policy question is how and by whom they will be paid, not whether. Basically, there are only two ways. The costs can be 'externalized'—that is, transferred to various segments of the community in the form of damage costs to human health, property, and ecosystems. Or they can 'internalized'—paid by the enterprise.

We move towards attacking the sources and not the effects. But we also meet environmental questions in our markets, among our own employees and in our local environment. This definitely provides experiences that underline the need for a more complete and comprehensive thinking about the systems of which environment becomes an integral part. We also, as industry, meet the problems of international relations and environment, unfortunately very often in the way of hidden trade barriers or difficulties in co-operation between authorities.

Rolf Marstrander
Director, Environment Affairs, Norsk Hydro
WCED Public Hearing, Oslo, 24–25 June 1985

The enterprise may invest in measures to prevent the damages and, if the market for its product allows, pass the costs along to the consumer. Or it may invest in measures to restore unavoidable damage—replanting forests, restocking fish, rehabilitating land after mining. Or it may compensate victims of health and property damage. In these cases, too, the costs may be passed on to the consumer.

Enterprises may be encouraged to invest in preventive, restorative, or compensatory measures with subsidies of various kinds. Indeed, in most industrialized and many developing countries, subsidies are a common way of encouraging companies to invest in measures needed to prevent external damage. But in this case, of course, it is the taxpayer who pays, rather than the consumer of the product. Moreover, if the subsidies are large and paid to industries operating in an international market, they can lead to trade distortions and should be avoided.

In 1972, the member countries of OECD agreed to base their environmental policies on a Polluter Pays Principle (PPP).[30] Essentially an economic efficiency measure, PPP is intended to encourage industries to internalize environmental costs and reflect them in the prices of products. At the same time, state regulations in Council for Mutual Economic Assistance countries are carried out through government bodies that allow environmental concerns to be taken into account.

In the case of OECD, the guidelines on PPP were intended to discourage subsidies that could lead to distortions in trade. Countries agreed to phase out the use of subsidies over varying periods of time. (See Chapter 3 for the application of PPP to international trade and investment.)

Incentives to reduce pollution can be enhanced by other measures.

Energy and water pricing policies, for example, can push industries to consume less. Product redesign and technological innovations leading to safer products, more efficient processes, and recycling of raw materials can also be promoted by a more effective, integrated use of economic incentives and disincentives, such as investment tax breaks, low-interest loans, depreciation allowances, pollution or waste charges, and non-compliance fees.

Sometimes the way in which other policy objectives are promoted unintentionally reduces the effectiveness of environmental programmes. For example, subsidies on raw materials or water supply or energy to promote the development of industry in remote areas may well dilute the pressure to conserve resources. Governments should examine whether existing economic policies, instruments, or subsidies provided to various industry-based programmes and projects contribute effectively to the promotion of environmentally sound and resource-efficient practices.

Broaden Environmental Assessments

An increasing number of countries require that certain major investments be subject to an environmental impact assessment. A broader environmental assessment should be applied not only to products and projects, but also to policies and programmes, especially major macroeconomic, finance, and sectoral policies that induce significant impacts on the environment.

Many developing countries, particularly in Asia and Latin America, have adopted systems for environmental impact assessment. But the lack of institutional capacity and skilled personnel mean that these are often conducted by outside consultants, without quality checks. In some cases, government authorities would benefit from a second opinion on the environmental documentation they receive. Interested governments should create an independent international assessment body to help developing countries, upon request, evaluate the environmental impact and sustainability of planned development projects.

Encourage Action by Industry

Industry's response to pollution and resource degradation has not been and should not be limited to compliance with regulations. It should accept a broad sense of social responsibility and ensure an awareness of environmental considerations at all levels. Towards this end, all industrial enterprises, trade associations, and labour unions should establish company-wide or industry-wide policies concerning resource and environmental management, including compliance with the laws and requirements of the country in which they operate.

International trade associations play a major role in setting standards and disseminating information, which must be significantly expanded. They should establish and make widely available sectoral guidelines for assessing the sustainability and potential hazards of new facilities, for developing accident contingency plans, and for selecting pollution control or waste treatment technologies. Such key industry associations as the International Chamber of Commerce and the European Council of Chemical Manufacturers' Federation that have taken important and encouraging leadership roles in dealing with environmental issues should now take a lead in addressing the broader concerns inherent in sustainable development.

With limited resources at their disposal, small and medium-sized industries often find themselves unable to afford the changes necessary to meet environmental regulations and product controls. Small-scale businesses such as metal working, machine tools, printing, and tanning and dying are frequently among the worst offenders of environmental regulations in any country. New technologies, especially micro-electronics, already allow small industries inexpensive means to control an entire production process. Energy-saving biological systems may be well suited to the needs of small and medium-sized industries for pollution control or waste disposal.

Small and medium-scale enterprises, constituting the largest segment of industry in most nations, need information and may in some cases require financial and technical assistance from the public sector. Management and worker training can help them incorporate cleaner technologies and environmental planning into work patterns. Governments should encourage co-operative efforts among smaller firms—in joint research and development on environmental issues, for example, or joint use of pollution control or waste treatment facilities.

Increase Capacity to Deal with Industrial Hazards

Chemical products have greatly improved health and life expectancies; increased agricultural production; raised comfort, convenience, and the general quality of life; and expanded economic opportunities. The chemical industry is also one of the most dynamic sectors in most countries, including many developing ones. Yet this industry, together with its products, can have a particularly severe impact on the environment. It has given rise to a host of new problems both of product and process pollution. It continues to generate an increasingly wider range of products and wastes whose effects, especially long-term ones, on human health and the environment are not precisely known. Major accidents have taken place, and the safety record of the industry has been challenged in recent years.

In a world more and more dependent on chemical products and highly complex large-scale technologies, accidents with catastrophic consequences are likely to increase. Some of the heavy metals and non-metallic minerals, such as asbestos, also pose serious hazards to health and the environment. Various hazardous products and processes are already built into current systems of production and the technological structure of contemporary society, and it will be a long time before these can be replaced with less dangerous, inherently safer technologies and systems. Some highly toxic chemicals that are known to cause cancer and birth defects and have long-term genetic effects are already in the environment in significant concentrations, and may take decades to be diffused.

Chemicals

Chemicals represent about 10 per cent of total world trade in terms of value.[31] Some 70,000–80,000 chemicals are now on the market—and hence in the environment.[32] The figure is only an informed estimate because no complete inventory has been done. Some 1,000–2,000 new chemicals enter the commercial market each year, many without adequate prior testing or evaluation of effects.

According to a US National Research Council sample of 65,725 chemicals in common use, data required for complete health hazard evaluations were available for only 10 per cent of pesticides and 18 per cent of drugs. No toxicity data existed for nearly 80 per cent of the chemicals used in commercial products and processes inventoried under the Toxic Substances Control Act.[33] This situation is now beginning to change as governments move gradually from a system of post-market testing to one of pre-market testing of all new chemicals.

By 1986, more than 500 chemicals and chemical products had been banned altogether or had their uses severely restricted in the country of origin.[34] In addition, an unknown number of chemicals are withdrawn from clearance processes every year in the light of control agency concerns, or are never submitted to national control agencies for clearance. Some of these end up on the export market.

In industrial countries, in an increasingly interdependent and effective system, chemical control agencies share test results and notify

‘*The most explosive development in the establishment of chemical and pollutive industry has come in developing countries. This is an outright danger. The last accidents are but a few of those that may come. However, we recognize that considerable responsibility rests on the trade union movement in the individual countries in pressing for influence on authorities and managements to avoid both such accidents and investments from companies that do not follow acceptable standards.*

Technology development has improved environment in the industrial parts of the world. The new production and information systems make it more difficult, then, for the developing countries to use cheap labour as a means to attract industry to their countries. The future for these countries does not look very bright, unless the international society takes it upon itself to affect a sharing of production technology and resources. This is politically difficult indeed.’

Juul Bjerke
International Confederation of Free Trade Unions
WCED Public Hearing, Oslo, 24–25 June 1985

each other of new restrictions on chemicals. A ban or restriction in one country is thus often quickly followed by a review and appropriate action in the others.

Importing developing countries do not, as a rule, share in this system. Recently, some industrial countries undertook to require their industry to provide a one-time notification to importing countries of chemicals that they have formally banned or severely restricted. They agreed to provide prior notification of the proposed export/import of such chemicals and they also agreed to provide the importing country with the information that led them to ban or restrict the chemical, if it is requested. While the intent behind this system is laudable, it is difficult to see how it can work for importing countries that have no control institutions to receive the notification or professional capacity to assess the information.

Third World importers have no way to effectively control trade in chemicals that have been banned or severely restricted in exporting countries. Thus these countries badly need the infrastructure to assess the risks associated with chemical use. In view of the seriousness of this situation, the Commission recommends that all governments, particularly those of the major chemical-producing countries, should:

- undertake that no new chemicals be placed on international markets until the health and environmental impacts have been tested and assessed;

- reinforce on-going efforts to obtain international agreement on the selection of existing chemicals for priority testing, on criteria and procedures for their assessment, and on a system for international sharing of the tasks and the resources required;
- strictly regulate the export to developing countries of those chemicals for which authorization for domestic sale has not been sought or given, by extending requirements for prior notification and information exchange to them; and
- support the establishment in existing regional organizations of units qualified to receive such prior notification and information, to assess it and to advise governments in the region on the risks associated with the use of these chemicals, in order to permit individual governments to weigh these risks against benefits they may perceive from importation of the chemicals.

Consumer awareness should be increased. Governments should encourage the establishment of information centres on chemical products used by consumers and strengthen the international networks of information exchange, assessment, and data banks now evolving in the UN and elsewhere.[35] Another essential step is the adoption and enforcement of regulations on the packaging and labelling of chemicals whose use may be potentially harmful, to ensure that clear directions are provided in common local languages. Consumer unions and other non-governmental organizations should take the lead in collecting and distributing comparative risk information on ingredients in consumer products such as cleaning agents and pesticides.

The chemical producer and user industries, as the source of the risks associated with chemicals and as the greatest beneficiary of their use, should bear the responsibility for ensuring (and the liability for not ensuring) that their products meet the highest standards of safety, have the fewest adverse side effects on health and the environment, and are handled with appropriate care by workers and users. This will require the fullest possible disclosure of information about the properties and production processes of chemical substances and their comparative risks, not only to the regulatory authorities but also to the workers, consumers, and residents of the community in which a chemical industry operates.

Hazardous Wastes

Industrialized countries generate about 90 per cent of the world's hazardous wastes. Although all estimates have a wide margin of error, given considerable differences in definition of 'hazardous waste', in 1984 some 325 million to 375 million tons were generated world-wide,[36] around 5 million tons of which were in the newly industrialized and developing areas of the world.[37]

In OECD member countries alone, thousands of waste disposal sites exist, many of which are likely to require some form of remedial action. Clean-up is expensive: Estimates include $10 billion for the Federal Republic of Germany, more than $1.5 billion for the Netherlands, $20–100 billion for the United States, and at least $60 million for Denmark (in 1986 dollars).[38] A large number of potentially hazardous sites may also exist in concentrated industrial-urban areas in centrally planned economies as well as in developing countries. Some form of government intervention is required through regulatory action or financial support.

Waste management in developing countries suffers from a variety of problems. Frequent and heavy rains in the tropics, for instance, leach wastes into the soils under landfills or even cause them to overflow. With little or no pretreatment of wastes, this could contaminate water supplies or cause local people to be directly exposed to the wastes. Land-filling generally occurs close to industrial states that are surrounded by poor neighbourhoods or shanty towns.[39] These dangers point up the need for land use planning in developing countries, and the more urgent need to actually implement and enforce such plans.

The overriding policy objective must be to reduce the amount of waste generated and to transform an increasing amount into resources for use and reuse. This will reduce the volume that otherwise must be treated or disposed of through incineration, land disposal, or dumping at sea. This is first and foremost a problem of industrialized countries. But it is also a problem in NICs and developing countries, where rapid industrialization is bringing the same severe problems of hazardous waste management.

The amount of wastes crossing national frontiers is increasing and is likely to continue to do so. Between 1982 and 1983, wastes transported in Western Europe for disposal in another country virtually doubled, reaching some 250,000–425,000 tons (1–2 per cent of the total hazardous wastes generated).[40] This increase may be attributed partly to the availability of relatively low-cost, legal, land-based disposal facilities in some countries. For example, about 4,000 shipments of hazardous wastes went from the Netherlands to the German Democratic Republic in 1984. And the Federal Republic of Germany sent about 20,000 shipments to the German Democratic Republic the preceding year. International transport of wastes meant for disposal at sea, either by incineration or dumping, amounted to

> ❝*In industry, we feel it must now be made mandatory for any firm that is potentially polluting nature through liquid gas or particle emissions to enrol their staff in short but instructive courses of environmental education. Too often firms pollute not just through accident or design but through gross ignorance by the labour involved of the destructive effect on the environment.*❞
>
> Donald Aubrey
> *Society to Overcome Pollution*
> WCED Public Hearing, Ottawa, 26–27 May 1986

about 1.8 million tons in 1983.[41] Small and poor countries are especially vulnerable to offshore dumping, as has occurred in the waters of the Pacific and the Caribbean.

Some countries have recently proposed what amounts to a commodity trade in hazardous (including radioactive) wastes. Strengthened international co-operation in this area is vitally important, and several international bodies have taken up the matter.[42] An international agreement currently being developed by OECD is to be based on three important principles: equally strict controls on shipments to non-member countries; prior notification to and consent from the country of final destination, whether member or non-member country; and a guarantee of existence of adequate disposal facilities in the recipient country. The UN Environment Programme has drawn up extensive draft guidelines, but as of now there is no effective mechanism either to monitor or to control hazardous waste trade and dumping.[43] Governments and international organizations must more actively support efforts to achieve an effective international regime to control the transfrontier movement of hazardous wastes.

Industrial Accidents

Accidents involving toxic chemicals and radioactive materials can occur in plants in any region. According to a survey carried out by the US Environmental Protection Agency, 6,928 accidents of varying severity occurred at US plants between 1980 and 1985—an average of five a day.[44]

In 1984, liquid gas storage tanks exploded in Mexico City, killing 1,000 people and leaving thousands more homeless. Only months after the Bhopal tragedy in India, which killed over 2,000 people and injured 200,000 more, an accident at a plant in West Virginia in the United States operated by the parent company of the Bhopal facility resulted in emergency evacuation of residents and some health problems. The accidental release in 1976 of the highly toxic and mutagenic chemical dioxin at Seveso, Italy, and the ensuing saga of drums of contaminated soil being passed around Europe, also showed that in industrial countries regulations can be evaded and minimum safety standards breached.

In early November 1986, a fire at a warehouse of a chemicals manufacturer in Basel, Switzerland, sent toxic fumes into France and the Federal Republic of Germany and released toxic chemicals into the Rhine, causing massive fish kills and affecting the vital water supply in countries downstream, all the way to the Netherlands. Scientists investigating the Rhine agreed that it could be years before the damaged riverine ecosystems would return to their former status.[45]

Thus incidents at Mexico City, Bhopal, Chernobyl, and Basel—all occurring within the short lifetime of this Commission—raised public concern about industrial disasters. They also demonstrated the likelihood of significant increases in the frequency and magnitude of industrial accidents with catastrophic consequences.

These events point to the need to strengthen national capabilities and the framework for bilateral and regional co-operation. National and local governments should:

- survey hazardous industrial operations and adopt and enforce regulations or guidelines on the safe operation of industrial plants and on the transport, handling, and disposal of hazardous materials;
- adopt land use policies or regional development plans that would require or provide incentives to industries that have a high pollution or accident potential to locate away from population centres, and that would discourage people from moving close to plants and waste disposal sites;
- ensure that plant workers are provided with full information about the products and technologies they handle, and are given adequate training in safe operational procedures and emergency preparedness; and
- involve local governments and community residents in major siting decisions and emergency preparedness planning.

Increasingly, the consequences of accidents may seriously affect neighbouring countries. Nations should enter into arrangements with other nations that could be seriously affected by an accident in hazardous facilities located on its territory, under which they would agree to:

- notify each other of the location and essential characteristics of existing hazardous installations, an accident in which could spill

over and affect lives, property, and ecosystems in the other;
- prepare contingency plans covering potential accidents in these installations;
- provide prompt alert, full information, and mutual assistance in case of accidents;
- establish criteria for selection of sites for new hazardous facilities, which would then be subject to the above; and
- establish standards for the liability and compensation for any damage caused by transfrontier pollution.

Industrial accidents and their consequences are to a large extent unpredictable. In order to better identify risks, governments, international organizations, and industry itself should promote further development of technology/risk assessment methodologies, establish data banks on such assessments conducted, and make them easily available to all countries.

Strengthen International Efforts to Help Developing Countries

Pollution-intensive, resource-based industries are growing fastest in developing countries. These governments will thus have to substantially strengthen their environmental and resource management capabilities. Even where policies, laws, and regulations on the environment exist, they may not be consistently enforced. Many developing nations have begun to build up their educational and scientific infrastructure, but their technical and institutional capacity for making the most of imported or new technologies remains small. Some countries thus continue to depend on outside technical and managerial skills for the maintenance of industrial operations. For lack of capital, they often find that a new industry can only be started with the support of foreign aid, commercial loans, a direct investment, or a joint venture with a transnational corporation.

The importance of private investment and the key role of transnational corporations have already been highlighted. (See Chapter 3.) It is inconceivable that a successful transition to sustainable development can be achieved unless the policies and practices are reoriented around sustainable development objectives. Those external agencies that support and facilitate private investment, particularly export credit and investment insurance organizations, should also incorporate sustainable development criteria into their policies and practices.

The problems of developing-country governments are compounded by the vagaries of the international economic system, such as high debts, high interest rates, and declining terms of trade for commodities. These do not encourage hard-pressed governments to spend high proportions of their meagre resources on environmental protection and resource management. (See Chapter 3.)

The developing countries themselves will eventually have to bear the consequences of inappropriate industrialization, and the ultimate responsibility for ensuring the sustainability of their development rests with each government. They must define their own environmental goals and development objectives, and establish clear priorities among competing demands on their scarce resources. They will also need to search for more self-reliant means of industrial and technological development. The choices are theirs, but they will need all the assistance—technical, financial, and institutional—that the international community can muster to help them set an environmentally sound and sustainable course of development.

Large industrial enterprises, and transnational corporations in particular, have a special responsibility. They are repositories of scarce technical skills, and they should adopt the highest safety and health protection standards practicable and assume responsibility for safe plant and process design and for staff training. The transnationals should also institute environmental and safety audits of their plants measured against standards at other subsidiaries, not just against those of other local companies, which may have less stringent requirements. These audits and their follow-up should be made available to governments and other interested parties.

Particular care is required in dealing with toxic chemicals and hazardous wastes, and in contingency planning for accidents. The views of non-governmental organizations and the local community should be sought in planning new industrial facilities. The relevant national and local authorities must be fully informed about the properties, potentially harmful effects, and any potential risks to the community of the technology, process, or product being introduced. The necessary information should be disclosed to nearby residents in an easily understandable manner. The enterprises must co-operate with the local government and community in contingency planning and in devising clearly defined mechanisms for relief and compensation to pollution or accident victims.

Many developing countries need information on the nature of industry-based resource and environmental problems, on risks associated with certain processes and products, and on standards and other measures to protect health and ensure environmental sustainability. They also need trained people to apply such information to local circumstances. International trade associations and labour unions should develop special environmental training programmes for developing countries and disseminate information on pollution control, waste minimization, and emergency preparedness plans through local chapters.

Notes

The Commission accepts full responsibility for this chapter, but wishes to acknowledge that it draws on the report of its Advisory Panel on Industry. (See Annexe 2 for a list of members.)

1 As will be noted later in this chapter, the conventional classification of economic activities into three sectors—primary (agriculture and mining), secondary (manufacturing), and tertiary (commerce and other services)—has become increasingly ambiguous. Some economic activities cut across all three. Furthermore, the services sector has begun to occupy an important place of its own in industrialized economies. In this chapter, however, the term 'industry' will be used in the traditional sense to include mining and quarrying, manufacturing, construction, electricity, water, and gas.

2 GATT, *International Trade 1985-86* (Geneva: 1986).

3 UNIDO, *Industry in the 1980s: Structural Change and Interdependence* (New York: 1985).

4 See, for example, W.W. Leontief, *The Impact of Automation* (Oxford: Oxford University Press, 1986); F. Duchin, 'Automation and its Effects on Employment', in E. Collings and L. Tanner (eds.), *Employment Implications of the Changing Industrial Base* (New York: Ballinger Books, 1984); J. Rada, *The Impact of Microelectronics* (Geneva: ILO, 1980); and D. Werneke, *Microelectronics and Office Jobs* (Geneva: ILO, 1983).

5 UNIDO, *Industry and Development: Global Report 1985* (New York: 1985).

6 WHO, *Urban Air Pollution 1973-1980* (Geneva: 1984); World Resources Institute/International Institute for Environment and Development, *World Resources 1986* (New York: Basic Books, 1986).

7 The UN Commission on Transnational Corporations has been working on a comprehensive code since 1977 but the sections on environmental and consumer protection have been virtually agreed. For other examples, see FAO, 'Code of Conduct on the Distribution and Use of Pesticides', Rome, 1985; UNEP, 'Guidelines on Risk Management and Accident Prevention in the Chemical Industry', adopted in 1982; and OECD, 'Declaration of OECD Member Countries on International Investment and Multinational Enterprise', 1976, and 'Clarification of the Environmental Concerns Expressed in Paragraph 2 of the General Policies Chapter of the OECD Guidelines for Multinational Enterprises', Paris, 1985.

8 See, for example, International Chamber of Commerce, 'Environmental Guidelines for World Industry', Paris, 1976 (revised in 1981 and 1986); Hellenic Marine Environment Protection Association, 'To Save the Seas, Declaration of a Voluntary Commitment' and 'Guidelines for the Officers of HELMEPA Member Vessels', Athens, 1982; and US National Agricultural Chemicals Association, 'Guidelines on Labelling Practices for Pesticide Products in Developing Areas of the World', Washington, DC, 1985.

9 UNEP, *State of the Environment 1982* (Nairobi: 1982).

10 OECD, 'The Impact of Environmental Measures on the Rate of Economic Growth, Rate of Inflation, Productivity and International Trade', *Background Papers Prepared for the International Conference on Environment and Economics Vol. I* (Paris: 1984).

11 US Department of Commerce, 'Plant and Equipment Expenditures by Business for Pollution Abatement', *Survey of Current Business*, February 1986.

12 Japanese Ministry of International Trade and Industry, data compiled annually for the Industrial Structural Council, Tokyo, 1970–86.

13 The UN Economic Commission for Europe compiles and publishes a 'compendium of low- and non-waste technologies'. A special department in the French Ministry of Environment collects and disseminates information on clean processes and technologies ('les techniques propres').

14 UNIDO, *Industry in the 1980s*, op. cit.

15 N. Namiki, 'International Redeployment of Pollution-Intensive Industries and the Role of Multinational Corporations', prepared for WCED, 1986.

16 OECD, *Developments in Steel Making Capacity in Non-OECD Market Economy Countries* (Paris: 1985).

17 Namiki, op. cit.

18 UNIDO, *Industry in a Changing World* (New York: 1983).

19 OECD, *The State of the Environment 1985* (Paris: 1985).

20 'Industry Experience with Environmental Problem Solving', background paper prepared for the World Industry Conference on Environmental Management, organized by the International Chamber of Commerce and the UN Environmental Programme, Versailles, 14–16 November 1984.

21 Ibid.

22 UNEP, *The World Environment 1972–1982* (Nairobi: 1982).

23 V. Anikeev, Director of the Department on Environment and Rational Use of Natural Resources, GOSPLAN, during a visit by WCED to the GOSPLAN headquarters, Moscow, 12 December 1986.

24 P.F. Drucker, 'The Changed World Economy', *Foreign Affairs*, Spring 1986.

25 E.D. Larson et al., 'Beyond the Era of Materials', *Scientific American*, June 1986.

26 Drucker, op. cit.

27 For a discussion of various possibilities for industrial application of biotechnology, see J. Elkington, *Double Dividends? US Biotechnology and Third World Development*, WRI Papers, No. 2 (Washington, DC: World Resources Institute, 1986).

28 The 1986 annual report of the Japanese Environment Agency to the Parliament dealt extensively with this topic of the potential environmental impacts and risks posed by the new technologies. *Quality of the Environment in Japan 1986* (Tokyo: 1987).

29 The US Government recently announced a comprehensive regulatory policy for ensuring the safety of biotechnology research and products. See 'Coordinated Framework for Regulation of Biotechnology', *Federal Register*, 26 June 1986.

30 See OECD, 'Guiding Principles Concerning International Economic Aspects of Environmental Policies', Council Recommendation C(72)128, Paris, 26 May 1972.

31 OECD, *Economic Aspects of International Chemicals Control* (Paris: 1983).

32 The Conservation Foundation, 'Chemicals Policy in the Global Environment', prepared for WCED, 1986.

33 National Research Council, *Toxicity Testing* (Washington, DC: National Academy Press, 1984).

34 See 'Consolidated List of Products Whose Consumption and/or Sale Have Been Banned, Withdrawn, Severely Restricted or Not Approved by Governments', compiled by the UN, 1st revised edition, DIESA/WP/1, 1986.

35 Notable examples include the International Programme on Chemical Safety (UNEP/WHO/ILO), International Register of Potentially Toxic Chemicals (UNEP), International Agency for Research on Cancer (WHO), and the UN's 'Consolidated List', op. cit.

36 H. Yakowitz, 'Global Aspects of Hazardous Waste Management', prepared for WCED, 1985; US Congress, Office of Technology Assessment, *Superfund Strategy* (Washington, DC: US Government Printing Office, 1985). US estimates include wastewater in very dilute form. The result is a much larger estimate of total hazardous wastes for the United States than for other countries.

37 Some other sources quote figures as high as 34 million tons for Brazil alone, and 22 million and 13.6 million tons for Mexico and India, respectively. See H. J. Leonard, 'Hazardous Wastes: The Crisis Spreads', *National Development*, April 1986.

38 Estimates quoted in an OECD Secretariat paper, Paris, 1986.

39 UNEP, 'Transfrontier Movements of Hazardous Wastes With Regard to Developing Countries', prepared for the Working Group of Experts on Environmentally Sound Management of Hazardous Wastes, Munich, 1984.

40 Yakowitz, op. cit.

41 OECD, Background Papers for Conference on International Cooperation Concerning Transfrontier Movements of Hazardous Wastes, Basel, Switzerland, 26–27 March 1985.

42 See EEC, 'Supervision and Control of Transfrontier Shipments of Hazardous Waste', Council Directive, Brussels, December 1984; OECD, Resolution of the Council C(85)100, Paris, June 1985.

43 UNEP, 'Transfrontier Movements', op. cit. See also M.J. Suess and J.W. Huismans (eds.), *Management of Hazardous Waste: Policy Guidelines and Code of Practice* (Copenhagen: WHO Regional Office for Europe, 1983).

44 Preliminary findings of a study conducted for US Environmental Protection Agency, 'Acute Hazardous Data Base', Washington, DC, 1985, quoted in Yakowitz, op. cit.

45 See, for example, *La Suisse*, 3–9 November; *Die Welt*, 10 November; *Die Zeit*, 14 November; *Der Spiegel*, 17 November; *International Herald Tribune*, 14–16 November 1986.

9

THE URBAN CHALLENGE

By the turn of the century, almost half the world will live in urban areas—from small towns to huge megacities.[1] The world's economic system is increasingly an urban one, with overlapping networks of communications, production, and trade.[2] This system, with its flows of information, energy, capital, commerce, and people, provides the backbone for national development. A city's prospects—or a town's—depend critically on its place within the urban system, national and international. So does the fate of the hinterland, with its agricultural, forestry, and mining, on which the urban system depends.

In many nations, certain kinds of industries and service enterprises are now being developed in rural areas. But they receive high-quality infrastructure and services, with advanced telecommunications systems ensuring that their activities are part of the national (and global) urban-industrial system. In effect, the countryside is being 'urbanized'.

I. THE GROWTH OF CITIES

This is the century of the 'urban revolution'. In the 35 years since 1950, the number of people living in cities almost tripled, increasing by 1.25 billion. In the more developed regions, the urban population nearly doubled, from 447 million to 838 million. In the less developed world, it quadrupled, growing from 286 million to 1.14 billion. (See Table 9.1.)

Over only 60 years, the developing world's urban population increased tenfold, from around 100 million in 1920 to close to 1 billion in 1980. At the same time, its rural population more than doubled.

- In 1940, only one person in eight lived in an urban centre, while about one in 100 lived in a city with a million or more inhabitants (a 'million city').
- By 1960, more than one in five persons lived in an urban centre, and one in 16 in a 'million city'.
- By 1980, nearly one in three persons was an urban dweller and one in 10 a 'million city' resident.[3]

TABLE 9.1

Population Living in Urban Areas, 1950–2000

Region	1950	1985	2000
	(per cent)		
World Total	29.2	41.0	46.6
More Developed Regions	53.8	71.5	74.4
Less Developed Regions	17.0	31.2	39.3
Africa	15.7	29.7	39.0
Latin America	41.0	69.0	76.8
(Temperate South America)	(64.8)	(84.3)	(88.6)
(Tropical South America)	(35.9)	(70.4)	(79.4)
Asia	16.4	28.1	35.0
(China)	(11.0)	(20.6)	(25.1)
(India)	(17.3)	(25.5)	(34.2)
	(million)		
World Total	734.2	1,982.8	2,853.6
More Developed Regions	447.3	838.8	949.9
Less Developed Regions	286.8	1,144.0	1,903.7
Africa	35.2	164.5	340.0
Latin America	67.6	279.3	419.7
Asia	225.8	791.1	1,242.4

Source: 'Urban and Rural Population Projections, 1984', Unofficial Assessment, Population Division, UN, New York.

The population of many of sub-Saharan Africa's larger cities increased more than sevenfold between 1950 and 1980—Nairobi, Dar es Salaam, Nouakchott, Lusaka, Lagos, and Kinshasa among them.[4] (See Table 9.2.) During these same 30 years, populations in many Asian and Latin American cities (such as Seoul, Baghdad, Dhaka, Amman, Bombay, Jakarta, Mexico City, Manila, Sao Paulo, Bogota, and Managua) tripled or quadrupled. In such cities, net immigration has usually been a greater contributor than natural increase to the population growth of recent decades.

In many developing countries, cities have thus grown far beyond anything imagined only a few decades ago—and at speeds without historic precedent. (See Box 9-1.) But some experts doubt that developing nations will urbanize as rapidly in the future as in the last 30–40 years, or that megacities will grow as large as UN projections suggest. Their argument is that many of the most powerful stimuli

TABLE 9.2

Examples of Rapid Population Growth in Third World Cities
(in millions)

City	1950	Most Recent Figure	UN Projection For 2000
Mexico City	3.05	16.0 (1982)	26.3
Sao Paulo	2.7	12.6 (1980)	24.0
Bombay	3.0 (1951)	8.2 (1981)	16.0
Jakarta	1.45	6.2 (1977)	12.8
Cairo	2.5	8.5 (1979)	13.2
Delhi	1.4 (1951)	5.8 (1981)	13.3
Manila	1.78	5.5 (1980)	11.1
Lagos	0.27 (1952)	4.0 (1980)	8.3
Bogota	0.61	3.9 (1985)	9.6
Nairobi	0.14	0.83 (1979)	5.3
Dar es Salaam	0.15 (1960)	0.9 (1981)	4.6
Gter. Khartoum	0.18	1.05 (1978)	4.1
Amman	0.03	0.78 (1978)	1.5
Nouakchott	0.0058	0.25 (1982)	1.1
Manaus	0.11	0.51 (1980)	1.1
Santa Cruz	0.059	0.26 (1976)	1.0

Source: Recent census data used whenever possible; if none available, an estimate by the city government or a local research group has been used. UN projections for the year 2000 from Department of International Economic and Social Affairs, *Estimates and Projections of Urban, Rural and City Populations 1950–2025* (the 1982 Assessment), ST/ESA/SER.R/58, New York, 1985 and from UN, *Urban, Rural and City Populations 1950–2000* (as Assessed in 1978), Population Studies No. 68 (New York, 1980). Other data from J. E. Hardoy and D. Satterthwaite, *Shelter: Need and Response* (Chichester, UK: John Wiley & Sons, 1981), with some figures updated with more recent census data.

to rapid urbanization in the past have less influence today, and that changing government policies could reduce the comparative attractiveness of cities, especially the largest cities, and slow rates of urbanization.

The urban population growth rate in developing countries as a whole has been slowing down—from 5.2 per cent per annum in the late 1950s to 3.4 per cent in the 1980s.[5] It is expected to decline even further in the coming decades. Nevertheless, if current trends hold, Third World cities could add a further three-quarters of a billion people by the year 2000. Over the same time, the cities of the industrial world would grow by a further 111 million.[6]

These projections put the urban challenge firmly in the developing countries. In the space of just 15 years (or about 5,500 days), the developing world will have to increase by 65 per cent its capacity to

Box 9-1. Dominating Cities

Nairobi, Kenya: In 1975, Nairobi had 57 per cent of all Kenya's manufacturing employment and two-thirds of its industrial plants. In 1979, Nairobi contained around 5 per cent of the national population.

Manila, Philippines: Metropolitan Manila produces one-third of the nation's gross national product, handles 70 per cent of all imports, and contains 60 per cent of the manufacturing establishments. In 1981, it contained around 13 per cent of the national population.

Lima, Peru: The metropolitan area of Lima accounts for 43 per cent of gross domestic product, for four-fifths of bank credit and consumer goods production, and for more than nine-tenths of capital goods production in Peru. In 1981, it was home to around 27 per cent of Peruvians.

Lagos, Nigeria: In 1978, Lagos' metropolitan area handled over 40 per cent of the nation's external trade, accounted for over 57 per cent of total value added in manufacturing, and contained over 40 per cent of Nigeria's highly skilled workers. It contains only some 5 per cent of the national population.

Mexico City, Mexico: In 1970, with some 24 per cent of Mexicans living there, the capital contained 30 per cent of the manufacturing jobs, 28 per cent of employment in commerce, 38 per cent of jobs in services, 69 per cent of employment in national government, 62 per cent of national investment in higher education, and 80 per cent of research activities. In 1965, it contained 44 per cent of national bank deposits and 61 per cent of national credits.

Sao Paulo, Brazil: Greater Sao Paulo, with around one-tenth of Brazil's national population in 1980, contributed one-quarter of the net national product and over 40 per cent of Brazil's industrial value-added.

Source: J.E. Hardoy and D. Satterthwaite, 'Shelter, Infrastructure and Services in Third World Cities', *Habitat International,* Vol. 10, No. 4, 1986.

produce and manage its urban infrastructure, services, and shelter—merely to maintain present conditions. And in many countries, this must be accomplished under conditions of great economic hardship and uncertainty, with resources diminishing relative to needs and rising expectations.

The Crisis in Third World Cities

Few city governments in the developing world have the power, resources, and trained staff to provide their rapidly growing populations with the land, services, and facilities needed for an adequate human life: clean water, sanitation, schools, and transport. The result is mushrooming illegal settlements with primitive facilities, increased overcrowding, and rampant disease linked to an unhealthy environment.

'Given the distribution of incomes, given the foreseeable availability of resources—national, local, and world-wide—given present technology, and given the present weakness of local government and the lack of interest of national governments in settlement problems, I don't see any solution for the Third World city.

Third World cities are and they will increasingly become centres of competition for a plot to be invaded where you can build a shelter, for a room to rent, for a bed in a hospital, for a seat in a school or in a bus, essentially for the fewer stable adequately paid jobs, even for the space in a square or on a sidewalk where you can display and sell your merchandise, on which so many households depend.

The people themselves organize and help construct most new housing units in Third World cities and they do so without the assistance from architects, planners, and engineers, nor from local or national governments. Furthermore, in many cases, national and local governments are frequently harassing these groups. The people themselves are becoming increasingly the true builders and designers of Third World cities and quite often the managers of their own districts.'

Jorge Hardoy
International Institute for Environment and Development
WCED Public Hearing, Sao Paulo, 28–29 Oct 1985

In most Third World cities, the enormous pressure for shelter and services has frayed the urban fabric. Much of the housing used by the poor is decrepit. Civic buildings are frequently in a state of disrepair and advanced decay. So too is the essential infrastructure of the city; public transport is overcrowded and overused, as are roads, buses and trains, transport stations, public latrines, and washing points. Water supply systems leak, and the resulting low water pressure allows sewage to seep into drinking water. A large proportion of the city's population often has no piped water, storm drainage, or roads.[7]

A growing number of the urban poor suffer from a high incidence of diseases; most are environmentally based and could be prevented or dramatically reduced through relatively small investments. (See Box 9-2.) Acute respiratory diseases, tuberculosis, intestinal parasites, and diseases linked to poor sanitation and contaminated drinking water (diarrhoea, dysentery, hepatitis, and typhoid) are usually endemic; they are one of the major causes of illness and death, especially among children. In parts of many cities, poor people can expect to see one in four of their children die of serious malnutrition

---

Box 9-2. Environmental Problems in Third World Cities

Out of India's 3,119 towns and cities, only 209 had partial and only 8 had full sewage and sewage treatment facilities. On the river Ganges, 114 cities each with 50,000 or more inhabitants dump untreated sewage into the river every day. DDT factories, tanneries, paper and pulp mills, petrochemical and fertilizer complexes, rubber factories, and a host of others use the river to get rid of their wastes. The Hoogly estuary (near Calcutta) is choked with untreated industrial wastes from more than 150 major factories around Calcutta. Sixty per cent of Calcutta's population suffer from pneumonia, bronchitis, and other respiratory diseases related to air pollution.

Chinese industries, most of which use coal in outdated furnaces and boilers, are concentrated around 20 cities and ensure a high level of air pollution. Lung cancer mortality in Chinese cities is four to seven times higher than in the nation as a whole, and the difference is largely attributable to heavy air pollution.

In Malaysia, the highly urbanized Klang Valley (which includes the capital, Kuala Lumpur) has two to three times the pollution levels of major cities in the United States, and the Klang river system is heavily contaminated with agricultural and industrial effluents and sewage.

Sources: Centre for Science and Environment, *State of India's Environment: A Citizens' Report* (New Delhi: 1983); V. Smil, *The Bad Earth: Environmental Degradation in China* (London: Zed Press, 1986); Sahabat Alam Malaysia, *The State of Malaysian Environment 1983–84—Towards Greater Environmental Awareness* (Penang, Malaysia: 1983).

---

before the age of five, or one adult in two suffering intestinal worms or serious respiratory infections.[8]

Air and water pollution might be assumed to be less pressing in Third World cities because of lower levels of industrial development. But in fact hundreds of such cities have high concentrations of industry. Air, water, noise, and solid waste pollution problems have increased rapidly and can have dramatic impacts on the life and health of city inhabitants, on their economy, and on jobs. Even in a relatively small city, just one or two factories dumping wastes into the only nearby river can contaminate everyone's drinking, washing, and cooking water. Many slums and shanties crowd close to hazardous industries, as this is land no one else wants. This proximity has magnified the risks for the poor, a fact demonstrated by great loss of life and human suffering in various recent industrial accidents.

The uncontrolled physical expansion of cities has also had serious implications for the urban environment and economy. Uncontrolled development makes provision of housing, roads, water supply, sewers, and public services prohibitively expensive. Cities are often built on the most productive agricultural land, and unguided growth results in the unnecessary loss of this land. Such losses are most serious in nations with limited arable land, such as Egypt. Haphazard development also consumes land and natural landscapes needed for urban parks and recreation areas. Once an area is built up, it is both difficult and expensive to re-create open space.

In general, urban growth has often preceded the establishment of a solid, diversified economic base to support the build-up of housing, infrastructure, and employment. In many places, the problems are linked to inappropriate patterns of industrial development and the lack of coherence between strategies for agricultural and urban development. The link between national economies and international economic factors has been discussed in Part I of this report. The world economic crisis of the 1980s has not only reduced incomes, increased unemployment, and eliminated many social programmes. It has also exacerbated the already low priority given to urban problems, increasing the chronic shortfall in resources needed to build, maintain, and manage urban areas.[9]

The Situation in Industrial World Cities

The Commission's focus on the urban crisis in developing countries is not meant to imply that what transpires in the cities of the industrial world is not of crucial importance to sustainable development globally. It is. These cities account for a high share of the world's resource use, energy consumption, and environmental pollution. Many have a global reach and draw their resources and energy from distant lands, with enormous aggregate impacts on the ecosystems of those lands.

Nor is the emphasis on Third World cities meant to imply that problems within the cities of industrialized countries are not serious. They are. Many face problems of deteriorating infrastructure, environmental degradation, inner-city decay, and neighbourhood collapse. The unemployed, the elderly, and racial and ethnic minorities can remain trapped in a downward spiral of degradation and poverty, as job opportunities and the younger and better-educated individuals leave declining neighbourhoods. City or municipal governments often face a legacy of poorly designed and maintained public housing estates, mounting costs, and declining tax bases.

But most industrial countries have the means and resources to tackle inner-city decay and linked economic decline. Indeed, many have succeeded in reversing these trends through enlightened policies, co-operation between the public and private sectors, and significant investments in personnel, institutions, and technological innovation.[10] Local authorities usually have the political power and credibility to take initiatives and to assess and deploy resources in innovative ways reflecting unique local conditions. This gives them a capacity to manage, control, experiment, and lead urban development. In centrally planned economies, the ability to plan and implement plans for urban development has been significant. The priority given to collective goods over private consumption may also have increased the resources available for urban development.

The physical environment in many cities of the industrial world has improved substantially over the decades. According to the historical records of many major centres—like London, Paris, Chicago, Moscow, and Melbourne—it was not too long ago that a major part of their population lived in desperate circumstances amid gross pollution. Conditions have improved steadily during the past century, and this trend continues, although the pace varies between and within cities.

In most urban areas, almost everyone is served by refuse collection today. Air quality has generally improved, with a decline in the emission of particles and sulphur oxides. Efforts to restore water quality have met with a mixed record of success because of pollution from outside of cities, notably nitrates and other fertilizers and pesticides. Many coastal areas, however, close to major sewage outlets, show considerable deterioration. There is rising concern about chemical pollutants in drinking water and about the impacts of toxic wastes on groundwater quality. And noise pollution has tended to increase.

Motor vehicles greatly influence environmental conditions in the cities of the industrial world. A recent slowdown in the growth rate of vehicle numbers, stricter emission standards for new vehicles, the distribution of lead-free gasoline, improvements in fuel efficiency, improved traffic management policies, and landscaping have all helped reduce the impacts of urban traffic.

Public opinion has played a critical role in the drive to improve urban conditions. In some cities, public pressure has triggered the abandonment of massive urban development projects, fostered residential schemes on a more human scale, countered indiscriminate demolition of existing buildings and historic districts, modified proposed urban highway construction, and led to transformation of derelict plots into playgrounds.

The problems that remain are serious but they affect relatively limited areas, which makes them much more tractable than those of

'Large cities by definition are centralized, manmade environments that depend mainly on food, water, energy, and other goods from outside. Smaller cities, by contrast, can be the heart of community-based development and provide services to the surrounding countryside.

Given the importance of cities, special efforts and safeguards are needed to ensure that the resources they demand are produced sustainably and that urban dwellers participate in decisions affecting their lives. Residential areas are likely to be more habitable if they are governed as individual neighbourhoods with direct local participation. To the extent that energy and other needs can be met on a local basis, both the city and surrounding areas will be better off.'

'Sustainable Development and How to Achieve It'
Global Tomorrow Coalition
WCED Public Hearing, Ottawa, 26–27 May 1986

Cairo or Mexico City, for example. Certain aspects of urban decline even provide opportunities for environmental enhancement. The exodus of population and economic activities, while creating severe economic and social difficulties, reduces urban congestion, allows new uses for abandoned buildings, protects historic urban districts from the threat of speculative demolition and reconstruction, and contributes to urban renewal. The de-industrialization of these cities is often counterbalanced by the growth of the services sector, which brings its own problems. But this trend creates opportunities to remove heavy industrial pollution sources from residential and commercial areas.

The combination of advanced technology, stronger national economies, and a developed institutional infrastructure give resilience and the potential for continuing recovery to cities in the industrial world. With flexibility, space for manoeuvre, and innovation by local leadership, the issue for industrial countries is ultimately one of political and social choice. Developing countries are not in the same situation. They have a major urban crisis on their hands.

II. THE URBAN CHALLENGE IN DEVELOPING COUNTRIES

Settlements—the urban network of cities, towns, and villages—encompass all aspects of the environment within which societies' economic and social interactions take place. Internationally, the major cities of the world constitute a network for the allocation of investment and for the production and sale of most goods and services. These centres are the first to be plugged into this network, through air- and seaports and telecommunications. New technologies usually arrive and are first put into practice in large and then smaller cities. Only if centres are firmly connected to this network can they hope to attract investment in technologies and manufacturing goods for world markets. Nationally, cities are veritable incubators of economic activities. Some enterprises are large-scale but the vast majority are small, doing everything from selling snack foods to mending shoes and building houses. The growth of these activities is the foundation of the domestic economy.

National Urban Strategies

The natural evolution of this network of settlements, however, has caused apprehension in most developing countries. Of particular concern has been the phenomenal growth of often one or two major cities. In some countries, the desire to limit this growth has led to spatial policies designed to accelerate the development of secondary centres. Underlying this has been a particular concern that unbalanced growth is increasing interregional disparities and creating economic and social imbalances that can have serious consequences in terms of national unity and political stability.

Although far from conclusive, the available evidence suggests that most attempts by central governments to balance spatial development have been both expensive and ineffective. Major macroeconomic, social, and sectoral policies have often been directly opposed to the decentralization policy. Investments supported by governments and aid agencies have followed the same centralizing logic as private investments, and have built transportation facilities, educational and health institutions, and urban infrastructure and services where the demand exists—in the major city. Rural-urban migration has followed the same pattern. A major reason why so many migrants in recent decades went to cities such as Nairobi, Manila, Lagos, Mexico City, Sao Paulo, Rangoon, or Port au Prince was the dominant role each centre came to play in its national economy.

The macroeconomic and pricing policies pursued by governments further reinforced this concentration. The major cities, often the capital, usually receive a disproportionately large share of the total national expenditure on education and on subsidies to reduce the prices of water, corn, electric power, diesel fuel, and public transport. Railroad freight rates sometimes favour routes that pass through the

❝We see that the increasing urban drift is inevitable: There are alot of 'push' factors working in the rural areas. Rural pluralization is caused by absence of land reform, by the increase of absentee landownership, by the displacement of the Green Revolution.

Besides the 'push' factors of the rural areas, there are, of course, the 'pull' factors, the glamour of the Big City, the higher pay of urban jobs as compared to rural income possibilities. So the informal sector of Jakarta has grown; maybe from the 7 million population of Jakarta, 3 or 4 million—at least two-thirds—are the result of the urban drift.❞

George Adicondro
Director, Irian Jaya Rural Community Development Foundation
WCED Public Hearing, Jakarta, 26 March 1985

capital. Property taxes in the city and surrounding districts may be undervalued. New or expanded industries given a boost by the import substitution policies are encouraged to establish in or near the capital.[11]

Agricultural and food policies have also tended to promote rapid growth of larger cities. Low or even negative economic supports for agricultural products have driven smallholders off their land and added to the numbers of the rural poor. Urban food prices, held low by subsidies, have served to attract many of them to cities. In recent years, however, some developing countries have found it possible to begin to shift more income from the major cities to the rural areas and smaller towns. In some cases, policies to promote small landholdings and intensive farming have had this effect. Increasing production, a growth in agricultural employment, and higher average incomes have stimulated the development of small and intermediate centres in the agricultural regions they serve.[12]

There are some important lessons to be learned about spatial strategies for urban development:

- Nothing much short of coercion will prevent the growth of the major city in the early stages of development.
- The key to successful intervention is timing, to encourage deconcentration only when the advantages of concentration are diminishing.
- Avoid policy interventions that increase the attractiveness of the major city, particularly subsidies on food and energy, overly generous provision of urban infrastructure and other services, and excessive concentration of administrative power in the capital.

- The best way to encourage the growth of secondary centres is to build on the natural economic advantages of their regions, especially in resource processing and marketing, and the decentralized provision of government services.
- Rural and urban development strategies and approaches should be complementary rather than contradictory: The development of secondary centres is to the direct economic benefit of the resource areas they serve.

The job opportunities and housing provided by cities are essential to absorb the population growth that the countryside cannot cope with; as long as price controls and subsidies do not interfere, the urban market should offer advantages to rural producers. But there are obviously conflicts of interest between developing country city-dwellers and farmers. A major thrust of the discussion on food security (see Chapter 5) was to assert the importance of decisively turning the 'terms of trade' in favour of farmers, especially small farmers, through pricing and exchange rate policies. Many developing countries are not implementing such policies, partly for fear of losing the support of politically powerful urban factions. Thus they fail both to stem urban drift and to improve food security.

These considerations can provide the basis for developing an explicit national settlements strategy and policies within which innovative and effective local solutions to urban problems can evolve and flourish. Every government has such a strategy in effect, but it is most often implicit in a range of macroeconomic, fiscal, budget, energy, and agricultural polices. These policies have usually evolved incrementally in response to the pressures of the day and, almost invariably, they contradict each other and the stated settlement goals of the government. A national urban strategy could provide an explicit set of goals and priorities for the development of a nation's urban system and the large, intermediate, and small centres within it. Such a strategy must go beyond physical or spatial planning. It requires that governments take a much broader view of urban policy than has been traditional.

With an explicit strategy, nations can begin to reorient those central economic and major sectoral policies that now reinforce megacity growth, urban decline, and poverty. They can likewise promote more effectively the development of small and intermediate urban centres, the strengthening of their local governments, and the establishment of services and facilities needed to attract development initiatives and investment. Ministries of Planning, Finance, Industry, Agriculture, and so on would have clear goals and criteria against which to assess the effects of their policies and expenditures on urban development. Contradictory policies and programmes could be changed. At the very least, the spatial biases inherent in macroeconomic and fiscal policies, annual budgets, pricing structures, and sectoral investment plans could be exposed and assessed. Within such a strategy, the traditional tools of urban policy, including land use planning and control, would stand a better chance of being effective.

The formulation of such a strategy is clearly a central government responsibility. Beyond this, however, the role of central governments should be primarily to strengthen the capacity of local governments to find and carry through effective solutions to local urban problems and stimulate local opportunities.

Strengthening Local Authorities

The institutional and legal structures of local government in most developing nations are inadequate for these purposes. In most African and Asian nations the structure of urban government goes back to the colonial period and was designed to deal with predominantly rural and agricultural societies. It was never intended to cope with rapid urbanization or to manage cities of several million inhabitants. Newly independent governments inherited a framework of laws and procedures totally inappropriate to deal with the urban processes they were about to confront. Yet in many nations, this inherited framework remains largely in place.

Where the immediate colonial past is less evident, as in most Latin American nations, the political, institutional, and legal frameworks for local government are often just as inappropriate and inadequate. As in Asia and Africa, most are based on models imported from Europe or North America. This has made it difficult for them to influence the direction of urbanization and to manage the problems of large, rapidly expanding urban centres. It has created cities that are energy- and material-intensive and dependent on imports, and that add to the burden on the national economy, including pressures on trade and balance of payments.

Urban development cannot be based on standardized models, imported or indigenous. Development possibilities are particular to each city and must be assessed within the context of its own region. What works in one city may be totally inappropriate in another. Although technical help from central agencies may be needed, only a strong local government can ensure that the needs, customs, urban forms, social priorities, and environmental conditions of the local area are reflected in local plans for urban development. But local

'A lot of youth in the Third World countries and even adults are unemployed. We want simple technologies whereby one particular person can do a kind of a job that could have provided job opportunities to several hundreds. What are we doing with the surplus potential, energy? So again I say that development is people, it is not high technology, it is not modernization, it is not Westernization. But it should be culturally relevant.'

Jan Selego
World Vision International
WCED Public Hearing, Nairobi, 23 Sept 1986

authorities have not been given the political power, decision-making capacity, and access to revenues needed to carry out their functions. This leads to frustration, to continuing criticism of local government for insufficient and inefficient services, and to a downward spiral of weakness feeding on weakness.

The lack of political access to an adequate financial base is a major weakness of local government in many developing countries. Most local governments have difficulties getting enough revenue to cover their operating expenses, let alone to make new investments to extend services and facilities. Even richer city governments have access to the equivalent of only $10–50 per inhabitant to invest each year. Despite these weaknesses, the trend in recent decades has been for national governments to reduce the financial capacity of local governments in real terms.

The result is growing centralization and continuing weaknesses at both the central and local level. Instead of doing a few things well, central authorities end up doing too many things, none of them well. Human and financial resources get stretched too thin. Local governments do not gain the expertise, authority, and credibility needed to deal with local problems.

To become key agents of development, city governments need enhanced political, institutional, and financial capacity, notably access to more of the wealth generated in the city. Only in this way can cities adapt and deploy some of the vast array of tools available to address urban problems—tools such as land title registration, land use control, and tax sharing.

Self-Reliance and Citizen Involvement

In most developing countries between one-fourth and one-half of the economically active urban population cannot find adequate, stable livelihoods. With few jobs available in established businesses or government services, people have to find or create their own sources of income. These efforts have resulted in the rapid growth of what has been termed the 'informal sector', which provides much of the cheap goods and services essential to city economies, business, and consumers.

Thus, while many poor people may not be officially employed, most are working—in unregistered factories and construction firms, selling goods on street corners, making clothes in their homes, or as servants or guards in better-off neighbourhoods. Most of the so-called unemployed are in fact working 10–15 hours a day, six to seven days a week. Their problem is not so much underemployment as underpayment.

Most house building, maintenance, or upgrading in the cities of developing countries is done outside official plans and usually in illegal settlements. This process mobilizes untapped resources, contributes to capital formation, and stimulates employment. These informal-sector builders represent an important source of urban employment, in particular for low and unskilled labour. They are not capital- or technology-intensive, they are not energy-intensive, and as a rule they do not impose a drain on foreign exchange. In their way, they contribute their share to attaining some of the nation's major development objectives. Moreover, they are flexible in responding to local needs and demands, catering in particular to poorer households, which usually have nowhere else to turn. Many governments have begun to see the wisdom of tolerating rather than quashing their work. Large-scale bulldozing of squatter communities is now rarer, although it still happens.

Governments should give more support to the informal sector, recognizing its vital functions in urban development. Some governments have done so, facilitating loans and credit to small entrepreneurs, building co-operatives, and neighbourhood improvement associations. Providing tenure to those living in illegal settlements is basic to this process, as is easing some building and housing regulations.

Multilateral and bilateral development assistance agencies should follow suit, and some are beginning to do so. Non-governmental and private voluntary organizations are springing up in many countries to provide cost-effective channels for assistance, ensuring that it gets to those who can use it. A much larger proportion of assistance could be channelled directly through these organizations.

The above measures would also reinforce self-reliance and local governance by the poor in their own neighbourhood associations. Left to their own devices, the poor in many Third World cities have organized to fill gaps in services left by the local government. Among other things, community groups mobilize and organize fund-raising or mutual self-help to deal with security, environmental, and health problems within the immediate area.

Governments should move from a position of neutrality or antagonism to active support for such efforts. A few have actually institutionalized such programmes so that public ministries or agencies work continuously with community organizations. In the Indian city of Hyderabad, for example, an Urban Community Development Department set up by the municipal corporation works directly with community groups and non-government organizations in poorer neighbourhoods. By 1983, some 223 organizations had been formed by residents in low-income areas, plus 135 youth organizations and 99 women's groups.[13] In this way governments can become partners and sponsors of the people who are the main builders of their cities.

Housing and Services for the Poor

In most developing-world cities, there is little low-cost housing. Generally those on low incomes either rent rooms—whether in tenements or cheap boarding-houses, or in someone else's house or shack—or they build or buy a house or shack in an illegal settlement. There are many kinds and degrees of illegality, and these influence the extent to which governments tolerate the existence of such settlements, or even provide them with public services and facilities.

Whatever form it takes, low-income accommodation generally shares three characteristics. First, it has inadequate or no infrastructure and services—including piped water, sewers, or other means of hygienically disposing of human wastes. Second, people live in crowded and cramped conditions under which communicable diseases can flourish, particularly when malnutrition lowers resistance. Third, poor people usually build on land ill-suited for human habitation: floodplains, dusty deserts, hills subject to landslide, or next to polluting industries. They choose these sites because the land's low commercial value means they stand a better chance of not being evicted.

Landownership structures and the inability or unwillingness of governments to intervene in these structures are perhaps the main factors contributing to 'illegal' settlements and chaotic urban sprawl. When half or more of a city's workforce has no chance of obtaining a legal plot on which a house can be built, let alone of affording to

❛The shantytowns have found their own technique, their own resources without any assistance from anyone else, and they solved their housing problems. The real problem is not that. It is the poverty, the lack of planning, the lack of technical assistance, the lack of financing to buy construction materials, the lack of urban equipment.

To change this housing policy for human settlements, they should stimulate self-construction, instead of financing these large housing complexes. It would have been much better and would have cost less to help the people to carry out the self-construction.

Generally speaking, it seems clear that without meeting the basic needs of human beings, concern for the environment has to be secondary. Man has to survive, answer, and attend first to his basic survival needs— food, housing, sanitation—and then to the environment.❜

Walter Pinto Costa
President, Environmental and Sanitation Association
WCED Public Hearing, Sao Paulo, 28–29 Oct 1985

buy or rent a house legally, the balance between private landownership rights and the public good must be quickly rethought.

Given urbanization trends in most developing countries, there is no time to wait for slow and uncertain programmes. Government intervention must be reoriented so that limited resources are put to maximum effect in improving housing conditions for the poor. The options for intervention are many (see Box 9-3), but governments should be guided by these seven priorities:

- provide legal tenure to those living in 'illegal' settlements, with secure titles and basic services provided by public authorities;
- ensure that the land and other resources people need to build or improve their housing are available;
- supply existing and new housing areas with infrastructure and services;
- set up neighbourhood offices to provide advice and technical assistance on how housing can be built better and cheaper, and on how health and hygiene can be improved;
- plan and guide the city's physical expansion to anticipate and encompass needed land for new housing, agricultural land, parks, and children's play areas;
- consider how public intervention could improve conditions for tenants and those living in cheap rooming or boarding-houses; and
- change housing finance systems to make cheap loans available to lower-income and community groups.

Box 9-3. Three Ways to Use $20 Million to Improve Conditions in a City of 1 Million

Option 1:

Build 2,000 public housing units for poor families (with an average of six family members), each costing $10,000. Conditions are improved for 12,000 people, but little cost recovery is possible for poor families. If the city's population grows at 5 per cent annually, 630,000 new inhabitants will be added over 10 years, so only a tiny fraction of total population will have benefited.

Option 2:

Establish a 'site-and-service scheme', whereby poor families are responsible for building their houses on an allocated site supplied with piped water, connection to a sewer system, and electricity, roads, and drainage. At $2,000 per plot, this means housing for some 60,000 people—about 10 per cent of the city's population growth over 10 years.

Option 3:

Allocate $100,000 to a neighbourhood organization representing 1,000 poor households (6,000 people) in an existing low-income settlement. It chooses to improve drainage and roads, build a health clinic, establish a co-operative to produce inexpensive building materials and components, and reblock the settlement to improve access roads and provide 50 new plots. With $10 million, 100 such community initiatives are supported, reaching 600,000 people and providing 5,000 new housing plots. Many new jobs are stimulated. The remaining $10 million is spent on installing piped water; at $100 per household, all 600,000 people reached.

Most cities urgently need a large and continuous increase in the availability of cheap housing plots convenient to the main centres of employment. Only government intervention can achieve this, but no general prescriptions are possible. Societies differ too much in how they view private landownership and land use rights, in how they use different instruments such as direct grants, tax write-offs, or deduction of mortgage interest, and in how they treat land speculation, corruption, and other undesirable activities that often accompany processes of this kind. Although the means are particular to each nation, the end must be the same: governments ensuring that there are cheaper, better-serviced, better-located, legal alternatives to illegal plots. If this need is not met, the uncontrolled growth of cities—and its accompanying high costs—will not be stopped.

Besides land, building materials are another major cost for people putting up their own houses. Government support for the production of materials and of certain structural components, fixtures, and fittings could reduce housing costs and create many jobs. Small neighbourhood workshops often have cost advantages because of the low cost of transport from the workshop to the building site.

The majority of building codes and standards are ignored because following them would produce buildings too expensive for most people. A more effective approach might be to set up neighbourhood offices to provide technical advice on how health and safety can be improved at minimum cost. Good professional advice can lower building costs and improve quality, and might be more effective than prescribing what can or cannot be built.

Many poor people rent accommodation; half or more of a city's entire population may be tenants. Increasing the availability of house sites, materials, and credits does little for those who must rent. One possibility is financial support to non-governmental, non-profit organizations to purchase and develop property specifically for rental units. A second is support for tenants to buy out landlords and convert tenancy into co-operative ownership.

Governments, especially those strapped for resources, may claim that piped water supplies and sewage disposal systems are too expensive. As a consequence, poor people may have to pay water vendors far more per litre of water than middle- or upper-income groups pay public agencies to pipe water into their homes. Western water-borne sewage systems and treatment plants may be prohibitively expensive. But other techniques and systems cost between one-tenth and one-twentieth as much per household, and most of these use much less water. Moreover, lower-cost technology can be upgraded over time, as money becomes available.[14]

Major improvements can be made relatively cheaply in all these areas. But costs will remain low only if low-income groups are encouraged to participate fully in defining what they need, in deciding what they will contribute to the new services, and in doing the job with their own hands. This co-operation depends on establishing the new relationship between citizens and government called for earlier.

Tapping More Resources

The available resources in or close to cities are often underused. Many landowners leave well-located sites undeveloped in order to benefit later from their increasing value as the city grows. Many public agencies have land that could be put to better use, such as the area next to stations and harbours controlled by railway and port authorities. Several countries have introduced special programmes to encourage public and private co-operation in the development of such lands, a trend that should be encouraged. There is a general

'I'm an expert in slum dwelling. We're establishing a small, tiny organization trying to organize slum dwellers, because we see so many slums. Slums in the city, slums in the villages, slums in the forests.

I have worked for four years to motivate my fellow slum dwellers to become transmigrants, and they finally migrated to ten places all over Indonesia. They are still in very good communication with me. They're still sending me letters, and they say that life is not better in the transmigration areas. Living in the shadows in the urban slums or living in the shadows in the transmigration site is just the same.

When I go back to my people, the slum dwellers, tonight they will ask me what I have got from this meeting in the big hotel. They won't ask for information, just 'have you brought some money for us to build new houses?' **'**

Syamsuddin Nainggolan
Founder, Yayasan Panca Bakti
WCED Public Hearing, Jakarta, 26 March 1985

need to find innovative and effective ways of pooling land for the common good. Most cities have mechanisms for acquiring land either at market rates (which means that schemes are never implemented), or at arbitrarily low confiscatory rates (where the alliance of political forces and landlords blocks the acquisition anyway).

Governments should also consider supporting urban agriculture. This may have less relevance in cities where land markets are highly commercialized and land for housing is in short supply. But in most cities, especially those with less commercialized land markets, considerable potential exists. Many African cities already realize this. Urban agriculture, especially on city fringes, is undertaken by people as a way to feed themselves. In other instances, the process is more commercialized, with enterprises specializing in vegetable production for sale within the city.

Officially sanctioned and promoted urban agriculture could become an important component of urban development and make more food available to the urban poor. The primary purposes of such promotion should be to improve the nutritional and health standards of the poor, help their family budgets (50–70 per cent of which is usually spent on food), enable them to earn some additional income, and provide employment. Urban agriculture can also provide fresher and cheaper produce, more green space, the clearing of garbage dumps, and recycling of household waste.[15]

Another poorly used resource is solid wastes, the disposal of which has become a major problem in many cities, with much of it dumped and uncollected. Promoting the reclamation, reuse, or recycling of materials can reduce the problem of solid waste, stimulate employment, and result in savings of raw materials. Composting can support urban agriculture. If a municipal government lacks the resources to collect household wastes regularly, it can support existing community-based schemes. In many cities, literally thousands of people already make a living sorting through wastes by hand on municipal tips. Investing in a more capital-intensive, automatic recycling plant could be doubly counterproductive if it unnecessarily consumes scarce capital or if a plant would destroy many people's livelihoods. But an immediate need here is to give health advice and provide health care services to those who are making a living off municipal tips.[16]

III. INTERNATIONAL CO-OPERATION

The future will be predominantly urban, and the most immediate environmental concerns of most people will be urban ones. The effectiveness of efforts to improve urban life depends largely on the health of national economies. In many developing countries, this is linked closely to the state of the world economy. An improvement in international economic relations (see Chapter 3) would perhaps do more than anything else to enhance the capacity of developing countries to address their linked urban and environmental problems. But beyond that is the need to strengthen co-operation among developing countries and to increase various types of direct support from the international community.

Co-operation Among Developing Countries

Developing countries can do a great deal together to develop the policy concepts, programmes, and institutions needed to tackle the urban crisis they share. Although the management problems confronting Caracas, Dakar, or Delhi have little relevance to those confronting London or Paris, the cities of Latin America, West Africa, or South Asia have much in common. As they formulate broad national urban strategies, it is important that they share experiences on the management of their growing megacities, on the development of small and intermediate centres, on strengthening local government, on upgrading illegal settlements, on crisis-response measures, and on a range of other problems that are more or less unique to the Third World.

Further research could provide the basis for rethinking the Third World city. It could also feed in-country training programmes (or, for smaller nations, regional training programmes) for city and municipal government staff. Good policy proposals and good training courses depend on good local information and analysis; far too little of all three of these is found within developing countries and cities.

International Support

A greater flow of international resources is required to support the efforts of developing countries to tackle the unfolding urban crisis. An agreed definition of 'urban development assistance' does not exist, but the Development Assistance Committee recently estimated that total bilateral and multilateral aid for urban programmes averaged about $900 million per year over 1980–84.[17] It is also estimated that to date less than 5 per cent of the developing world's urban population has been reached by a housing or neighbourhood up-grading project sponsored by a development assistance agency. This level of support needs to be increased significantly. Moreover, the scope of support should be broadened and its quality and terms improved.

In addition, development assistance agencies should increase aid and technical assistance in three areas:

- to set up infrastructure funds for local governments;
- to undertake tasks such as reorganizing local tax assessments and collection, preparing or updating maps of property ownership, and setting up technical teams to advise households and community groups on improving housing;
- for in-country training courses and on-the-job training for local officials.

Part of the increased aid should go directly to community groups, using intermediaries such as national or international non-governmental organizations. Several bilateral aid programmes have already demonstrated the cost-effectiveness of this approach; various such groups have been responsible for many successful community-based schemes to improve housing and provide basic services. They are generally more successful at reaching the poorest. More aid should also go to supporting independent research groups working in housing and urban issues, particularly those providing advice to local governments and community groups; many are doing so already, especially in Latin America.

International co-operation can also contribute to developing low

Box 9-4. Misunderstanding Women's Needs in Housing Projects

Housing projects often use a gridiron layout that does not allow women to work in their house and at the same time keep an eye on their own or their neighbours' children. House designs and plot sizes rarely consider the fact that many women will want to use their houses as workshops (to make clothes, for instance) or as shops, which in fact are often forbidden in low-income housing projects. Application procedures for low-income housing sometimes require 'husbands' to apply; this excludes women-headed households—between 30 and 50 per cent of all households. Women's special needs in different cultures are ignored—in Islamic societies, for example, women's need for private open space within the house is rarely considered in house designs, while their need for relatively sheltered pathways to get to shops and clinics is not acknowledged in site layouts.

Source: Based on C.O.N. Moser, 'Housing Policy: Towards a Gender Awareness Approach', Working Paper No. 71, Development Planning Unit, London, 1985.

cost technologies for urban needs and studying ways of meeting the housing needs of women. (See Box 9-4.)

Many technical agencies within the UN system have the appropriate knowledge bases to play a valuable role in advising and supporting governments, notably the UN Centre for Human Settlements (UNCHS, or Habitat). They should identify the information and guidelines that city governments need and the form in which it can be made accessible and usable by them. This could be patterned, for example, upon the ongoing efforts to prepare guidebooks for community workers on identifying disease vectors and mobilizing communities to deal with them, and on interventions to promote child survival and health. More generally, Habitat can strengthen international co-operation at the global level, as in the UN International Year of Shelter for the homeless. The capacity of the UN system to provide leadership on human settlements issues through Habitat needs to be strengthened.

Notes

1 This chapter draws heavily on four background papers prepared for WCED: I. Burton, 'Urbanization and Development', 1985; J.E. Hardoy and D. Satterthwaite, 'Shelter, Infrastructure and Services in Third World Cities', 1985 (printed in *Habitat International*, Vol. 10, No. 4, 1986); J.E. Hardoy and D. Satterthwaite, 'Rethinking the Third World City', 1986; and I. Sachs, 'Human Settlements: Resource and Environmental Management', 1985.

2 See J. Jacobs, *Cities and the Wealth of Nations* (New York: Random House, 1984).

3 UN, *The Growth in the World's Urban and Rural Population 1920-1980*, Population Studies No. 44 (New York: 1969); UN, *Urban Rural and City Populations 1950-2000* (as assessed in 1978), Population Studies No. 68 (New York: 1980).

4 The expansion of 'city' or 'metropolitan area' boundaries accounts for some of the population growth in Table 9.2. The UN projections are based on extrapolating past trends. This method often provides a poor guide to future trends, especially long-term ones. But the data base with which to make better projections is not available.

5 UNCHS (Habitat) position paper for October 1986 DAC meeting on Urban Development, OECD document DAC (86)47, 27 August 1986.

6 Department of International Economic and Social Affairs, 'Urban and Rural Population Projections, 1984' (unofficial assessment), UN, New York, 1986.

7 J.E. Hardoy and D. Satterthwaite, *Shelter: Need and Response; Housing, Land and Settlement Policies in Seventeen Third World Nations* (Chichester, UK: John Wiley & Sons, 1981). For the situation in Sao Paulo, see J. Wilheim, 'Sao Paulo: Environmental Problems of the Growing Metropolis', submitted to WCED Public Hearings, Sao Paulo, 1985.

8 J.E. Hardoy and D. Satterthwaite, 'Third World Cities and the Environment of Poverty', *Geoforum*, Vol. 15, No. 3, 1984. See also World Social Prospects Association, *The Urban Tragedy* (Geneva: UNITAR, 1986).

9 See O. Sunkel, 'Debt, Development and Environment', submitted to WCED Public Hearings, Sao Paulo, 1985; R. Jordan S., 'Population and the Planning of Large Cities in Latin America', paper submitted to the International Conference on Population and the Urban Future, Barcelona, Spain, 19-22 May 1986.

10 G. Scimemi, 'Citta e Ambiente', DAEST, Istituto Universitario di Architettura, Venezia, 1987. See also, *The State of the Environment in OECD Member Countries* (Paris: OECD, 1979 and 1985).

11 I. Scott, *Urban and Spatial Development in Mexico* (London: Johns Hopkins University Press, 1982).

12 See Chapter 8 in J.E. Hardoy and D. Satterthwaite (eds.), *Small and Intermediate Urban Centres; Their Role in Regional and National Development in the Third World* (London: Hodder and Stoughton, 1986).

13 UNCHS, 'Habitat Hyderabad Squatter Settlement Upgrading Project, India', project monograph produced for the International Year of Shelter for the Homeless, Nairobi, 1986.

14 J. M. Kalbermatten et al., *Appropriate Technology for Water Supply and Sanitation; a Summary of Technical and Economic Options* (Washington, DC: World Bank, 1980).

15 D. Silk, 'Urban Agriculture', prepared for WCED, 1985.

16 N. Khouri-Dagher, 'Waste Recycling: Towards Greater Urban Self-Reliance', prepared for WCED, 1985.

17 See draft annotated agenda for October 1986, DAC Meeting on Urban Development, OECD document DAC (86)15. The World Bank definition of urban development assistance was used, which includes alleviating poverty and promoting urban efficiency, shelter, urban transport, integrated urban development, and regional development on secondary cities.

Part III

COMMON ENDEAVOURS

10

MANAGING THE COMMONS

The traditional forms of national sovereignty are increasingly challenged by the realities of ecological and economic interdependence. Nowhere is this more true than in shared ecosystems and in 'the global commons'—those parts of the planet that fall outside national jurisdictions. Here, sustainable development can be secured only through international co-operation and agreed regimes for surveillance, development, and management in the common interest. But at stake is not just the sustainable development of shared ecosystems and the commons, but of all nations whose development depends to a greater or lesser extent on their rational management.

By the same token, without agreed, equitable, and enforceable rules governing the rights and duties of states in respect of the global commons, the pressure of demands on finite resources will destroy their ecological integrity over time. Future generations will be impoverished, and the people who suffer most will be those who live in poor countries that can least assert their own claims in a free-for-all.

Management of the various commons—the oceans, outer space, and Antarctica—is at different stages of evolution, as is the very 'commonality' of these areas. In the Law of the Sea, the international community has developed one of the most ambitious and advanced of international conventions ever for the seas and the sea-bed. But a few countries have so far declined to adhere to the multilateral regime that had been the subject of protracted global negotiations, and this is blocking implementation of certain key aspects. Boundaries have been drawn on the oceans to separate the common seas from national Exclusive Economic Zones (EEZs), but as the common and claimed waters form interlocked ecological and economic systems, and as the health of one depends on the health of the other, both are discussed in this chapter. As for outer space, the least tapped global commons, discussion of joint management has only just begun. Antarctica has been covered for over a quarter of a century by a binding Treaty. Many states that are not party to it feel they should by right have a stake in the management of what they see as a part of the global commons.

I. OCEANS: THE BALANCE OF LIFE

In the Earth's wheel of life, the oceans provide the balance.[1] Covering over 70 per cent of the planet's surface, they play a critical role in maintaining its life-support systems, in moderating its climate, and in sustaining animals and plants, including minute, oxygen-producing phytoplankton. They provide protein, transportation, energy, employment, recreation, and other economic, social, and cultural activities.

The oceans also provide the ultimate sink for the by-products of human activities. Huge, closed septic tanks, they receive wastes from cities, farms, and industries via sewage outfalls, dumping from barges and ships, coastal run-off, river discharge, and even atmospheric transport. In the last few decades, the growth of the world economy, the burgeoning demand for food and fuel, and accumulating discharges of wastes have begun to press against the bountiful limits of the oceans.

The oceans are marked by a fundamental unity from which there is no escape. Interconnected cycles of energy, climate, marine living resources, and human activities move through coastal waters, regional seas, and the closed oceans. The effects of urban, industrial, and agricultural growth are contained within no nation's Exclusive Economic Zone; they pass through currents of water and air from nation to nation, and through complex food chains from species to species, distributing the burdens of development, if not the benefits, to both rich and poor.

Only the high seas outside of national jurisdiction are truly 'commons'; but fish species, pollution, and other effects of economic development do not respect these legal boundaries. Sound management of the ocean commons will require management of land-based activities as well. Five zones bear on this management: inland areas, which affect the oceans mostly via rivers; coastal lands—swamps, marshes, and so on—close to the sea, where human activities can directly affect the adjacent waters; coastal waters—estuaries, lagoons, and shallow waters generally—where the effects of land-based activities are dominant; offshore waters, out roughly to the edge of the continental shelf; and the high seas, largely beyond the 200-mile EEZs of coastal states' control.

Major fisheries are found mostly in offshore waters, while pollution affecting them comes mostly from inland sources and is concentrated in coastal waters. Formal international management is essential in the areas beyond the EEZs, although greater international co-operation,

'The world's environmental problems are greater than the sum of those in each country. Certainly, they can no longer be dealt with purely on a nation-state basis. The World Commission on Environment and Development must strike at this fundamental problem by recommending specific ways for countries to co-operate to surmount sovereignty, to embrace international instruments in order to deal with global threats. The growing trend towards isolationism demonstrates that the current rhythm of history is out of harmony with human aspirations, even with its chances for survival.

The challenge ahead is for us to transcend the self-interests of our respective nation-states so as to embrace a broader self-interest — the survival of the human species in a threatened world.'

Hon. Tom McMillan
Minister of Environment, Government of Canada
WCED Public Hearing, Ottawa, 26–27 May 1986

including improved frameworks to coordinate national action, is needed for all areas.

The Balance Under Threat

Today, the living resources of the sea are under threat from over-exploitation, pollution, and land-based development. Most major familiar fish stocks throughout the waters over the continental shelves, which provide 95 per cent of the world's fish catch, are now threatened by overfishing.

Other threats are more concentrated. The effects of pollution and land development are most severe in coastal waters and semi-enclosed seas along the world's shore-lines. The use of coastal areas for settlement, industry, energy facilities, and recreation will accelerate, as will the upstream manipulation of estuarine river systems through dams or diversion for agriculture and municipal water supplies. These pressures have destroyed estuarine habitats as irrevocably as direct dredging, filling, or paving. Shore-lines and their resources will suffer ever increasing damage if current, business-as-usual approaches to policy, management, and institutions continue.

Certain coastal and offshore waters are especially vulnerable to ecologically insensitive onshore development, to competitive over-fishing, and to pollution. The trends are of special concern in coastal areas where pollution by domestic sewage, industrial wastes, and pesticide and fertilizer run-off may threaten not only human health but also the development of fisheries.

Even the high seas are beginning to show some signs of stress from the billions of tons of contaminants added each year. Sediments brought to the oceans by great rivers such as the Amazon can be traced for as much as 2,000 kilometres out to sea.[2] Heavy metals from coal-burning plants and some industrial processes also reach the oceans via the atmosphere. The amount of oil spilled annually from tankers now approaches 1.5 million tons.[3] The marine environment, exposed to nuclear radiation from past nuclear weapons tests, is receiving more exposure from the continuing disposal of low-level radioactive wastes.

New evidence of a possible rapid depletion of the ozone layer and a consequent increase in ultraviolet radiation poses a threat not only to human health but to ocean life. Some scientists believe that this radiation could kill sensitive phytoplankton and fish larvae floating near the ocean's surface, damaging ocean food chains and possibly disrupting planetary support systems.[4]

High concentrations of substances such as heavy metals, organochlorines, and petroleum have been found on the oceans' surface. With continued accumulation, these could have complex and long-lasting effects.[5] The sea-floor is a region of complex physical, chemical, and biological activity where microbial processes play a major role, but as yet serious damage is known to have occurred only in very localized regions. Although these findings are encouraging, given accelerating pressures and the inadequacy of present data they provide no grounds for complacency.

Oceans Management

Looking to the next century, the Commission is convinced that sustainable development, if not survival itself, depends on significant advances in the management of the oceans. Considerable changes will be required in our institutions and policies and more resources will have to be committed to oceans management.

Three imperatives lie at the heart of the oceans management question:

- The underlying unity of the oceans requires effective global management regimes.
- The shared resource characteristics of many regional seas make forms of regional management mandatory.
- The major land-based threats to the oceans require effective national actions based on international co-operation.

Mutual dependence has increased in recent years. The Law of the Sea Convention, with the establishment of the 200-mile EEZs, has put an additional 35 per cent of the oceans' surface under national control with regard to management of natural resources. It has also provided an institutional setting that could lead to better management of these areas, given that single governments may be expected to manage more rationally resources over which they have sole control. However, this expectation ignores the realities of short-sighted political and economic goals.

An international ecosystem approach is required for the management of these resources for sustained use. Significant gains have been made in past decades, nationally and internationally, and many essential components have been put in place. But they do not add up to a system that reflects the imperatives mentioned above. Where the EEZs of several states come together in semi-enclosed or regional seas, integrated management requires varying degrees of international co-operation, such as joint monitoring and research on migratory species and measures to combat pollution and regulate actions whose effects reach across boundaries.

When it comes to the high seas beyond national jurisdiction, international action is essential. The sum of the multiple conventions and programmes now in place do not and cannot represent such a regime. Even the separate UN programmes cannot easily be coordinated, given the structure of the United Nations.[6]

The Commission believes that a number of actions are urgently needed to improve regimes for oceans management. Thus the Commission proposes measures to:

- strengthen capacity for national action, especially in developing countries;
- improve fisheries management;
- reinforce co-operation in semi-enclosed and regional seas;
- strengthen control of ocean disposal of hazardous and nuclear wastes; and
- advance the Law of the Sea.

National Action

Coastal governments should launch an urgent review of the legal and institutional requirements for integrated management of their EEZs, and of their roles in arrangements for international co-operation. This review should be undertaken within the framework of a clear statement of national goals and priorities. Reducing overexploitation of fisheries in coastal and offshore waters might be one such goal. The rapid clean-up of municipal and industrial pollution discharging into critical marine habitats could be another. Others might include strengthening national research and management capacity, and producing an inventory of coastal and marine resources.

Given the increased pressures on coastal and marine resources projected through the year 2000, all coastal states should have a complete inventory of these assets. Drawing on senior experts from national and international agencies, nations could deploy the latest satellite mapping and other techniques to put together an inventory of these resources and then monitor changes in them.

Many developing countries will require assistance to strengthen their legal and institutional frameworks needed for integrated management of coastal resources. Many small island and maritime developing countries lack the economic or military means to prevent the exploitation of their coastal resources or the pollution of their waters by powerful countries or companies. This has become a major concern in the Pacific in particular, and threatens the political stability of the region. International development banks and development assistance agencies should establish programmes to support the development of this institutional capacity.

Fisheries Management

World fisheries have been expanding since the Second World War, with the global catch rising at a steady 6–7 per cent annually from 20 million to 65 million tons between 1950 and 1969. But after 1970, as more and more stocks were depleted, the average annual growth in catches fell to only about 1 per cent. (See Table 10.1.) With conventional management practices, the growth era in fisheries is over. Even assuming restored productivity in now depleted stocks, and an increased harvest from underutilized fisheries, FAO sees only a gradual increase in catches, perhaps rising from current levels of over 80 million tons to about 100 million. This does not augur well for future food security, especially in low-income countries where fish are a principal source of animal protein and where millions secure their livelihoods from fisheries activities.[7]

Overexploitation threatens many stocks as economic resources. Several of the world's largest fisheries—the Peruvian anchoveta, several North Atlantic herring stocks, and the Californian sardine—have collapsed following periods of heavy fishing. In some of the areas affected by these collapses, and in other rich fisheries such as the Gulf of Thailand and off West Africa, heavy fishing has been followed by marked changes in species composition.[8] The reasons for these changes are not well understood, and more research is needed into the responses of marine resources to exploitation so that managers

TABLE 10.1

World Fish Catch in Major Fisheries, 1979–84 (thousand tons)

Fishery	1979	1980	1981	1982	1983	1984
N. Atlantic	14,667	14,676	14,489	13,597	13,891	13,940
N. Pacific	20,303	20,733	21,908	22,603	23,666	26,416
Cent. Atlantic	6,064	6,867	6,833	7,239	7,210	7,164
Cent. Pacific	7,536	7,910	8,478	8,175	7,848	8,531
Indian Ocean	3,541	3,693	3,728	3,852	4,061	4,362
South Atlantic	4,420	3,895	4,037	4,340	4,314	3,957
South Pacific	7,242	6,619	7,240	8,328	6,724	8,684
Inland	7,240	7,603	8,138	8,455	9,131	9,716
Total*	71,014	71,996	74,850	76,590	76,846	82,770
Developed	37,143	38,234	38,890	39,265	39,991	42,412
Developing	33,871	33,758	35,961	37,326	36,855	40,358
Developing countries' catch as per cent of world total	47.7	46.9	48.0	48.7	48.0	48.8

* Columns do not add to totals due to rounding.

Source: Based on data in FAO, *Yearbooks of Fishery Statistics* (Rome: 1979–84).

can receive better scientific advice. Greater support for such work is urgently needed, and this support must include additional assistance to developing countries in increasing their research capacity and their knowledge of their own resources.

One factor leading to the establishment of extended EEZs was the concern of coastal states, both industrialized and developing, over the depletion of fisheries off their coasts. A large number of conventions had been established covering most major fisheries, but they proved inadequate in most cases. Participating countries were in general unable to overcome the difficulties of allocating shares to limited common resources. Improved management was seen as an urgent need, and open access was perceived as the main obstacle to it.

The advent of extended EEZs under the Law of the Sea Convention was expected to solve or at least alleviate the problem. Coastal states were required to introduce effective conservation and management of the living resources in their EEZs. They could also control the activities of foreign fishermen and develop their own fisheries.

Industrial countries have been much more successful in doing this

> **'***The opinion of the public is what you see here in this room. You see important leaders from all over Brazil, from all over the country that have come here, from the rubbermen that was under a palmtree yesterday and was here speaking to the U.N. Commission and leaders that are independent. The Brazilian population yearned to have someone to speak to. Someone who will listen, who will not sort of mystify things, and someone who will not trick them. So there is an enormous expectation with regards to the seriousness of your Commission.***'**
>
> Randau Marques
> *Journalist*
> WCED Public Hearing, Sao Paulo, 28-29 Oct 1985

than developing countries. In the north-west Atlantic, the annual catch by long-range fleets has declined from over 2 million tons before 1974 to around a quarter of a million tons in 1983, and the share of the catch taken by the United States and Canada has risen from under 50 per cent to over 90 per cent.

Yet long-range industrial fishing fleets still catch about 5 million tons annually in developing regions. Off West Africa, for example, over half the total catch is still taken by such fleets.[9] This is due partly to the fact that many of the biggest resources lie off thinly populated areas—the western edge of the Sahara and off Namibia. But it is also due to the common lack of locally available capital, and to a shortage of local expertise in many technical aspects of fisheries, especially processing and marketing.

Coastal developing countries can usually obtain some modest revenue in the form of licence fees, but this represents only a fraction of what they could earn from a full national use of the resource. Another 10-15 million tons of so far underutilized or unexploited resources could be added to the existing fisheries off their coasts.[10] There is a pressing need for these resources to be managed sustainably, for the benefit of developing countries and in ways that help to meet global nutritional needs.

Whaling offers another example. Recognizing that the history of whaling up to the 1960s was that of overexploitation, the International Whaling Commission (IWC), the main international body regulating whaling, has taken a series of conservation measures since the early 1970s and now all stocks that are below a certain level have been classified as protected from commercial whaling.

In its early days, the IWC was dominated by whaling nations. After 1979, non-whaling nations became an increasingly significant majority of the membership. This change was reflected in the IWC's decisions, which increasingly opted in cases of scientific doubt for a cautious approach and the reduction of catch levels or the cessation of whaling altogether on certain stocks.

This trend culminated in the moratorium decision of 1982. Members have the right to object and continue commercial whaling or to catch whales for scientific purposes. There is a strongly held view in conservation circles that whaling for scientific purposes can be used as a loophole by whaling nations. Permissions for such hunting should be stringently applied by IWC members, or the IWC's credibility will be undermined.

An important political factor in recent developments has been the ability of the US Government to invoke legislation that enables contracts for fishing in US waters to be withheld from nations that undermine marine conservation agreements. The value of such fishery concessions is large and the legislation has significant political and economic leverage. Another important factor has been the strength of the non-governmental organizations (NGOs) in organizing support for anti-whaling actions, lobbying governments and organizing boycotts of fish and other products from whaling nations.

By early 1987, whaling was restricted to scientific catches by Iceland and the Republic of Korea and to a small catch by Norway, which continued to object to the moratorium, but which planned to halt its commercial whaling following the 1987 season. And there were catches by Japan and the Soviet Union. The Soviet Union had indicated it would observe the moratorium after the 1987 Antarctic season, and Japan had withdrawn its objection to the moratorium with effect from 1988. However, Japan may continue whaling for scientific purposes.[11] In addition, some whaling was being performed by native peoples in the Soviet Union and Alaska.

If the moratorium is observed and whaling for scientific purposes is not abused, commercial whaling will no longer be a major threat to the conservation of whale stocks taken as a whole. The annual rate of increase of these stocks, however, is unlikely to exceed a few per cent. Thus substantial whale populations will probably not be observed much before the second half of the next century.

Co-operation on Regional Seas

A large number of agreements have been entered into on regional seas. The Commission has not attempted to evaluate them all, but given the Commission's origin in the UN Environment Programme (UNEP) Governing Council and the General Assembly resolution, it has given special attention to UNEP's Regional Seas Programme. This programme now brings together over 130 states bordering 11 different shared seas around the world, states that have an interest in co-operating for their own and mutual benefit. UNEP provides the initial impetus by bringing governments together to develop a flexible legal framework within which further agreements can be negotiated as needs require and politics allow. UNEP also provides some initial seed money for programme development, but the governments of the region themselves are meant to take over funding and management, drawing on the technical advice of UN and other agencies. The result is a gradually evolving action-oriented programme rooted in the needs of the regions as perceived by the governments concerned. Fourteen UN agencies and over 40 international and regional organizations participate in the world-wide programme.

The political strategy behind the programme and the requirement that management and financing be undertaken by the participating countries have clearly been crucial to its success. But it is one thing to contribute a few million dollars for research, and quite another to incorporate the resulting findings into land-based development plans and to enforce strong pollution control programmes. The massive US-Canadian clean-up of the Great Lakes over the past 15 years cost $8.85 billion for partial treatment of municipal and industrial wastes.[12] Huge investments will also be required to roll back land-based pollution along UNEP's regional seas. Yet nowhere have the sums been committed under agreed schedules to construct the necessary urban and industrial pollution control systems and to underwrite policies to control agricultural run-off. The programme now has to confront the regional seas challenge through the year 2000—moving beyond general agreement on goals and research to a solid schedule of investment on a scale that will make a difference.

Measures to Control Ocean Disposal of Waste

The Convention on the Prevention of Marine Pollution by Dumping of Wastes and Other Matter (London Dumping Convention), which has world-wide application, was concluded in November 1972 and entered into force on 30 August 1975.[13] Its political evolution parallels that of the International Whaling Commission. Initially, it consisted largely of dumping states, but non-dumping states are now in the majority. At present it has 61 contracting parties, and secretariat facilities are provided by the International Maritime Organization. The dumping of wastes is regulated by the three annexes to the

'Why must we gamble with the lives of innocent children in order to generate plutonium for bombs? Even to contemplate dumping radioactive waste in waters that belong to all of us as part of our global heritage is an outrage. For us to make such important decisions on behalf of future generations without taking into account the morality of using international waters as an exclusive rubbish bin is an arrogant act.'

Peter Wilkinson
Greenpeace
WCED Public Hearing, Oslo, 24–25 June 1985

Convention[14]: on extremely dangerous substances including high-level radioactive wastes, the dumping of which is prohibited (Annex I); on somewhat less noxious substances, the dumping of which can be permitted only by 'prior special permit' (Annex II); and all other substances, which can be dumped only after a general permit has been obtained from national authorities (Annex III). Although the Convention applies to all wastes dumped deliberately at sea, the ocean disposal of radioactive wastes has attracted the most attention. It is this question that the Commission considers here.

Prior to 1983, Belgium, the Netherlands, Switzerland, and the United Kingdom had been dumping low-level wastes regularly at the north-east Atlantic dumpsite in international waters off the coast of Spain. Despite protests from representatives of these nations at the London Dumping Convention meeting that they would ignore a moratorium resolution on low-level wastes and carry out dumping during 1983, a de facto moratorium—which all countries honour but to which some have not formally agreed—went into and remains in effect. Under it, no disposal should take place until it can be demonstrated that it is environmentally safe.

In 1985, the London Dumping Convention voted to extend indefinitely the moratorium on the ocean dumping of low-level radioactive wastes.[15] As a result, the burden of proof that such activities are safe was effectively reversed, being put on those nations who want to dump. This revolutionary reversal, though not binding, reflects the changed composition of the London Dumping Convention.

In 1986, the London Dumping Convention established an intergovernmental panel of experts to examine the issue of comparative risks of land- and sea-based options for disposal of radioactive waste. Without prejudging this assessment, the Commission would urge all states to continue to refrain from disposing of either low- or high-level wastes at sea or in the sea-bed. Moreover, it would seem prudent to anticipate continuing opposition to sea dumping and to actively pursue the siting and development of environmentally safe, land-based methods of disposal.

Several other conventions regulate the dumping of wastes in the north-east Atlantic and North Sea, the Mediterranean Sea, and the Baltic Sea. Most of the Regional Seas Conventions also include a general provision calling on contracting parties to take all appropriate measures to prevent and reduce pollution caused by dumping.

Land-based sources of nuclear waste have become significant in the North Sea, where high levels of radioactivity have been found in fish, and could threaten other seas.[16] The Convention for the Prevention of Marine Pollution from Land-Based Sources (Paris Convention) was ratified in 1978 by eight states and the European Economic Community. While it has achieved some international co-operation, its silence on nuclear plants and its acceptance of the 'best available technology' principle in determining permitted levels of radioactive discharges clearly needs to be reviewed.

The Law of the Sea Convention requires states to establish national laws and regulations to 'prevent, reduce and control pollution of the marine environment from dumping'. It also requires express prior approval by the coastal state for dumping in the territorial sea, in the EEZs, and onto the continental shelf. The legislative history of this Article indicates that coastal states have not only the right to act but a duty to do so. States also have an obligation under the Law of the Sea to ensure that their activities do not injure the health and environment of neighbouring states and the commons.

The Commission encourages the London Dumping Convention to reaffirm the rights and responsibilities of states to control and regulate dumping within the 200-mile EEZ. It is urgent that they do so, as oceans and food chains respect no boundaries.

Moreover, all states should undertake to report releases of toxic and radioactive substances from land-based sources into any body of water to the appropriate Convention Secretariat so that they may begin to report on the aggregate releases into various seas. Competent authorities must be designated to keep records of the nature and quantities of wastes dumped. Beyond that, regional institutions should forward this information to the London Dumping Convention secretariat.

The Law of the Sea

The United Nations Conference on the Law of the Sea was the most ambitious attempt ever to provide an internationally agreed regime for the management of the oceans. The resulting Convention represents a major step towards an integrated management regime for the oceans. It has already encouraged national and international action to manage the oceans.[17]

The Convention reconciled widely divergent interests of states, and established the basis for a new equity in the use of the oceans and their resources. It confirmed that coastal states are empowered to exercise sovereignty over their territorial sea, sea-bed and subsoil, and the superjacent air space, up to a distance of 12 nautical miles. It redefined the rights of coastal states concerning the continental shelf. It established Exclusive Economic Zones of up to 200 nautical miles within which the coastal state may exercise sovereign rights with regard to the management of national resources, living and non-living, in the waters, sea-bed, and subsoil.

The Convention removed 35 per cent of the oceans as a source of growing conflict between states. It stipulates that coastal states must ensure that the living resources of the EEZs are not endangered by overexploitation. Thus, not only do governments now have the legal power and the self-interest to apply sound principles of resource management within this area, but they have an obligation to do so. The Convention calls for regional co-operation in formulating and implementing conservation and management strategies for living marine resources, including co-operation in the exchange of scientific information, the conservation and development of stocks, and the optimum use of highly migratory species.

Similarly, coastal states now have a clear interest in the sound management of the continental shelf and in the prevention of pollution from land- and sea-based activities. Under the Convention, coastal states may adopt laws and regulations for their EEZs compatible with international rules and standards to combat pollution from vessels.

The Convention also defines the waters, sea-bed, and subsoil beyond the limits of national jurisdiction, and recognizes this as international. Over 45 per cent of the planet's surface, this sea-bed area and its resources are declared to be the 'common heritage of mankind', a concept that represents a milestone in the realm of international co-operation. The Convention would bring all mining activities in the sea-bed under the control of an International Seabed Authority.

By early 1987, the Convention had been signed by 159 nations, and 32 countries had ratified it. However, a small number of significant states had indicated that they were unlikely to ratify it.[18] The reasons for this rest largely with the regime proposed to manage the common sea-bed.

Despite this, many of the Convention's other provisions have been broadly accepted and have already entered into international law and practice in various ways. This process should be encouraged, especially as regards those provisions that relate to the environment. This Commission believes that the Convention should be ratified by the major technological powers and come into force. Indeed, the most significant initial action that nations can take in the interests of the oceans' threatened life-support system is to ratify the Law of the Sea Convention.

II. SPACE: A KEY TO PLANETARY MANAGEMENT

Outer space can play a vital role in ensuring the continued habitability of the Earth, largely through space technology to monitor the vital signs of the planet and aid humans in protecting its health. According to the 1967 Outer Space Treaty, outer space, including the moon and other celestial bodies, is not subject to national appropriation by claim of sovereignty, by means of use of occupation, or by any other means. The UN Committee on the Peaceful Uses of Outer Space has been labouring to see that these ideals remain on the agenda. This Commission, in view of these developments, considers space as a global commons and part of the common heritage of mankind.

The future of the space as a resource will depend not so much on technology as on the slow and difficult struggle to create sound international institutions to manage this resource. It will depend most of all upon humanity's ability to prevent an arms race in space.

Remote Sensing from Space

If humanity is going to respond effectively to the consequences of changes human activity has induced—the build-up of atmospheric carbon dioxide, depletion of stratospheric ozone, acid precipitation, and tropical forest destruction—better data on the Earth's natural systems will be essential.

Today several dozen satellites contribute to the accumulation of new knowledge about the Earth's systems—for example, about the spread of volcanic gases, enabling scientists for the first time to describe the specific links between a major natural disturbance of the upper atmosphere and changes in the weather thousands of miles away.[19]

6We need a kind of new earth/space monitoring system. I think that it goes farther than simply an earth environmental system. It's a combined earth/space monitoring system, a new agency that would have the resources to be able to monitor, report, and recommend in a very systematic way on the earth/space interaction that is so fundamental to a total ecological view of the biosphere.9

Maxwell Cohen
University of Ottawa
WCED Public Hearing, Ottawa, 26–27 May 1986

Satellites also played a key scientific role after the 1986 discovery of a 'hole' in the ozone layer over Antarctica. When ground-based observers noted this phenomenon, archived satellite data were examined and provided a record of seasonal ozone fluctuation extending back nearly a decade.[20] And scientists have been able to follow closely the unfolding of the drought in the Sahel region of Africa in the 1980s. Satellite-generated maps correlating rainfall patterns and biomass have served as a tool in understanding droughts and helped in the targeting of relief aid.

Recently, an international and interdisciplinary group of scientists has proposed a major new initiative—the International Geosphere-Biosphere Programme—to be co-ordinated through the International Council of Scientific Unions. It would investigate the biosphere using many technologies, including satellites. This proposal seemed in 1987 to be gaining momentum; it was already influencing the budget decisions of several nations on allocations for future satellite launches and is increasing coordination between existing efforts.

The primary frustration about this wealth of data is that the information is dispersed among governments and institutions, rather than being pooled. UNEP's Global Environment Monitoring System is a modest effort to pool space data relevant to the Earth's habitability. It should be strengthened. But most such efforts are underfunded, undercoordinated, and inadequate to the tasks.

The primary responsibility for action rests initially with national governments, co-operating to pool, store, and exchange data. In time, international efforts might be funded through some direct global revenue source or through contributions from individual nations. (See Chapter 12.)

The Geosynchronous Orbit

From an economic point of view, the most valuable part of the

Earth's orbital space is the geosynchronous orbit, a band of space 36,000 kilometres above the equator.[21] Most communication and many weather satellites—as well as many military ones—are in geosynchronous orbit. To prevent signals to and from the satellites interfering with one another, satellites must be placed some distance apart, effectively limiting the number that can use this valuable band to 180. Thus, the geosynchronous orbit is not only a valuable but also a scarce and limited global resource.

The growth in satellite communication traffic during the 1970s led to many predictions that slots would soon be saturated. Thus conflict emerged over the use and ownership of the geosynchronous orbit, largely between industrial nations that have the capacity to put satellites in this orbit and the equatorial developing nations that do not but that lie beneath this band of space.

The first effort to devise a property regime for geosynchronous orbit was the 1976 Bogota Declaration, signed by seven equatorial countries.[22] These countries declared that the orbits above them were extensions of their territorial airspace. The Bogota Declaration has been challenged by some nations that see it as contradicting the 'non-appropriation' principle of the Outer Space Treaty. Another group of developing countries proposed a licensing system for the use of geosynchronous orbits.[23] Countries would be awarded slots that could then be sold, rented, or reserved for future use.

Another way of managing this resource and capturing its rental value for the common interest would be for an international body to own and license the slots to bidders at an auction. Such an alternative would be analogous to the Seabed Authority in the Law of the Sea Convention.

Industrial countries have opposed the creation of a property rights regime for geosynchronous orbit, especially a regime that granted rights to slots to countries that cannot now use them. They argue that a regime of prior allocation would drive up costs and reduce the incentive of the private sector to develop and use this orbit. Others, who see a rapidly growing role for satellite communications, argue that regulatory regimes should be established before competition makes such a step more difficult.

Since satellite communications involve the use of radio waves, a de facto regime for the parcelling out of slots in geosynchronous orbit has emerged through the activities of the International Tele-communications Union (ITU) in the past several years. The ITU allocates the use of the radio waves (those parts of the electromagnetic spectrum used for communication).[24] The highly technical character of the task of parcelling out radio waves, combined with the fact that strict compliance is necessary to allow any user to enjoy access to this resource, has produced a successful international resource regime, based on three regional conferences, for effective management of the resource.[25] Whether this approach will endure depends in large part upon the perceived justice of the decisions reached by the regional conferences.

The Pollution of Orbital Space

Debris in orbit is a growing threat to human activities in space. In 1981, a panel of experts convened by the American Institute of Aeronautics and Astronautics concluded that the growth of space debris could pose 'an unacceptable threat' to life in space within a decade.[26] This debris consists of spent fuel tanks, rocket shells, satellites that no longer function, and shrapnel from explosions in space; it is concentrated in the region between 160 and 1,760 kilometres above the Earth.

With greater care in the design and disposal of satellites, much of it could be avoided. However, the creation of debris is an integral and unavoidable consequence of the testing and use of space weapons. The contribution of military activities to the Earth's 'debris belt' could grow greatly if plans to place large numbers of satellite-based weapons and weapons-related sensors are realized.

The most important measure to minimize space debris, therefore, is to prevent the further testing and deployment of space-based weapons or weapons designed for use against objects in space.

Clean-up would be expensive. It has been proposed that the major powers lead an international effort to retrieve the larger pieces of space debris from orbit. Such work would involve the design, construction, and launch of vehicles that could manoeuvre in space and grapple with large, jagged, tumbling space objects. The proposal has elicited little enthusiasm.

Nuclear Power in Orbit

Many spacecraft are nuclear-powered and threaten contamination if they fall to the Earth.[27] There are two basic approaches to the problem: Ban or regulate. The option of banning all radioactive materials from space is the simplest to enact. It would eliminate the problem and would also severely stunt the further development of space-based warfare systems. A total ban should exempt scientific uses in deep-space, as small amounts of fissionable materials have

> *'Utilization of spacecraft for solving the problems of forestry provides a good example of the peaceful use of space. Taking into account the interests of the present and future generations, there is no other more favourable area of space technology application than environmental protection, to study the natural resources of Earth and control their rational utilization and reproduction. We think that in the forthcoming years international co-operaton in this field will be further expanded '*

L. E. Mikhailov
USSR State Committee on Forestry
WCED Public Hearing, Moscow, 11 Dec 1986

been essential for the powering of deep-space probes. A ban on reactors in space would be easy to monitor, because reactors produce waste heat detectable by infrared sensors at great distances. Verifying the absence of small nuclear power systems would be more difficult, but still possible.

A wide variety of methods are available for regulating the use of radioactive materials in space. The most important include limiting the size of reactors permitted in orbit, requiring shielding around radioactive material sufficient to withstand re-entry into the Earth's atmosphere, and requiring deep-space disposal of spacecraft that contain radioactive material. All are technologically feasible, but would add cost and complexity to missions. Nevertheless, these measures should be implemented as a minimum step.

Towards a Space Regime

Soon after the aeroplane was invented, it became obvious that collisions would occur unless a general air traffic control regime was established. This model offers a useful way to think about the need for and contents of a space regime. The creation of 'rules of the road' for orbital space could ensure that the activities of some do not degrade the resource for all.

Orbital space cannot be effectively managed by any one country acting alone. The inherently international character of orbital space has been recognized by a majority of nations in the Outer Space Treaty. The international community should seek to design and implement a space regime to ensure that space remains a peaceful environment for the benefit of all.

An essential step towards efficient management of the space resource is to abandon the notion that because outer space in general is unlimited, orbital space can absorb all human activity. Because of the speeds involved, orbital space is for practical purposes much 'closer' than the atmosphere. A system of space traffic control in which some activities were forbidden and others harmonized cuts a middle path between the extremes of a sole Space Authority and the present near anarchy.

The electromagnetic spectrum has been effectively regulated by international agreement, and through this regulation has begun to emerge the beginnings of a space regime for geosynchronous orbital space. An extension of this type of approach to control debris and the use of nuclear materials in orbit is the next logical step.

A fine balance must be struck between regulating activities too late and regulating non-existent activities too soon. Regulating activities on the Moon, for example, beyond the general principles laid out in the Outer Space Treaty is clearly premature. But regulating space debris and nuclear materials in Earth orbit is clearly overdue.

III. ANTARCTICA:
TOWARDS GLOBAL CO-OPERATION

The Antarctic continent—larger than the United States and Mexico combined—for over a generation has been managed under a regime of multilateral co-operation that has secured environmental protection. Signed on 1 December 1959, the Antarctic Treaty has been the vehicle for a number of important initiatives in pursuit of its two primary objectives: to maintain Antarctica for peaceful uses only, prohibiting all military activities, weapons testing, nuclear explosions, and disposal of radioactive wastes; and to promote freedom of scientific investigation in Antarctica and international co-operation to that end.[28]

The fact that the 'question of Antarctica' is today on the UN agenda[29] indicates the reality that there is a debate in the international community over the future management of the continent. Under the combined pressures of economic, technological, environmental, and other trends, there are new initiatives to establish a regime for minerals exploitation. New questions about equitable management are presenting challenges that may reshape the political context of the continent within the next decade.[30]

During the forthcoming period of change, the challenge is to ensure that Antarctica is managed in the interests of all humankind, in a manner that conserves its unique environment, preserves its value for scientific research, and retains its character as a demilitarized, non-nuclear zone of peace.

Responsibility for guiding change at present rests initially with the countries party to the Antarctic Treaty.[31] Eighteen nations now enjoy full decision-making status under the Treaty, with these Consultative Parties exercising their rights and carrying out their obligations in peaceful co-operation despite their divergent views on the territorial claims to parts of the continent. An additional 17 nations have observer status at the biennial Antarctic Treaty System (ATS) meetings.

The Antarctic Treaty is open to accession by any state that is a member of the United Nations, and by others invited to accede. To become a Consultative Party, a state must demonstrate concrete interest in Antarctica by conducting substantial scientific research there. The Treaty nations feel that this system is applied flexibly and opens the Treaty to all nations with a genuine interest in Antarctica. Many developing nations without the resources to conduct research on the continent feel that this condition effectively excludes most of the world's nations.[32]

But the question of participation is not polarized between industrial and developing countries. Not all industrialized countries are members of the Treaty, and Argentina, Brazil, Chile, China, India, and Uruguay have consultative status under it, while several additional developing countries have acceded to it. However, the overwhelming majority of developing countries, including all those of Africa, remain outside the arrangements.

There is furthermore no general agreement as to whether Antarctica is part of the international commons. For example, seven states maintain territorial claims. Moreover, many developing countries reject the idea that what they regard as the common heritage of mankind should be managed by some countries to the exclusion of others. Many of them see the Antarctic Treaty System as the exclusive preserve of the rich and technologically advanced countries. Some object to what they consider the exclusivity of the Treaty System, with countries self-appointed to determine the future of the continent. Although the Consultative Parties assert that they have managed Antarctica in the interests of all peoples, several nations maintain that these interests should not be defined by the Consultative Parties alone; this view has gained many new sources of expression since 1959. Despite the present debate over the continent's future, many nations outside the Treaty have recognized the trusteeship role played by the Treaty nations in protecting the environment of Antarctica.[33]

The Commission does not propose to adjudicate the status of Antarctica. But it sees it as essential that the continent be managed

Box 10-1. Antarctica's Unique Treaty Arrangements

Under the Antarctic Treaty, the seven states claiming territory there have agreed with non-claimant parties to the Treaty to set aside the disputed territorial status of Antarctica in order to carry out agreed-upon activities in the area.

While the Treaty is in force, no acts or activities taking place will 'constitute a basis for asserting, supporting, or denying a claim to territorial sovereignty in Antarctica', nor may any new claim, or enlargement of an existing claim, be asserted.

Decisions are taken by consensus, which guarantees to both claimant and non-claimant states that no activity or management practice prejudicial to their position on the territorial status of Antarctica will be approved. The Treaty provides for on-site inspection at any time in any or all areas of Antarctica by designated nationals of the Consultative Parties.

Source: Based on L. Kimball, 'Testing the Great Experiment', *Environment*, September 1985.

and protected in a responsible manner that takes into account the common interests at stake. It notes also that the legal and management regimes are in the midst of a process of change leading to wider participation.

The Antarctic Treaty Consultative Parties have endeavoured to demonstrate a strong concern for the protection of the continent's environment and the conservation of its natural resources. (See Box 10-1.) In 1964, they adopted the 'Agreed Measures for the Conservation of Antarctic Fauna and Flora',[34] which amount to a conservation protocol to the Treaty. At subsequent biennial meetings, they have continued to develop environmental principles and measures to guide the planning and execution of their activities. Additional measures would improve the scope and effectiveness of environmental protection, and it would be useful to consider means to ensure that the record of compliance with these measures is widely known.

The Consultative Parties have also played a leading role in the promulgation of two important international conventions relating to conservation of living resources: the 1972 Convention on the Conservation of Antarctic Seals and the 1980 Convention on the Conservation of Antarctic Marine Living Resources.[35] The second arose out of concern that the depletion of Antarctic fish stocks, particularly shrimp-like krill, could have severe and unpredictable effects on related and dependent species. It adopts an 'ecosystem approach' to resource management.[36]

Taken together, these legal instruments and accompanying protocols and recommendations, along with the non-governmental body the Scientific Committee on Antarctic Research (SCAR), constitute what is referred to as the Antarctic Treaty System. This system demonstrates the evolution that has taken place under the Antarctic Treaty since it entered into force.

Several international NGOs have begun to monitor the adequacy of and compliance with environmental protection and conservation measures in Antarctica and have frequently been critical of these measures. They have also sought observer status at ATS meetings and greater involvement in the formulation and review of Antarctic policies. Some UN agencies are concerned with southern hemisphere meteorology, oceanography, or fishing and have become involved in Antarctic science and politics. A concrete result of this interest has been invitations extended to the Food and Agriculture Organization, the Intergovernmental Oceanographic Commission, the International Union for the Conservation of Nature and Natural Resources, IWC, SCAR, the Scientific Committee on Oceanic Research, and the World Metereorogical Organization to attend as observers meetings of the Commission for the Conservation of Antarctic Marine Living Resources (CCAMLR). The European Economic Community is also a CCAMLR member as a result of its member states ceding competence to it with respect to fisheries management policies.

For the ATS to remain viable into the next century, it will need to continue to evolve and adapt itself to deal with new issues and new circumstances. Although the Treaty could run indefinitely, in 1991 any of the Consultative Parties may call for a general conference of the signatory nations to review its operation.

Guard Present Achievements

Although further change in the management status of Antarctica is inevitable, it is essential that such change not jeopardize the achievements of the Treaty System in the areas of peace, science, conservation, and environment. Antarctica has been an agreed zone of peace for nearly 30 years, free of all military activities, nuclear tests, and radioactive wastes. This is a foundation on which humanity must build.

Cooperation in scientific investigation has steadily expanded; it must be further strengthened, especially concerning Antarctica's role in global atmospheric and oceanic circulation and world climate. At the same time, more efforts should be made to secure full participation in such research. Means must be found to expand consultation and participation and to extend the benefits of international co-operation

'The most cruel environmental threat comes from the environmental movement itself as we see the animal rights laws systematically destroy our way of life and violate our right as aboriginal peoples to our traditions and values. Yet our people, including the Arctic people, need development. The challenge is to find strategies for development that meet the needs of the people and the environment.'

Rhoda Inuksu
Inuit Indian
WCED Public Hearing, Ottawa, 26–27 May 1986

in Antarctic science and technology to the international community as a whole.

Several suggestions along these lines have been made. They include establishing a fund to facilitate the participation of interested developing countries in Antarctic science, and inviting more scientists from developing nations to join projects and visit scientific stations. Given the costly technologies involved in Antarctic science, possibilities should be explored for sharing Antarctic base and logistics capabilities with interested non-consultative states. The right to consultative status could be extended to states participating in scientific activities on a joint basis.

As Antarctic activities multiply, sound conservation will also require increased data collection, monitoring, and environmental assessment. The interactive and cumulative effects of these projects must be carefully reviewed and areas of unique scientific and environmental value protected.

Anticipate Pressures for Mineral Development

Minerals of various kinds are known to exist in Antarctica, but the minerals talks have triggered false assumptions about the imminence of their development. Even given the most optimistic growth trends, it seems clear that more accessible sources will be developed elsewhere long before Antarctica attracts major investment. Only two minerals have been found that might exist in concentrations suitable for exploitation—coal in the Transantarctic Mountains and iron in the Prince Charles Mountains. Mining them would be a fool's venture.[37] The costs would be prohibitive, and sufficient coal and iron can be found closer to the main markets.

Circumstantial evidence suggests the existence of offshore oil and gas, but no deposits have yet been discovered. The Federal Republic of Germany, France, Japan, the United Kingdom, and the USSR have surveyed Antarctica's continental shelves. The surveys were of a scientific nature, but, coinciding as they did with the first serious discussions of a minerals regime, were viewed by some observers as signalling commercial interests.

The 18 Consultative Parties are conducting negotiations among themselves to complete an agreed legal framework for determining the environmental acceptability of possible minerals exploration and development in Antarctica and to govern any such activities.[38] Treaty members felt that it would be more difficult to agree on such a regime after actual finds have been made. The negotiations in many ways are an expression of the idea that prevention is better than cure, forethought preferable to afterthought.

Antarctica is an enormous continent where claims to sovereignty are in dispute and where there are no agreed legal bases for issuing licences, leasing or selling mineral rights, or receiving royalty payments. These delicate questions have now been raised and will not lie silent until they have been answered within an internationally agreed framework. Until these matters are resolved, and protection of the Antarctic environment is assured, it seems unlikely that any nation or group of nations will be able to invest securely in developing the continent's mineral resources.[39]

Given the absence of technologies tested in the ultimate extremities of Antarctic conditions, the lack of agreement on procedures to assess and take account of the impacts of any development, and the sparse data base, it could take a generation or more of dedicated research and technological development to ensure that minerals exploitation would not destroy the Antarctic's fragile ecosystem and its place in global environmental processes. Thus it is important that no minerals activity takes place until these conditions have changed, and then only in consonance with a regime that guarantees implementation of the most stringent standards needed to protect the continent's environment and share the proceeds equitably.

Promote Evolution of Antarctic Treaty System

In the years ahead, activities in Antarctica will expand in kind and scale, as will the numbers of participants in such activities. Further efforts must be made to ensure effective management of those activities and an orderly expansion of participation in such management. A variety of options are being discussed by the international community. More effective management, including expanded participation, could evolve gradually through the existing Treaty System. But given the extent of probable change and the lure of mineral wealth, however

Some unique objects like Lake Baikal and Siberia, the Great Lakes in Africa and North America, are part of our global patrimony. They are some of the absolute values our planet possesses and their significance transcends any national boundaries. We should learn how to foresee their future and how to anticipate the after-effects of large-scale engineeriong projects.

Since people's interests vary, it cannot be taken for granted that people will accept scholars' recommendations and come to agreement on that score. And their agreement is of special importance in situations where global problems are involved and where the human race as a whole may be threatened with perils generated by the absence of such agreement.

What is needed today is the moulding of a new ethos and new arrangements for building an understanding among people, countries, and regions. And as a first step we should produce new knowledge, concentrate our research efforts on maintaining life on Earth, and develop a system distributing and disseminating knowledge and new moral criteria in a way that makes it available to billions of people who inhabit our planet.

Academician N. N. Moiseev
USSR Academy of Sciences
WCED Public Hearing, Moscow, 8 Dec 1986

remote, such an approach could be too slow to retain political support. Another is that the above goals might be reached through the negotiation of an entirely new system. However, neither of these approaches would be free of difficulty. Yet another alternative would be to intensify efforts to make the Treaty System more universal, more open, and responsive to expressions of concrete and legitimate concern and interest in Antarctica.

Establish a Means for More Effective Communication

As activities under the different treaties increase, so does the importance of coordination among the advisory and decision-making authorities responsible for various areas. Antarctica may require the establishment of somewhat more formal institutions than have governed the first generation of activities, in order to foster better communication and coordination both within and outside the Treaty System.

Antarctica is on the agenda of the UN General Assembly and will probably remain so. Nothing will happen, however, unless the participants in the debate find terms of reference that can command broad-based support and an agreed-upon means to explore and give effect to improved management.

To focus on longer-term strategies to preserve and build on the achievements of the existing Treaty System, nations must create the means to foster dialogue among politicians, scientists, environmentalists, and industries from countries within and outside it. A good place to start would be the development of closer working relationships between the parties to Antarctic regimes and the international organizations within and outside the UN system that have responsibilities for science and technology, conservation, and environmental management.

National policy processes could also be structured to provide for dialogue with concerned industries, public interest organizations, and expert advisors, perhaps through an Antarctic advisory committee. The US Government has been in the forefront of those countries appointing industry and public interest advisors to its delegations to Consultative Parties meetings. Australia, Denmark, and New Zealand have more recently followed suit.

Hammering out an internationally supported consensus on Antarctica is a huge task requiring time and patience. And the lure of minerals increases with every new rumour of a find. Yet such a consensus is the only way to prevent a tragic plundering of the silent continent, and to maintain Antarctica as a symbol of peaceful international co-operation and environmental protection.

Notes

1 This section draws on F. Szekely, 'The Marine and Coastal Environment', prepared for WCED, 1986; J. Beddington, 'Whaling', prepared for WCED, 1986; and V. Sebek, 'Policy Paper on Dumping', prepared for WCED, 1986.

2 M.W. Holdgate et al., 'The Marine Environment', in *The World Environment 1972–1982* (Dublin: Tycooly International Publishing Ltd., 1982).

3 See National Academy of Sciences, *Oil in the Sea* (Washington, DC: National Academy Press, 1985); and OECD, *Maritime Transport, 1984* (Paris: 1985).

4 'Scientists Closer to Identifying Cause of Antarctic Ozone Depletion', *National Science Foundation News*, 20 October 1986; Ad Hoc Working Group of Legal and Technical Experts for the Elaboration of a Protocol on the Control of Chlorofluorocarbons to the Vienna Convention for the Protection of the Ozone Layer (Vienna Group), 'Report of the Second Part of the Workshop on the Control of Chlorofluorocarbons, Leesburg, USA', UNEP/WG.151/Background 2, Na.86-2184, UNEP, Nairobi, 15 October 1986; A.S. Miller and I.M. Mintzer, *The Sky Is the Limit: Strategies for Protecting the Ozone Layer*, WRI Research Report No. 3 (Washington, DC: World Resources Institute, 1986).

5 GESAMP in a recent evaluation of the present state of the health of the oceans. 'The Health of the Oceans', Regional Seas Reports and Studies No. 16, UNEP, Nairobi, 1982.

6 M. Bertrand, 'Some Reflections on Reform of the United Nations', Joint Inspection Unit, United Nations, Geneva, 1985.

7 E.P. Eckholm, *Down to Earth* (London: Pluto Press, Ltd., 1982).

8 J.A. Gulland and S. Garcia, 'Observed Patterns in Multispecies Fisheries,' in R.M. May (ed.), *Exploitation of Marine Communities* (Berlin: Springer-Verlag, 1984); FAO, 'Review of the State of World Fishery Resources', Fisheries Circular 710 (rev.4), Rome, 1985.

9 Dr J. Gulland, Marine Resources Assessment Group, Imperial College of Science and Technology, London, personal communication, 20 January 1987.

10 FAO, op. cit.

11 IWC, *Report of the IWC 36th Session, 1986* (Cambridge: forthcoming).

12 *Report on Great Lakes Water Quality; Great Lakes Water Quality Board Report to the International Joint Commission* (Windsor, Ont.: IJC, 1985).

13 IMO, 'The Provisions of the London Dumping Convention, 1972', and Decisions made by the Consultative Meetings of Contracting Parties, 1975-84.

14 Dumping in the Convention means any deliberate disposal at sea of material and substances of any kind, form, or description from vessels, aircraft, platform, or other artificial structures, as well as the disposal of vessels, aircraft, platforms, or other artificial structures themselves.

15 Twenty-five nations, led by Spain, Australia, and New Zealand, supported the resolution, while Canada, France, South Africa, Switzerland, the United Kingdom, and the United States voted against.

16 U. Grimas and A. Svansson, *Swedish Report on the Skagerak* (Stockholm: National Environmental Protection Board, 1985).

17 United Nations. Final Act of the Third Conference on the Law of the Sea. Montego Bay, Jamaica, December 1982. In its final form, the Convention is composed of 17 main parts (320 articles), dealing with the territorial sea and contiguous zone; straits used for international navigation; archipelagic states; exclusive economic zone; continental shelf; high seas; regime of islands; enclosed or semi-enclosed seas; right of access of land-locked states to and from the sea and freedom of transit; the area, protection, and preservation of the marine environment; marine scientific research; development and transfer of marine technology; settlement of disputes; general provisions; and final provisions. There are nine annexes to the Convention: highly migratory species; Commission on the Limits of the Continental Shelf; basic conditions of prospecting; exploration and exploitation; statute of the International Tribunal for the Law of the Sea; Statute of the Enterprise; conciliations; arbitration; and special arbitration and participation by international organizations. Under the Convention, coastal states may adopt laws and regulations in the EEZ compatible with international rules and standards to combat pollution from vessels.

18 Among other things, declaration by the President of the United States, on 9 July 1982, and *L.O.S. Bulletin*, July 1985, issued by the Office of the Special Representative of the Secretary General for the Law of the Sea Convention.

19 W. Sullivan, 'Eruption in Mexico Tied to Climate Shift Off Peru,' *New York Times*, 12 December 1982.

20 R. Kerr, 'Taking Shots at Ozone Hole Theories,' *Science*, 14 November 1986.

21 When the speed of a satellite matches the speed of the planet's rotation, the satellite is stationary relative to particular places on the Earth. There is only one band or

arc, directly above the equator, where it is possible to achieve geosynchronous orbit.

22 The general case for a regulatory regime and several alternative regimes are spelled out in K.G. Gibbons, 'Orbital Saturation: The Necessity for International Regulation of Geosynchronous Orbits', *California Western International Law Journal*, Winter 1979.

23 A summary of Third World views is found in H.J. Levin, 'Orbit and Spectrum Resource Strategies: Third World Demands', *Telecommunications Policy*, June 1981.

24 The allocation is done every 10 years at World Administrative Radio Conferences (WARCs), the last of which was held in 1979. US Congress, Office of Technology Assessment, *Radiofrequency Use and Management: Impacts from the World Administrative Radio Conference of 1979* (Washington, DC: US Government Printing Office, 1980).

25 These conferences are described in G. Coding, Jr., 'The USA and the 1985 Space WARC', and A.M. Rutkowski, 'Space WARC: The Stake of the Developing Countries, the GEO and the WARC-ORB 85 Conference', *Space Policy*, August 1985.

26 AIAA Technical Committee on Space Systems, 'Space Debris', July 1981.

27 The United States has launched 23 spacecraft that relied at least in part upon nuclear power sources: one source was a reactor; the rest were radioactive materials the decay heat of which is converted into electricity (thermoelectric generators). By the end of 1986 the Soviet Union had launched 31 nuclear-powered spacecraft, almost all of which contained fission reactors, and it currently operates all of the reactor-powered satellites.

28 'Antarctic: A Continent in Transition', Fact Sheet Folio, International Institute for Environment and Development, London, 1986.

29 In 1983, the Seventh Summit Conference of the Non-Aligned Countries included a paragraph on Antarctica in its communique. That same year, the question of Antarctica was put on the agenda of the UN General Assembly. The debate resulted in a consensus resolution asking for the elaboration of a special report by the Secretary General, which was debated by the UN General Assembly at its 39th Session in November 1984. The consensus has not been maintained. At subsequent General Assembly sessions, resolutions on Antarctica have been passed over the objections of the parties to the Treaty, most of whom chose not to participate in the vote.

30 L. Kimball, 'Testing the Great Experiment', *Environment*, September 1985.

31 'Antarctic Treaty', concluded 1 December 1959 and entered into force 23 June 1961, summarized in M.J. Bowman and D.J. Harris (eds.), *Multilateral Treaties Index and Current Status* (London: Butterworths, 1984).

32 They include the original seven claimants: Argentina, Australia, Chile, France, New Zealand, Norway, and the United Kingdom; an additional five who were original signatories: Belgium, Japan, South Africa, USSR, and the United States; plus six who have since acceded to the Treaty and become full Consultative Parties: Poland (1977), the Federal Republic of Germany (1981), Brazil and India (1983), and China and Uruguay (1985). Any country can accede to the Treaty, becoming a full 'Consultative Party' providing, and during such time as, it demonstrates an interest in the continent through the presence of a substantial scientific activity. Seventeen other countries have acceded to the Treaty, but do not hold consultative status. Since 1983, they have been invited to attend Antarctic Treaty meetings as observers.

33 Both in their declaration of principles concerning the environment and in the text of the Convention on the Conservation of Antarctic Marine Living Resources, the Consultative Parties insist that the primary responsibility for these matters lies with them by virtue of their status as Consultative Parties, a proposition that Parties to the Convention who are not also Parties to the Treaty are obliged to affirm.

34 'Agreed Measures for the Conservation of Antarctic Fauna and Flora', agreed 2–13 June 1984, reprinted in W.M. Bush (ed.), *Antarctica and International Law* (London: Oceana Publications, 1982).

35 'Convention for the Conservation of Antarctic Seals', concluded 11 February 1972 and entered into force 11 March 1978, summarized in Bowman and Harris, op. cit.; 'Convention on the Conservation of Antarctic Marine Living Resources', concluded 20 May 1980 and entered into force 7 April 1981, summarized in ibid. See also J.N. Barnes, 'The Emerging Convention on the Conservation of Antarctic Marine Living Resources: An Attempt to Meet the New Realities of Resource Exploitation in the Southern Ocean', in J.I. Charney (ed.), *New Nationalism and the Use of Common Spaces* (Totowa, NJ: Allenheld Publishers, 1982).

36 J.R. Beddington and R.M. May, 'The Harvesting of Interacting Species in a Natural Ecosystem', *Scientific American*, November 1982.

37 J.H. Zumberge, 'Mineral Resources and Geopolitics in Antarctica', *American Scientist*, January–February 1979; G. Pontecorvo, 'The Economics of the Resources of Antarctica', in Charney, op. cit.

38 L. Kimball, 'Unfreezing International Cooperation in Antarctica', *Christian Science Monitor*, 1 August 1983.

39 D. Shapley, 'Antarctic Up for Grabs', *Science 82*, November 1982.

11

PEACE, SECURITY, DEVELOPMENT, AND THE ENVIRONMENT

Among the dangers facing the environment, the possibility of nuclear war, or military conflict of a lesser scale involving weapons of mass destruction, is undoubtedly the gravest. Certain aspects of the issues of peace and security bear directly upon the concept of sustainable development. Indeed, they are central to it.

Environmental stress is both a cause and an effect of political tension and military conflict.[1] Nations have often fought to assert or resist control over raw materials, energy supplies, land, river basins, sea passages, and other key environmental resources. Such conflicts are likely to increase as these resources become scarcer and competition for them increases.

The environmental consequences of armed conflict would be most devastating in the case of thermo-nuclear war. But there are damaging effects too from conventional, biological, and chemical weapons, as well as from the disruption of economic production and social organization in the wake of warfare and mass migration of refugees. But even where war is prevented, and where conflict is contained, a state of 'peace' might well entail the diversion into armament production of vast resources that could, at least in part, be used to promote sustainable forms of development.

A number of factors affect the connection between environmental stress, poverty, and security, such as inadequate development policies, adverse trends in the international economy, inequities in multi-racial and multi-ethnic societies, and pressures of population growth. These linkages among environment, development, and conflict are complex and, in many cases, poorly understood. But a comprehensive approach to international and national security must transcend the traditional emphasis on military power and armed competition. The real sources of insecurity also encompass unsustainable development, and its effects can become intertwined with traditional forms of conflict in a manner that can extend and deepen the latter.

I. ENVIRONMENTAL STRESS AS A SOURCE OF CONFLICT

Environmental stress is seldom the only cause of major conflicts within or among nations. Nevertheless, they can arise from the marginalization of sectors of the population and from ensuing violence. This occurs when political processes are unable to handle the effects of environmental stress resulting, for example, from erosion and desertification. Environmental stress can thus be an important part of the web of causality associated with any conflict and can in some cases be catalytic.

Poverty, injustice, environmental degradation, and conflict interact in complex and potent ways. One manifestation of growing concern to the international community is the phenomenon of 'environmental refugees'.[2] The immediate cause of any mass movement of refugees may appear to be political upheaval and military violence. But the underlying causes often include the deterioration of the natural resource base and its capacity to support the population.

Events in the Horn of Africa are a case in point. In the early 1970s, drought and famine struck the nation of Ethiopia. Yet it has been found that the hunger and human misery were caused more by years of overuse of soils in the Ethiopian highlands and the resulting severe erosion than by drought. A report commissioned by the Ethiopian Relief and Rehabilitation Commission found: 'The primary cause of the famine was not drought of unprecedented severity, but a combination of long-continued bad land use and steadily increased human and stock populations over decades'.[3]

Wars have always compelled people to leave their homes and their lands, to become refugees. Also, the wars in our time have forced large numbers of people to leave their homelands. In addition, we now have the phenomenon of environmental refugees. In 1984–85, some 10 million Africans fled their homes, accounting for two-thirds of all refugees worldwide. Their flight was not surprising in a region where 35 million suffered from famine. Many of them swarmed into cities. But many others moved across national boundaries, heightening interstate tensions. Cote d'Ivoire, Ghana, and Nigeria have been generous in welcoming refugees from the desertified Sahel. Tanzania, Zambia, and Zimbabwe have also been receiving large numbers of refugees. Yet, the Cote d'Ivoire, for instance, which depends for much of its export revenues on timber, is suffering rapid deforestation caused in part by land hunger, and one-third of landless people are immigrants. Agriculture destroys 4.5 times as much forestland in the Cote d'Ivoire as logging does.[4]

Almost 1 million Haitian 'boat people', one-sixth of the entire populace, have fled that island nation, an exodus fuelled in large part by environmental degradation. Haiti suffers some of the world's most severe erosion, down to bedrock over large parts of some regions, so that even farmers with reasonable amounts of land cannot make a living. According to a US Agency for International Development (USAID) report, 'The social and economic effects of environmental degradation are great, and contribute to the growing outflow from rural areas. Thousands of rural Haitians leave their homes each year for Port au Prince, other Caribbean islands and the United States in search of employment and better living conditions.'[5] El Salvador, one of the most troubled nations of Central America, is also one of the most environmentally impoverished, with some of the worst erosion rates in the region. 'The fundamental causes of the present conflict are as much environmental as political, stemming from problems of resource distribution in an overcrowded land,' according to a draft USAID environmental profile of El Salvador.[6]

South Africa reveals similar problems. The inhuman policy of apartheid is at the core of the state of political conflict in Southern Africa. One of the many ways by which apartheid institutionalizes both conflict and environmental degradation is by allocating, through the 'homelands' system, 14 per cent of the nation's land to 72 per cent of the population.[7] Young working-age blacks flee the overcultivated and overgrazed 'homelands' to seek work in the cities, where, on top of the squalor of overcrowded townships, they encounter extreme socio-economic inequality and racial segregation. They fight back. Repression intensifies, and the victims seek refuge over the border—whereupon the South African regime widens the conflict into neighbouring states. The entire region is becoming caught up in the ensuing violence, which could well ignite wider conflict drawing in major powers.

In addition to the interrelated problems of poverty, injustice, and environmental stress, competition for non-renewable raw materials, land, or energy can create tension. It was the quest for raw materials that underlay much of the competition between colonial powers and the subjugation of their holdings. Conflicts in the Middle East inevitably contain the seeds of great power intervention and global conflagration, in part because of the international interest in oil.

As unsustainable forms of development push individual countries up against environmental limits, major differences in environmental endowment among countries, or variations in stocks of usable land and raw materials, could precipitate and exacerbate international

'*How can the world of nature and the community of peoples with their national economies be harmonized? Posing the question this way suggests that the two are separate. But not so. Humanity, the human species, exists and is supported within the world of nature. And I mean that not figuratively but literally.*

We are deep-air animals living inside an ecological system. We draw boundaries, of course, on the ecosphere for national and regional purposes. But it is all of one piece.

*When, therefore, we optimistically declare that economic development and environmental maintenance can go along hand in hand, this qualifier must immediately be added: only if the maintenance of the ecosphere is made the first priority. Economic development must be secondary, guided by strict ecological standards. These fundamental ideas are far from being universally accepted.***'**

Stanley Rowe
Saskatchewan Environmental Society
WCED Public Hearing, Ottawa, 26–27 May 1986

tension and conflict. And competition for use of the global commons, such as ocean fisheries and Antarctica, or for use of more localized common resources in fixed supply, such as rivers and coastal waters, could escalate to the level of international conflict and so threaten international peace and security.

Global water use doubled between 1940 and 1980, and it is expected to double again by 2000, with two-thirds of the projected water use going to agriculture. Yet 80 countries, with 40 per cent of the world's population, already suffer serious water shortage.[8] There will be growing competition for water for irrigation, industry, and domestic use. River water disputes have already occurred in North America (the Rio Grande), South America (the Rio de la Plata and Parana), South and South-east Asia (the Mekong and the Ganges), Africa (the Nile), and the Middle East (the Jordan, Litani, and Orontes, as well as the Euphrates).

Fisheries, whether coastal or oceanic, are fundamental to the diets of many countries. For some countries, fishing is a key economic sector, and overfishing poses immediate dangers to several national economies. In 1974 Iceland, largely dependent on its fishing industry, found itself embroiled with the United Kingdom in a 'cod war'. Similar tensions exist in the Japanese and Korean seas and on both sides of the South Atlantic. The 1986 declaration of an exclusive fishery zone around the Falkland/Malvinas Islands has further

> *'Today we cannot secure security for one state at the expense of the other. Security can only be universal, but security cannot only be political or military, it must be as well ecological, economical, and social. It must ensure the fulfilment of the aspirations of humanity as a whole.'*
>
> A. S. Timoshenko
> *Institute of State and Law, USSR Academy of Sciences*
> WCED Public Hearing, Moscow, 11 Dec 1986

unsettled relations between Britain and Argentina. Disputes over fishing rights in the South Pacific and the search for tuna by distant-water fleets led to increased competition for diplomatic and fisheries advantages by the major powers in that region in 1986. Fisheries-related disputes may well become more frequent as nations harvest fish stocks beyond the level of sustainable yields.

Environmental threats to security are now beginning to emerge on a global scale. The most worrisome of these stem from the possible consequences of global warming caused by the atmospheric build-up of carbon dioxide and other gases.[9] (See Chapter 7.) Any such climatic change would quite probably be unequal in its effects, disrupting agricultural systems in areas that provide a large proportion of the world's cereal harvests and perhaps triggering mass population movements in areas where hunger is already endemic. Sea levels may rise during the first half of the next century enough to radically change the boundaries between coastal nations and to change the shapes and strategic importance of international waterways—effects both likely to increase international tensions. The climatic and sea-level changes are also likely to disrupt the breeding grounds of economically important fish species. Slowing, or adapting to, global warming is becoming an essential task to reduce the risks of conflict.

II. CONFLICT AS A CAUSE OF UNSUSTAINABLE DEVELOPMENT

Arms competition and armed conflict create major obstacles to sustainable development. They make huge claims on scarce material resources. They pre-empt human resources and wealth that could be used to combat the collapse of environmental support systems, the poverty, and the underdevelopment that in combination contribute so much to contemporary political insecurity. They may stimulate an ethos that is antagonistic towards co-operation among nations whose ecological and economic interdependence requires them to overcome national or ideological antipathies.

The existence of nuclear weapons and the destructive potential inherent in the velocity and intensity of modern conventional warfare have given rise to a new understanding of the requirements for security among nations. In the nuclear age nations can no longer obtain security at each other's expense. They must seek security through co-operation, agreements, and mutual restraint; they must seek common security.[10] Hence interdependence, which is so fundamental in the realm of environment and economics, is a fact also in the sphere of arms competition and military security. Interdependence has become a compelling fact, forcing nations to reconcile their approach to 'security'.

Nuclear War—Threat to Civilization

The likely consequences of nuclear war make other threats to the environment pale into insignificance. Nuclear weapons represent a qualitatively new step in the development of warfare. One thermonuclear bomb can have an explosive power greater than that of all the explosives used in wars since the invention of gunpowder. In addition to the destructive effects of blast and heat, immensely magnified by these weapons, they introduce a new lethal agent—ionizing radiation—that extends lethal effects over both space and time.

In recent years, scientists have in addition called our attention to the prospect of 'nuclear winter'. It has been most authoritatively explored by some 300 scientists from the United States, the USSR, and more than 30 other countries—working on a collaborative basis in some cases across ideological divides.[11]

The theory contends that the smoke and dust ejected into the atmosphere by a nuclear war could absorb enough solar radiation to remain aloft for some time, preventing sunlight from reaching the surface of the earth, causing a widespread and prolonged cooling of land areas. There would be severe repercussions for plant life generally and for agriculture in particular, disrupting the production of food to sustain survivors of the war. Great uncertainties remain about the scale and linkages determining environmental effects, but large-scale environmental perturbations are considered probable. A nuclear war cannot be won, and must never be fought. In the aftermath, there would be no difference between so-called victor and vanquished. The nuclear-weapon states must spare no effort to conclude a verifiable agreement on banning all nuclear weapon tests.

The findings on nuclear winter are vitally important too for non-aligned nations, predominantly in the South, which are not

'All youth organizations believe that environmental issues stand high on the priority list of global problems. However, their solution depends on the preservation of peace on our planet. The quest of solutions to ecological problems is impossible without the curbing of the arms race, for the arms race absorbs tremendous intellectual and material resources of mankind. The solution of ecological problems also depends on the way of life of young people and their value orientaton.'

Dr. I. I. Russin
Moscow State University
WCED Public Hearing, Moscow, 8 Dec 1986

parties to the East-West conflict. They cannot expect to avoid the potentially disastrous environmental consequences of nuclear war in the northern hemisphere. The aftermath of such a war would envelop the world. There is a danger that nuclear weapons will spread to more and more countries and be used in what begins as a limited regional conflict. Beyond the five recognized nuclear-weapon states, at least six others have a widely acknowledged potential nuclear weapons capability; a dozen others are not far behind. The nuclear-weapon states cannot expect the non-nuclear-weapon states to abstain from exercising the nuclear option in the absence of real progress on the road to nuclear disarmament. It is imperative, therefore, that the probable consequences of nuclear war be recognized universally and that all states become involved in efforts to prevent the proliferation— and above all the use—of nuclear weapons.

Other Weapons of Mass Destruction

Other forms of war and other weapons of mass destruction have large-scale effects on both human societies and the human environment. Biological warfare could release new agents of disease that would prove difficult to control. Recent advances in biotechnology multiply the potentially lethal applications of such weapons. Likewise, the deliberate manipulation of the environment (for example, through artificial earthquakes and floods) would have consequences far beyond the borders of those involved in a conflict, were they ever used. Chemical agents can seriously damage the environment, as demonstrated by the defoliants used in South-east Asia. The dangerous and environmentally unpredictable consequences of biological and chemical weapons have led to international agreements banning their use.[12] But there is need for further efforts to strengthen the regimes to which these agreements contribute. In particular, the Geneva protocol prohibiting the use of chemical weapons should be supplemented by agreements prohibiting the production and stockpiling of such weapons.

Military applications of new technologies now threaten to make outer space a focus of international competition and conflict. (See Chapter 10.) Most countries in the international community see space as a global commons that should benefit humanity as a whole and be preserved from military competition—a feeling reflected in the 1967 Outer Space Treaty, under which nations agreed not to deploy weapons of mass destruction there. Governments should now agree on measures to prevent an arms race in space and stop it on Earth. Failing such agreement, the arms race could expand, with dire consequences for humanity.

The Costs of the 'Arms Culture'

The absence of war is not peace; nor does it necessarily provide the conditions for sustainable development. Competitive arms races breed insecurity among nations through spirals of reciprocal fears. Nations need to muster resources to combat environmental degradation and mass poverty. By misdirecting scarce resources, arms races contribute further to insecurity.

The coexistence of substantial military spending with unmet human needs has long evoked concern. President Eisenhower, for example, observed at the end his term in office that 'every gun that is made, every warship launched, every rocket fired represents, in the final analysis, a theft from those who hunger and are not fed, who are cold and are not clothed'.[13]

Global military spending in 1985 was well in excess of $900 billion.[14] This was more than the total income of the poorest half of humanity. It represented the equivalent of almost $1,000 for every one of the world's 1 billion poorest. Put another way, military spending surpassed the combined gross national products of China, India, and the African countries south of the Sahara. Moreover, global military spending has risen not only absolutely but proportionately—from an estimated 4.7 per cent of world output in 1960 to over 6 per cent—representing an increase of about 150 per cent in real (constant price) terms. Three-quarters of current expenditure is in the industrial world.[15]

The true cost of the arms race is the loss of what could have been produced instead with scarce capital, labour skills, and raw materials. The plants that manufacture weapons, the transport of those weapons, and the mining of minerals for their production all place enormous demands on energy and mineral resources and are a major contributor to pollution and environmental deterioration.

The distorting effects of the 'arms culture' are most striking in the deployment of scientific personnel. Half a million scientists are employed on weapons research world-wide, and they account for around half of all research and development expenditure.[16] This exceeds the total combined spending on developing technologies for new energy sources, improving human health, raising agricultural productivity, and controlling pollution. Military research and development—$70–80 billion world-wide in 1984—is growing at twice the rate of military spending as a whole.[17] At the same time, there is a paucity of resources available for monitoring global climatic change, for surveying the ecosystems of disappearing rain forests and spreading deserts, and for developing agricultural technologies appropriate to rainfed, tropical agriculture.

Nations are seeking a new era of economic growth. The level of spending on arms diminishes the prospects for such an era—especially one that emphasizes the more efficient use of raw materials, energy, and skilled human resources. It also has a bearing, albeit indirect, on the willingness of rich countries to provide development assistance to developing countries. Clearly, there is no simple correspondence between reduced defence spending and increased aid. There are other reasons aside from domestic resource constraints for a reluctance to expand aid, and nations cannot wait for disarmament before devoting more resources to ensuring sustainable development. Nonetheless, increased defence spending puts pressure on other budgetary items, and aid is an easy target, despite being a relatively small outlay for most donor countries.[18]

Although redeployment is clearly possible, resources currently employed in military applications cannot be redeployed quickly or easily elsewhere—in other sectors or other countries. There are technical problems in achieving such a transformation, not least the contribution made by military spending to jobs in economies with high unemployment. And beyond the technical problems are questions of political will. Nonetheless, some countries—China, Argentina, and Peru, for example—have recently shown that it is both technically and politically possible to make substantial shifts from military to civilian spending within a short time.[19]

World Armaments and the Growth of the 'Arms Culture'

Traditionally, nations have adhered to an 'arms culture'. They find themselves locked into arms competitions fuelled among other things

❝I have here listened to people speaking about financial crises, famine, pollution, and social injustice at various levels. As an ecologist, I cannot see any of these questions without linking them to the armaments question and to the nuclear issue.

Poverty generates tensions and conflicts, urban and rural violence. The indigenous people are still awaiting solutions for their problems. All this depends on money and nevertheless we are spending money on our nuclear programmes. They say that this has peaceful objectives. This is not true because precious money is being spent on this.

The greatest crime: the death of hope, the death of all of the rights we all have, especially that of the young of believing in a future, the hope for a normal life, a difficult life but something that appears as a challenge to live it the best we can. We have a right to this chance.❞

Cacilda Lanuza
Brazilian Ecological Movement
WCED Public Hearing, Sao Paulo, 28–29 Oct 1985

by powerful vested interests in the 'military-industrial complex' as well as in the armed forces themselves. Industrial nations account for most of the military expenditures and the production and transfer of arms in international society. However, the influence of this 'arms culture' is not confined to these nations. It is present also in the developing world, fostered both by the desire of many governments to seek security through acquisition of arms and by a burgeoning world arms trade.

Since the early 1960s, military spending in developing countries as a whole has increased fivefold. Their share of total spending increased from under one-tenth to almost a quarter of a far larger total.[20] Some developing countries, such as the Republic of Korea, have achieved a high level of development in spite of military spending. But systematic analysis suggests that increases in military spending have had negative effects on economic performance.[21]

Moreover, defence expenditure is one of the most import-intensive of activities, usually creating a large secondary demand for imported spares, ammunition, servicing, training, and fuel. It has been estimated that 20 per cent of the external debt acquired by non-oil developing countries in the decade to 1982 could be attributed to arms import.[22] And high levels of arms spending motivated by a variety of reasons have undoubtedly contributed to the severity of the crises of development in Africa, where military spending rose, in real terms, by 7.8 per cent per annum between 1971 and 1982, and arms imports rose by 18.5 per cent.[23] It should be noted in this connection that in the case of the Frontline States they have been compelled to expand their armed forces because of the threat from South Africa.

The development of an 'arms culture' in many developing countries presents particular dangers in the context of environmental and poverty-induced stresses. There are already numerous simmering disputes in the Third World—over 40 unresolved—many arising from boundaries defined in colonial times.

Sophisticated weapons can help convert the potential into actual conflict. According to the UN Group of Governmental Experts on the Relationship Between Disarmament and Development: 'There can no longer be the slightest doubt that resource scarcities and ecological stresses constitute real and imminent threats to the future well-being of all people and nations. These challenges are fundamentally non-military and it is imperative that they be addressed accordingly. If this is not recognized, ... there is a grave risk that the situation will deteriorate to the point of crisis where, even with low probability of success, the use of force could be seen as a way to produce results quickly enough. This is far from being a remote possibility. In recent years, there has been a marked tendency in international relations to use or to threaten to use military force in response to non-military challenges to security.'[24]

The situation in many developing countries presents particular dangers in the context of environmental and poverty-induced stresses. Large-scale movements of refugees, competition for scarce water and fertile lands, deposits of oil and raw materials, ill-defined boundaries, and so on all add to tensions and increase possibilities for conflict. The importation of armaments by developing countries has increased also because of these real or potential conflicts. It is sometimes encouraged by the arms manufacturers because of the important profits that can themselves sustain the manufacture of arms in the exporting countries. The export of arms has been evaluated at more than $35 billion annually. The arms trade is estimated to have absorbed over $300 billion over the last two decades, three-quarters in the form of sales to developing countries.[25]

III. TOWARDS SECURITY AND SUSTAINABLE DEVELOPMENT

Principles

The first step in creating a more satisfactory basis for managing the interrelationships between security and sustainable development is to

'Environment must also be an approach to development. Environment is a social justice issue and environment even is a peace and security issue. The barriers to achieving sustainable development are great, as might be expected in a major historical transformation, but they are far from insurmountable.

We approach the millennium in a world in which global interdependence is the central reality, but where absolute poverty and environmental degradation cloud our vision of a common future, and where a geopolitical climate dominated by nuclear terrorism and increasing militarization saps the idealism of the young and the will to dream in us all.'

Ralph Torrie
*On Behalf of Canadian Environment,
Development, and Peace Organizations*
WCED Public Hearing, Ottawa, 26–27 May 1986

broaden our vision. Conflicts may arise not only because of political and military threats to national sovereignty; they may derive also from environmental degradation and the pre-emption of development options.

There are, of course, no military solutions to 'environmental insecurity'. And modern warfare can itself create major internationally shared environmental hazards. Furthermore, the idea of national sovereignty has been fundamentally modified by the fact of interdependence in the realm of economics, environment, and security. The global commons cannot be managed from any national centre: The nation state is insufficient to deal with threats to shared ecosystems. Threats to environmental security can only be dealt with by joint management and multilateral procedures and mechanisms.

Co-operative Management

Already, environmental stresses are encouraging co-operation among nations, giving some indication of ways to proceed. Antarctica is subject to a far-reaching agreement that provides a collective approach to management. (See Chapter 10.) There are now various institutional systems, often of complex and advanced form, to foster bilateral and regional co-operation for marine fisheries in order to regulate maximum sustainable yields and the distribution of catches. One of the main threats to the oceans—the dumping of highly toxic wastes— has so far been managed by the London Dumping Convention. As for international water bodies, impressive progress has been made by the bilateral US-Canadian Commission for the Great Lakes. The Mediterranean Convention, only one of the many such treaties concluded within the context of the UN Environment Programme's Regional Seas Programme, brings together coastal nations in an arrangement to monitor and combat pollution at sea.

Some of the most challenging problems require co-operation among nations enjoying different systems of government, or even subject to antagonistic relations. The 1986 Chernobyl reactor accident in the Soviet Union has resulted in two agreements covering international co-operation in cases of such accidents. In the future, the nation concerned will immediately alert neighbouring states; they, in turn, will offer assistance at cost and free of liability.[26] The 1979 Convention on Transboundary Pollution has provided a framework for monitoring and assessing damage from pollutants causing acid rain in Europe.[27]

Co-operation on environmental issues among developing countries has often been made difficult by poor communications. Nonetheless, many now participate in the Regional Seas Programme. The nations of the Sahel have formed a regional organization to deal with desertification, and there is emerging a body of successful case histories with respect to river-basin development: Witness the joint-management programmes in Africa for the Senegal River Basin.

The Importance of Early Warning

Since it is often uncertainty and insecurity that prompts international conflict, it is of the utmost importance that governments become aware of imminent environmental stress before the damage actually threatens core national interests. Governments are usually not well equipped with this kind of foresight.

It would be highly desirable if the appropriate international organizations, including appropriate UN bodies and regional organizations, were to pool their resources—and draw on the most sophisticated surveillance technology available—to establish a reliable early warning system for environmental risks and conflict. (See Chapter 12.) Such a system would monitor indicators of risks and potential disputes, such as soil erosion, growth in regional migration, and uses of commons that are approaching the thresholds of sustainability. The organizations would also offer their services for helping the respective countries to establish principles and institutions for joint management.

Disarmament and Security

Action to reduce environmental threats to security requires a re-

Box 11-1. Spending on Military Versus Environmental Security

The world spent well over $900 billion on military purposes in 1985, more than $2.5 billion a day. The real cost is what the same resources might otherwise be used for:

- An Action Plan for Tropical Forests would cost $1.3 billion a year over the course of five years. This annual sum is the equivalent of half a day of military expenditure worldwide.
- Implementing the UN Action Plan for Desertification would cost $4.5 billion a year during the last two decades of this century—the equivalent of less than two days of military spending.
- One of the greatest environmental hazards in the Third World is lack of clean water for household use, contributing to 80 per cent of disease. The UN Water and Sanitation Decade, although given only a small fraction of support needed, would have cost $30 billion a year during the 1980s. This is the approximate equivalent of 10 days of military spending.
- To supply contraceptive materials to all women already motivated to use family planning would cost an additional $1 billion per year on top of the $2 billion spent today. This additional $1 billion is the equivalent of 10 hours of military spending.

Sources: International Task Force, *Tropical Forests A Call for Action* (Washington, DC: World Resources Institute, 1985); Dr. M.K. Tolba, 'Desertification and the Economics of Survival', *UNEP Information 86/2*, 25 March 1986; A. Agarwal et al., *Water Sanitation and Health for All?* (London: IIED/Earthscan, 1981); World Bank, *World Development Report 1984* (New York: Oxford University Press, 1984).

definition of priorities, nationally and globally. Such a redefinition could evolve through the widespread acceptance of broader forms of security assessment and embrace military, political, environmental, and other sources of conflict.

A broader approach to security assessment would no doubt find many cases in which national, regional, and global security could be enhanced through expenditures quite small in relation to the levels of military spending. Four of the most urgent global environmental requirements—relating to tropical forests, water, desertification, and population—could be funded with the equivalent of less than one month's global military spending. (See Box 11-1.) It is difficult to shift budgetary resources, but individual governments have already shown that transformation is possible, given political will. In some of the countries most seriously affected by environmental stress and poverty, the sums required to alleviate these conditions are small in relation to what is now spent on disaster relief, let alone military activities.[28] However, these sums must be spent quickly, before deteriorating conditions require much larger expenditures.

But in terms of the aggregate resources involved in arms spending and the potential threat to the environment from war, the greatest need is to improve relations among those major powers capable of deploying weapons of mass destruction. This is needed to achieve agreement on tighter control over the proliferation and testing of various types of weapons of mass destruction—nuclear and non-nuclear—including those that have environmental implications.[29]

A substantial number of agreements already show the potential for negotiated, multilateral solutions. President Reagan and General Secretary Gorbachev made substantial progress towards strategic arms agreement, which must be carried forward to reverse the alarming trends of several decades. Apparently, the two major powers came close to agreeing on intermediate range systems in Europe, to be followed by agreements banning forward deployment of shorter range systems. It would alleviate significantly the pressures exercised by nuclear weapons on the security order in Europe. In addition, they are moving towards a 50 per cent reduction agreement on strategic systems, followed by total elimination agreements. They also need to agree on effective measures to prevent an arms race in space. Successful negotiations would contribute significantly to stemming the spread of nuclear weapons as the major nuclear-weapon states would deliver on their promise to build down their nuclear arsenals. Such progress is consistent with the basic needs of our times and the right of humanity to have the spectre of nuclear destruction removed from the face of the Earth.

Nations must turn away from the destructive logic of an 'arms culture' and focus instead on their common future. The level of armaments and the destruction they could bring about bear no relation to the political conflict that triggered the arms competition in the first place. Nations must not become prisoners of their own arms race. They must face the common danger inherent in the weapons of the nuclear age. They must face the common challenge of providing for sustainable development and act in concert to remove the growing environmental sources of conflict.

Notes

1 For some preliminary analyses along these lines, see L. Timberlake and J. Tinker, 'Environment and Conflict: Links Between Ecological Decay, Environmental Bankruptcy and Political and Military Instability', Earthscan Briefing Document, Earthscan, London, 1984; N. Myers, 'The Environmental Dimension to Security Issues', *The Environmentalist*, Winter 1986; R.H. Ullman, 'Redefining Security', *International Security*, Summer 1983; and A.H. Westing (ed.), *Global Resources and International Conflict* (Oxford: Oxford University Press, 1986).

2 E. El-Hinnawi, *Environmental Refugees* (Nairobi: UNEP, 1985).

3 Relief and Rehabilitation Commission, 'Drought and Rehabilitation in Wollo and Tigrai', Addis Ababa, 1975.

4 L. Timberlake, *Africa in Crisis* (London: International Institute for Environment and Development/Earthscan, 1985).

5 Project Paper for Haiti Agroforestry Outreach Project (Project 521-0122), US Agency for International Development, Washington, DC, 1981.

6 National Park Service/US Man and the Biosphere Secretariat, 'Draft Environmental Profile of El Salvador', Bureau of Science and Technology, US Agency for International Development, Washington, DC, April 1982. See also T.P. Anderson, *The War of the Dispossessed: Honduras and El Salvador 1969* (Lincoln, Neb.: University of Nebraska Press, 1981); W.H. Durham, *Scarcity and Survival in Central America: Ecological Origins of the Soccer War* (Stanford, Calif.: Stanford University Press, 1979).

7 D. Smith, 'Update: Apartheid in South Africa', Queen Mary College, London, 1984.

8 M. Falkenmark, 'New Ecological Approach to the Water Cycle: Ticket to the Future', *Ambio*, Vol. 13, No. 3, 1984; S. Postel, *Water: Rethinking Management in an Age of Scarcity*, Worldwatch Paper 62 (Washington, DC: Worldwatch Institute, 1984).

9 B. Bolin et al., *The Greenhouse Effect: Climatic Change and Ecosystems* (Chichester, UK: John Wiley & Sons, 1986); National Research Council, *Changing Climate* (Washington, DC: National Academy Press, 1983); S. Seidel and D. Keyes, *Can We Delay a Greenhouse Warming?* (Washington, DC: US Environmental Protection Agency, 1983).

10 Independent Commission on Disarmament and Security Issues under the Chairmanship of Olof Palme, *Common Security* (London: Pan Books, 1982).

11 SCOPE, *Environmental Consequences of Nuclear War* (Chichester, UK: John Wiley & Sons, 1985). Some of the other major studies on the nuclear winter scenario are R. Turco et al., 'Nuclear Winter: Global Consequences of Multiple Nuclear Explosions', *Science*, 23 December 1983; P. Ehrlich et al., *The Cold and the Dark: The World After Nuclear War* (New York: W.W. Norton, 1984); ; M.A. Hartwell and T.C. Hutchinson, *Environmental Consequences of Nuclear War, Volume II: Ecological and Agricultural Effects* (Chichester, UK: John Wiley & Sons, 1985); National Research Council, *The Effects on the Atmosphere of a Major Nuclear Exchange* (Washington, DC: National Academy Press, 1985); A. Ginsberg et al., 'Global Consequences of a Nuclear War: A Review of Recent Soviet Studies', *World Armaments and Disarmament, SIPRI Yearbook 1985* (London: Taylor & Francis, 1985); A.B. Pittock et al., *Environmental Consequences of Nuclear War, Volume I: Physical and Atmospheric Effects* (Chichester, UK: John Wiley & Sons, 1986); S.L. Thompson and S.H. Schneider, 'Nuclear Winter Reappraised', *Foreign Affairs*, Summer 1986. The effects of nuclear war are explored in Y.I. Chazor et

al., *The Danger of Nuclear War: Soviet Physicians' Viewpoint* (Moscow: Novosti Press, 1982); S. Glasstone and P.J. Dolan (eds.), *The Effects of Nuclear Weapons*, 3rd ed. (Washington, DC: US Government Printing Office, 1977); National Academy of Sciences, *Long-term Worldwide Effects of Multiple Nuclear Weapon Detonations* (Washington, DC: National Academy Press, 1975); US Congress, Office of Technology Assessment, *The Effects of Nuclear War* (Washington, DC: US Government Printing Office, 1980); UN, *Comprehensive Study of Nuclear Weapons* (A/35/392) (New York: 1980); World Health Organization, *Effects of Nuclear War on Health and Health Services* (Geneva: 1984).

12 Outright banning of particularly lethal weapons has its origin in the St. Petersburg Declaration banning the use of 'dum-dum bullets' and the Hague war rules outlining the use of shaped charges (1899). Also relevant are the Geneva Protocol banning the military use of chemical and bacteriological weapons (1925); the Convention on the Prohibition of the Development, Production, and Stockpiling of Bacteriological and Toxin Weapons (1975); and the Convention on the Prohibition of Military or Any Other Hostile Use of Environmental Modification Techniques (1978).

13 The Eisenhower quote is taken from his final, valedictory, address (speech to the American Society of Newspaper Editors, Washington, DC, April 1953), which also includes the more famous reference to the 'military-industrial complex'.

14 Estimates from R.L. Sivard, *World Military and Social Expenditures* (Washington, DC: World Priorities, Inc., 1986). More details in M. Brzoska et al., 'World Military Expenditure and Arms Production', *SIPRI Yearbook*, op. cit. The figure of total military spending is necessarily approximate because of the enormous problems of aggregating spending in different—and often non-convertible—currencies and from countries with different statistical conventions. According to Sivard, total military spending in 1983 was $728 billion. On the basis of trends and preliminary data, a figure of at least $900 billion and possibly $1,000 billion in current prices and exchange rates seems appropriate for 1986.

15 Sivard, 1986 edition, op. cit.; *SIPRI Yearbook*, op. cit.

16 Sivard, 1986 edition, op. cit.; *SIPRI Yearbook*, op. cit.

17 M. Ackland-Hood, 'Military Research and Development Expenditure', *SIPRI Yearbook*, op. cit.

18 According to calculations based on OECD Development Assistance Committee data, which are not universally accepted, together with Sivard, total non-military development aid measured in net concessional flows from industrial to developing countries represents roughly 5 per cent of the amount spent by all industrial countries on armaments. For the United States, foreign aid accounts for 4 per cent of armaments spending, and for the USSR, 1.5 per cent. In Austria, Denmark, the Netherlands, Norway, and Sweden, by contrast, the proportion is close to 30 per cent, and it is over 10 per cent for Australia, Belgium, Canada, France, FRG, and Switzerland.

19 According to L.R. Brown et al., in *State of the World 1986* (London: W.W. Norton, 1986), China in 1972 spent 14 per cent of its gross national product (GNP) on military purposes, one of the highest levels in the world. Since 1970 (except for 1979), the government has systematically reduced this until by 1985 it amounted to only 7.5 per cent. In mid-1985 the government announced it would cut the armed forces to 3.2 million, a drop of 24 per cent. In Argentina, by 1984 new President Raul Alfonsin had cut arms outlays to half their peak level of 1980 (nearly 4 per cent of GNP) by reordering priorities and shifting resources to social programmes. Peruvian President Alan Garcia Perez, on taking office in mid-1985, announced he would reduce military outlays, which then totalled 5 per cent of

GNP, or one-quarter of the federal budget. First he cancelled half the order for 26 French Mirage fighter planes.

20 Over 1960-81, Third World military expenditures grew by some 7 per cent per year, as compared with 3.7 per cent in the industrial world. In 1960, Third World military expenditures accounted for less than one-tenth of the global total, but in 1981 for more than one-fifth of a far larger total. R. L. Sivard, *World Military and Social Expenditures* (Washington, DC: World Priorities, Inc., 1985).

21 L. Taylor, 'Military Economics in the Third World', prepared for The Independent Commission on Disarmament and Security Issues, 1981.

22 R. Tullberg, 'Military Related Debt in Non-Oil Developing Countries', *SIPRI Yearbook*, op. cit.

23 R. Luckham, 'Militarization in Africa', *SIPRI Yearbook*, op. cit.

24 I. Thorsson et al., *Relationship Between Disarmament and Development*, Disarmament Study Review No.5 (A/36/536) (New York: UN Department of Political and Security Council Affairs, 1982).

25 Arms exports from Brown et al., op cit., based on US Arms Control and Disarmament Agency; estimate of cumulative spending on the arms trade in Sivard, 1985 edition, op. cit.

26 'Negotiations on Agreement Concerning Nuclear Safety Reach Consensus', press release (PR8-86/17), IAEA, 15 August 1986.

27 'Convention on Long-Range Transboundary Air Pollution', concluded 13 November 1979 and entered into force 16 March 1983, summarized in M.J. Bowman and D.J. Harris (eds.), *Multilateral Treaties: Index and Current Status* (London: Butterworths, 1984).

28 The amount that the United Nations has recently budgeted for Ethiopia to cater for anti-erosion, reforestation, and related measures under its Anti-Desertification Plan suggests that no more than $50 million a year would have been required to counter much of the highlands' problem if the investment had been undertaken in due time. By contrast, the amount required to counter Ethiopia's famine during 1985 amounted to $500 million for relief measures alone. Between 1976 and 1980 Ethiopia spent an average of $225 million a year on military activities.

29 Among international treaties specifically designed to protect the global commons from militarization are the Antarctic Treaty (1959); the Moscow Treaty Banning Nuclear Weapons Tests in the Atmosphere, in Outer Space and Under Water (1963); the Outer Space Treaty (1967); the Treaty of Tlatelolco (1967); the Treaty on the Non-Proliferation of Nuclear Weapons (1968); and the Sea-Bed Treaty (1971).

12

TOWARDS COMMON ACTION:
PROPOSALS FOR INSTITUTIONAL
AND LEGAL CHANGE

In the middle of the 20th century, we saw our planet from space for the first time. Historians may eventually find that this vision had a greater impact on thought than did the Copernican revolution of the 16th century, which upset humans' self-image by revealing that the Earth is not the centre of the universe. From space, we see a small and fragile ball dominated not by human activity and edifice but by a pattern of clouds, oceans, greenery, and soils. Humanity's inability to fit its activities into that pattern is changing planetary systems fundamentally. Many such changes are accompanied by life-threatening hazards, from environmental degradation to nuclear destruction. These new realities, from which there is no escape, must be recognized—and managed.

The issues we have raised in this report are inevitably of far-reaching importance to the quality of life on earth—indeed, to life itself. We have tried to show how human survival and well-being could depend on success in elevating sustainable development to a global ethic. In doing so, we have called for such major efforts as greater willingness and co-operation to combat international poverty, to maintain peace and enhance security world-wide, and to manage the global commons. We have called for national and international action in respect of population, food, plant and animal species, energy, industry, and urban settlements. The previous chapters have described the policy directions required.

The onus for action lies with no one group of nations. Developing countries face the challenges of desertification, deforestation, and pollution, and endure most of the poverty associated with environmental degradation. The entire human family of nations would suffer from the disappearance of rain forests in the tropics, the loss of plant and animal species, and changes in rainfall patterns. Industrial nations face the challenges of toxic chemicals, toxic wastes, and acidification. All nations may suffer from the releases by industrialized countries of carbon dioxide and of gases that react with the ozone layer, and from any future war fought with the nuclear arsenals controlled by those nations. All nations will also have a role to play in securing peace, in changing trends, and in righting an international economic system that increases rather than decreases inequality, that increases rather than decreases numbers of poor and hungry.

The time has come to break out of past patterns. Attempts to maintain social and ecological stability through old approaches to development and environmental protection will increase instability. Security must be sought through change. The Commission has noted a number of actions that must be taken to reduce risks to survival and to put future development on paths that are sustainable.

Without such reorientation of attitudes and emphasis, little can be achieved. We have no illusions about 'quick-fix' solutions. We have tried to point out some pathways to the future. But there is no substitute for the journey itself, and there is no alternative to the process by which we retain a capacity to respond to the experience it provides. We believe this to hold true in all the areas covered in this report. But the policy changes we have suggested have institutional implications, and it is to these we now turn—emphasizing that they are a complement to, not a substitute for, the wider policy changes for which we call. Nor do they represent definitive solutions, but rather first steps in what will be a continuing process.

In what follows we put forward, in the first place, what are essentially conceptual guidelines for institutions at the national level. We recognize that there are large differences among countries in respect of population size, resources, income level, management capacity, and institutional traditions; only governments themselves can formulate the changes they should make. Moreover, the tools for monitoring and evaluating sustainable development are rudimentary and require further refinement.

We also address, in more specific terms, the question of international institutions. The preceding chapters have major implications for international co-operation and reforms, both economic and legal. The international agencies clearly have an important role in making these changes effective, and we endeavour to set out the institutional implications, especially as regards the United Nations system.

I. THE CHALLENGE FOR INSTITUTIONAL AND LEGAL CHANGE

Shifting the Focus to the Policy Sources

The next few decades are crucial for the future of humanity. Pressures on the planet are now unprecedented and are accelerating at rates and scales new to human experience: a doubling of global population in a few decades, with most of the growth in cities; a five- to tenfold increase in economic activity in less than half a century; and the resulting pressures for growth and changes in agricultural, energy, and industrial systems. Opportunities for more sustainable forms of growth and development are also growing. New technologies and potentially unlimited access to information offer great promise.

Each area of change represents a formidable challenge in its own right, but the fundamental challenge stems from their systemic character. They lock together environment and development, once thought separate; they lock together 'sectors', such as industry and agriculture; and they lock countries together as the effects of national policies and actions spill over national borders. Separate policies and institutions can no longer cope effectively with these interlocked issues. Nor can nations, acting unilaterally.

The integrated and interdependent nature of the new challenges and issues contrasts sharply with the nature of the institutions that exist today. These institutions tend to be independent, fragmented, and working to relatively narrow mandates with closed decision processes. Those responsible for managing natural resources and protecting the environment are institutionally separated from those responsible for managing the economy. The real world of interlocked economic and ecological systems will not change; the policies and institutions concerned must.

This new awareness requires major shifts in the way governments and individuals approach issues of environment, development, and international co-operation. Approaches to environment policy can be broadly characterized in two ways. One, characterized as the 'standard agenda', reflects an approach to environmental policy, laws, and institutions that focuses on environmental effects. The second reflects an approach concentrating on the policies that are the sources of those effects.[1] These two approaches represent distinctively different ways of looking both at the issues and at the institutions to manage them.

The effects-oriented 'standard agenda' has tended to predominate

'In the case of environmental problems, it is obvious that the problems cannot be solved by one group, one group working in separation. You cannot say because people are dying of poisoning, it is the Ministry of Health that will solve it. Or to say because it comes from factories, it is the Ministry of Industry. That is impossible.

I think the problems need a more holistic approach. The United Nations Organization, as a professional organization, has developed this fragmentation. It started automatically with no bad intention at all. But at the same time, the member countries requested and national bodies also requested entry points in recipient countries. So WHO corresponds with the Ministry of Health, UNESCO corresponds with the Ministry of Education, FAO corresponds with the Ministry of Agriculture—the fragmentation is getting worse.'

Speaker from the floor, government agency
WCED Public Hearing, Jakarta, 26 March 1985

as a result of growing concerns about the dramatic decline in environmental quality that the industrialized world suffered during the 1950s and 1960s. New environmental protection and resource management agencies were added on to the existing institutional structures, and given mainly scientific staffs.[2]

These environment agencies have registered some notable successes in improving environmental quality during the past two decades.[3] They have secured significant gains in monitoring and research and in defining and understanding the issues in scientific and technical terms. They have raised public awareness, nationally and internationally. Environmental laws have induced innovation and the development of new control technologies, processes, and products in most industries, reducing the resource content of growth.[4]

However, most of these agencies have been confined by their own mandates to focusing almost exclusively on the effects. Today, the sources of these effects must be tackled. While these existing environmental protection policies and agencies must be maintained and even strengthened, governments now need to take a much broader view of environmental problems and policies.

Central agencies and major sectoral ministries play key roles in national decision making. These agencies have the greatest influence on the form, character, and distribution of the impacts of economic activity on the environmental resource base. It is these agencies, through their policies and budgets, that determine whether the environmental resource base is enhanced or degraded and whether the planet will be able to support human and economic growth and change into the next century.

The mandated goals of these agencies include increasing investment, employment, food, energy, and other economic and social goods. Most have no mandate to concern themselves with sustaining the environmental resource capital on which these goals depend. Those with such mandates are usually grouped in separate environment agencies or, sometimes, in minor units within sectoral agencies. In either case, they usually learn of new initiatives in economic and trade policy, or in energy and agricultural policy, or of new tax measures that will have a severe impact on resources, long after the effective decisions have been taken. Even if they were to learn earlier, most lack the authority to ensure that a given policy is implemented.

Environmental protection and sustainable development must be an integral part of the mandates of all agencies of governments, of international organizations, and of major private-sector institutions. These must be made responsible and accountable for ensuring that their policies, programmes, and budgets encourage and support activities that are economically and ecologically sustainable both in the short and longer terms. They must be given a mandate to pursue their traditional goals in such a way that those goals are reinforced by a steady enhancement of the environmental resource base of their own national community and of the small planet we all share.

New Imperatives for International Co-operation

National boundaries have become so porous that traditional distinctions between local, national, and international issues have become blurred. Policies formerly considered to be exclusively matters of 'national concern' now have an impact on the ecological bases of other nations' development and survival. Conversely, the growing reach of some nations' policies—economic, trade, monetary, and most sectoral policies—into the 'sovereign' territory of other nations limits the affected nations' options in devising national solutions to their 'own' problems. This fast-changing context for national action has introduced new imperatives and new opportunities for international co-operation.

The international legal framework must also be significantly strengthened in support of sustainable development. Although international law related to environment has evolved rapidly since the 1972 Stockholm Conference, major gaps and deficiencies must still be overcome as part of the transition to sustainable development. Much of the evidence and conclusions presented in earlier chapters of this report calls into question not just the desirability but even the feasibility of maintaining an international system that cannot prevent one or several states from damaging the ecological basis for development and even the prospects for survival of any other or even all other states.

However, just at the time when nations need increased international co-operation, the will to co-operate has sharply declined. By the mid-1980s, multilateral institutions were under siege for many, and often contradictory, reasons. The UN system has come under increasing attack for either proposing to do too much or, more frequently, for apparently doing too little. Conflicting national interests have blocked significant institutional reforms and have increased the need for fundamental change.[5] By the mid-1980s, funds for many international organizations had levelled off or declined in both relative and absolute terms.

Bilateral development assistance has declined as a percentage of gross national product (GNP) in many industrial countries, falling even further below the targets proposed in the early 1970s.[6] The benefits and effectiveness of aid have come under serious question, in part because of criticism based on environmental considerations.[7] Yet, sustainable development creates the need for even greater international aid and co-operation.

Nations must now confront a growing number, frequency, and scale of crises. A major reorientation is needed in many policies and institutional arrangements at the international as well as national level. The time has come to break away. Dismal scenarios of mounting destruction of national and global potential for development—indeed, of the Earth's capacity to support life—are not inescapable destiny. One of the most hopeful characteristics of the changes the world is racing through is that invariably they reflect great opportunities for sustainable development, providing that institutional arrangements permit sustainable policy options to be elaborated, considered, and implemented.

II. PROPOSALS FOR INSTITUTIONAL AND LEGAL CHANGE

The ability to choose policy paths that are sustainable requires that the ecological dimensions of policy be considered at the same time as the economic, trade, energy, agricultural, industrial, and other dimensions—on the same agendas and in the same national and international institutions. That is the chief institutional challenge of the 1990s.

There are significant proposals for institutional and legal change in previous chapters of our report. The Commission's proposals for institutional and legal change at the national, regional, and international levels are embodied in six priority areas:

- getting at the sources,
- dealing with the effects,
- assessing global risks,
- making informed choices,
- providing the legal means, and
- investing in our future.

Together, these priorities represent the main directions for institutional and legal change needed to make the transition to sustainable development. Concerted action is needed under all six.

Getting at the Sources

National Policies and Institutions

The way countries achieve sustainable development will vary among the many different political and economic systems around the world. Governments differ greatly in their capacity to monitor and evaluate sustainable development, and many will need assistance. Several features should be common to most countries.

Sustainable development objectives should be incorporated in the terms of reference of those cabinet and legislative committees dealing with national economic policy and planning as well as those dealing with key sectoral and international policies. As an extension of this, the major central economic and sectoral agencies of governments should now be made directly responsible and fully accountable for ensuring that their policies, programmes, and budgets support development that is ecologically as well as economically sustainable.

Where resources and data permit, an annual report and an audit on changes in environmental quality and in the stock of the nation's environmental resource assets are needed to complement the traditional annual fiscal budget and economic development plans.[8] These are essential to obtain an accurate picture of the true health and wealth of the national economy, and to assess progress towards sustainable development.[9]

Governments that have not done so should consider developing a 'foreign policy for the environment'.[10] A nation's foreign policy needs to reflect the fact that its policies have a growing impact on the environmental resource base of other nations and the commons, just as the policies of other nations have an impact on its own. This is true of certain energy, agricultural, and other sectoral policies discussed

*'All governments should develop a 'foreign policy for the environment'
as one major way of improving the international co-ordination of national
environmental policies.*

*But in the long-term perspective, and here I think the World Com-
mission could have an important message, I think that it will be politically sound and wise to get support from the NGOs to prepare for
changes that have to take place anyway sooner or later. So I think it
would be politically wise to look into that in a much broader way than
what has been done so far.'*

Mats Segnestam
Swedish Society for the Conservation of Nature
WCED Public Hearing, Oslo, 24-25 June 1985

in this report, as well as certain foreign investment, trade, and development assistance policies and those concerning the import or
export of hazardous chemicals, wastes, and technology.

Regional and Interregional Action

The existing regional and subregional organizations within and outside the UN system need to be strengthened and made responsible
and accountable for ensuring that their programmes and budgets
encourage and support sustainable development policies and practices. In some areas, however, especially among developing countries,
new regional and subregional arrangements will be needed to deal
with transboundary environmental resource issues.

Some countries already enjoy comparatively well developed bilateral and regional structures, although many of them lack the mandate and support required to carry out the greatly expanded role they
must assume in the future. These include many specialized bilateral
organizations such as the Canada/USA International Joint Commission; subregional agencies in Europe such as the different Com-
missions for the Rhine River, the Danube River, and the Baltic Sea;
and organizations such as the Council of Mutual Economic Assistance
(CMEA), the Organisation for Economic Co-operation and Development (OECD), and the European Economic Community. These
bodies provide member countries with a strong foundation on which
to build. Although most of them have effective programmes for international co-operation on environmental protection and natural
resources management, these programmes will need to be
strengthened and adapted to new priorities. The regional organizations in particular need to do more to integrate environment

fully in their macroeconomic, trade, energy, and other sectoral programmes.

Similar organizations among developing countries should be strengthened, particularly at bilateral and subregional levels. Organizations such as the Organization of African Unity, the Southern Africa Development Coordination Conference, the Gulf Cooperation Council, the Arab League, the Organization of American States, the Association of South East Asian Nations, and the South Asian Association for Regional Cooperation could work together to develop contingency plans and the capacity to respond quickly to critical situations and issues. They need in such bodies to develop comparable economic and environmental statistics, base-line quantity and quality surveys of shared resources, and early-warning capabilities to reduce environment and development hazards. They could develop and apply in concert basic common principles and guidelines concerning environmental protection and resource use, particularly with respect to foreign trade and investment. In this respect, developing countries have much to gain through sharing their common experiences and taking common action.

A new focus on the sustainable use and management of transboundary ecological zones, systems, and resources is also needed. There are, for example, over 200 distinct biogeographic zones in the world. Moreover, most non-island countries in the world share at least one international river basin. The entire national territories of nearly one-quarter of those countries is part of an international river basin. Yet over one-third of the 200 major international river basins in the world are not covered by any international agreement, and fewer than 30 have any co-operative institutional arrangements. These gaps are particularly acute in Africa, Asia, and Latin America, which together have 144 international river basins.[11]

Governments, directly and through the UN Environment Programme (UNEP) and the International Union for the Conservation of Nature and Natural Resources (IUCN), should support the development of regional and subregional co-operative arrangements for the protection and sustained use of transboundary ecological systems with joint action programmes to combat common problems such as desertification and acidification.

Global Institutions and Programmes

At the global level, an extensive institutional capacity exists that could be redirected towards sustainable development. The United Nations, as the only intergovernmental organization with universal member-

'In retrospect, even if the institutional and policy goals of the decade had been achieved, one is left with the feeling that most developing countries would be only marginally better off than they are today. The reason for this is a striking and humbling one. Although governments, environmentalists, and the aid agencies kept their eye on the environmental ball during the 1970s and the early 1980s, recent events have starkly demonstrated that they were watching the wrong ball. While the world was worrying about the environmental impacts of investments, controlling pollution, and conserving resources, we collectively failed to notice the dramatic decline in what had complacently been called 'renewable resources'.'

David Runnals
International Institute for Environment and Development
WCED Public Hearing, Ottawa, 26–27 May 1986

ship, should clearly be the locus for new institutional initiatives of a global character.

Although the funds flowing to developing countries through UN programmes represents a relatively small portion of total official development assistance (ODA) flows, the UN can and should be a source of significant leadership in the transition to sustainable development and in support of developing countries in effecting this transition. Under existing conditions the UN system's influence is often fragmented and less effective than it might be because of the independent character of the specialized agencies and endemic weaknesses of co-ordination. However, recent moves towards organizational reform and greater economy and efficiency could improve the capacity of the UN to provide this leadership, and should include sustainable development as an important criterion.

All major international bodies and agencies of the UN system should be made responsible and accountable for ensuring that their programmes and budgets encourage and support development policies and practices that are sustainable. Governments, through parallel resolutions in the respective governing bodies, should now begin to reorient and refocus the mandates, programmes, and budgets of key agencies to support sustainable development. They should also insist on much greater coordination and co-operation among them.

Each agency will need to redeploy some staff and financial resources to establish a small but high-level centre of leadership and expertise. That centre should be linked to the programme planning and budget processes.

Each agency should be directly responsible for ensuring that the environmental and resource aspects of programmes and projects are properly taken into account when they are being planned, and that the financial resources needed are provided directly from its own budget. In line with these new responsibilities, the following bodies should also assume full financial responsibility within their own budgets for certain programmes presently supported by the Environment Fund of UNEP: the World Health Organisation on 'Environmental Health', the Food and Agriculture Organisation (FAO) on 'Agricultural Chemicals and Residues', the UN Disaster Relief Office on 'Natural Disasters', the UN Industrial Development Organisation on 'Industry and Transport', the International Labour Organisation on 'Working Environment', the UN Department for Disarmament Affairs on 'Arms Race and the Environment', the Department for International Economic and Social Affairs on 'Environmental Aspects of Development Planning and Cooperation', the UN Educational, Scientific, and Cultural Organisation (UNESCO) on 'Education', and the UN Development Programme (UNDP) on 'Technical Cooperation'. UNEP (discussed extensively in the next section) should continue to co-operate closely with these agencies and help identify new programme needs and monitor performance.

As in each agency, there is also a need for a high-level centre of leadership for the UN system as a whole with the capacity to assess, advise, assist, and report on progress made and needed for sustainable development. That leadership should be provided by the Secretary-General of the United Nations Organisation.

Governments at the UN General Assembly should therefore take the necessary measures to reinforce the system-wide responsibility and authority of the UN Secretary-General concerning interagency co-ordination and co-operation generally, and for achieving sustainable development specifically. This will require that the representatives of those same governments in the governing bodies of all major UN organizations and specialized agencies take complementary measures. This could be done as an integral part of the parallel resolutions just proposed on building sustainable development objectives and criteria into the mandates, programmes, and budget of each agency.

To help launch and guide the interagency co-ordination and co-operation that will be needed, the UN Secretary-General should constitute under his chairmanship a special UN Board for Sustainable Development. The principal function of the Board would be to agree on combined tasks to be undertaken by the agencies to deal effectively with the many critical issues of sustainable development that cut across agency and national boundaries.

Dealing With the Effects

Governments should also strengthen the role and capacity of existing environmental protection and resource management agencies.[12]

National Environmental Protection and Natural Resources Management Agencies

Strengthening of environmental agencies is needed most urgently in developing countries. Those that have not established such agencies should do so as a matter of priority. In both cases, bilateral and multilateral organizations must be prepared to provide increased assistance for institutional development. Some of this increased financial support should go to community groups and non-governmental organizations (NGOs), which are rapidly emerging as important and cost-effective partners in work to protect and improve the environment locally and nationally, and in developing and implementing national conservation strategies.

Industrialized countries also need greatly strengthened environmental protection and resource management agencies. Most face a continuing backlog of pollution problems and a growing range of environment and resource management problems too. In addition, these agencies will be called upon to advise and assist central economic and sectoral agencies as they take up their new responsibilities for sustainable development. Many now provide institutional support, technical advice, and assistance to their counterpart agencies in developing countries, and this need will grow. And, almost inevitably, they will play a larger and more direct role in international co-operation, working with other countries and international agencies trying to cope with regional and global environmental problems.

Strengthen the United Nations Environment Programme

When UNEP was established in 1972, the UN General Assembly gave it a broad and challenging mandate to stimulate, coordinate, and provide policy guidance for environmental action throughout the UN system.[13] That mandate was to be carried out by a Governing Council of 58 member states, a high-level UN interagency Environment Coordination Board (ECB),[14] a relatively small secretariat located in Nairobi, and a voluntary fund set initially at a level of $100 million for the first five years. UNEP's principal task was to exercise leadership and a catalytic influence on the programmes and projects of other international organizations, primarily in but also outside the UN system. Over the past 10 years, the Environment Fund has levelled off at around $30 million annually, while its range of tasks and activities have increased substantially.

This Commission has recommended a major reorientation and refocusing of programmes and budgets on sustainable development in and among all UN organizations. Within such a new system-wide commitment to and priority effort on sustainable development, UNEP should be the principal source on environmental data, assessment, reporting, and related support for environmental management as well as be the principal advocate and agent for change and co-operation on critical environment and natural resource protection issues. The major priorities and functions of UNEP should be:

- to provide leadership, advice, and guidance in the UN system on restoring, protecting, and improving the ecological basis for sustainable development;
- to monitor, assess, and report regularly on changes in the state of the environment and natural resources (through its Earthwatch programme);
- to support priority scientific and technological research on critical environmental and natural resource protection issues;
- to develop criteria and indicators for environmental quality standards and guidelines for the sustainable use and management of natural resources;
- to support and facilitate the development of action plans for key ecosystems and issues to be implemented and financed by the governments directly concerned;
- to encourage and promote international agreements on critical issues identified by Earthwatch and to support and facilitate the development of international law, conventions, and co-operative arrangements for environmental and natural resource conservation and protection;
- to support the development of the institutional and professional capacity of developing countries in all of these areas and help them develop specific programmes to deal with their problems and advise and assist development assistance agencies in this respect; and
- to provide advice and assistance to the United Nations Development Programme, the World Bank, and other UN organizations and agencies regarding the environmental dimensions of their programmes and technical assistance projects, including training activities.

Focus on Environmental Protection Issues. UNEP has been a key agent in focusing the attention of governments on critical environmental problems (such as deforestation and marine pollution), in helping develop many global and regional action plans and strategies (as on desertification), in contributing to the negotiation and implementation of international conventions (on Protection of the Ozone Layer, for example), and in preparing global guidelines and principles for action by governments (such as on marine pollution from land-based sources). UNEP's Regional Seas Programme has been particularly successful, and could serve as a model for some other areas of special concern, especially international river basins.

UNEP's catalytic and co-ordinating role in the UN system can and should be reinforced and extended. In its future work on critical environmental protection issues, UNEP should focus particularly on:

- developing, testing, and helping to apply practical and simple methodologies for environmental assessment at project and national levels;
- extending international agreements (such as on chemicals and hazardous wastes) more widely;
- extending the Regional Seas Programme;
- developing a similar programme for international river basins; and
- identifying the need for and advising other UN organizations and agencies in establishing and carrying out technical assistance and training courses for environmental protection and management.

Priority to Global Environmental Assessment and Reporting. Although more is known about the state of the global environment now than a decade ago, there are still major gaps and a limited international capability for monitoring, collecting, and combining basic and comparable data needed for authoritative overviews of key environmental issues and trends. Without such, the information needed to help set priorities and develop effective policies will remain limited.

UNEP, as the main UN source for environmental data, assessment, and reporting, should guide the global agenda for scientific research and technological development for environmental protection. To this end, the data collection, assessment, and state of the environment reporting functions (Earthwatch) of UNEP need to be significantly strengthened as a major priority. The Global Environment Monitoring System should be expanded as rapidly as possible, and the development of the Global Resource Information Database should

'The environment has quickly deteriorated in certain areas and we don't know where to put the thresholds for nature's tolerance. We must move very fast towards a consensus on the necessity for taking urgent action. There is a strong popular support for this in our country. The findings of several opinion polls tell us that ecological issues have heightened priority. People feel anxious about the legacy our generation will be passing on to the next one. A new environmental awareness has germinated among large sections of the community and mainly among young people.'

Dr. Imre V. Nagy
National Environment Protection Committee
of the Patriotic People's Front, Hungary
WCED Public Hearing, Moscow, 8 Dec 1986

be accelerated to bridge the gap between environmental assessment and management. Special priority should be accorded to providing support to developing countries to enable them to participate fully in and derive maximum benefits from these programmes

Strengthen International Environmental Co-operation. The UNEP Governing Council cannot fulfil its primary role of providing leadership and policy guidance in the UN system nor have a significant influence on national policies unless governments increase their participation and the level of representation. National delegations to future meetings should preferably be led by Ministers, with their senior policy and scientific advisers. Special provisions should be made for expanded and more meaningful participation by major non-governmental organizations at future sessions.

Increase the Revenue and Focus of the Environment Fund. The UNEP voluntary funding base of $30 million annually is too limited and vulnerable for an international fund dedicated to serving and protecting the common interests, security, and future of humanity. Six countries alone provided over 75 per cent of the 1985 contributions to the Environment Fund (the United States, Japan, USSR, Sweden, the Federal Republic of Germany, and the United Kingdom).[15] Considering the critical importance of renewed efforts on environmental protection and improvement, the Commission appeals to all governments to substantially enlarge the Environment Fund both through direct contributions by all members of the UN and through some of the sources cited later in this chapter in the section 'Investing in Our Future'.

A substantial enlargement of the Environment Fund seems unlikely in the current climate of financial austerity. Any additional funds made available by states for UN development programmes and activities will likely be channelled largely through UNDP and the development programmes of other UN agencies. Moreover, as recommended earlier, the budgets of all of those agencies should be deployed so that environmental considerations are built into the planning and implementation of all programmes and projects.

The Environment Fund can be made more effective by refocusing the programme on fewer activities. As other UN agencies assume full responsibility for certain activities now provided through the Environment Fund and finance them entirely from their own budgets, some resources will be released for other purposes. These should be concentrated on the principal functions and priority areas identified earlier.

Expanding support and co-operation with NGOs capable of carrying out elements of UNEP's programme will also increase the effectiveness of the Environment Fund. Over the last decade, non-governmental organizations and networks have become increasingly important in work to improve environmental protection locally, nationally, and internationally. However, financial support from the Environment Fund for co-operative projects with NGOs declined in both absolute and relative terms in the last 10 years, from $4.5 million (23 per cent of the Fund) in 1976 to $3.6 million (13 per cent) in 1985.[16] The amount and proportion of Environment Fund resources for co-operation and projects with NGOs should be significantly increased by using the capacities of those NGOs that can contribute to UNEP's programmes on a cost-effective basis.

Assessing Global Risks

The future—even a sustainable future—will be marked by increasing risk.[17] The risks associated with new technologies are growing.[18] The numbers, scale, frequency, and impact of natural and human-caused disasters are mounting.[19] The risks of irreversible damage to natural systems regionally (for example through acidification, desertification, or deforestation) and globally (through ozone layer depletion or climate change) are becoming significant.[20]

Fortunately, the capacity to monitor and map Earth change and to assess risk is also growing rapidly. Data from remote sensing platforms in space can now be merged with data from conventional land-based sources. Augmented by digital communications and advanced information analysis, photos, mapping, and other techniques, these data can provide up-to-date information on a wide variety of resource, climatic, pollution, and other variables.[21] High-speed data communications technologies, including the personal computer, enable this information to be shared by individuals as well as corporate and governmental users at costs that are steadily falling. Concerted efforts should be made to ensure that all nations gain access to them and the information they provide either directly or through the UNEP Earthwatch and other special programmes.

Governments, individually and collectively, have the principal responsibility to collect this information systematically and use it to assess risks, but to date only a few have developed a capacity to do so. Some intergovernmental agencies have a capacity to collect and assess information required for risk assessment, such as FAO on soil and forest cover and on fisheries; the World Meteorological Organization on climate; UNEP on deserts, pollutants, and regional seas. Quasi-governmental organizations like IUCN have a similar capacity. These are only a few examples from a long list. But no intergovernmental agency has been recognized as the centre of leadership to stimulate work on risk assessment and to provide an authoritative source of reports and advice on evolving risks. This gap needs to be filled both within and among governments. Beyond our proposal that the global environment assessment and reporting functions of UNEP should be significantly strengthened, the Commission would now propose that UNEP's Earthwatch be recognized as the centre of leadership on risk assessment in the UN system.

But neither UNEP nor other intergovernmental organizations can be expected to carry out these important functions alone. To be effective, given the politically sensitive nature of many of the most critical risks, intergovernmental risk assessment needs to be supported by independent capacities outside of government. Several national science academies and international scientific groups—such as the Internation Council of Scientific Unions and its Scientific Committee on Problems of the Environment, with special programmes such as the newly inaugurated International Geosphere-Biosphere Programme (see Chapter 10); the Man and the Biosphere Programme of UNESCO; quasi-governmental bodies such as IUCN; and certain industry groups and NGOs—are active in this field. But, again, there is no recognized international non-governmental centre of leadership through which they efforts of these groups can be focused and co-ordinated.

During the 1970s, the growing capacity of computers led various governments, institutes, and international bodies to develop models for integrated policy analysis. They have provided significant insights and offer great promise as a means of anticipating the consequences of interdependent trends and of establishing the policy options to address them.[22] Without suggesting any relationship between them, early attempts were all limited by serious inconsistencies in the methods and assumptions employed by the various sources on which they depended for data and information.[23] Although significant improvements have been made in the capability of models and other techniques, the data base remains weak.[24]

There is an urgent need to strengthen and focus the capacities of these and other bodies to complement and support UNEP's monitoring and assessment functions by providing timely, objective, and authoritative assessments and public reports on critical threats and risks to the world community. To meet this need, we recommend the establishment of a Global Risks Assessment Programme:

- to identify critical threats to the survival, security, or well-being of all or a majority of people, globally or regionally;
- to assess the causes and likely human, economic, and ecological consequences of those threats, and to report regularly and publicly on their findings;
- to provide authoritative advice and proposals on what should or must be done to avoid, reduce, or, if possible, adapt to those threats; and
- to provide an additional source of advice and support to governments and intergovernmental organizations for the implementation of programmes and policies designed to address such threats.

The Global Risk Assessment Programme would not require the creation of a new international institution as such, as it should function primarily as a mechanism for co-operation among largely non-governmental national and international organizations, scientific bodies, and industry groups. To provide intellectual leadership and guide the programme, there should be a steering group composed of eminent individuals who together would reflect a broad cross-section of the major areas of knowledge, vocations, and regions of the world, as well as the major bodies active in the field.

The steering group would serve as the focal point for identifying the risks to be addressed by the programme, agreeing on the research needed to assess those risks, and co-ordinating the work among the various participating bodies. It could form special consortia and task forces made up of experts from these bodies and it would also establish special expert and advisory groups consisting of world-known authorities in specialized areas of science, economics, and law. The steering group would be responsible for the overall evaluation of results, for their wide dissemination, and for follow-up activities.

The steering group would also be charged with helping mobilize funds for implementing the programme through contributions by the Environment Fund of UNEP, states, foundations, and other private sources. Funding would principally be for the purpose of financing the various activities that would be carried out by other organizations as part of the programme, with only a small portion required to meet the costs of the steering group.

Making Informed Choices

As is evident from this report, the transition to sustainable development will require a range of public policy choices that are inherently complex and politically difficult. Reversing unsustainable development policies at the national and international level will require immense efforts to inform the public and secure its support. The scientific community, private and community groups, and NGOs can play a central role in this.

Increase the Role of the Scientific Community and Non-Governmental Organizations

Scientific groups and NGOs have played—with the help of young people[25]—a major part in the environmental movement from its earliest beginnings. Scientists were the first to point out evidence of significant environmental risks and changes resulting from the growing intensity of human activities. Other non-governmental organizations and citizens' groups pioneered in the creation of public awareness and political pressures that stimulated governments to act. Scientific and non-governmental communities played a vital role in the United Nations Conference on the Human Environment in Stockholm.[26]

These groups have also played an indispensable role since the Stockholm Conference in identifying risks, in assessing environmental impacts and designing and implementing measures to deal with them, and in maintaining the high degree of public and political interest required as a basis for action. Today, major national 'State of the Environment' reports are being published by some NGOs (in Malaysia, India, and the United States, for instance).[27] Several international NGOs have produced significant reports on the status of and prospects for the global environment and natural resource base.[28]

The vast majority of these bodies are national or local in nature, and a successful transition to sustainable development will require

'If the NGO community is to translate its commitment to sustainable development into effective action, we will need to see a matching level of commitment from the governmental and intergovernmental communities, in genuine partnership with NGOs. The success and cost-effectiveness of NGO action is to an important degree a function of their spontaneity and freedom of action.

Both among NGOs and amongst governments, we must find ways to engender a new period of international co-operation. The urgency of our tasks no longer permits us to spill our energies in fruitless and destructive conflict. Whilst we fight our wars of ideology on the face of this planet, we are losing our productive relationship with the planet itself.'

David Bull
Environment Liaison Centre
WCED Public Hearing, Nairobi, 23 Sept 1986

substantial strengthening of their capacities. To an increasing extent, national NGOs draw strength from association with their counterparts in other countries and from participation in international programmes and consultations. NGOs in developing countries are particularly in need of international support—professional and moral as well as financial—to carry out their roles effectively.

Many international bodies and coalitions of NGOs are now in place and active. They play an important part in ensuring that national NGOs and scientific bodies have access to the support they require. These include regional groups providing networks linking together environment and development NGOs in Asia, Africa, Eastern and Western Europe, and North and South America. They also include a number of regional and global coalitions on critical issues such as pesticides, chemicals, rain, seeds, genetic resources, and development assistance. A global network for information exchange and joint action is provided through the Environment Liaison Centre (ELC) in Nairobi. ELC has over 230 NGO member groups, with the majority from developing countries, and is in contact with 7,000 others.

Only a few international NGOs deal on a broad basis with both environment and development issues, but this is changing rapidly. One of them, the International Institute for Environment and Development, has long specialized in these issues and pioneered the conceptual basis for the environment/development relationship. Most of them work with and support related organizations in the developing world. They facilitate their participation in international activities and their links with counterparts in the international community. They provide instruments for leadership and co-operation among a wide variety of organizations in their respective constituencies. These capabilities will be ever more important in the future. An increasing number of environment and development issues could not be tackled without them.

NGOs should give a high priority to the continuation of their present networking on development co-operation projects and programmes, directed at the improvement of the performance of NGO bilateral and multilateral development programmes. They could increase their efforts to share resources, exchange skills, and strengthen each other's capacities through greater international co-operation in this area. In setting their own house in order, 'environment' NGOs should assist 'development' NGOs in reorienting projects that degrade the environment and in formulating projects that contribute to sustainable development. The experience gained would provide a useful basis for continuing discussions with bilateral and multilateral agencies as to steps that these agencies might take to improve their performance.

In many countries, governments need to recognize and extend NGOs' right to know and have access to information on the environment and natural resources; their right to be consulted and to participate in decision making on activities likely to have a significant effect on their environment; and their right to legal remedies and redress when their health or environment has been or may be seriously affected.

NGOs and private and community groups can often provide an efficient and effective alternative to public agencies in the delivery of programmes and projects. Moreover, they can sometimes reach target groups that public agencies cannot. Bilateral and multilateral development assistance agencies, especially UNDP and the World Bank, should draw upon NGOs in executing programmes and projects. At the national level, governments, foundations, and industry should also greatly extend their co-operation with NGOs in planning, monitoring, and evaluating as well as in carrying out projects when they can provide the necessary capabilities on a cost-effective basis. To this end, governments should establish or strengthen procedures for official consultation and more meaningful participation by NGOs in all relevant intergovernmental organizations.

International NGOs need substantially increased financial support to expand their special roles and functions on behalf of the world community and in support of national NGOs. In the Commission's view, the increased support that will allow these organizations to expand their services represents an indispensable and cost-effective investment. The Commission recommends that these organizations be accorded high priority by governments, foundations, and other private and public sources of funding.

Increase Co-operation with Industry

Industry is on the leading edge of the interface between people and the environment. It is perhaps the main instrument of change that affects the environmental resource bases of development, both positively and negatively. (See Chapter 8.) Both industry and government, therefore, stand to benefit from working together more closely.

World industry has taken some significant steps through voluntary guidelines concerning industry practices on environment, natural resources, science, and technology. Although few of these guidelines have been extended to or applied regionally in Africa, Asia, or Latin America, industry continues to address these issues through various international associations.

These efforts were advanced significantly by the 1984 World Industry Conference on Environmental Management (WICEM).[29] Recently, as a follow-up to WICEM, several major corporations from a number of developed countries formed the International Environment Bureau to assist developing countries with their environment/development needs. Such initiatives are promising and should be encouraged. Co-operation between governments and industry would be further facilitated if they established joint advisory councils for sustainable development—for mutual advice, assistance, and co-operation in helping to shape and implement policy, laws, and regulations for more sustainable forms of development. Internationally, governments in co-operation with industry and NGOs should work through appropriate regional organizations to develop basic codes of conduct for sustainable development, drawing on and extending relevant existing voluntary codes, especially in Africa, Asia, and Latin America.

The private sector also has a major impact on development through commercial bank loans from within and outside countries. In 1983, for example, the proportion of the total net receipts of developing countries from private sources, mostly in the form of commercial bank loans, was greater than all ODA that year. Since 1983, as indebtedness worsened, commercial bank lending to developing countries has declined.[30]

Efforts are being made to stimulate private investment. These efforts should be geared to supporting sustainable development. The industrial and financial corporations making such investments, and the export credit, investment insurance, and other programmes that facilitate them, should incorporate sustainable development criteria into their policies.

Providing the Legal Means

National and international law has traditionally lagged behind events. Today, legal regimes are being rapidly outdistanced by the accelerating pace and expanding scale of impacts on the environmental base of development. Human laws must be reformulated to keep human activities in harmony with the unchanging and universal laws of nature. There is an urgent need:

- to recognize and respect the reciprocal rights and responsibilities of individuals and states regarding sustainable development,
- to establish and apply new norms for state and interstate behaviour to achieve sustainable development,
- to strengthen and extend the application of existing laws and international agreements in support of sustainable development, and
- to reinforce existing methods and develop new procedures for avoiding and resolving environmental disputes.

Recognizing Rights and Responsibilities

Principle 1 of the 1972 Stockholm Declaration said that 'Man has the fundamental right to freedom, equality and adequate conditions of life, in an environment of a quality that permits a life of dignity and well-being'.[31] It further proclaimed the solemn responsibility of governments to protect and improve the environment for both present and future generations. After the Stockholm Conference, several states recognized in their Constitutions or laws the right to an adequate environment and the obligation of the state to protect that environment.

Recognition by states of their responsibility to ensure an adequate environment for present as well as future generations is an important step towards sustainable development. However, progress will also be facilitated by recognition of, for example, the right of individuals to know and have access to current information on the state of the environment and natural resources, the right to be consulted and to participate in decision making on activities likely to have a significant effect on the environment, and the right to legal remedies and redress for those whose health or environment has been or may be seriously affected.

⁶What are we to do? It is axiomatic that we as individuals or groups of individuals share territory in resources. We need to define common norms of behaviour. This is true whether we are speaking of a family, small town, a province or country, or the world community. However, the definition of common norms of behaviour is not in itself sufficient for the creation of a body of rules and regulation.

To operate effectively, certain basic conditions must be fulfilled: the existence of a general will among members of the community to accept and adhere to regulations; the existence of a political framework not only for defining and quantifying common behaviour or norms, but also for adopting existing rules to change within the community; a means of determining compliance with international rules and regulations; and, finally, the means for enforcement.⁹

Fergus Watt
World Association of World Federalists
WCED Public Hearing, Ottawa, 26–27 May 1986

The enjoyment of any right requires respect for the similar rights of others, and recognition of reciprocal and even joint responsibilities. States have a responsibility towards their own citizens and other states:

- to maintain ecosystems and related ecological processes essential for the functioning of the biosphere;
- to maintain biological diversity by ensuring the survival and promoting the conservation in their natural habitats of all species of flora and fauna;
- to observe the principle of optimum sustainable yield in the exploitation of living natural resources and ecosystems;
- to prevent or abate significant environmental pollution or harm;
- to establish adequate environmental protection standards;
- to undertake or require prior assessments to ensure that major new policies, projects, and technologies contribute to sustainable development; and
- to make all relevant information public without delay in all cases of harmful or potentially harmful releases of pollutants, especially radioactive releases.

It is recommended that governments take appropriate steps to recognize these reciprocal rights and responsibilities.[32] However, the wide variation in national legal systems and practices makes it impossible to propose an approach that would be valid everywhere. Some countries have amended their basic laws or constitution; others

❛Law does not stand alone. It depends on the functioning of many things. Experience from the past 15 years of development has taught us that there is a danger that bureaucracy with all its strength coming from the West, in Indonesia's case because of the oil and gas revenues, will strangle the community with so many laws. They have, for instance, laws that ask every gathering of five or more people to have permission from the police. Sometimes I feel that maybe the best government is the one who governs the least. In this case, I feel that sometimes the Asian countries learn from each other.❜

Adi Sasono
Institute for Development Studies
WCED Public Hearing, Jakarta, 26 March 1985

are considering the adoption of a special national law or charter setting out the rights and responsibilities of citizens and the state regarding environmental protection and sustainable development. Others may wish to consider the designation of a national council or public representative or 'ombudsman' to represent the interests and rights of present and future generations and act as an environmental watchdog, alerting governments and citizens to any emerging threats.

A Universal Declaration and a Convention on Environmental Protection and Sustainable Development

Building on the 1972 Stockholm Declaration, the 1982 Nairobi Declaration, and many existing international conventions and General Assembly resolutions, there is now a need to consolidate and extend relevant legal principles in a new charter to guide state behaviour in the transition to sustainable development. It would provide the basis for, and be subsequently expanded into, a Convention, setting out the sovereign rights and reciprocal responsibilities of all states on environmental protection and sustainable development. The charter should prescribe new norms for state and interstate behaviour needed to maintain livelihoods and life on our shared planet, including basic norms for prior notification. consultation, and assessment of activities likely to have an impact on neighbouring states or global commons. These could include the obligation to alert and inform neighbouring states in the event of an accident likely to have a harmful impact on their environment. Although a few such norms have evolved in some bilateral and regional arrangements, the lack of wider agreement on such basic rules for interstate behaviour undermines both the sovereignty and economic development potential of each and all states.

We recommend that the General Assembly commit itself to preparing a universal Declaration and later a Convention on environmental protection and sustainable development. A special negotiating group could be established to draft a Declaration text for adoption in 1988. Once it is approved, that group could then proceed to prepare a Convention, based on and extending the principles in the Declaration, with the aim of having an agreed Convention text ready for signature by states within three to five years. To facilitate the early launching of that process the Commission has submitted for consideration by the General Assembly, and as a starting point for the deliberations of the special negotiating group, a number of proposed legal principles embodied in 22 Articles that were prepared by its group of international legal experts. These proposed principles are submitted to assist the General Assembly in its deliberations and have not been approved or considered in detail by the Commission. A summary of the principles and Articles appears as Annexe 1 of this report.

Strengthen and Extend Existing International Conventions and Agreements

In parallel, governments should accelerate their efforts to strengthen and extend existing and more specific international conventions and co-operative arrangements by:

- acceding to or ratifying existing global and regional conventions dealing with environment and development, and applying them with more vigour and rigour;
- reviewing and revising those relevant conventions that need to be brought in line with the latest available technical and scientific information; and
- negotiating new global and regional conventions or arrangements aimed at promoting co-operation and co-ordination in the field of environment and development (including, for example, new conventions and agreements on climate change, on hazardous chemicals and wastes, and on preserving biological diversity).

It is recommended that the UNEP secretariat, in close co-operation with the IUCN Environmental Law Centre, should help in these efforts.

Avoiding and Settling Environmental Disputes

Many disputes can be avoided or more readily resolved if the principles, rights, and responsibilities cited earlier are built into national and international legal frameworks and are fully respected and implemented by many states. Individuals and states are more reluctant to act in a way that might lead to a dispute when, as in many national legal systems, there is an established and effective capacity as well as ultimately binding procedures for settling disputes. Such a capacity and procedures are largely lacking at the international level, particularly on environmental and natural resource management issues.[33]

It is recommended that public and private organizations and NGOs help in this area by establishing special panels or rosters of experts with experience in various forms of dispute settlement and special competence on the legal and substantive aspects of environmental protection, natural resources management, and sustainable development. In addition, a consolidated inventory and referral system or network for responding to requests for advice and assistance in avoiding or resolving such disputes should be established.

To promote the peaceful and early settlement of international disputes on environmental and resource management problems, it is recommended that the following procedure be adopted. States should be given up to 18 months to reach mutual agreement on a solution or on a common dispute settlement arrangement. If agreement is not reached, then the dispute can be submitted to conciliation at the request of any one of the concerned states and, if still unresolved, thereafter to arbitration or judicial settlement.

This proposed new procedure raises the possibility of invoking a binding process of dispute settlement at the request of any state. Binding settlement is not the preferred method for settling international disputes. But such a provision is now needed not only as a last resort to avoid prolonged disputes and possible serious environmental damage, but also to encourage and provide an incentive for all parties to reach agreement within a reasonable time on either a solution or a mutually agreed means, such as mediation.

The capabilities of the Permanent Court of Arbitration and the International Court of Justice to deal with environmental and resource management problems also should be strengthened. States should make greater use of the World Court's capacity under Article 26 of its Statute to form special chambers for dealing with particular cases or categories of cases, including environmental protection or resource management cases. The Court has declared its willingness and readiness to deal with such cases fully and promptly.

Investing in Our Future

We have endeavoured to show that it makes long-term economic sense to pursue environmentally sound policies. But potentially very

❝First, if the problems of environmental degradation and of poverty, particularly in the Third World, are to be solved, a continued economic development is essential. Second, we must reconcile environmental protection with economic growth. There is a growing consensus that this is perfectly possible and desirable. Third, there is also a great consensus that the application of strict environmental standards is good for economic growth, as well as for the environment, and that they encourage innovation, promote inventiveness and efficiency, and generate employment. Fourth, to achieve the goals of sustainable development, good environment, and decent standards of life for all involves very large changes in attitude.❞

Stanley Clinton-Davis
Commissioner for Environment, European Economic Community
WCED Public Hearing, Oslo, 24–25 June 1985

large financial outlays will be needed in the short term in such fields as renewable energy development, pollution control equipment, and integrated rural development. Developing countries will need massive assistance for this purpose, and more generally to reduce poverty. Responding to this financial need will be a collective investment in the future.

National Action

Past experience teaches us that these outlays would be good investments. By the late 1960s, when some industrial countries began to mount significant environmental protection programmes, they had already incurred heavy economic costs in the form of damage to human health, property, natural resources, and the environment. After 1970, in order to roll back some of this damage, they saw expenditures on environmental pollution measures alone rise from about 0.3 per cent of GNP in 1970 to somewhere between 1.5 per cent and, in some countries, 2.0 per cent around the end of the decade. Assuming low levels of economic growth in the future, these same countries will probably have to increase expenditures on environmental protection somewhere between 20 to 100 per cent just to maintain current levels of environmental quality.[34]

These figures relate only to expenditures to control environmental pollution. Unfortunately, similar figures are not available on the level of expenditures made to rehabilitate lands and natural habitats, re-establish soil fertility, reforest areas, and undertake other measures to restore the resource base. But they would be substantial.

Nations, industrial and developing, that did not make these investments have paid much more in terms of damage costs to human health, property, natural resources, and the environment. And these costs continue to rise at an accelerating pace. Indeed, countries that have not yet instituted strong programmes now face the need for very large investments. Not only do they need to roll back the first generation of environmental damage, they also need to begin to catch up with the rising incidence of future damage. If they do not, their fundamental capital assets, their environmental resources, will continue to decline.

In strictly economic terms, the benefits of these expenditures have been generally greater than the costs in those countries that have made them.[35] Beyond that, however, many of these countries found that economic, regulatory, and other environmental measures could be applied in ways that would result in innovation by industry. And those companies that did respond innovatively are today often in the forefront of their industry. They have developed new products, new processes, and entire plants that use less water, energy, and other resources per unit of output and are hence more economic and competitive.

Nations that begin to reorient major economic and sectoral policies along the lines proposed in this report can avoid much higher future levels of spending on environmental restoration and curative measures and also enhance their future economic prospects. By making central and sectoral agencies directly responsible for maintaining and enhancing environmental and resource stocks, expenditures for environmental protection and resource management would gradually be built into the budgets of those agencies for measures to prevent damage. The unavoidable costs of environmental and resource management would thus be paid only once.

International Action

Developing countries, as stated earlier, need a significant increase in financial support from international sources for environmental restoration, protection, and improvement and to help them through the necessary transition to sustainable development.

At the global level, there is an extensive institutional capacity to channel this support. This consists of the United Nations and its specialized agencies; the multilateral development banks, notably the World Bank; other multilateral development co-operation organizations, such as those of the European Economic Community;

national development assistance agencies, most of whom co-operate within the framework of the Development Assistance Committee of OECD or of the Organization of Petroleum-Exporting Countries; and other international groups, such as the Consultative Group on International Agricultural Research, that play an important role and influence on the quality and nature of development assistance. Together, the development organizations and agencies are responsible for the transfer of about $35 billion of ODA annually to developing countries. In addition, they are the source of most technical assistance and policy advice and support to developing countries.

These organizations and agencies are the principal instruments through which the development partnership between industrial and developing countries operates and, collectively, their influence is substantial and pervasive. It is imperative that they play a leading role in helping developing countries make the transition to sustainable development. Indeed, it is difficult to envisage developing countries making this transition in an effective and timely manner without their full commitment and support.

Reorienting Multilateral Financial Institutions. The World Bank, International Monetary Fund (IMF), and regional Development Banks warrant special attention because of their major influence on economic development throughout the world. As indicated in Chapter 3, there is an urgent need for much larger flows of concessional and nonconcessional finance through the multilateral agencies. The role of the World Bank is especially important in this respect, both as the largest single source of development lending and for its policy leadership, which exerts a significant influence on both developing countries and donors. The World Bank has taken a significant lead in reorienting its lending programmes to a much higher sensitivity to environmental concerns and to support for sustainable development. This is a promising beginning. But it will not be enough unless and until it is accompanied by a fundamental commitment to sustainable development by the World Bank, and by the transformation of its internal structure and processes so as to ensure its capacity to carry this out. The same is true of other multilateral development banks and agencies.

The IMF also exerts a major influence on the development policies of developing countries and, as described in Chapter 3, there is deep concern in many countries that the conditions that accompany its lending are undermining sustainable development. It is therefore essential that the IMF, too, incorporate sustainable development objectives and criteria into its policies and programmes.

Several countries have already formally instructed their representatives on the Board of the World Bank to ensure that the environmental impacts of projects proposed for approval have been assessed and adequately taken into account. We recommend that other governments take similar action, not only with regard to the World Bank but also in the Regional Banks and the other institutions. In this way they can support the ongoing efforts within the Banks and other institutions to reorient and refocus their mandates, programmes, and budgets to support sustainable development. The transition to sustainable development by the development assistance agencies and the IMF would be facilitated by the establishment of a high-level office in each agency with the authority and resources to ensure that all policies, projects, and loan conditions support sustainable development, and to prepare and publish annual assessments and reports on progress made and needed. A first step is to develop simple methodologies for such assessments, recognizing that they are at present experimental and need further work.

In making these changes, the multilateral financial institutions fortunately have some base on which to build. In 1980, they endorsed a Declaration of Environmental Policies and Procedures Relating to Economic Development. Since then they have been meeting and consulting through the Committee of International Development Institutions on the Environment (CIDIE).[36] Some have articulated clear policies and project guidelines for incorporating environmental concerns and assessments into their planning and decision making, but only a few have assigned staff and resources to implementing them, notably the World Bank, which is now considering even further institutional changes to strengthen this work. Overall, as pointed out by the UNEP Executive Director in his statement reviewing the first five years of work, 'CIDIE has not yet truly succeeded in getting environmental considerations firmly ingrained in development policies. There has been a distinct lack of action by several multilaterals.' CIDIE members have 'gone along with the Declaration in principle more than in major shifts in action.'[37]

In order to marshal and support investments in conservation projects and national conservation strategies that enhance the resource base for development, serious consideration should be given to the development of a special international banking programme or facility[38] linked to the World Bank. Such a special conservation banking programme or facility could provide loans and facilitate joint financing arrangements for the development and protection of critical habitats and ecosystems, including those of international significance,

‘We must have a true participation of all of the society in the decision making and more particularly in the allocation of resources. And why so? Because all of us are perfectly aware that there will never be sufficient resources for everything that we wish, but if the population participates in the decision making it will benefit those who need the most and it will express their thought about the allocation of resources and it will give us the certainty that that which is being done is the legitimate aspiration of the people.’

Aristides Marques
National Council for Urban Development
WCED Public Hearing, Brasilia, 30 Oct 1985

supplementing efforts by bilateral aid agencies, multilateral financial institutions, and commercial banks.

In the framework of the Council of Mutual Economic Assistance, there has been since the early 1970s a Committee for Environmental Protection with the participation of the heads of appropriate organizations in the member states. This Committee coordinates the relevant research and development programmes and, in some cases, organizes technical assistance for the interested member states, involving the Investment Bank of CMEA.

Reorienting Bilateral Aid Agencies. Bilateral aid agencies presently provide nearly four times as much total ODA as is provided by international organizations. As indicated in Chapter 3, a new priority and focus in bilateral aid agencies is needed in three main areas:

- new measures to ensure that all projects support sustainable development;
- special programmes to help restore, protect, and improve the ecological basis for development in many developing countries; and
- special programmes for strengthening the institutional and professional capacities needed for sustainable development.

Proposals for special bilateral aid programmes in the areas of agriculture, forestry, energy, industry, human settlements, and genetic resources are made in earlier chapters of this report. The first two priority areas in this chapter also contain proposals for strengthening the institutional and professional capacities in developing countries. The focus here is therefore on the first area: new measures to ensure that all bilateral aid projects support sustainable development.

Over the past decade, bilateral aid agencies have gradually given more attention to the environmental dimensions of their programmes and projects. A 1980 survey of the environmental procedures and practices of six major bilateral aid agencies indicated that only one, the US Agency for International Development, had systematic and enforceable procedures backed by the staff resources necessary to carry them out.[39] Since then, others have made some progress on the policy level, increased funds for environmental projects, and produced guidelines or checklists to guide their programmes. However, a 1983 study of those guidelines concluded that there was little evidence of their systematic application.[40]

An important step towards concerted action was taken in 1986 with the adoption by OECD of a recommendation to member governments to include an environmental assessment policy and effective procedures for applying it in their bilateral aid programmes.[41] It is based on a detailed analysis and studies carried out by a joint group of governmental experts from both the Development Assistance Committee and the Environmental Committee.[42] The recommendation includes proposals for adequate staff and financial resources to undertake environmental assessments and a central office in each agency to supervise implementation and to assist developing countries wishing to improve their capacities for conducting environmental assessments. We urge all bilateral aid agencies to implement this recommendation as quickly as possible. It is essential, of course, that this should not reduce aid flows in the aggregate or slow disbursements or represent a new form of aid conditionality.

New Sources of Revenue and Automatic Financing. We have made a series of proposals for institutional change within and among the organizations and specialized agencies of the UN system in the sections on 'Getting at the Sources' and 'Dealing with the Effects'. Most of those changes will not require additional financial resources but can be achieved through a reorientation of existing mandates, programmes, and budgets and a redeployment of present staff. Once implemented, those measures will make a major difference in the effective use of existing resources in making the transition to sustainable development.

Nevertheless, there is also a need to increase the financial resources for new multilateral efforts and programmes of action for environmental protection and sustainable development. These new funds will not be easy to come by if the international organizations through which they flow have to continue to rely solely on traditional sources of financing: assessed contributions from governments, voluntary contributions by governments, and funds borrowed in capital markets by the World Bank and other international financial institutions.

Assessed contributions from governments have traditionally been used largely for the administrative and operating costs of international organizations; they are not intended for multilateral assistance. The total assessed contributions from governments are much smaller than the amount provided through voluntary contributions and the prospects of raising significant additional funds through assessed contributions are limited.

Voluntary contributions by governments give the overall revenue system some flexibility, but they cannot be adjusted readily to meet new or increased requirements. Being voluntary, the flow of these funds is entirely discretionary and unpredictable. The commitments are also extremely short-term, as pledges are normally made only one or two years in advance. Consequently, they provide little security or basis for effective planning and management of international actions requiring sustained, longer-term efforts. Most of the limited funds provided so far for international environmental action have come through voluntary contributions, channelled principally through UNEP and NGOs.

Given the current constraints on major sources and modes of funding, it is necessary to consider new approaches as well as new sources of revenue for financing international action in support of sustainable development. The Commission recognizes that such proposals may not appear politically realistic at this point in time. It believes, however, that—given the trends discussed in this report—the need to support sustainable development will become so imperative that political realism will come to require it.

The search for other, and especially more automatic, sources and means for financing international action goes almost as far back as the UN itself. It was not until 1977, however, when the Plan of Action to Combat Desertification was approved by the UN General Assembly that governments officially accepted, but never implemented, the principle of automatic transfers. That Plan called for the establishment of a special account that could draw resources not only from traditional sources but also from additional measures of financing, 'including fiscal measures entailing automaticity'.[43]

Since then, a series of studies and reports[44] have identified and examined a growing list of new sources of potential revenue, including:
- revenue from the use of international commons (from ocean

'The problems of today do not come with a tag marked energy or economy or CO_2 or demography, nor with a label indicating a country or a region. The problems are multi-disciplinary and transnational or global.

The problems are not primarily scientific and technological. In science we have the knowledge and in technology the tools. The problems are basically political, economic, and cultural.'

Per Lindblom
International Federation of Institutes of Advanced Studies
WCED Public Hearing, Oslo, 24–25 June 1985

fishing and transportation, from sea-bed mining, from Antarctic resources, or from parking charges for geostationary communications satellites, for example);

- taxes on international trade (such as a general trade tax; taxes on specific traded commodities, on invisible exports, or on surpluses in balance of trade; or a consumption tax on luxury goods); and
- international financial measures (a link between special drawing rights and development finance, for example, or IMF gold reserves and sales).

In its 1980 report, the Brandt Commission called for raising additional funds from more automatic sources such as those cited above. In its follow-up report in 1983, the Brandt Commission strongly urged that these most 'futuristic' of all the Report's proposals not be lost completely from view.[45] Nevertheless, they again sank below the short-term horizon of the international agenda.

The World Commission on Environment and Development was specifically given the mandate by the UN General Assembly to look once again beyond that limited horizon. We have done so and, given the compelling nature, pace, and scope of the different transitions affecting our economic and ecological systems as described in this report, we consider that at least some of those proposals for additional and more automatic sources of revenue are fast becoming less futuristic and more necessary. This Commission particularly considers that the proposals regarding revenue from the use of international commons and natural resources now warrant and should receive serious consideration by governments and the General Assembly.

III. A CALL FOR ACTION

Over the course of this century, the relationship between the human world and the planet that sustains it has undergone a profound change. When the century began, neither human numbers nor technology had the power to radically alter planetary systems. As the century closes, not only do vastly increased human numbers and their activities have that power, but major, unintended changes are occurring in the atmosphere, in soils, in waters, among plants and animals, and in the relationships among all of these. The rate of change is outstripping the ability of scientific disciplines and our current capabilities to assess and advise. It is frustrating the attempts of political and economic institutions, which evolved in a different, more fragmented world, to adapt and cope. It deeply worries many people who are seeking ways to place those concerns on the political agendas.

We have been careful to base our recommendations on the realities of present institutions, on what can and must be accomplished today. But to keep options open for future generations, the present generation must begin now, and begin together, nationally and internationally.

To achieve the needed change in attitudes and reorientation of policies and institutions, the Commission believes that an active follow-up of this report is imperative. It is with this in mind that we call for the UN General Assembly, upon due consideration, to transform this report into a UN Programme of Action on Sustainable Development. Special follow-up conferences could be initiated at the regional level. Within an appropriate period after the presentation of the report to the General Assembly, an international Conference could be convened to review progress made and promote follow-up arrangements that will be needed over time to set benchmarks and to maintain human progress within the guidelines of human needs and natural laws.

The Commissioners came from 21 very different nations. In our discussions, we disagreed often on details and priorities. But despite our widely differing backgrounds and varying national and international responsibilities, we were able to agree to the lines along which institutional change must be drawn.

We are unanimous in our conviction that the security, well-being, and very survival of the planet depend on such changes, now.

Notes

1 The characteristics and differences of the two approaches are described in our inaugural report, 'Mandate for Change: Key Issues, Strategy and Workplan', Geneva, 1985.

2 L.G. Uy, 'Combating the Notion of Environment as Additionality: A study of the Integration of Environment and Development and a Case for Environmental Development as Investment', Centre for Environmental Studies, University of Tasmania, Hobart, Tasmania, 1985 (to be published).

3 OECD, *Environment and Economics, Vols. I* and *II,* Background Papers for the International Conference on Environment and Economics (Paris: 1984).

4 OECD, 'The Impact of Environmental Policies on Industrial Innovation', in *Environment and Economics, Vol. III,* op cit.

5 R. Bertrand, 'Some Reflections on Reform of the United Nations', Joint Inspection Unit, UN, Geneva, 1985.

6 V. Fernando, 'Development Assistance, Environment and Development', prepared for WCED, Geneva, 1985.

7 'List of Projects with Possible Environmental Issues', transmitted to Congress by US Agency for International Development, 1987, as included in Public Law 99-591.

8 L. Gagnon, Union Quebecoise pour la Conservation de la Nature, Quebec, 'Pour Une Revision des Sciences Economiques', submitted to WCED Public Hearings, Ottawa, 1986. See also the review of the state-of-the art concerning natural resource accounts, including detailed case studies from Norway and France, in OECD, *Information and Natural Resources* (Paris: 1986).

9 T. Friend, 'Natural Resource Accounting and its Relationship with Economic and Environmental Accounting', Statistics Canada, Ottawa, September 1986.

10 The need for an explicit 'foreign policy for environment' was raised in different ways in the discussion at many WCED public hearings, but originally in a joint submission by Nordic NGOs to the Public Hearings in Oslo, 1985.

11 See 'Report of the Secretary-General: Technical and Economic Aspects of International River Basin Development', UN E/C.7/35, New York, 1972. An updated list of relevant international agreements was provided by the IUCN Environmental Law Centre. See also Department of Technical Cooperation for Development, *Experiences in the Development and Management of International River and Lake Basins,* Proceedings of the UN Interregional Meeting of International River Organizations held at Dakar, Senegal, in May 1981 (New York: UN, 1983).

12 In 1982, there were environment and natural resource management agencies operating in 144 countries. At the time of the 1972 Stockholm Conference, only 15 industrial countries and 11 developing countries had such agencies. World Environment Center, *World Environment Handbook* (New York: 1985).

13 See General Assembly resolution 2997 (XXVII) of 15 December 1972 on 'Institutional and financial arrangements for international environmental co-operation'.

14 The Environment Coordination Board was abolished in 1977 and its functions assumed by the Administrative Committee on Coordination (ACC). See General Assembly Resolution 32/197, Annex, para 54. The ACC subsequently established a Committee of Designated Officials for Environmental Matters (DOEM).

15 In addition to the Environment Fund there were 18 special Trust Funds with

contributions totalling $5-6 million in 1985. See UNEP, *1985 Annual Report* (Nairobi: 1986).

16 Ibid., Annex V, Table 8.

17 J. Urquhart and K. Heilmann, *Risk Watch: The Odds of Life* (Bicester, UK: Facts on File, 1984).

18 'Risk Assessment and Risk Control', *Issue Report*, Conservation Foundation, Washington, DC, 1985; C. Schweigman et al., ' "Agrisk", Appraisal of Risks in Agriculture in Developing Countries', University of Groningen, The Netherlands, 1981.

19 A. Wijkman and L. Timberlake, *Natural Disasters: Acts of God and Acts of Man?* (London: Earthscan for the International Institute for Environment and Development and the Swedish Red Cross, 1984).

20 WMO, *A Report of the International Conference on the Assessment of the Role of Carbon Dioxide and of Other Greenhouse Gases in Climate Variations and Associated Impacts*, Villach, Austria, 9-15 October 1985, WMO No.661 (Geneva: WMO/ICSU/UNEP, 1986).

21 For an overview of the current technological capabilities and possibilities, see A. Khosla, 'Decision Support Systems for Sustainable Development', prepared for WCED, 1986.

22 See M.C. McHale et al., *Ominous Trends and Valid Hopes: A Comparison of Five World Reports* (Minneapolis, Minn.: Hubert Humphrey Institute of Public Affairs) for a comparison of *North-South: A Programme for Survival* (Cambridge, Mass.: MIT Press, 1980); World Bank, *World Development Report 1980* (Washington, DC: 1980); US Department of State and Council on Environmental Quality, *Global 2000 Report to the President: Entering the Twenty-First Century* (Washington, DC: US Government Printing Office, 1980); IUCN/WWF/UNEP, *World Conservation Strategy* (Gland, Switzerland: 1980); and OECD, *Interfutures: Facing the Future, Mastering the Probable and Managing the Unpredictable* (Paris: 1979). See also D. Meadows et al., *Groping in the Dark—The First Decade of Global Modelling* (Chichester, UK: John Wiley & Sons, 1982) for an analysis of various models.

23 See G.O. Barney, Study Director, *Global 2000 Report*, op. cit.

24 See OCED, *Economic and Ecological Interdependence* (Paris: 1982).

25 The importance of involving youth in nature conservation and environmental protection and improvement activities was emphasized in many presentations at WCED Public Hearings. See, for example, the report 'Youth Nature Conservation Movement in the Socialist Countries' to the Public Hearing at Moscow, December 1986.

26 For an overview of the role and contribution of NGOs to environment and development action at the national and international levels, see 'NGOs and Environment-Development Issues', report to WCED by the Environment Liaison Centre, Nairobi, 1986. It includes a selection of 20 case studies of successful NGO environmental action around the world.

27 NGOs in Chile, Colombia, the Federal Republic of Germany, and Turkey have also published 'State of the Environment' reports. Official reports have appeared in Australia, Austria, Canada, Denmark, Finland, France, Ireland, Israel, Japan, the Netherlands, the Philippines, Poland, Spain, Sweden, the United States, and Yugoslavia.

28 See, for example, the annual *State of the World* report by Worldwatch Institute, the *World Resources Report* by World Resources Institute and the International Institute for Environment and Development, and the *World Conservation Strategy* by IUCN.

29 *Report of the World Industry Conference on Environmental Management*, sponsored by the International Chamber of Commerce and UNEP, 1984; see particularly the principles adopted by OECD in 1985 as a clarification of the OECD Guiding Principles for Multinational Enterprises in *International Legal Materials*, Vol. 25, No. 1 (1986); see also the presentation to WCED Public Hearings, Oslo, June 1985, on 'World Industry Conference Follow-Up' by the Chairman of the Environment Committee of the International Chamber of Commerce.

30 See P.S. Thacher, 'International Institutional Support: The International System, Funding and Technical Assistance', presented to the World Conservation Strategy Conference, Ottawa, Canada, June 1986.

31 United Nations, *Report of the United Nations Conference on the Human Environment*, document A/Conf.48/14/Rev 1, Chapter 1 (New York: 1972).

32 These and other principles have been developed as proposed Articles for a Convention in the report to WCED by its Experts Group on Environmental Law. Their report also contains a commentary on the legal precedents and references for each Article. See *Legal Principles for Environmental Protection and Sustainable Development* (Dordrecht, The Netherlands: Martinus Nijhoff, in press).

33 For an overview of dispute settlement procedures, mechanisms, and needs, see R.E. Stein and G. Grenville-Wood, 'The Settlement of Environmental Disputes: A Forward Look', prepared for WCED, 1985.

34 OECD, *Environment and Economics, Vol. I*, op. cit.

35 OECD, *Environment and Economics*, Results of the International Conference on Environment and Economics (Paris: 1985).

36 For a summary report on the work of the Committee of International Development Institutions on the Environment, see UNEP, *1985 Annual Report*, op. cit.

37 Statement by Dr M.K. Tolba, UNEP Executive Director, at the opening of the sixth session of CIDIE, hosted by the Organization of American States, Washington, DC, June 1985.

38 A proposal for a world conservation bank was made by M. Sweatman of the International Wilderness Leadership Foundation at the WCED Public Hearings, Ottawa, 1986.

39 R.D.G. Johnson and R.O. Blake, *Environmental and Bilateral Aid* (London: International Institute for Environment and Development, 1980).

40 J. Horberry, *Environmental Guidelines Survey: An Analysis of Environmental Procedures and Guidelines Governing Development Aid* (London: IIED and IUCN, 1983).

41 'Environmental Assessment of Development Assistance Projects and Programmes', OECD Council Recommendation C(85)104 (Paris: OECD, 20.6.85); 'Measures Required to Facilitate the Environmental Assessment of Development Assistance Projects and Programmes', OECD Council Recommendation C(86)26 (final), OECD, Paris, 20 November 1986.

42 'Final Report on Environmental Assessment and Development Assistance' *OECD Environment Monograph* No 4 (Paris: OECD, 1986).

43 *Report of the United Nations Conference on Desertification*, document A/CONF.74/36 (New York: UN, 1977).

44 See, for example, E.B. Steinberg and J.A. Yager, 'New Means of Financing International Needs', *The Brookings Institution*, Washington, DC, 1978; 'Additional Measures and Means of Financing for the Implementation of the Plan of Action to Combat Desertification', document UNEP/GC.6/9/Add.1., 1978; UN, 'Study on Financing the United Nations Plan of Action to Combat Desertification: Report

of the Secretary-General', General Assembly document A/35/396, 1980; Dag Hammarskjold Foundation, 'The Automatic Mobilization of Resources for Development', *Development Dialogue*, No. 1, 1981; UN, 'Study on Financing the Plan of Action to Combat Desertification: Report of the Secretary-General', General Assembly document A/36/141, 1981.

45 Independent Commission on International Development Issues, *North-South: A Programme for Survival* (London: Pan Books, 1980); *Common Crisis, North-South: Cooperation for World Recovery* (London: Pan Books, 1983).

ANNEXE 1

SUMMARY OF PROPOSED LEGAL PRINCIPLES FOR ENVIRONMENTAL PROTECTION AND SUSTAINABLE DEVELOPMENT ADOPTED BY THE WCED EXPERTS GROUP ON ENVIRONMENTAL LAW*

I. GENERAL PRINCIPLES, RIGHTS, AND RESPONSIBILITIES

Fundamental Human Right

1. All human beings have the fundamental right to an environment adequate for their health and well-being.

Inter-Generational Equity

2. States shall conserve and use the environment and natural resources for the benefit of present and future generations.

Conservation and Sustainable Use

3. States shall maintain ecosystems and ecological processes essential for the functioning of the biosphere, shall preserve biological diversity, and shall observe the principle of optimum sustainable yield in the use of living natural resources and ecosystems.

Environmental Standards and Monitoring

4. States shall establish adequate environmental protection standards and monitor changes in and publish relevant data on environmental quality and resource use.

---

* This summary is based on the more detailed legal formulations in the report to the Commission by the international legal experts group. (See Annexe 2 for a list of group members.) It highlights only the main thrusts of the principles and Articles and is not a substitute for the full text, published in *Legal Principles for Environmental Protection and Sustainable Development* (Dordrecht, The Netherlands: Martinus Nijhoff Publishers, in press).

Prior Environmental Assessments

5. States shall make or require prior environmental assessments of proposed activities which may significantly affect the environment or use of a natural resource.

Prior Notification, Access, and Due Process

6. States shall inform in a timely manner all persons likely to be significantly affected by a planned activity and to grant them equal access and due process in administrative and judicial proceedings.

Sustainable Development and Assistance

7. States shall ensure that conservation is treated as an integral part of the planning and implementation of development activities and provide assistance to other States, especially to developing countries, in support of environmental protection and sustainable development.

General Obligation to Co-operate

8. States shall co-operate in good faith with other States in implementing the preceding rights and obligations.

II. PRINCIPLES, RIGHTS, AND OBLIGATIONS CONCERNING TRANSBOUNDARY NATURAL RESOURCES AND ENVIRONMENTAL INTERFERENCES

Reasonable and Equitable Use

9. States shall use transboundary natural resources in a reasonable and equitable manner.

Prevention and Abatement

10. States shall prevent or abate any transboundary environmental interference which could cause or causes significant harm (but subject to certain exceptions provided for in Art. 11 and Art. 12 below).

Strict Liability

11. States shall take all reasonable precautionary measures to limit the risk when carrying out or permitting certain dangerous but beneficial activities and shall ensure that compensation is provided should substantial transboundary harm occur even when the activities were not known to be harmful at the time they were undertaken.

Prior Agreements When Prevention Costs Greatly Exceed Harm

12. States shall enter into negotiations with the affected State on the equitable conditions under which the activity could be carried out when planning to carry out or permit activities causing transboundary harm which is substantial but far less than the cost of prevention. (If no agreement can be reached, see Art. 22.)

Non-Discrimination

13. States shall apply as a minimum at least the same standards for environmental conduct and impacts regarding transboundary natural resources and environmental interferences as are applied domestically (i.e., do not do to others what you would not do to your own citizens).

General Obligation to Co-operate on Transboundary Environmental Problems

14. States shall co-operate in good faith with other States to achieve optimal use of transboundary natural resources and effective prevention or abatement of transboundary environmental interferences.

Exchange of Information

15. States of origin shall provide timely and relevant information to the other concerned States regarding transboundary natural resources or environmental interferences.

Prior Assessment and Notification

16. States shall provide prior and timely notification and relevant information to the other concerned States and shall make or require an environmental assessment of planned activities which may have significant transboundary effects.

Prior Consultations

17. States of origin shall consult at an early stage and in good faith with other concerned States regarding existing or potential transboundary interferences with their use of a natural resource or the environment.

Co-operative Arrangements for Environmental Assessment and Protection

18. States shall co-operate with the concerned States in monitoring, scientific research and standard setting regarding transboundary natural resources and environmental interferences.

Emergency Situations

19. States shall develop contingency plans regarding emergency situations likely to cause transboundary environmental interferences and shall promptly warn, provide relevant information to and co-operate with concerned States when emergencies occur.

Equal Access and Treatment

20. States shall grant equal access, due process and equal treatment in administrative and judicial proceedings to all persons who are or may be affected by transboundary interferences with their use of a natural resource or the environment.

III. STATE RESPONSIBILITY

21. States shall cease activities which breach an international obligation regarding the environment and provide compensation for the harm caused.

IV. PEACEFUL SETTLEMENT OF DISPUTES

22. States shall settle environmental disputes by peaceful means. If mutual agreement on a solution or on other dispute settlement arrangements is not reached within 18 months, the dispute shall be submitted to conciliation and, if unresolved, thereafter to arbitration or judicial settlement at the request of any of the concerned States.

ANNEXE 2

THE COMMISSION AND ITS WORK

The World Commission on Environment and Development was created as a consequence of General Assembly resolution 38/161 adopted at the 38th Session of the United Nations in the fall of 1983. That resolution called upon the Secretary-General to appoint the Chairman and Vice-Chairman of the Commission and in turn directed them to jointly appoint the remaining members, at least half of whom were to be selected from the developing world. The Secretary General appointed Mrs. Gro Harlem Brundtland of Norway, then leader of the Norwegian Labour Party, as Chairman and Dr. Mansour Khalid, the former Minister of Foreign Affairs from Sudan, as Vice-Chairman. They together appointed the remaining members of the Commission.

The Commission has functioned as an independent body. All its members have served the Commission in their individual capacities, not as representatives of their governments. The Commission has thus been able to address any issues, to solicit any advice, and to formulate and present any proposals and recommendations that it considered pertinent and relevant.

In pursuing its mandate, the Commission has paid careful attention to the Terms of Reference suggested by the General Assembly in Resolution 38/161 and has operated in close collaboration with the Intergovernmental Inter-sessional Preparatory Committee of the Governing Council of the UN Environment Programme, which has itself been preparing an intergovernmental report on environmental perspectives to the year 2000 and beyond.

After the Commission's report has been discussed by UNEP's Governing Council, it is to be submitted to the General Assembly of the United Nations for its consideration during its 42nd Session in the fall of 1987.

The Commissioners

Chairman

Gro Harlem Brundtland, Norway. Prime Minister, Vice President Socialist International from 1986, Leader of the Labour Party from 1981, Member of Parliament from 1977, Minister of Environment 1974–79, Associate Director Oslo School Health Services 1968–74.

Vice-Chairman

Mansour Khalid, Sudan. Deputy Prime Minister 1976, Minister of Education 1975–76, President, UN Security Council 1972, Minister of Foreign Affairs 1971–75, Minister of Youth and Social Affairs 1969–71.

Members

Susanna Agnelli, Italy. Italian Senator, writer, Under-Secretary of State for Foreign Affairs, Member of the Independent Commission on International Humanitarian Issues, Member of the European Parliament 1979–81, Mayor of Monte Argentario 1974–84, Member of Chamber of Deputies 1976–83.

Saleh Abdulrahman Al-Athel, Saudi Arabia. President of King Abdulaziz City for Science and Technology; Vice-President for Graduate Studies and Research, King Saud University 1976–84; Dean, College of Engineering, King Saud University 1975–76.

Pablo Gonzalez Casanova, Mexico.* Professor of Political and Social Sciences, National Autonomous University of Mexico, President of the Latin American Association of Sociology.

Bernard T. G. Chidzero, Zimbabwe. Minister of Finance, Economic Planning and Development; Chairman, Development Committee (the World Bank and the International Monetary Fund); Member, UN Committee for Development Planning; Member, Board of the World Institute for Development Economics and Research; Director, Commodities Division, United Nations Conference on Trade and Development (UNCTAD) 1968–77; Deputy Secretary General, UNCTAD 1977–80.

Lamine Mohamed Fadika, Cote d'Ivoire. Minister of Marine Affairs, Chairman of the National Council for Environment, Secretary of State for Marine Affairs 1974–76.

---

* In August 1986, for personal reasons, Pablo Gonzalez Casanova ceased to participate in the work of the Commission.

Volker Hauff, Federal Republic of Germany. Member of Parliament; Vice Chairman, Social Democratic Party Parliamentary Group, Responsible for Environment; Minister for Transportation 1980–82; Minister for Research and Technology 1979–80; Parliamentary Secretary of State for Science Research and Technology 1972–78.

Istvan Lang, Hungary. Secretary General of the Hungarian Academy of Sciences; Deputy Secretary General 1970–85, and Executive Secretary 1963–70, Section of Biology, Hungarian Academy of Sciences; Research Institute of Soil Science and Agricultural Chemistry, Hungarian Academy of Sciences 1955–63.

Ma Shijun, Peoples Republic of China. Director of the Research Center of Ecology, Academia Sinica, Chairman of the Commission of Environmental Sciences, President of the Ecological Society of China.

Margarita Marino de Botero, Colombia. Chairman, Fundacion El Colegio de Villa de Leyva (The Green College); Director General, National Institute of Renewable Natural Resources and the Environment (INDERENA) 1983–86; Director, Office of International Affairs, INDERENA 1978–83; Regional Consultant, United Nations Environment Programme 1973–77.

Nagendra Singh, India. President of the International Court of Justice, President of IMO Assembly 1959, President of ILO Maritime Session 1971, President of the Indian Academy of Environmental Law and Research, President of the National Labour Law Association of India, Life Member of the Board of Governors of the International Council for Environmental Law, Member of the Permanent Court of Arbitration, Deputy Chairman of CEPLA (IUCN), Chancellor of the University of Goa, Fellow of the British Academy.

Paulo Nogueira-Neto, Brazil. Federal District Secretary of Environment, Science and Technology, National Council of Environment; Federal Secretary of the Environment 1974–86; Associate Professor, Department of Ecology, University of Sao Paulo; President, Association for the Defence of the Environment 1954–83; President, Sao Paulo State Forest Council 1967–74.

Saburo Okita, Japan. President, International University; Advisor to the Ministry of Foreign Affairs; Advisor to the Environment Agency; Executive Committee Member of the Club of Rome; Chairman, World Wildlife Fund Japan; Chairman, Advisory Committee for External Economic Issues 1984–85; Government Representative for External Economic Relations 1980-81; Foreign Minister 1979-80; Member of the Pearson Commission 1968-69.

Shridath S. Ramphal, Guyana. Secretary General of the Commonwealth of Nations, Minister for Foreign Affairs 1972-75, Minister of Justice 1973-75, Minister of State for Foreign Affairs 1967-72, Attorney General 1966-72.

William Doyle Ruckelshaus, United States. Attorney, Perkins, Coie; Administrator, U.S. Environmental Protection Agency 1970-73, 1983-84; Senior Vice President for Law and Corporate Affairs, Weyerhaeuser Company 1976-83; Acting Director of the Federal Bureau of Investigation 1973; Deputy Attorney General, US Department of Justice 1973.

Mohamed Sahnoun, Algeria. Algerian Ambassador to the United States; Chief of Algerian Permanent Mission to the United Nations 1982-84; Algerian Ambassador, Paris 1979-82; Algerian Ambassador, Bonn 1975-79; Deputy Secretary General Arab League 1973-74; Deputy Secretary General, Organization of African Unity 1964-73.

Emil Salim, Indonesia. Minister of State for Population and the Environment; Minister of State for Development Supervision and the Environment 1978-83; Member People's Consultative Assembly 1977-87; Minister of Communications 1973-78; Minister of State for Administrative Reform; Deputy Chairman, National Planning Board 1971-81.

Bukar Shaib, Nigeria. Minister of Agriculture, Water Resources and Rural Development 1983-86; Special Advisor to the President of Nigeria 1980-83; Nigerian Ambassador to Rome 1979; Permanent Secretary, Federal Ministry of Agriculture and Water Resources 1968-78.

Vladimir Sokolov, USSR. Director, Institute of Evolutionary Animal Morphology and Ecology, USSR Academy of Sciences; Professor and Head of Department of Vertebrate Zoology, Faculty of Biology, Moscow State University; Deputy Chairman, Section of Chemical and Technological and Biological Sciences, Presidium, USSR Academy of Sciences.

Janez Stanovnik, Yugoslavia. Member, Presidium of the Socialist Republic of Slovenia; Professor, University of Ljubljana; Executive Secretary, UN Economic Commission for Europe 1967-83; Member of the Federal Cabinet and Federal Executive Council 1966-67.

Maurice Strong, Canada. President, American Water Development, Inc.; former Under-Secretary General and Special Advisor to the Secretary-General of the United Nations; Executive Director of the United Nations Office for Emergency Operations in Africa 1985-86; Chairman of the Board, Petro-Canada 1976-78; Executive Director, United Nations Environment Programme 1973-75; Secretary General, United Nations Conference on the Human Environment 1970-72.

Jim MacNeill, Canada. Secretary General of the Commission and ex officio member; Director of Environment, OECD 1978-84; Secretary (Deputy Minister), Canadian Ministry of State for Urban Affairs 1974-76; Canadian Commissioner General, UN Conference on Human Settlements 1975-76; Assistant Secretary, Canadian Ministry of State for Urban Affairs 1972-74.

The Commission's Mandate

The Commission's Mandate, officially adopted at its Inaugural Meeting in Geneva on 1-3 October 1984, states:

The World Commission on Environment and Development has been established at a time of unprecedented growth in pressures on the global environment, with grave predictions about the human future becoming commonplace.

The Commission is confident that it is possible to build a future that is more prosperous, more just, and more secure because it rests on policies and practices that serve to expand and sustain the ecological basis of development.

The Commission is convinced, however, that this will not happen without significant changes in current approaches: changes in perspectives, attitudes and life styles; changes in certain critical policies and the ways in which they are formulated and applied; changes in the nature of co-operation between governments, business, science and people; changes in certain forms of international co-operation which have proved incapable of tackling many environment and development issues; changes, above all, in the level of understanding and commitment by people, organizations and governments.

The World Commission on Environment and Development therefore invites suggestions, participation and support in order to assist it urgently:

1. to re-examine the critical issues of environment and development and to formulate innovative, concrete and realistic action proposals to deal with them;

2. to strengthen international co-operation on environment and development and to assess and propose new forms of co--operation that can break out of existing patterns and influence policies and events in the direction of needed change; and

3. to raise the level of understanding and commitment to action on the part of individuals, voluntary organizations, businesses, institutes and governments.

The Commission solicits the views of those individuals, scientific institutes, non-governmental organizations, specialized agencies and other bodies of the United Nations, and national governments concerned with environment and development issues. It requests their support and it will facilitate their participation in the work of the Commission. It wishes especially to hear the views of youth.

In fulfilling its tasks, the Commission will pay careful attention to the Terms of Reference suggested by the General Assembly of the United Nations in resolution 38/161, in which the General Assembly welcomed the establishment of the Commission.

The Commission's Work

In May 1984, an Organizational Meeting of the Commission was held in Geneva to adopt its rules of procedure and operation and to appoint a Secretary General to guide its work. In July 1984, a Secretariat was established in Geneva, temporarily at the Centre de Morillon and later at the Palais Wilson. Members of the Secretariat have included:

Secretary General:
Jim MacNeill

Senior Professional Staff:
Nitin Desai, Senior Economic Advisor
Vitus Fernando, Senior Programme Officer
Branislav Gosovic, Senior Programme Officer
Marie-Madeleine Jacquemier, Finance and Administrative Officer
Kazu Kato, Director of Programmes
Warren H. Lindner, Secretary of the Commission and Director of Administration
Elisabeth Monosowski, Senior Programme Officer
Gustavo Montero, Programme Planning Officer
Shimwaayi Muntemba, Senior Programme Officer
Janos Pasztor, Senior Programme Officer
Peter Robbs, Senior Public Information Advisor

Vicente Sanchez, Director of Programmes
Linda Starke, Editor
Peter Stone, Director of Information
Edith Surber, Finance and Administrative Officer

General Services and Support Staff:

Brita Baker	Christel Ollesch
Elisabeth Bohler-Goodship	Ellen Permato
Marie-Pierre Destouet	Guadalupe Quesada
Marian Doku	Mildred Raphoz
Tamara Dunn	Evelyn Salvador
Teresa Harmand	Iona D'Souza
Aud Loen	Kay Streit
Jelka de Marsano	Vicky Underhill
Chedra Mayhew	Shane Vanderwert

The Commission held its first official meeting in Geneva on 1–3 October 1984. During that meeting, the Commission agreed upon its Mandate, the key issues it would address in the course of its deliberations, the strategy it would employ to achieve its objectives, and the workplan and timetable that would be used to guide its work. Immediately following that meeting, the Commission publicly released its principal working document, 'Mandate for Change'.

At its Inaugural Meeting, the Commission selected eight key issues for analysis during the course of its work:

- Perspectives on Population, Environment, and Sustainable Development;
- Energy: Environment and Development;
- Industry: Environment and Development;
- Food Security, Agriculture, Forestry, Environment, and Development;
- Human Settlements: Environment and Development;
- International Economic Relations, Environment, and Development;
- Decision Support Systems for Environmental Management; and
- International Cooperation.

It agreed that it would examine these issues from the perspective of the year 2000 and beyond and from the perspective of their common sources in economic, social, and sectoral policies.

At its Inaugural Meeting, the Commission also decided that its processes would be open, visible, and participatory and that in conducting its work, strategies would be employed to ensure it of receiving the broadest range of views and advice on the key issues it was addressing.

The Commission therefore decided that it would hold deliberative meetings in all regions of the world and that it would take the occasion of those meetings to get a first-hand view of environment and development issues in those regions. It also decided to use these visits to hold open Public Hearings where senior government representatives, scientists and experts, research institute staff, industrialists, representatives of non-governmental organizations, and the general public could openly express their concerns to the Commission and submit their views and advice on issues of common concern.

These Public Hearings, which are a unique feature of the Commission, have become its 'trademark', demonstrating both to the Commissioners and the participants that the issues addressed by the Commission are indeed of global concern and do transcend national boundaries and different cultures. Hundreds of organizations and individuals gave testimony during the Public Hearings and over 500 written submissions, constituting more than 10,000 pages of material, were received by the Commission in connection with them. The Public Hearings have been of immeasurable benefit to the Commissioners and the Secretariat, and the gratitude of the Commission is extended to all who contributed to their success.

Deliberative meetings, site visits, and/or Public Hearings of the Commission were held in Jakarta, Indonesia, 27–31 March 1985; Oslo, Norway, 21–28 June 1985; Sao Paulo and Brasilia, Brazil, 25 October–4 November 1985; Vancouver, Edmonton, Toronto, Ottawa, Halifax, and Quebec City, Canada, 21–31 May 1986; Harare, Zimbabwe, 15–19 September and Nairobi, Kenya, 20–23 September 1986; Moscow, USSR, 6–12 December 1986; and Tokyo, Japan, 23–28 February 1987. Special working group meetings of the Commission were also held in Geneva, Moscow, and Berlin (West).

To further widen its base of information and advice, the Commission appointed a group of expert Special Advisors to assist it and the Secretariat in the analysis of the key issues. These included Edward S. Ayensu on Food Security and Forestry, Gamani Corea on International Economic Relations, Gordon T. Goodman on Energy, Ashok Khosla on Decision Support Systems for Environmental Management, Robert D. Munro on International Co-operation and Law, Michael Royston on Industry, and Guy-Olivier Segond on Youth. Johan Jorgen Holst served as Special Advisor to the Chairman and guided the work on Environment and Security.

The Chairman was also advised by Hans Christian Bugge and Morten Wetland. Later in its work, the Commission appointed Lloyd Timberlake as Special Editorial Advisor.

To assist it in its work in three of the key issue areas—Energy, Industry, and Food Security—the Commission constituted Advisory Panels of leading experts to advise it on the recommendations and conclusions it should consider making. The chairmen and members of these were:

Advisory Panel on Energy:

Chairman:
  Enrique Iglesias (Uruguay), Foreign Minister of Uruguay
Members:
  Abdlatif Y. Al-Hamad (Kuwait)
  Toyoaki Ikuta (Japan)
  Gu Jian (China)
  Al Noor Kassum (Tanzania)
  Ulf Lantzke (deceased) (Federal Republic of Germany)
  Wangari Maathai (Kenya)
  David J. Rose (deceased) (United States)
  Prem Shankar Jha (India)
  Carl Tham (Sweden)
  Gyorgy Vajda (Hungary)

Advisory Panel on Industry:

Chairman:
  Umberto Colombo (Italy), President of ENEA
Members:
  Betsy Ancker-Johnson (United States)
  M.J. Flux (United Kingdom)
  Arnoldo Jos Gabaldon (Venezuela)
  Alexander C. Helfrich (Netherlands)
  Charles Levinson (Canada)
  Finn Lied (Norway)
  George P. Livanos (Greece)
  Mohamed Mazouni (Algeria)
  Thomas McCarthy (United States)
  Jose E. Mindlin (Brazil)
  Keichi Oshima (Japan)
  Roger Strelow (United States)
  Naval Tata (India)
  Erna Witoelar (Indonesia)

Advisory Panel on Food Security:

Chairman:
    M.S. Swaminathan (India), Director General of the International
    Rice Research Institute
Members:
    Nyle Brady (United States)
    Robert Chambers (United Kingdon)
    K. Chowdhry (India)
    Gilberto Gallopin (Argentina)
    Joe Hulse (Canada)
    Kenneth King (Guyana)
    V. Malima (Tanzania)
    Samir Radwan (Eygpt)
    Lu Liang Shu (China)

The reports of the three Advisory Panels were submitted to the
Commission for its consideration during its meeting in Canada in
May of 1986 and have since been published under the titles *Energy
2000*, *Industry 2000*, and *Food 2000*.

The Commission was also assisted in its review of legal rights and
principles by a group of international legal experts chaired by
Robert Munro (Canada) with Johan G. Lammers (Netherlands) as
Rapporteur. The members of the group included Andronico Adede
(Kenya), Francoise Burhenne (Federal Republic of Germany),
Alexandre-Charles Kiss (France), Stephen McCaffrey (United States),
Akio Morishima (Japan), Zaki Mustafa (Sudan), Henri Smets (Be-
lqium), Robert Stein (United States), Alberto Szekely (Mexico),
Alexandre Timoshenko (USSR), and Amado Tolentino (Philippines).
Their report was submitted to and considered by the Commission
during its meeting in Harare in September 1986. It will be published
under the title *Legal Principles for Environmental Protection and
Sustainable Development*.

During the course of its work, the Commission also engaged
experts, research institutes, and academic centres of excellence from
around the globe to prepare more than 75 studies and reports relating
to the eight key issues for the Commission's review and consideration.
These studies and reports provided an invaluable resource base for
the final reports of the Commission's Advisory Panels and for the
final chapters of this report.

Financial Contributions

Initial funding to permit the Commission to commence its work came from the governments of Canada, Denmark, Finland, Japan, the Netherlands, Norway, Sweden, and Switzerland. Each of these 'sponsoring' governments had been instrumental in the creation of the Commission and during the course of the Commission's work each increased their contribution beyond their original pledge.

In addition to the 'sponsoring' group of countries, the Commission has also received untied financial contributions from the governments of Cameroon, Chile, the Federal Republic of Germany, Hungary, Oman, Portugal, and Saudi Arabia. Significant contributions have also been received from the Ford Foundation and the John D. and Catherine MacArthur Foundation, as well as from NORAD and SIDA.

Other Contributions

The City and Canton of Geneva restored and furnished one wing of the Palais Wilson and provided that to the Commission's Secretariat free of rent and utilities. The local costs of the Commission's meetings in Indonesia, Brazil, Zimbabwe, and the USSR were covered by the host governments. The costs of the Commission's working group meeting in Moscow were also covered by the Soviet Government. The costs of the working group meeting in Berlin (West) were covered by the Federal Republic of Germany. The Arab Fund for Economic and Social Development hosted and covered all of the costs of a meeting in Kuwait of the Advisory Panel on Energy. The accounts of the Commission have been audited by Hunziker and Associates of Geneva.

The Commission's sincere appreciation is extended to all the governments, foundations, and institutes that provided the financial and other support necessary for it to complete its work, including those that contributed funds too late to be acknowledged here.

Further Activities

Between the issuance of this report and its consideration by the UN General Assembly during its 42nd Session in the fall of 1987, the Commission will be meeting at a series of regional presentational meetings with senior governmental representatives, the business and scientific communities, non-governmental organizations, and the press to discuss this report and, it is hoped, to build a body of public and governmental support for the recommendations and conclusions.

There are no plans for the Commission to continue after its report has been considered by the General Assembly, and it will officially cease its operations on 31 December 1987.

TOKYO DECLARATION

At the close if its final meeting, in Tokyo, the Commission issued the following as the Toyko Declaration, dated 27 February 1987:

The World Commission on Environment and Development was constituted in 1984 as an independent body by the United Nations General Assembly and set out to:

(a) re-examine the critical issues of environment and development, and formulate innovative, concrete, and realistic action proposals to deal with them;

(b) strengthen international co-operation on environment and development, and assess and propose new forms of co-operation that can break out of existing patterns and influence policies and events in the direction of needed change; and

(c) raise the level of understanding and commitment to action on the part of individuals, voluntary organizations, business, institutes, and governments.

As we come in Toyko to the end of our task, we remain convinced that it is possible to build a future that is prosperous, just, and secure.

But realizing this possibility depends on all countries adopting the objective of sustainable development as the overriding goal and test of national policy and international co-operation. Such development can be defined simply as an approach to progress which meets the needs of the present without compromising the ability of future generations to meet their own needs. A successful transition to a sustainable development through the year 2000 and beyond requires a massive shift in societal objectives. It also requires the concerted and vigorous pursuit of a number of strategic imperatives.

The World Commission on Environment and Development now calls upon all the nations of the World, both jointly and individually, to integrate sustainable development into their goals and to adopt the following principles to guide their policy actions.

1. Revive Growth

Poverty is a major source of environmental degradation which not only affects a large number of people in developing countries but also undermines the sustainable development of the entire community of nations—both developing and industrialized. Economic growth must be stimulated, particularly in developing countries, while enhancing the environmental resource base. The industrialized countries can, and must contribute to reviving world economic growth. There must be urgent international action to resolve the debt crisis; a substantial increase in the flows of development finance; and stabilization of the foreign exchange earnings of low-income commodity exporters.

2. Change the Quality of Growth

Revived growth must be of a new kind in which sustainability, equity, social justice, and security are firmly embedded as major social goals. A safe, environmentally sound energy pathway is an indispensable component of this. Education, communication, and international co-operation can all help to achieve those goals. Development planners should take account in their reckoning of national wealth not only of standard economic indicators, but also of the state of the stock of natural resources. Better income distribution, reduced vulnerability to natural disasters and technological risks, improved health, preservation of cultural heritage—all contribute to raising the quality of that growth.

3. Conserve and Enhance the Resource Base

Sustainability requires the conservation of environmental resources such as clean air, water, forests, and soils; maintaining genetic diversity; and using energy, water and raw materials efficiently. Improvements in the efficiency of production must be accelerated to reduce per capita consumption of natural resources and encourage a shift to non-polluting products and technologies. All countries are called upon to prevent environmental pollution by rigorously enforcing environmental regulations, promoting low-waste technologies, and anticipating the impact of new products, technologies and wastes.

4. Ensure a Sustainable Level of Population

Population policies should be formulated and integrated with other economic and social development programmes—education, health care, and the expansion of the livelihood base of the poor. Increased access to family planning services is itself a form of social development that allows couples, and women in particular, the right to self-determination.

5. Reorient Technology and Manage Risks

Technology creates risks, but it offers the means to manage them. The capacity for technological innovation needs to be greatly enhanced in developing countries. The orientation of technology development in all countries must also be changed to pay greater regard to environmental factors. National and international institutional mechanisms are needed to assess potential impacts of new technologies before they are widely used. Similar arrangements are required for major interventions in natural systems, such as river diversion or forest clearance. Liability for damages from unintended consequences must be strengthened and enforced. Greater public participation and free access to relevant information should be promoted in decision-making processes touching on environment and development issues.

6. Integrate Environment and Economics in Decision-Making

Environmental and economic goals can and must be made mutually reinforcing. Sustainability requires the enforcement of wider responsibilities for the impacts of policy decisions. Those making such policy decisions must be responsible for the impact of those decisions upon the environmental resource capital of their nations. They must focus on the sources of environmental damage rather than the symptoms. The ability to anticipate and prevent environmental damage will require that the ecological dimensions of policy be considered at the same time as the economic, trade, energy, agricultural, and other dimensions. They must be considered on the same agendas and in the same national and international institutions.

7. Reform International Economic Relations

Long term sustainable growth will require far-reaching changes to produce trade, capital, and technology flows that are more equitable and better synchronized to enviromental imperatives. Fundamental improvements in market access, technology transfer, and international finance are necessary to help developing countries widen their opportunities by diversifying their economic and trade bases and building their self-reliance.

8. Strengthen International Co-operation

The introduction of an environmental dimension injects an additional element of urgency and mutual self-interest, since a failure to address the interaction between resource degradation and rising poverty will spill over and become a global ecological problem. Higher priorities must be assigned to environmental monitoring, assessment, research and development, and resource management in all fields of international development. This requires a high level of commitment by all countries to the satisfactory working of multilateral institutions; to the making and observance of international rules in fields such as trade and investment; and to constructive dialogue on the many issues where national interests do not immediately coincide but require negotiation to be reconciled. it requires also a recognition of the essential importance of international peace and security. New dimensions of multilateralism are essential to sustainable human progress.

The Commission is convinced that if we can make solid progress towards meeting these principles in the balance of this century, the next century can offer a more secure, more prosperous, more equitable, and more hopeful future for the whole human family.

Acknowledgements

Since its creation in late 1983, the Commission has received advice and support from thousands of individuals, institutes, and organizations the world over, many of whom are listed here. Many people laboured long hours in preparing submissions for the public hearings, reports for the Advisory Panels, and studies for submission to the Commission. Without their dedication, co-operation, and advice, as well as that of the Special Advisors and the Chairmen and members of the Advisory Panels and Legal Expert Group, this report would not have been possible. The Commission's sincerest appreciation is extended to them all. (Affiliations and titles are as of the date of communication with the Commission; verification of all the following names and titles was not possible, and the Commission apologizes for any inaccuracies.)

Thomas Aarnio, Ministry of the Environment, Finland
Aziz Ab'Saber, University of Sao Paulo, Brazil
Muchtar Abas, Indonesia
A.H. Abbott, Deputy Minister, Department of the Environment, Nova Scotia, Canada
Krisno Abinto, WALUBI, Indonesia
Tatjana Adamova, USSR State Committee for Science and Technology
Kath Adams, Earthscan, United Kingdom
Patricia Adams, Director, Third World Research, Energy Probe, Canada
Adebayo Adedeji, Executive Secretary, Economic Commission for Africa, Ethiopia
George Adicondro, Director, Irian Jaya Rural Development Foundation, Indonesia
Erwin Adriawan, Biological Science Club, Indonesia

Anil Agarwal, Centre for Science and Environment, India
Agriculture Canada, Government of Canada
Maria Aguri Yoshioka, Companhia de Tecnologia de Saneamento Ambiental (CE-TESB), Brazil
Robert Aiken, Ambio, Sweden
Shukhrat Akhundzhanov, USSR Academy for Foreign Trade
Tutty Alawiyah, Universitas Islam As. Syafi, Indonesia
Waldemar Albano, Jr., Chairman, Cotia City Council, Sao Paulo, Brazil
Geroncio Albuquerque Rocha, ex-President of the National Association of Geologists, Brazil
Kalimardin Algamar, BPPT, Indonesia
Mary Allegretti, Institute for Socio-Economic Studies, Brazil
Vanessa Allison, Canada
Tisna Amidjaja, Ketua LIPI, Indonesia
Djoko Aminoto, Chairman of the Board, Bina Desa, Indonesia
B.D. Amoa, All Africa Council of Churches, Kenya
David Anderson, Resource and Economic Development Division, Alberta, Canada
Sergio Roberto de Andrade Leite, President, Association for the Ecology and Environment of Araraquara (SEMARA), Brazil
David Claudia Andujar, Coordinator, Commission for the Creation of the Yanomani Park, Brazil
M. Appelberg, National Swedish Environment Protection Board, Sweden
E. Apter, Department of Political Science, Yale University, USA
A. Arbatov, Head, Department of Natural Resources, Scientific Institute of Systematic Research, USSR
June Archibald, Foreign Aid Issues Research Framework, Canada
Tom Chr. Arelsen, Environment and Youth, Norway
Kai Arne Armann, Future in Our Hands, Norway
A. Arismunandar, Pertambangan & Energi, Indonesia
Association of Peel People, Canada
Association of Universities and Colleges in Canada, Canada
Donald Aubrey, Research Coordinator, STOP, Canada
Achoka Aworry, The Kenya Energy Non-governmental Organization, Kenya
Aminuddin Aziz, MUI, Indonesia

A.G. Babaev, Director, Institute of Desert, USSR
Thomas Bachman, Berlin (West)
Lisa Bader, Canada
Lynda Baiden, Department of Environment, Nova Scotia, Canada
Yves Bajard, First Watercount Group, Canada
W. Banage, University of Zambia
Patrick Banda, Zimbabwe
J. Banyopadhyay, Research Foundation for Science and Technology and Natural Resource Policy, India
Remy Barre, Conservatoire National des Arts de Metiers, France
Ken de la Barre, New England Environmental Conference, Tufts University, USA
Marcia Marli Battaglia, Companhia de Tecnologia de Saneamento Ambiental (CE-TESB), Brazil
Beatrice Bazar, President, Canadian Association for the Club of Rome, Canada
Roger Beardmore, Regional Director, Conservation and Protection Service, Environment Canada—Atlantic Region, Canada
Suzanne Beaudoin, Text Processing Operator, Intergovernmental Affairs Directorate, Ottawa, Canada
John Beddington, Imperial College, United Kingdom

B.M. Bel'kov, Chief of State Committee for Nature Protection of the Byelorussian S.S.R., USSR

Jean Belanger, Canadian Chemical Producers Association, Canada

Sharon Belaschuk, Information Division, Government of Alberta, Canada

Julie Bell, Ministry of Environment, Toronto, Canada

Robert Bellerive, Translator, Translation Bureau, Quebec, Canada

Bjorn Bergmann-Paulsen, Nordic Experts Group, Norway

Einar J. Berntsen, Norwegian Hydrological Committee, Norway

Rosalie Bertell, President of the Board of Directors, International Institute of Concern for Public Health, Canada

Torolf Berthelsen, Statens Institut for Stralehygiene, Norway

I. Bertilsson, Environment Coordinator, African Development Bank, Cote d'Ivoire

Alexandre Bezeredi, Officer, Western Europe II Relations Division, Canada

Malur Bhagavan, SAREC, Sweden

Harry Bhaskara, The Jakarta Post, Indonesia

Paolo Bifani, France

Bimo, Vice Director, Yatasan Indonesia Sejahtera, Indonesia

S. Bistron, Research Scientist, Institute of Environmental Science and Technology, Poland

Juul Bjerke, Chief Economist, Norwegian Federation of Trade Unions, Norway

Lars Bjorkbom, Ministry for Foreign Affairs, Sweden

Francis Blanchard, Director General, International Labour Office, Switzerland

Roland Segurd Blinstrup, Regional Representative, Brazilian Society for the Defense of Flora and Fauna, Brazil

Andreas Blom, Blom Fiskeoppdrett, Norway

Stephane Blondin, Canada

Michael Bloomsfield, Harmony Foundation of Canada, Canada

Ole Bockman, Norsk Viftefabrikk, Norway

Ragnar Boge, Swedish National Institute of Radiation Protection, Sweden

Boediono, UGM/Bappenas, Indonesia

Peter von Boguslawsky, Ministry of the Environment, Finland

Jacob Bomann-Larsen, Future in Our Hands, Norway

Alexander Bonilla, Regional Coordinator, Central American University Project on Ecology and Agrochemics, Brazil

Knut Bonke, Kvaerner Brug A/S, Norway

Alexander Borodin, USSR State Committee for Science and Technology, USSR

Jean-Luc Bourdages, Comite pour une strategie quebecoise de conservation, Canada

Eugenia Bovina, USSR State Committee for Science and Technology

T.I. Bozhinov, Chairman, Committee for Environment Protection, Bulgaria

Francisco Bozzano-Barnes, Canada

Jim Bradley, Minister of the Environment for Ontario, Canada

Victor Bravo, Instituto de Economia Energetica, Argentina

Brazilian Association of Sanitary and Environmental Engineering, Brazil

Robert Brennan, Graduate Student, School of Community and Regional Planning, Canada

W.A. Bridgeo, Saint Mary's University, Canada

Marina Brisotti, Companhia de Tecnologia de Saneamento Ambiental (CETESB), Brazil

Denies Bristo, Communications Branch, Ottawa, Canada

British Columbia Watershed Protection Alliance, Canada

Clayton Broddy, Canada

David Brooks, Friends of the Earth, Canada

Lester Brown, President, Worldwatch Institute, USA

Paul Brown, Professor, School of Public Administration, Dalhousie University, Canada

Geoffrey Bruce, Vice-President, Canadian International Development Agency, Canada
Louis Bruyere, President, Native Council of Canada
Alexander Bryce, Consellor, Canadian Mission, Geneva, Switzerland
P.V.R. Bubrahmanyam, National Environmental Engineering Research Institute, India
Tubagus Budi, Angkatan Bersenjata, Indonesia
David Bull, Executive Director, Environment Liaison Centre, Kenya
Hubert Bunce, Reid, Collins and Associates Limited, Canada
Hayden Burgess, World Council of Indigenous Peoples, Canada
M. Burhan, FISIP UI, Indonesia
Francoise Burhenne, IUCN Environmental Law Centre, Federal Republic of Germany
Wolfgang Burhenne, IUCN Environmental Law Centre, Federal Republic of Germany
Ian Burton, Director, IFIAS, Canada
Butantan Museum Institute, Brazil
John G. Butt, Minister of Environment, Newfoundland, Canada

Vincent Cable, Aide to Commissioner Ramphal, United Kingdom
Charles Caccia, Member of Parliament, House of Commons, Ottawa, Canada
Andrea Sardro Calabi, President, Social and Economic Institute, Planning Ministry, Brazil
Canadian Chemical Producers' Association (CCPA), Canada
Canadian National Institute for the Blind, Canada
Canadian Nuclear Association, Canada
Canadian University Service Overseas, Canada
Canadian Wildlife Federation, Canada
Onelia Cardettini, France
Cloe Cardoso Pinto, Chairman, Cloe-Misael Foundation, Brazil
Carleton University students, Canada
Shirley Carr, Canadian Labour Congress/National Survival Institute, Canada
Jacques Carriere, Chief, Translation Bureau, Quebec, Canada
Jenny Carter, World Hunger, Canada
Celia G. Castello, Companhia de Tecnologia de Saneamento Ambiental (CETESB), Brazil
Margaret Catley-Carlson, President, Canadian International Development Agency, Canada
Cherga de Jesus Cavalcanti Vasques, Movement in the Defense of Life, Brazil
Magda Cawley, Office of the Regional Director General, Pacific and Yukon Region, Canada
Carlos Celsa, Companhia de Tecnologia de Saneamento Ambiental (CETESB), Brazil
Flora Maria Cerqueira Ribeira de Souza, Center of Environmental Resources of the State of Bahia, Brazil
Michael Chadwick, Beijer Institute, Sweden
B. Chakalall, Caribbean Conservation Association, Barbados
Chen Changdu, Professor, University of Beijing, China
John G. Charbonneau, Advisor, International Programme Branch, Intergovernmental Affairs Directorate, Canada
P. Chauraya, Zimbabwe
E.N. Chidumayo, Conservator of Natural Resources, Zambia
L. Chikwavaire, Project Officer, Zimbabwe Women's Bureau, Zimbabwe
Victoria Chitepo, Minister of Natural Resources and Tourism, Zimbabwe
Abdul M. Choudhury, Ambassador of Bangladesh, Chairman, Intergovernmental Inter-sessional Preparatory Committee, Kenya
Christian Farmers Federation, Canada
J. Chuto, Designer, Design Office for Atmosphere Protection, Poland

Adolph Ciborowski, Ministry of Regional Economy and Environmental Protection, Poland

D. Cichy, Research Scientist, Institute of School Programmes, Poland

Jose Thiago Cintra, CLEE, Mexico

Joe Clark, Secretary of State for External Affairs, Canada

Jack Clements, Senior Environmental Advisor, Canada

Alain Clerc, Scientific Advisor, Office federal de la Protection de l'Environnement, Switzerland

Stanley Clinton-Davis, Commissioner for Environment, European Economic Commission, Belgium

Maxwell Cohen, University of Ottawa, Canada

Carol Collier, Coordinator, Department of Regional Industrial Expansion, Quebec, Canada

Antoinette K. Colosurdo, Companhia de Tecnologia de Saneamento Ambiental (CETESB), Brazil

Comisao do Meio Ambiente da Baixada Santista, Brazil

Commission of Enquiry on Unemployment Insurance, Canada

Committee for the Defense of the Billings Dam, Brazil

Companhia Energetica de Sao Paulo, Brazil

Companhia de Tecnologia de Saneamento Ambiental, Brazil

Shirley A.M. Conover, Environmental Scientist and Consultant, Canada

Carol Conrad, Director, Policy and Planning Department of Development, Nova Scotia, Canada

Conservation Council of Ontario, Canada

Alberto Contar, President, Maringa Association for Environmental Protection and Education (ADEAM), Brazil

Thomas Coon, Indigenous Survival International, Canada

Tim Cooper, National Co-ordinator, Christian Ecology Group, England

Charles Corea, India

Jose Pedro de Oliveira Costa, Executive Secretary, Secretaria Especial do Meio Ambiente (SEMA), Brazil

Council for Mutual Economic Assistance, USSR

Robert Coupland, University of Saskatchewan, Canada

John E. Cox, Ottawa, Canada

Barbara Coyne, Executive Assistance, Ministry of Environment, Toronto, Canada

Alistair D. Crerar, Chief Executive Officer, Environment Council of Alberta, Canada

Crossroads Resource Group, Canada

Christopher Cudmore, Canada

Ignas da Cunha, Assistant to the Director, Social Research and Development Agency, Indonesia

Joao Pedro Cuthi Dias, Secretary for Environment of the State of Mato Grosso do Sul, Brazil

Graham Daborn, Acadia University, Nova Scotia, Canada

D.C. Danha, Executive Director, African Development Bank, Cote d'Ivoire

Danisworo, IAI, Indonesia

P. Darangwa, Zimbabwe .

Stan Darling, Member of Parliament, Chairman, House of Commons, Special Committee on Acid Rain, Canada

Ray Dart, Canada

Dilip Das, India

Patrick Davidson, Canada

Kenneth G. Davis, President, Canadian Foundation for World Development, Canada

Scott Davis, Foreign Aid Issues Research Framework, Canada

Claude E. Delisle, Ecole Polytechnique de Montreal, Canada
Wandy Demaine, Western and Northern Region, Alberta, Canada
Micheline Demers, Direction des Communications, Ministere des Relations Internationales, Quebec, Canada
Michael Dence, Royal Society of Canada,
Department of Environment, Government of Newfoundland and Labrador, Canada
Department of Fisheries and Oceans, Canada
Department of Physics, Carleton University, Canada
Department of Renewable Resources, Government of the Yukon, Canada
Doris Derry, Western and Northern Region, Alberta, Canada
Alain Desautels, Reviser, Translation Bureau, Quebec, Canada
Richard Deschenes, Head, Transportation Section, Quebec, Canada
Daniel Deudney, USA
Gordon Devies, Association of Canadian Engineering Consultants, Canada
Marion Dewer, International Institute of Concern for Public Health, Canada
Emmy Dharsono, Coordinator, SKEPHI, Indonesia
Eberhard Diepgen, Governing Mayor of Berlin (West)
Dave Dilks, Foreign Aid Issues Research Framework, Canada
N.H. Dini, WALHI, Indonesia
Direction des Reserves Ecologiques et des Sites Naturels, Ministere de l'Environnement du Quebec, Canada
A. Djali, BATAN, Indonesia
Achmad Djen, The Indonesian Environmental Forum, Indonesia
Artur Joao Donato, President, Industrial Federation of the State of Rio de Janeiro and the Industrial Center of Rio de Janeiro, Brazil
R.S. Dorney, Consulting Ecologist, Ecoplans Ltd., Canada
Odd Einar Dorum, Leader of the Norwegian Liberal Party, Norway
Marc Dourojeanni, Colegio de Ingenieros, Peru
Harald Dovland, Norsk Institut for Luftforskning, Norway
Therese Drapeau, Service des Communications, Environment Canada
Felicia Duarte, Movement in Defense of Life, Brazil
Daniel Dubeau, Directeur de l'Environnement, Hydro-Quebec, Canada
Clement Dugas, Environment Canada
Julian Dumanski, Agricultural Institute of Canada
A. Dunkel, Director-General, General Agreement on Tariffs and Trade, Switzerland
O.P. Dwivedi, Chairman, Department of Political Studies, University of Guelph, Canada
Sidsel Dyekjaer-Hansen, Danish UN Association, Denmark

EDPRA Consulting Inc., Canada
Wayne Easter, President, National Farmers' Union, Canada
Ecole Nationale d'Economie Appliquee, Senegal
Joseph R. Egan, Egan Associates, USA
N.S. Egorov, Deputy Minister, Higher and Specialized Secondary Education of the USSR
Bertil Eidsberg, Vennersborg, Norway
Constanje Eisenbart, FEST, Federal Republic of Germany
Anton Eliassen, Norwegian Meteorological Institute, Norway
J.R. Ellin, Vice-Chairman, Voluntary Planning Board, Nova Scotia, Canada
John Elkington, Director, Bioresources Ltd, United Kingdom
Kenneth C. Emberley, Manitoba Environmental Council Land Use Committee, Canada
Sabine Emmerich, Berlin (West)

R.J. Engelhard, Staff Member, The Beijer Institute Centre for Energy and Development in Africa, Kenya
Environment Component, Public Service Alliance of Canada
Environmental and Energy Study Institute, USA
Environmental Health Directorate, Health Protection Branch, Minister of National Health and Welfare, Canada
Environmental Quality Committee of the Alberta Fish and Game Association, Canada
George Erasmus, Indigenous Survival International, Canada
Karina Eriksson, Ministry of Agriculture, Sweden
Alan Ernest, Foreign Aid Issues Research Framework, Canada
European Environmental Bureau, Brussels
John Evans, Canada
S.A. Evteyev, Deputy Chairman, Scientific Council on the Biosphere, USSR Academy of Sciences

Anthony J.Fairclough, Acting Director General, Commission of the European Communities, Belgium
Hugh Fairn, Chairman, Land Resources Coordinating Council, Voluntary Planning Board, Nova Scotia, Canada
T.L. de Fayer, Canada
Anwar Fazal, IOCU Regional Director for Asia/Pacific, Malaysia
A. Fazelyanov, Aide to Commissioner Sokolov, USSR
Federal Environmental Assessment Review Office, Government of Canada
Pedro Antonio Federsoni, Jr, Head of Museum, Brazil
Fabio Feldman, Coordinator, Lawyers' Association of Brazil
Douglas Ferguson, student, North Toronto Collegiate, Canada
Maxime Ferrari, Director, UNEP Regional Office for Africa, Kenya
Janine Ferretti, The Pollution Probe Foundation, Canada
Erik Fiil, Head of Division, Danish International Development Agency, Denmark
Flying Tomato Production, Canada
Foreign Aid Issues Research Framework, Canada
Richard Fort, Ministry of the Environment, Norway
Theodora Carroll Foster, EDPRA Consulting, Inc., Canada
James Francois, Executive Director, Watershed Association Development Enterprises, Nova Scotia, Canada
Marcel Frenette, Professeur Titulaire, Dept de Genie Civil, Universite Laval, Canada
Alexander G. Friedrich, Chairman, German Foundation for International Development, Berlin (West)
I.T. Frolov, Academy of Sciences of the USSR
Risuko Fukuda, Social Cooperation Division, Ministry of Foreign Affairs, United Nations Bureau, Japan
Fundacion para la Defensa del Ambiente (FUNAM), Argentina

Richard Gaechter, Ambassador of Switzerland, Kenya
Gilles Gagnon, Service de la Recherche Applique, Ministere de l'Energie et des Resources, Canada
Luc Gagnon, Comite pour une strategie quebecoise de conservation, Canada
Julio M.G. Gaiger, President, National Indian Support Association, Brazil
Gary Gallon, Canada
Raul Ximenes Galvao, University of Sao Paulo, Brazil
I.P. Garbouchev, Bulgarian Academy of Sciences, Bulgaria
Rolando Garcia, Centre for Advanced Studies, IPN, Mexico
Jerry Garvey, Communications Consultants Ltd., Canada
T. Gedamu, Senior Economic Advisor, African Development Bank, Cote d'Ivoire

Richard Gendron, Mouvement Ecologique Collegial de Sherbrooke, Canada
Robert Geraghty, Deputy Minister, Department of Housing, Government of Nova
Scotia, Canada
Steinar Gil, Ministry of Foreign Affairs, Norway
Michael Gilbertson, Contaminants Evaluation Officer, Fisheries and Oceans, Canada
J.W. Giles, Associate Deputy Minister, Ministry of Environment, Ontario, Canada
Libuse Gilka, Society for Understanding Nutrition, Canada
Marcelle Girard, Service de Communications, Environment Canada
Thomas Gladwin, Associate Professor, New York University, USA
Harris R. Gleckman, Transnational Affairs Officer, Centre on Transnational Cor-
porations, United Nations, USA
Global Tomorrow Coalition, USA
E. Gobena, Conference Organizer, UNEP, Kenya
Lorraine Goddard, Administration Officer, Intergovernmental Affairs Directorate,
Canada
Maynari Goes, President, Camara Municipal de Campos do Jordao, Brazil
Jose Goldemberg, Companhia Energetica de Sao Paulo, Brazil
Bernice Goldsmith, student, North Toronto Collegiate, Canada
Maria de Lourdes Passos Gomes Nahas, Companhia de Tecnologia de Saneamento
Ambiental (CETESB), Brazil
John Gordon, Environment Analyst Conservation and Protection Service, En-
vironment Canada—Atlantic Region, Canada
Steve Gorman, Scheduling Officer, Office of the Deputy Minister, Ottawa, Canada
Debbie Goryk, Western and Northern Region, Alberta, Canada
Laurie Gourlay, Canada
Odd Grann, Secretary General, Norwegian Red Cross, Norway
Douglas R. Grant, Scientist, International Union for Quaternary Research, Canada
Fitzhugh Green, Aide to Commissioner Ruckelshaus, USA
Greenpeace, United Kingdom
Dolores Gregory, Aide to Commissioner Ruckelshaus, USA
Lucio Grinover, Director, Faculty of Architecture and Urban Planning of the
University of Sao Paulo, Brazil
Gary Gurbin, Parliamentary Secretary to the Minister of Environment, Canada
Ibsen de Gusmao Camara, President, Brazilian Foundation for the Preservation of
Nature, Brazil
Z. Gyimesi, Director of the Central Research Institute for Physics, Hungary

Ismid Hadad, Chief Editor, PRISMA Institute for Economic and Social Research,
Education & Information, Indonesia
Ahmed Hagag, Ambassador of Egypt, Kenya
Bertil Hagerhall, Ministry of Agriculture, Sweden
Laura Hahn, Canada
Peter Hall, Department of Geography, University of Reading, United Kingdom
Betty Hamilton, Environment Canada, Atlantic Region, Canada
H.L. Hammond, Forester Silva Ecosystem Consultants Ltd., Canada
Ole Jorgen Hansen, Miljoverndepartementet, Norway
Svein Hansen, Aide to the Chairman, Norway
Arthur J. Hanson, Association of Universities and Colleges in Canada
Halle Jorn Hanssen, NORAD/DUH, Norway
Hanswarh, EMDI, Indonesia
Estu Sinar Harapan, Indonesia
Jorge Hardoy, International Institute for Environment and Development, Argentina
Kenneth Hare, Provost of Trinity College, University of Toronto, Canada
Jennifer Harker, Senior Environmental Planner, M.M. Dillon Ltd., Canada

Jorgen Hartnak, Ministry of Environment, Denmark
Nashihin Hasan, Chairman of the Board, WALHI, Indonesia
Erkki Hasanen, The Academy of Finland, Finland
Michio Hashimoto, Environmental Science Policy Unit, Tsukuba University, Japan
Zentaro Hashimoto, Assistant of Vice Minister, Environment Agency, Japan
Frederic Hauge, Environment and Youth, Norway
Heather Hawrys, Administrative Assistant, Ministry of Environment, British Columbia, Canada
Janice Hayes, Ottawa Convention Services Ltd., Canada
Ivan Head, International Development Research Center, Canada
Carl-Geran Heden, Karolinska Institute, Sweden
Robert van Heecheren, The Netherlands
Marianne Heiberg, Norwegian Institute of International Affairs, Norway
Dieter Heinrich, World Association of World Federalists, Netherlands
Morten Helle, Statens Forurensningstilsyn, Norway
Bo Herrlander, Flakt Industri AB, Sweden
Farida Hewitt, Foreign Aid Issues Research Framework, Canada
Nicholas Highton, Beijer Institute, Sweden
Stuart B. Hill, Ecological Agriculture Projects, MacDonald College McGill University, Canada
Janus Hillgard, Greenpeace, Denmark
Dorothy Hogben, Communications Branch, Ottawa, Canada
Miriam Holland, Canada
C.S. Holling, Institute of Animal Resources Ecology, University of British Columbia, Canada
Sidney Holt, International League for the Protection of Cetaceans, United Kingdom
Erika Horvath, Canada
P. Hosia, Zimbabwe
E. Howard-Clinton, Economic Affairs Officer, Economic Commission for Africa, Ethiopia
Nay Htun, Director, UNEP Regional Office for Asia and Pacific, Thailand
Donald Huisingh, North Carolina State University, USA
Eric Hulten, Norsk Rad, Sweden
Michael Humphries, Chairman, Islands Trust, The Wilderness Advisory Committee, Canada
George Hyfantis, Advanced Waste Management Systems, Inc., USA
Erik Hyrhaug, New Thinking, Norway
Thomas Hysing, Norwave, Norway

M. Ibrahim, Badan Litbank DepTan, Indonesia
Eva Ikonen, The Academy of Finland, Finland
Toshiyuki Inamura, Minister of State, Director of the Environment Agency, Japan
Indigenous Survival International, Canada
Rhoda Inuksu, President, Inuit Tapirisat of Canada
Uzuki Isomura, Visitors Receiving Section, International Department, International Hospitality and Conference Service Assocation, Ministry of Foreign Affairs, Japan
Institute for Environmental Protection and Control in Mato Grosso do Sul (INAMB), Brazil
International Chamber of Commerce, France
International Council of Scientific Unions, France
International Development Research Centre, Canada
International Federation of Institutes for Advanced Study, Canada
International Union of Geological Sciences, Canada
Colin Isaacs, Pollution Probe Foundation, Canada

N. Islam, Assistant Director General, Food and Agriculture Organization of the United Nations, Italy
I.D. Ivanov, Institute of World Economy and International Relations, USSR
Y.A. Izrael, Chairman, State Committee on Hydrometeorology and Control of the Environment, USSR

J. Jakobsche, Advisor to the Chairman of the Planning Commission, Council of Ministers, Poland
Neil Jamieson, East West Centre, Hawaii
Bhupendra Jasani, Stockholm International Peace Research Institute, Sweden
R.D. Jenny, Indonesia
Gregory Jeffs, Canada
Hira Jhamtani, Biological Science Club, Indonesia
Svein Steve Johansen, Norwegian Institute for Water Research, Norway
Jan Johansen, Statens Forurensningstilsyn, Norway
Thomas Johansson, University of Lund, Sweden
Alf Johnels, Naturhistoriska Riksmuseet, Sweden
P.M. Johnson, Chairman Advisory Committee and Trustee, The Elsa Animal Appeal, Kenya
Down Jones, Foreign Services Community Association, Ottawa, Canada
Karen Jorgensen, Ministry of the Environment, Norway
Irwan Julianto, KOMPAS, Indonesia
Calestous Juma, Science and Policy Research Unit (SPRU), Sussex University, United Kingdom
Moch. Jusuf, Antara, Indonesia

T.O. Kaazik, Deputy Director of Vocational Training Institute for High Ranking Officials of Council of Ministers of the Estonian SSR, USSR
Wartono Kadri, Dep. Kehutanan, Indonesia
A.M. Kaidala, Acting-Chief, Agro-Industrial Committee of the USSR Department of Nature Protection, Reserves, Forestry and Animal Husbandry, USSR
Yolanda Kakabadse, Director, Fundacion Natura, Ecuador
Fumio Kaneko, Assistant Director, International Department, International Hospitality and Conference Service Association, Ministry of Foreign Affairs, Japan
Yoshikazu Kaneko, Director, Social Cooperation Division, Ministry of Foreign Affairs, United Nations Bureau, Japan
Kartjono, Manager, Research and Communication, Bina Swadaya, Indonesia
Roger Kasperson, Clark University, USA
J.A. Katili, Pertambangan & Energi, Indonesia
Kativik Environmental Quality Commission, Canada
Aristides Katoppo, Director, Sinah Kasih Publishing Group, Indonesia
Pekka Kauppi, Ministry of Environment, Finland
Issei Kawakatsu, Deputy Director, Social Cooperation Division, Ministry of Foreign Affairs, United Nations Bureau, Japan
Joe Keeper, Northern Flood Committee (Cree Indian Bands), Canada
Terry A. Kelly, Chief, Administration, Text, Processing Communications and Support Services, Canada
Kenyan and Kenya-Based NGOs, Kenya
Esther Kienholz, Western and Northern Region, Alberta, Canada
Gustav A. Kienitz, Berlin (West)
Sheila Kieren, Special Assistant, Office of the Minister of the Environment, Ottawa, Canada
Keikichi Kihara, Professor, College of Arts and Sciences, Chiba University, Japan

Denise Killanova Mattas, Director, Department for Education and Culture, Municipality of Vargem Grande Paulista, Brazil
Lee Kimball, International Institute for Environment and Development, USA
J.P. Kimmins, Professor of Forest Ecology, University of British Columbia, Canada
Taijiro Kimura, Social Cooperation Division, Ministry of Foreign Affairs, United Nations Bureau, Japan
Yuji Kimura, Assistant Director, International Affairs, Environment Agency, Japan
Jim Kingham, Director General, Ontario Region, Environment Canada
M.F. Kismadi, Aide to Commissioner Salim, Indonesia
Chuck Knight, Mayor, City of Fort McMurray, Alberta, Canada
Osamu Kobayashi, Director of the Environment Protection Department, Tokyo Electric Power Co. Ltd., Japan
Tatyana Kodhiat, The Indonesian Environmental Forum, Indonesia
Kodhyat, Institute for Indonesian Tourism Studies, Indonesia
Yoshihiro Kogane, Vice President, Nikko Research Center Ltd., Japan
Ole Andreas Kongsgaarden, Elkem A/S Fiskaa Verk, Norway
Sergei Korneev, USSR Academy for Foreign Trade
L.N. Krasavina, Moscow Financial Institute, USSR
Ailton Krenak, Coordinator, Indian Nations' Union, Brazil
Bjornulf Kristiansen, Norwegian Farmers' Union, Norway
Sergei Kromov, USSR Academy of Sciences
Joseph J. Krop, Society for Clinical Ecology, Canada
A. Kubozono, Director, International Affairs Division, National Aerospace Development Agency, Japan
Yuri Kurdas, USSR State Committee for Science and Technology
Paul Kuzmin, USSR State Committee for Science and Technology
Kari Kveseth, Royal Norwegian Council of Scientific and Industrial Research, Norway
B. Kwenda, Conference Organizer, Harare International Conference Centre, Zimbabwe
Monique Lachance, Coordination Sectorielle, Ministere des Relations Internationales, Quebec, Canada
Poka Laenui, World Council of Indigenous Peoples, Canada
J. Laine, E & RS 300, Canada
Nicolau Laitano, Director, Center for Environmental Protection, Alto Urugai Catarinense—Vale do Rio de Peixe, Jabora, Santa Catarina, Brazil
Cindy Lamson, Institute for Resource and Environmental Studies, Dalhousie University, Nova Scotia, Canada
Gundrun Landbo, Chief, Information NORAD, Norway
Cacilda Lanuza, Actress, Member of the Seiva Ecological Movement, and Member of the Brazilian Ecological Movement, Brazil
David Large, Voluntary Planning Board, Nova Scotia, Canada
I.A. Latysjev, Institute for East Studies, USSR
John. A. Laurmann, Gas Research Institute, USA
Guy LeBlanc, Minister of Environment, Nova Scotia, Canada
Gerald Leach, International Institute for Environment and Development, United Kingdom
Jose Leal, Economic Commission for Latin America, Chile
V.A. Legasov, Member of the Academy of Sciences of the USSR
Jeffrey Leonard, Conservation Foundation, USA
Don Lesh, Global Tomorrow Coalition, USA
Gilles Lessard, International Development Research Center, Canada
Arturo Leyser, Berlin (West)
Tek-Tjeng Lie, National Institute for Cultural Studies, Indonesia
Mara Liliana, Vice-President, National Council for Protection Medium, Director of National Council for Water, Romania

Clifford Lincoln, Environment Minister of Quebec, Canada
Per Lindblom, Deputy Director, IFIAS, Sweden
Gotz Link, Programme Officer, German Foundation for International Development, Berlin (West)
Mr Liphuko, Department of Regional and Town Planning, Ministry of Local Government and Lands, Botswana
Fu Lixiun, People's Republic of China
Maurice Lloyd, Manager, Atlantic Region UMA Group, Nova Scotia, Canada
Yedo Lobao, Congressman, Legislative Assembly, Brazil
Marianne Loe, Norsk Folkeljelp, Norway
A.A. Loedin, Libang DepKes, Indonesia
Martin Loer, Protokoll des Landes Berlin (West)
J. Lofblad, General Secretary, International Federation of Building and Woodworkers, Norway
John Logsden, Director of Programme in Science and Technology and Public Policy, George Washington University, USA
Bindu Lohani, Chairman, Environmental Engineering Division, Asian Institute of Technology, Thailand
Aage Lomo, Federation of Norwegian Industries, Norway
Susy Cristina Lopes Moco, Companhia de Tecnologia de Saneamento Ambiental (CETESB), Brazil
Jocelyne Louis-Seize, Text Processing Operator, Intergovernmental Affairs Directorate, Ottawa, Canada
Asbjorn Lovbraek, Christian Michelsen Institut, Norway
Tom Lovejoy, Vice-President of the World Wildlife Fund-US, USA
L. Luctacz, Professor, University of Warsaw, Poland
Svante Lundkvist, Swedish Minister of Agriculture, Sweden
Jose A. Lutzemberger, President, AGAPAN de Porto Alegre, Uniao Ecologica, Brazil
Ned Lynch, Director, International Programme Branch, Intergovernmental Affairs Directorate, Canada
Finn Lynge, Inuit Circumpolar Conference Environmental Commission, Denmark

M.A.L. Mabagunji, Department of Geography, Ibadan University, Nigeria
Nydia MacCool, Ottawa Convention Services, Ltd. Canada
Peter MacKellar, Director, Energy and Environment Division, Ottawa, Canada
Andrew MacKay, President, Dalhousie University, Nova Scotia, Canada
A.R. MacKinnon, Director, Centre for International Programs, Canada
Norman MacNeill, Deputy Minister, Department of Development, Government of Nova Scotia, Canada
Lucie MacRillo, Administrative Operations, Ottawa, Canada
Vera Luiza Visockis Maceda, Brazil
Paulo Afonso Leme Machado, Professor of Environmental Law, Brazil
Andrew H. Macpherson, Canada
Marc Magali, Co-Presidente, Societe pour Vaincre la Pollution, Canada
Burhan Magenda, Faculty of Political and Social Sciences, University of Indonesia
Sophie Mair, Canada
Vladimir Maksimov, USSR Academy for Foreign Trade
Carl Goran Maler, Sweden
Halfdan Mahler, Director-General, World Health Organization, Switzerland
Kathini Maloba, The International Federation of Plantation, Agricultural and Allied Workers, Kenya
Zephaniah Mandirahwe, Zimbabwe
Leif Manger, Norwegian Association for Development Research, Norway

Elisabeth Mann Borgese, Dalhousie University, Institute for Resource and Environment Studies, Canada
William Mansfield, Deputy Executive Director, UNEP, Kenya
Audrey Manzer, Chairman, Dartmouth Lakes Advisory Board, Nova Scotia, Canada
Andi Mappasala, Chairman, Yayasan Tellung Poccoe, Indonesia
Ninuk Mardiana, KOMPAS, Indonesia
Mahar Mardjono, Chairman, FISKA, Indonesia
Pierre de Margerie, The Toronto Issues Exploration Group, Canada
M.H. Maria, KOMPAS, Indonesia
D.J. Marquardt, Director, Administrative Operations, Canada
Aristides Marques, National Council for Urban Development, Brazil
B.E. Marr, Deputy Minister, Ministry of Environment, British Columbia, Canada
Andre Marsan, Andre Marsan & Associates, Canada
Rolf Marstrander, Director, Environmental Affairs, Norsk Hydro, Norway
R.B. Martin, Principal Ecologist, Department of National Parks and Wildlife Management, Zimbawbe
Andre Martin, Service des Relations Publiques, Hydro-Quebec, Canada
Maureen Martinauck, Information Directorate, Toronto, Canada
Esperanza Martinez, Executive Director, Society for the Defense of Nature in Pachamamata Camaccuna, Ecuador
Soedarno Martosewojo, Indonesia
A. Mascarenhas, Regional Director of the Conservation for Development Center, IUCN, Zimbabwe
Sergei Maslov, USSR Academy for Foreign Trade
Joel Matheson, Minister of Mines and Energy, Government of Nova Scotia, Canada
T.I. Mathew, International Labour Office, Switzerland
Kazuo Matsushita, Assistant of Vice Minister, Environment Agency, Japan
I. Matsvairo, Zimbabwe
Denise V. Mattos, Director, Education and Culture Department of the Municipality of Varge en Grande Paulista, Brazil
Tom McCarthy, Chairman, Environment Committee, International Chamber of Commerce, France
Donna McConnell, Department of Environment, Nova Scotia, Canada
Donald McCracken, Foreign Aid Issues Research Framework, Canada
Donna McCready, Research Coordinator, Department of Environment, Nova Scotia, Canada
Jane McDowell, Communications Officer, Intergovernmental Affairs Directorate, Canada
A.D. McIntyre, Department of Agriculture and Fisheries for Scotland, Marine Laboratory, United Kingdom
A.J. McIntyre, Canada
Alister McIntyre, Deputy Secretry-General, United Nations Conference on Trade and Development, Switzerland
Keith L. McIntyre, Mohawk College of Applied Arts and Technology, Canada
Suzanne McLennan, Charter Division, Ottawa, Canada
Tom McMillan, Minister of the Environment, Government of Canada
Jeffrey A. McNeely, International Union for the Conservation of Nature and Natural Resources, Switzerland
Harvey Mead, Union Quebecoise pour la Conservation de la Nature, Canada
J.A. de Medicis, Ambassador of Brazil, Former Chairman, Intergovernmental Intersessional Preparatory Committee, Kenya
Evan Mehlum, Norwave A/S, Norway
Meizar, SKREPP, Indonesia
Guillermo Gallo Mendoza, Fundacion Bariloche, Argentina

Gray Merriam, Professor of Biology, Carleton University, Canada
Joyce Michells, Head, Correspondence, Conservation and Protection, Ottawa, Canada
Andrew Michrowski, President, Planetary Association for Clean Energy, Canada
Bogadur Mickailov, USSR State Committee for Science and Technology
L.E. Mikhailov, Deputy Chairman, USSR State Committee on Forestry
Simon Miles, Conservation Council of Ontario, Canada
Kenton Miller, Director General, International Union for the Conservation of Nature
    and Natural Resources, Switzerland
Betty Mindlin, Institute for Economic Research, Brazil
Abdul Samad Minty, Anti-Apartheid Movement, United Kingdom
Irving Mintzer, World Resources Institute, USA
Barbara Mitchell, International Institute for Environment and Development, United
    Kingdom
Debbie Mitchell, Department of Environment, Nova Scotia, Canada
R. Mkwanazi, Zimbabwe
Adhi Moersid, IAI, Indonesia
N.N. Moiseyev, Member, Academy of Sciences of the USSR
Dag Moller, Fiskeridirektoratets Havforskningsinstitutt, Norway
B.A. Molski, Professor, Botanical Garden of the Polish Academy of Sciences, Warsaw,
    Poland
Olga Monakova, USSR Academy of Sciences
Marcello Monteiro de Carvalho, Attorney-at-Law, Brazil
Estanislau Monteiro de Oliveira, Secretaria Especial do Meio Ambiente (SEMA),
    Brazil
Raul A. Montenegro, President, Asociacion Argentina de Ecologia, Argentina
Andre Franco Montoro, Governor, Sao Paulo, Brazil
Laurindo S. Moreira, Miguelopolis, Brazil
Joao Eduardo Moritz, President, Brazilian National Federation of Engineers, Brazil
Omar Morrinez-Legeretta, Mexico
Karen Morrison, Canada
Joao Eduardo Mortiz, President, Brazilian National Federation of Engineers, Brazil
Ted Moses, Grand Chief/Chairman, Grand Council of the Crees, Canada
Movement for the Defense of Life, Santos, Brazil
T.P.Z. Mpofu, Director of Natural Resources, Ministry of Natural Resources and
    Tourism, Zimbabwe
P. Muchanyuka, Zimbabwe
Simon Muchiru, Environment Liaison Centre, Kenya
Robert Mugabe, Prime Minister, Zimbabwe
Kartono Muhamad, FISKA, Indonesia
Paul Muldoon, Social Sciences and Humanities Research Council of Canada
Harald Muller, Hessische Stiftung Friedens- und Konfliktforschung, Federal Republic
    of Germany
Ingrid Munro, UN Centre for Human Settlements (Habitat), Kenya
David A. Munro, Secretary-General, Conference on Conservation and Development,
    Canada
Laura Murphy, The Indonesian Environmental Forum, Indonesia
Charles M. Musial, President, New Waterford Fish and Game Association, Canada
Rahab W. Mwatha, Secretary, The Greenbelt Movement, Kenya
Norman Myers, Environmental Consultant, United Kingdom

NATUR & UNGDOM, Norway
William Nagle, World Resources Institute, USA
I.V. Nagy, President, Environment Protection Committee of the Patriotic People's
    Front, Hungary

Syamsuddin Nainggolan, Yayasan Panca Bakti, Indonesia
P.K.R. Nair, International Council for Research on Agroforestry (ICRAF), Kenya
Lance Nale, Executive Director, Voluntary Planning Board, Department of Development, Nova Scotia, Canada
Nobuyoshi Namiki, Member of Board of Directors, Japan Economic Research Centre, Japan
David Nantes, Minister of Municipal Affairs, Government of Nova Scotia, Canada
National Agency of Environmental Protection, Denmark
National Council of Rubber Tappers of Brazil
National Survival Institute, Canada
Yoshihiro Natori, Assistant Director, International Affairs, Environment Agency, Japan
Natural Resources Defense Council, USA
Valerian Naumov, USSR State Committee for Science and Technology
Coleman Nee, Aide to Commissioner Ruckelshaus, USA
Neighborhood Association of Barra da Tijuca (AMABARRA), Brazil
Gordon Nelson, Faculty of Environmental Studies, University of Waterloo, Canada
Fiona Nelson, Chairperson, National Survival Institute, Canada
Jeremiah Niagah, Minister of Environment and Natural Resources, Kenya
Peter Nijhoff, Director, Nature and Environment, International Union for the Conservation of Nature and Natural Resources, Netherlands
Hiroshi Nishimiya, Social Cooperation Division, Ministry of Foreign Affairs, United Nations Bureau, Japan
Teshishige Nishio, Director, Public Information Office, Environment Agency, Japan
Garth Norris, Western and Northern Region, Alberta, Canada
North Toronto Collegiate, Canada
Norwegian Farmer's Union and the Agricultural Cooperative Organizations, Norway
S. Nugroho, LKBN Antara, Indonesia
Abdul Hakim Nusantara, SKREPP, Indonesia
Joseph S. Nye, Director, Centre for Science and International Affairs, USA
Julius K. Nyerere, former President, Tanzania

John O'Riordan, Director, Planning and Assessment, Ministry of Environment, British Columbia, Canada
Timothy O'Riordan, School of Environmental Sciences, University of East Anglia, United Kingdom
G.O.P. Obasi, Director General, World Meteorogical Organization, Switzerland
Hans Odendahl, Manager, Crawley-McCracken, Ottawa, Canada
Richard Odingo, Faculty of Arts and Social Sciences, University of Nairobi, Kenya
Kamil Oesman, Bird-Lovers Association of Indonesia
Paschalia Edith Ogaye, Breastfeeding Information Group, Kenya
Toshohisa Ohno, Visitors Receiving Section, International Hospitality and Conference Service Association, Ministry of Foreign Affairs, Japan
Oikos, Association for Defenders of the Earth, Brazil
Ibu Gedong Bagoes Oka, Indonesia
Luza Okiishi, Companhia de Tecnologia de Saneamento Ambiental (CETESB), Brazil
G. Okolotowicz, Research Scientist, Sea Fisheries Institute, Poland
Kare Olerud, Norwegian Society for the Conservation of Nature, Norway
Beatrice Olivastri, Executive Director, National Survival Institute, Canada
Maria Isabel Oliveira Vieira de Mendonca, Companhia de Tecnologia de Saneamento Ambiental (CETESB), Brazil
George Opundo, Ministry of Environment and Natural Resources, Kenya
O. Ooko-Ombaka, Public Law Institute, Kenya
Alex Orlov, USSR Academy for Foreign Trade

Celso Orsini, University of Sao Paulo, Brazil
Antonio Ortiz Mena, President, Inter-American Development Bank, USA
J.O. Oucho, Population Studies and Research Institute, Kenya
Joseph Ouma, Dean of School of Environmental Studies, Moi University, Kenya
Janette Outerkirk, Administrative Assistant, Office of the Deputy Minister, Ottawa, Canada
Lars Overein, Norwegian Institute for Water Research, Norway
Maureen Oxley, Canada

Maria Tereza Jorge Padua, General Secretary, Brazilian Institute for Forestry Development, Brazil
Waldemar Pailoli, President, Brazilian Association for the Protection of Nature, Brazil
G.K.C. Pardoe, United Kingdom
Leo Pare, Sous-Ministre, Ministere des Relations Internationales, Quebec, Canada
Regina Maria Passos Gomes, Companhia de Tecnologia de Saneamento Ambiental (CETESB), Brazil
Surendra Patel, Professor, University of Sussex, United Kingdom
Corry Patty, Indonesia
Torbjorn Paule, Norges Naturvernforbund, Norway
O. Pavlov, Aide to Commissioner Sokolov, USSR
J. Pawlak, Deputy Chief Inspector, State Inspectorate of Environment, Poland
Bing Pearl, Chief of Staff, Ministry of National Defence, Ottawa, Canada
Charles Pearson, The Johns Hopkins University, USA
Red Pedersen, Minister of Renewable Resources, Government of the Northwest Territories, Canada
Flavio Rios Peixoto da Silveira, Minister of Urban Development and Environment, Brazil
Austin Pelton, Minister of Environment, British Columbia, Canada
Maria Jose Pereira de Lacerda (Dede), resident of Gariroba shantytown, Brazil
Renat Perelet, Scientific Secretary, Institute for System Studies of the State Committee for Science and Technology and the USSR Academy of Sciences
Nadyr Sobral Peres de Souza, President, Regional Council for Environmental Defense (CONDEMA), Brazil
Permanent Assembly of Environmentalist Groups in Sao Paulo (APEDEMA), Brazil
Sigurd Peterson, President, Agricultural Institute of Canada, Canada
Leonid Petrenko, USSR State Committee for Science and Technology
Yuri Petrov, USSR Academy for Foreign Trade
Klaus Pfister, Ministry of Environment, Finland
M. Jean Piette, Director, Direction des Strategies et Politiques Environnementales, Quebec, Canada
Luis Carlos Pinheiro Machado, President, Brazilian Company of Farming/Ranching Research, Brazil
Dick Pitman, Zambesi Society and the Wildlife Society, Zimbabwe
Planetary Association for Clean Energy, Inc., Canada
George Pletiukhine, USSR State Committee for Science and Technology
Hasan Poerbo, PPLH ITB, Indonesia
P.I. Poletaev, Deputy Chairman, Commission on Environmental Protection and Rational Use of Natural Resources of the Presidium of the Council of Ministers, USSR
Pollution Probe Foundation, Canada
B.V. Pospelov, Institute for the Far-East, USSR
Luiz Augusto de Proenca Rosa, Federal University of Rio de Janeiro, Brazil
George Priddle, Chairman and Associate Professor, Faculty of Environmental Studies, Waterloo University, Canada

D.I. Protsenko, Chairman, State Committee on Natural Protection of the Ukranian SSR, USSR
Provinces of Alberta, British Columbia, Nova Scotia, Ontario, and Quebec, Canada
Public Advisory Committees to Environment Council of Alberta, Canada
Agus Puronomo, The Indonesian Environmental Forum, Indonesia

S.A. Qasim, Aide to Commissioner Al-Athel, Saudi Arabia
Irene Quellet, Administrative Assistant, Intergovernmental Affairs Directorate, Ottawa, Canada

T.W. Raintung, DGI, Indonesia
Jacub Rais, Bakosurtanal, Indonesia
Arcot Ramachandran, Executive Director, UN Centre for Human Settlements, Kenya
Hanna Rambe, Majalah Mutiara Indonesia
K.K.S. Rana, former Chairman, Intergovernmental Inter-sessional Preparatory Committee, Kenya
Paul Raskin, Energy Systems Research Group, USA
A. Ray, Fundamental Research Institute, Canada
Amalya Reddy, Department of Management Studies, Indian Institute of Science, India
William E. Rees, Associate Professor, School of Community and Regional Planning, University of British Columbia, Canada
Regional Development and Farming Systems Research Groups, Royal Tropical Institute, Netherlands
David Rehling, Danmarks Naturfredningsforening, Denmark
Julyan Reid, Director General, External Relations, Corporate Planning Environment, Canada
William K. Reilly, President, Conservation Foundation, USA
Magda Renner, President, Friends of the Earth, Brazil
Robert Repetto, World Resources Institute, USA
Ataide Ribeiro, City Councilman, Health and Environmental Council of Santana do Parnaiba, Brazil
Miles G. Richardson, President, Council of the Haida Nation, Canada
Peter Richetts, Saint Mary's University, Nova Scotia, Canada
Sheila Ritchie, Communications Branch, Pacific and Yukon Region, Canada
Filippo di Robilant, Aide to Commissioner Agnelli, Italy
Raymond Robinson, Federal Environmental Assessment Review Office, Canada
Henning Rodhe, Stockholms Universitet, Sweden
Nina Kvalheim Rong, Rong Laks A/S, Norway
E.F. Roots, Office of the Science Advisor, Canada
Imron Rosyadi, MUI, Indonesia
Rolf Svein Rougno, Ordforer, Norway
Sauli Rouhinen, Finnish Council for the Protection of the Environment, Finland
Stanley Rowe, Saskatchewan Environmental Society, Canada
Royal Society of Canada, Academy of Science, Canada
B.G. Rozanov, Moscow State University, USSR
David Runnalls, International Institute for Environment and Development, USA
I.I. Russin, Professor, Moscow State University, USSR

Ignacy Sachs, Centre International de Recherche sur l'environnement et le developpement, France
Roald Sagdeev, Institute of Space Research, USSR
Klaus A. Sahlgren, Executive Secretary, United Nations Economic Commission for Europe, Switzerland
William Saint, Executive Director, Ford Foundation, Kenya

Genevieve Sainte-Maire, Deputy Minister, Environment Canada
Mika Sakakibara, Student, Tokyo University of Agriculture and Technology, Japan
Salam, The Indonesian Environmental Forum, Indonesia
Dodok Sambodo, The Indonesian Environmental Forum, Indonesia
Plinio Sampaio Jr, Catholic University of Sao Paulo, Brazil
Richard Sandbrook, Executive Vice President, International Institute for Environment and Development/Earthscan, United Kingdom
Kirsten Sander, Greenpeace, Denmark
Sao Paulo Municipal Advisory Councils for Protection of the Environment (CONDEMA), Brazil
Sarlito Sarwono, Faculty of Psychology, University of Indonesia
Adi Sasono, Director, Institute for Development Studies, Indonesia
Eiko Sato, Visitors Receiving Section, International Department, International Hospitality and Conference Service Association, Ministry of Foreign Affairs, Japan
David Satterthwaite, International Institute for Environment and Development, United Kingdom
Phillip Saunders, International Centre for Ocean Development, Nova Scotia, Canada
Lee Schipper, Shell International Petroleum Company, United Kingdom
Wilhelm Schmid, Chef des Affaires internationales de l'Environnement, Departement Federal des Affaires Etrangres, Switzerland
Ted Schrecker, Dept. of Environment and Resource of Studies, Canada
Ilja Schwartz, USSR State Committee for Science and Technology
Gabriel Scimemi, Deputy Director, Environment Directorate, Organisation for Economic Co-operation and Development, Paris, France
Christopher Seebach, President, Aquarian Agency Ltd., Canada
Michael Sefali, Minister of Planning for Lesotho, SADCC Sector for Soil and Water Conservation and Land Utilization, Lesotho
Mats Segnestam, Swedish Society for the Protection of Nature, Sweden
Veronique Seifert, Earthscan, United Kingdom
Hans Martin Seip, Senter for Industriforskning, Norway
Rolf Selrod, Ministry of the Environment, Norway
A.P. Semyonov, Chief Technical Labour Inspector, Central Council of Trade Unions, USSR
Yuri Senkevich, Institute for Bio-Medicine, USSR
Sugeng Setiadi, Chairman of the Board, Yayasan Mandiri, Indonesia
V. Shakarov, Aide to Commissioner Sokolov, USSR
Ravi Sharma, Environment Liaison Centre, Kenya
Margarita Shatkovsky, Companhia de Tecnologia de Saneamento Ambiental (CETESB), Brazil
Kathleen Shaw, Legislative Committee, Canadian Federation of University Women, Canada
R.H. Shepherd, President, Syncrude Canada, Ltd., Canada
Steven Shrybman, Counsel, Canadian Environmental Law Association, Canada
M.R. Siahaan, DGI, Indonesia
Anton Sila, KNI, Indonesia
Jaime da Silva Araujo, National Council of Rubber Tappers, Brazil
Linus Simanjuntak, Chairman, YIH, Indonesia
Michael Simmons, The DPA Group, Nova Scotia, Canada
Janet Singh, Aide to Commissioner Ramphal, United Kingdom
Rosa Sirois, Environment Canada, Atlantic Region, Canada
J. Siuta, Deputy Director, Institute of Environmental Protection, Poland
R.W. Slater, Assistant Deputy Minister, Corporate Planning, Quebec, Canada
Fred Sleicher, Manager, Great Lakes Section, Ministry of the Environment, Ontario, Canada

Bruce M. Small, Pollution and Education Review Group, Board of Education for the City of Toronto, Canada

M.G. Smith, Department of Social Anthropology, Yale University, USA

Ian R. Smyth, Executive Director, Canadian Petroleum Association, Canada

H.M. Soedjono, MUI, Indonesia

Francisca Soee, Protokoll des Landes, Berlin (West)

Soeharto, President, Indonesia

Sugyanto Soegyoko, ITP, Indonesia

Retno Soetarjono, PSL UI, Indonesia

K. Soetrisno, Indonesia

Hardjanto Sostoharsono, Ditjen Tanaman Pangan, Indonesia

Aristides Arthus Soffiati Netto, President, North Fluminense Center for Conservation of Nature—City of Campos, Brazil

Arthur Soffiati, Sociedade Visconde de Sao Leopoldo, Brazil

W. Solodzuk, Deputy Minister, Environment Alberta, Canada

Atle Sommerfeldt, Mellomkirkelig Rad for Den Norske Kirke, Norway

Gunnar Sorbo, Christian Michelsens Institute, Norway

Southern African Development Coordinating Conference (SADCC), Botswana

Sonia F. de Souza, Agua Funda Anti-Pollution League, Brazil

John Spayne, Aide to Commissioner Khalid

J. Gustave Speth, President, World Resources Institute, USA

Robert E. Stein, President, Environmental Mediation International, USA

Mark Stephanson, Director of Community Relations, Manitoba Environment, Canada

Tom Stoel, Natural Resources Defense Council, USA

Hans Stoen, Ministry of the Environment, Norway

W. Stoermer, Aide to Commissioner Hauff, Federal Republic of Germany

Jane Stuart, Friends of the Earth Canada

Aca Sugandhy, IAP, Indonesia

Rosi Sularto, IAI, Indonesia

Sumartoyo, Bina Desa, Indonesia

Otto Sumarwoto, Lembaga Ekology—UNPAD, Indonesia

B.B. Sundaresen, National Environmental Engineering Research Institute, India

Osvaldo Sunkel, Joint ECLA/UNEP Unit on Development and Environment, Chile

Rakel Surlien, Minister of the Environment, Ministry of the Environment, Norway

K.H. Sutrisno, Vice-Director, Yayasan Indonesia Sejahtera Indonesia

M.S. Swaminathan, President, International Rice Research Institute, Philippines

Michael Sweatman, Director, International Wilderness Leadership Foundation, Canada

Bruce Switzer, Canada

Abdullah Syarwani, Executive Director, PKBI, Indonesia

Istvan Szabolcs, Institute for Soil Science and Agricultural Chemistry, Hungary

Francisco Szekely, Mexico

Erwin Szenes, Aide to Commissioner Lang, Hungary

A. Takats, Division Head, National Authority for Environment Protection and Nature Conservation, Hungary

Sergei Tamaev, USSR Academy for Foreign Trade

Carl Olaf Tamm, University of Uppsala, Sweden

Koichi Tani, Director, International Affairs Division, Environment Agency, Japan

Task Force on Water Use in Agriculture of the Agricultural Institute of Canada, Canada

Indra Tata, The Indonesian Environmental Forum, Indonesia

Dewi Tazkirawati, The Indonesian Environmental Forum, Indonesia

Bo Tengberg, Sweden

Peter Thacher, World Resources Institute, USA
Tom Thackeray, Director, Information Division, Government Alberta, Canada
Claes Thimren, Sweden
Vernon G. Thomas, Associate Professor, Department of Zoology, College of Biological
    Science, University of Guelph, Canada
Frank Thomas, President, Ford Foundation, Kenya
Jose Willibaldo Thome, President, Zoobotannical Foundation of Rio Grande do Sul,
    Brazil
Bruce Thompson, Canada
Jan Thompson, Aide to the Chairman, Norway
Craig Thorburn, The Indonesian Environmental Forum, Indonesia
Roland J. Thornhill, Minister of Development, Nova Scotia, Canada
Jon Tinker, Director, Earthscan, United Kingdom
Sediono Tjondronegoro, ASMEN RISTEK,Indonesia
Eileen Tobey, Communications Consultants Ltd., Canada
K. Toeti, TEMPO, Indonesia
Mostafa Tolba, Executive Director, United Nations Environment Programme, Kenya
Maja Tolstikova, USSR State Committee for Science and Technology
Ian Torrens, Organisation for Economic Co-operation and Development, France
Ralph Torrie, Canadian Environment, Development, and Peace Organizations, Canada
N. I. Towfiq, Aide to Commissioner Al-Athel, Saudi Arabia
Trent University students, Canada
Dina Trisundari, The Indonesian Environmental Forum, Indonesia
Irina Tropina, USSR State Committee for Science and Technology
M. Tsabit, WALHI, Indonesia
Kyai Tsabith, An-Nugoyah Pesantren, Indonesia
S. Tsikwa, Zimbabwe
Marina Tumarkina, Youth Environment Protection Council, Moscow State University,
    USSR
Frans Tumiwa, DGI, Indonesia
Nick Tywoniuk, Director General, Western and Northern Region, Alberta, Canada

UNESCO Canada MAB/NET, Canada
USSR Commission for UNEP, USSR
G.W. Uku, Chief of Protocol, Ministry of Foreign Affairs, Zimbabwe
Uniao Ecologica, Brazil
United Nations Conference on Trade and Development, Switzerland
United Nations Educational, Scientific and Cultural Organization, France
University of Laval, Faculty of Sciences and Engineering, Canada
US-Based International Development, Environment, and Population NGOs, USA
US Council for International Business and the Business Round Table, USA
G. Ya. Uskov, State Committee for Science and Technology, USSR

Marcia Valiante, Canadian Environmental Law Research Foundation, Canada
J.R. Vallentyne, Senior Scientist, Great Lakes Fisheries Research Branch, Ontario,
    Canada
Randall Van Holle, Carleton University, Canada
Julie Vanderschot, Projects Officer, Intergovernmental Affairs Directorate, Canada
David VanderZwaag, Assistant Professor, Dalhousie Law School, Nova Scotia,
    Canada
Nancy Vanstone, Programme Manager, Planning and Policy Development, Maritime
    Resources Management Services, Nova Scotia, Canada
Galina Varshavskaya, USSR

Nelson Vasconcelos, Director, Pollution Control, Companhia de Tecnologia de Saneamento Ambiental (CETESB), Brazil
Monique Vezina, Minister for External Relations, Canada
Jean-Pierre Vettovaglia, Minister, Mission permanente de la Suisse pres les organisations internationales, Switzerland
Valmira Vieira Mecenas, Secretary, Natural Resources, Technology, and Environment, Brazil
Raymond Vles, Friends of the Earth, Canada
Sharon Vollman, Office of the Regional Director General, Pacific and Yukon Region, Canada

Lars Walloe, Universitet of Oslo, Norway
Ingo Walter, New York University Graduate School of Business, USA
Kirsten Warnoe, Environmental Protection Agency, Denmark
Carol Warshawski, Senior Officer, Federal and Intergovernmental Affairs, Alberta, Canada
S.M. Washira, African Development Trust, Kenya
Mr. Ranjit Watson, Aide to Commissioner Ramphal
Fergus Watt, World Association of World Federalists, Canada
Helmust Weidner, International Institute for Environment and Society, Federal Republic of Germany
Pearl Weinberger, Department of Biology, University of Ottawa, Canada
Arthur W. Westing, Stockholm International Peace Research Institute, Sweden
Westman Media Cooperative Limited, Canada
Tim Wherle, student, Carleton University, Canada
Rodney White, Canada
Henrik Wickmann, Danish Environmental Protection Agency, Denmark
Widjanarka, KRAPP, Indonesia
John Wiebe, Director General, Pacific and Yukon Region, Canada
Ponna Wignaraja, Society for International Development, Italy
B. Widjanarko, Suara Karya, Indonesia
Widjarnarko, Coordinator, KRAPP, Indonesia
Wildlife Clubs of Kenya
Wildlife Habitat Canada
Jorge Wilheim, Secretary of the Planning Department of the City of Sao Paulo, Brazil
Peter Wilkinson, Greenpeace International, United Kingdom
Kare Willoch, Prime Minister of Norway, Norway
Ian Wilson, Canadian Nuclear Association, Canada
Howard Windsor, Environment Analyst, Canada
R. Winters, E & RS 300, Canada
Wahyu Wisaksono, Indonesia
Gunn Wisloff, President, YWCA, Norway
Erna Witoelar, WALHI, Indonesia
Z. Wojcik, Museum of the Earth, Poland
World Media Institute, Canada
World Resources Institute, USA
World Vision International, USA
Vera Wullur, Chairman, DNIKS, Indonesia
Brian Wynne, United Kingdom

Harvey Yakowitz, Organisation for Economic Cooperation and Development, France
Takashi Yamada, Assistant Director, External Relations Department, Japan
Ayako Yamada, Head of the Better Living Section, Shiga Prefectural Union of Agricultural Cooperatives, Japan

A.L. Yanshin, Vice-President, Academy of Sciences of the USSR
Debra Yatim, The Indonesian Environmental Forum, Indonesia
Judith Yaworski, President, Communications Consultants, Canada
Tokuhisa Yoshida, Deputy Director, International Affairs, Environment Agency, Japan⁻
Alex Yusutardi, The Indonesian Environmental Forum, Indonesia

V. Zagladin, USSR
M.T. Zen, BPPT, Indonesia
John Zetter, United Kingdom
Mr. Zidel, Chairman, MAB National Committee of the German Democratic Republic
Zimbabwe NGOs
Renat Zobnin, USSR Academy for Foreign Trade
Werner E. Zulauf, President Director, Companhia de Tecnologia de Saneamento Ambiental (CETESB), Brazil
Susilo Zumrotin, Executive Secretary, YLK—Indonesian Consumers Organisation, Indonesia
J. Zurek, Director, Institute of Environmental Protection, Poland
Shelley Zwicker, Environment Canada, Atlantic Region, Canada

INDEX